JOURNAL FOR THE STUDY OF THE NEW TESTAMENT
SUPPLEMENT SERIES

285

Editor
Mark Goodacre

Community–Identity Construction in Galatians

Exegetical, Social-Anthropological and Socio-Historical Studies

Atsuhiro Asano

T&T CLARK INTERNATIONAL
A Continuum imprint
LONDON • NEW YORK

Copyright © Atsuhiro Asano, 2005
A Continuum imprint

Published by T&T Clark International
The Tower Building, 11 York Road, London SE1 7NX
15 East 26th Street, Suite 1703, New York, NY 10010

www.tandtclark.com

British Library Cataloguing-in-Publication Data
A catalogue record for this book is available from the British Library

ISBN 056703027-X   (hardback)

Typeset by Data Standards Ltd, Frome, Somerset, BA11 1RE
Printed on acid-free paper in Great Britain by MPG Books Ltd,
Bodmin, Cornwall.

CONTENTS

ACKNOWLEDGEMENTS

This book is based upon a D. Phil. thesis submitted to the Faculty of Theology at the University of Oxford in the summer of 2003. My special appreciation goes first of all to my supervisor for the D. Phil. program, Professor Christopher Rowland at The Queen's College, for guiding me through this long academic journey with valuable guidance and much-needed encouragement. It has been an honour to study under his supervision. I also thank Professor Peter Clarke at King's College of London University, who kindly acted as a co-supervisor while I wrote the chapters on methodology, for providing me with insights into the areas of sociology and religious study. I would like to thank also the internal and external examiners of my *viva voce*, Professor Robert Morgan at Linacre College and Professor Philip Esler at St Andrew's University, respectively, for reading my thesis in entirety, attentively listening to my defences and arguments, and sharing their valuable insights with me. I thank also Ms Kim Kanouf and Rev. Tom Houston for reading earlier drafts to make suggestions for improving my English. I thank Professor Michael Wolter at Bonn University for his hospitality and allowing me to conduct research at the library of die evangelisch-theologische Fakultät. I would like also to show my sincere appreciation to Professor Shin Chiba and Chief Librarian Ms Yuki Nagano at International Christian University for their hospitality during my research on Mukyokai at the university. I thank Sasakawa Fund for financing the entire trip for my research on Mukyokai in Tokyo, Japan. I thank also Keiyu Publishing House and Dr Keisuke Nakazawa for funding my trips to various New Testament conferences both in Europe and in North America, which enabled me to present my thoughts reflected in the various chapters of this book to wider audiences. I also express my appreciation to The Queen's College for providing financial support for my research in various forms. My appreciation also goes to the editorial staff of T&T Clark/Continuum for their valuable suggestions and instructions. I would not have been able to complete the work without the encouragement of mentors and friends. I only have space to acknowledge a few, whose constant encouragement is responsible for its completion: Professor David Scholer, Professor Colin Brown, Ms Olive Brown, Dr David Parris, Dr Karl Pagenkemper, Dr Karen Maticich, Professor Mari Nishino, Professor Gohei Hata, Dr Hélène Deacon, Rev. Sally Norris, Mr Isao Hashimoto, Ms Noriko

Matsunaga, Rev. Kazuto Sakoda, the Houstons, Herr und Frau Hahn, and my dear students at TCI, to whom I express my sincere gratitude.

Cumnor Hill, Oxford

August, 2004

A. Asano

ABBREVIATIONS

AB	The Anchor Bible
ABD	Anchor Bible Dictionary
ASP	American Studies in Papyrology
ASTI	*Annual of the Swedish Theological Institute*
BAGD	A Greek-English Lexicon of the New Testament and Other Early Christian Literature
BARev	*Biblical Archaeology Review*
BEvT	Beiträge zur evangelischen Theologie
BibInt	*Biblical Interpretation*
BNTC	The Black Commentary
BTB	*Biblical Theology Bulletin*
BZ	Biblische Zeitschrift
BZNWKAK	Beihefte zur Zeitschrift für neutestamentlische Wissenschaft und die Kunde der älteren Kirche
CBQ	*Catholic Bible Quarterly*
CGTC	Cambridge Greek Testament Commentary
CH	*Church History*
EncJud	Encyclopedia Judaica
ESCA	*Encyclopedia of Social and Cultural Anthropology*
EvT	*Evangelische Theologie*
ExpTim	Expository Times
FRLANT	Forschungen zur Religion und Literatur des Alten und Neuen Testaments
GNT	Grundrisse zum Neuen Testament
HR	*History of Religions*
HTKNT	Herders theologischer Kommentar zum Neuen Testament
HTR	*Harvard Theological Review*
ICC	The International Critical Commentary
IVP	InterVarsity Press
JAAR	*Journal of American Academy of Religion*
JBL	*Journal of Biblical Literature*
JNES	*Journal of Near Eastern Studies*
JQR	*Jewish Quarterly Review*
JSJ	*Journal for the Study of Judaism in the Persian, Hellenistic and Roman Period*
JSNT	*Journal for the Study of the New Testament*

JSNTSup	Journal for the Study of the New Testament Supplement Series
JSSR	*Journal for the Scientific Study of Religion*
JTS	*Journal of Theological Studies*
LCL	Loeb Classic Library
Mohr	J.C.B. Mohr (Paul Siebeck)
NICNT	New International Commentary of the New Testament
NIDNTT	*New International Dictionary of New Testament Theology*
NIGTC	The New International Greek Testament Commentary
NovT	*Novum Testamentum*
NTG	Neue Theologische Grundrisse
NTOA	Novum Testamentum et Orbis Antiquus
NTR	New Testament Readings
NTS	*New Testament Studies*
NTT	New Testament Theology
OTP	*The Old Testament Pseudepigrapha*
RB	*Revue biblique*
RelSRev	*Religious Studies Review*
RHPR	*Revue d'histoire et de philosophie religieuse*
RHR	*Revue de l'histoire des religions*
SBLDS	Society of Biblical Literature Dissertation Series
SBLSP	Society of Biblical Literature Seminar Papers
SBS	Stuttgarter Bibelstudien
SBT	Studies in Biblical Theology
SIGC	Studien zur interkulturellen Geschichte des Christentums
SJT	*Scottish Journal of Theology*
SNTSMS	Society for New Testament Studies Monograph Series
SNTW	Study of the New Testament and its World
SP	Sacra Pagina
SR	*Studies in Religion / Sciences religieuses*
ST	*Studia Theologica*
TDNT	*Theological Dictionary of the New Testament*
TNTC	Tyndale New Testament Commentaries
UniT	Uni-Tachenbücher
WBC	Word Biblical Commentary
WBP	Word Books Press
WUNT	Wissenschaftliche Untersuchungen zum Neuen Testament
W/JKP	Westminster / John Knox Press
Zenshu	*Uchimura Kanzo Zenshu [all works of Kanzo Uchimura]*
ZNW	*Zeitschrift für die neutestamentliche Wissenschaft*

INTRODUCTION

This book considers issues of community–identity construction, with particular focus on the context and patterns thereof, as put forth in Paul's letter to the Galatians. Both the study of Galatians in particular and Pauline studies in general have been dominated since the Enlightenment by what is essentially a history of ideas; even the so-called 'New Perspective' on Paul's relation to the Torah may be thought of as essentially a reformulation of this discussion of ideas.[1] By focusing particularly on the issue of identity, I wish to offer to the 'sculpture' of the earliest Church shaped by many forerunners in the field of New Testament studies a new contour, i.e. a contour of the reality of religious experience. 'Community–identity construction' implies the involvement of some intentionality in forming and providing the identity of a particular community. As one thinks of 'identity' sociologically, i.e. in terms of features that distinguish a group of people from others,[2] the idea generally includes both ideological (or cognitive) features and the more concrete materiality of religion, such as distinct rituals and artefacts. In order to articulate this religio-social dimension of the recipient community of the letter, this essay employs social-scientific criticism.

There are generally two approaches that pervade the book. One is the application of social-anthropological theories on identity, which provide insights not only on the 'mechanism' of how community–identity is constructed but also on the nature of community–identity that gives insights to the relationship between communities involved in this study. Another approach is the comparative study, in which the Galatian

---

1. It is in this context that the value of social-scientific criticism has been recognized, because of its ability to look at the same texts from an entirely different perspective. Horsley, in his recent study of Mark's gospel, points out that conventional assumptions and approaches to the gospel, such as an emphasis on 'theology', which neglects politics and social issues, and the interest in fragmentary theological lessons instead of the whole story, hinder the reader from reaching the true picture of the gospel. Richard A. Horsley, *Hearing the Whole Story: The Politics of Plot in Mark's Gospel* (Louisville, KY: W/JKP, 2001), pp. ix-xv (Introduction: 'Rethinking Mark in Context').

2. Reginald Byron, 'Identity', in Alan Barnard and Jonathan Spencer (eds.), *ESCA* (London and New York: Routledge, 1996).

community and its founder, Paul, will be compared with the case of an emergent minority religious community in modern Japan as an analogy. The former (theories) will primarily aid in studying the context (or conditions) of community–identity construction (Part II). It is argued that Paul's effort of identity construction is at least partially conditioned by the pressure from his significant outgroups and that Paul's conflict with them can be understood in terms of varying, at times opposing, approaches to and expectations of community–identity construction. The latter (analogical case) will primarily be applied to a study of the patterns (or practical ways) of identity construction (Part III). The analogical case will be helpful in drawing out not only a conceptual type of identity (e.g. recreated worldview) but also tangible and physical types of identity (e.g. ritual and letter).

In the rest of the Introduction, I will first review the conventional ('theological' in Horsley's terms) approach to the Galatian study, particularly Paul's relation to the Torah, to illuminate how the discussion has been repeating itself and thereby limiting its interpretive value. Second, I will survey the relevant notable works in social-scientific criticism in order to show how the discipline has been helpful for Pauline studies in general, Galatians in particular, and therefore helpful for the present study. Then, I will clarify and explain the characteristic features of the present essay. Finally, the scope and structure of the essay will be outlined.

1. *Old and New Perspectives and Beyond*

a. *'Old' Perspectives*
The question of how Paul understood the Torah is one of the central concerns in Pauline studies, and therefore central to the study of Galatians as well. However, this conventional approach to the study focuses on the soteriological significance of the dichotomy between 'salvation by faith' and what is called 'works salvation'. It has been briefly suggested earlier that such an approach to understanding the letter of Galatians seems unduly repetitive. The following brief review of scholarship since the mid-nineteenth century pertinent to the issue of Paul's understanding of the Torah demonstrates the simple point that the present conventional discussion on the Torah adds very little to its precedents in the history of interpretation.[3] While Luther is chronologically clearly outside the scope of the review, his understanding of the Torah issue sets the course for all subsequent discussion. According to Luther, Paul's polemic against the

---

3. Cf. Francis Watson, *Paul, Judaism and the Gentiles: A Sociological Approach* (SNTSMS, 56; Cambridge: Cambridge University Press, 1986).

Torah is based on the supremacy of the new revelation of Christ in the eschatological transition.[4] The Torah's function remains as a 'hammer of death' for the unregenerate.[5] Baur articulates this negativity of the Torah within the broader framework of religious evolution. Therefore, spiritual and universalistic Christianity is said to have evolved from external and particularistic Judaism.[6] The Torah's negative nature is further articulated by Wrede, who points out its unfulfillability and inherently demanding nature. Wrede states, 'every "thou shalt" is done away' by the coming of Christ.[7] This problem of the Torah's nature to demand is even further expanded by Schürer in his description of 'Life under the Law' ('Das Leben unter dem Gesetz', i.e. the evil of the retribution system).[8] Bultmann's existential approach to the issue of the Torah is based on these negative views, especially the retribution system pointed out sharply by Schürer.[9] Schweitzer applied Luther's eschatological understanding of the Torah to his view of eschatology, arguing that the incompatibility of eschatology with the Torah is the basis of Paul's polemical attitude against it.[10] This debate over the Torah eventually does get challenged, however, by two Jewish scholars. Both Montefiore and Schoeps deny the conventional view of the Torah as a corpus of legalism, contending instead that Paul, the Diaspora Jew, misrepresents Rabbinic Judaism.[11]

4.   Hilton C. Oswald (ed.), *Luther's Works* (trans. Jaroslav Pelikan; 56 vols.; St Louis: Concordia, 1963), XXVI, p. 39.

5.   Ibid., p. 310.

6.   Ferdinand Christian Baur, *Das Christentum und die christliche Kirche der drei ersten Jahrhunderte* (Tübingen: L. Fr. Fues, 1860), pp. 5–22 (especially, pp. 6–7). Cf. also *idem, Paulus, der Apostel Jesu Christi: Sein Leben und Wirken, seine Briefe und seine Lehre* (2 vols.; Leipzig: Fues's Verlag, 2nd edn, 1866), II, pp. 224–32.

7.   W. Wrede, *Paul* (trans. E. Lummis; London: Philip Green, 1907), p. 126. Wrede also considers the pragmatic aspect of Paul's Law-free mission, which Dunn subsequently develops into the idea of 'identity markers'. James D.G. Dunn, *The Theology of Paul's Letter to the Galatians* (NTT; Cambridge: Cambridge University Press, 1993), pp. 78–79.

8.   Emil Schürer, *Geschichte des jüdischen Volkes im Zeitalter Jesu Christi* (4 vols.; Leipzig: J.C. Hinrichs'sche, 4th edn, 1907), II, pp. 545–79. Note that the later edition edits out the polemical expressions against the Torah that are characteristic of the original work. *Idem, The History of the Jewish People in the Age of Jesus Christ (175 BC–AD 135)* (rev. and ed. Geza Vermes, Fergus Millar and Matthew Black; 3 vols. in 4; Edinburgh: T. and T. Clark, 1979), II, p. 464, note 1, pp. 406–407, 486–87.

9.   Rudolf Bultmann, *Theologie des Neuen Testaments* (NTG; Tübingen: Mohr, 3rd edn, 1958), pp. 260–70.

10.   Albert Schweitzer, *Die Mystik des Apostels Paulus* (Tübingen: Mohr, 1930), pp. 186–93. He states, 'Paulus opfert das Gesetz der Eschatologie. Das Judentum gibt die Eschatologie auf und behält das Gesetz [Paul sacrifices the Torah for eschatology, whereas Judaism gives up eschatology and upholds the Torah]' (p. 90, author's translation).

11.   C.J.G. Montefiore, *Judaism and St. Paul: Two Essays* (London: Max Goschen, 1973), pp. 87–88, 93–94. H.J. Schoeps, *Paulus: Die Theologie des Apostels im Lichte der jüdischen Religionsgeschichte* (Tübingen: Mohr, 1959), Chapter 5, 'Die Gesetzeslehre des Apostels Paulus' (pp. 174–230, esp. 207–209).

b. *'New' Perspective and Beyond*

In 1977, Sanders published *Paul and Palestinian Judaism*, and it is generally considered to have inaugurated the 'New Perspective' regarding the issue of Paul's understanding of the Torah. His survey of Jewish texts written between 200 BCE and 200 CE brings him to a conclusion which is very close to the earlier proposals of Montefiore and Schoeps. In what is now known as 'covenantal nomism', according to Sanders, obedience to the Torah is a matter of maintenance of the covenant membership, rather than one of entrance into the covenant. The Torah provides the means for atonement which results in maintenance or restoration of the covenant relationship. Those who are covenantally maintained by obedience, atonement and God's mercy belong to the community which will finally be redeemed.[12] What then is Paul's polemic against the Torah? According to Sanders, it is based on the supremacy of Christ over the Torah.[13] Therefore, Sanders contributed to tone down the degree of negativity of the Torah expressed by Wrede by shifting the flow of Paul's logic from 'plight to solution' to 'solution to plight'. Sanders finally concludes that Judaism's errancy lies in the fact that 'it is not Christianity'.[14] After Sanders's covenantal nomism (and the prior contributions of Montefiore and Schoeps), many scholars joined the discussion by suggesting various alternative solutions for Paul's polemic. Moo aptly describes this scholarly *status quo* in his survey of the New Perspective. He says, 'Paul's polemic is left hanging in mid-air, and it is necessary either to accuse Paul of misunderstanding (or misrepresenting) his opponents, or to find new opponents for him to be criticizing'.[15] Dunn limits the Pauline polemic to 'works of the Law', which he argues to be circumcision, the Sabbath, and food regulations, and he maintains that these identity-markers hindered the Gentiles from appropriating salvation through Christ.[16] Setting aside the question of whether Paul's experience on the way to Damascus was conversion or a call to mission, Dunn comes very close to Baur on the pragmatic aspect of the polemic.[17] Paul's supposed misrepresentation of the Torah proposed by Schoeps is revisited by Räisänen, who argues the

---

12. E.P. Sanders, *Paul and Palestinian Judaism* (Minneapolis: Fortress, 1977), p. 422. Cf. Schoeps, *Paulus*, pp. 212, 224–30. Schoeps argues that Paul's Hellenistic understanding of the Law (νόμος) contradicts the Rabbinic understanding of the Torah.

13. E.P. Sanders, *Paul, the Law and the Jewish People* (Minneapolis: Fortress, 1983), p. 165. Cf. also Sanders, *Paul and Palestinian Judaism*, p. 485.

14. Sanders, *Paul and Palestinian Judaism*, pp. 551–52.

15. Douglas Moo, 'Paul and the Law in the Last Ten Years', *SJT* 40 (1987), pp. 287–307 (293).

16. Dunn, *Theology*, pp. 78–79.

17. Baur, *Das Christentum*, pp. 49–55.

polemic stems from Paul's intentional dichotomization in order to refute 'another gospel' (Gal. 1.6).[18]

Even after the inauguration of the 'New Perspective', we find Pauline scholarship repeatedly visiting different scholarly positions from the previous 150 years, oscillating between the old and the new interpretations of the Torah issue.[19] Wright exhibits his doubt of the significance of sociological (and for that matter rhetorical) considerations, and seeks to advance Pauline studies on the basis of the conventional approach.[20] However, in the end, his interpretive approach, i.e. the covenantal renewal scheme, only serves to mirror Schweitzer's theory of incompatibility between the Torah and eschatology. This phenomenon of an ongoing dialectic suggests that a conventional approach is of limited value in furthering our understanding of the Galatian letter.[21] Thus, it is suggested that one must find a way out by employing a different (truly new) perspective, one not dominated by the concern for doctrine. This recognition gave birth to the recent interest in social-scientific criticism.

2. *Social-Scientific Criticism in Pauline Studies*

Works that treat the letter to the Galatians entirely from a social-scientific perspective are still rare except for the recent work by Esler for the series

18. Heikki Räisänen, *Paul and the Law* (WUNT, 29; Tübingen: Mohr, 1987), p. 260. Cf. Schoeps, *Paulus*, p. 278. Schoeps argues that the reason for Paul's failure in his Jewish mission is not an insensitivity to the Jews and their culture as such, but that he misrepresents Judaism.

19. For example, Thomas Schreiner, *The Law and Its Fulfillment: A Pauline Theology of Law* (Grand Rapids: Baker, 1992), p. 119. Mark A. Seifrid, *Justification by Faith: The Origin and Development of a Central Pauline Theme* (Leiden: E.J. Brill, 1992), p. 132. While Moo does suggest a redirection for future scholarship on Pauline Law, which remains bound by the conventional theological approach, his insights describe the status quo and have little value for advancing the scholarship. Cf. Moo, 'Paul and the Law', p. 306.

20. N.T. Wright, *The Climax of the Covenant: Christ and the Law in Pauline Theology* (Minneapolis: Fortress, 1993), pp. 16–17. When Wright says 'Paul's thought forms/thought patterns', it seems to mean his theological reflection and inclinations.

21. This conclusion is shared (in a rather harsh way) by the reviewer of the work by Latto on Pauline theology, which focuses on the differences regarding anthropology between Paul and contemporary Judaism. This work, again, may simply be understood within Schweitzer's tension between eschatology and the Torah. Timo Latto, *Paulus und das Judentum: Anthropologische Erwägnungen* (Åbo: Åbo Akademis Förlag, 1991); reviewed by Russell Morton, 'Review: *Paulus und das Judentum*', *CBQ* 55 (1993), pp. 375–77.

of *New Testament Readings.*[22] Occasional applications are made, however, of various social-scientific theories on independent pericopae of Galatians, including Esler's article on the issue of table-fellowship,[23] and Elliot's exegesis on Gal. 3.1, which is based upon the idea of the 'evil eye'.[24] Esler's *Galatians* will be reviewed shortly and subsequently referred to frequently throughout the book. Because the Galatians study is understood as a part of the larger Pauline study, the review of the history and development of social-scientific criticism of Pauline studies feasibly touches on its contribution to the interpretation of the letter.

Early interest in or sensitivity to the social background of Pauline communities, or the primitive churches in general, is a component of the whole historical-critical method pioneered and developed by such scholars as Dibelius and Bultmann.[25] In his work *Licht vom Osten*, Deissmann investigates the social levels of the early church by isolating specific social locations amidst an entire social stratification (*Gesellschaftsschichten*), based upon the investigation of the then newly discovered texts.[26] Owing much to the Marxist scholars, represented by Kautsky, who describe the emergence of the early church in Marxist terms as a proletariat movement,[27] the issue of social level gained the attention of New Testament studies. This question of social level (here of Pauline

22. Philip F. Esler, *Galatians* (NTR; London and New York: Routledge, 1998).
23. Philip F. Esler, 'Making and Breaking an Agreement Mediterranean Style', *BibInt* 3.3 (1995), pp. 285–314. This article is expanded and included in the above work, *Galatians*, pp. 93–116.
24. John H. Elliott, 'Paul, Galatians, and the Evil Eye', *Currents in Theology and Mission* 17 (August 1990), pp. 262–73; cf. *idem*, 'The Evil Eye and the Sermon on the Mount: Contours of a Pervasive Belief in Social Scientific Perspective', *BibInt* 2 (March 1994), pp. 51–84; Susan Eastman, 'The Evil Eye and the Curse of the Law: Galatians 3.1 Revisited', *JSNT* 83 (2001), pp. 69–87.
25. Martin Dibelius, *Urchristentum und Kultur: Rektoratsrede gehalten bei der Stiftungsfeier der Universität am 22. November 1927* (Heidelberg: C. Winters Universitäts-buchhandlung, 1928). Cf. Rudolf Bultmann, *Die Geschichte der synoptischen Tradition* (Göttingen: Vandenhoeck & Ruprecht, 10th edn, 1995), pp. 6–8.
26. Adolf Deissmann, *Licht vom Osten: Das Neue Testament und die neuentdeckten Texte der hellenistisch-römischen Welt* (Tübingen: Mohr, 4th edn, 1923), pp. 6–7. This work has continually been re-evaluated since its publication. For criticism, cf. Nigel Turner, 'Second Thoughts: Papyrus Finds', *ExpTim* LXXVI (1964), pp. 44–48; Abraham J. Malherbe, *Social Aspects of Early Christianity* (Philadelphia: Fortress, 1983), pp. 36–45. An even earlier study and directly pertinent to Galatians may be found in *die Provinzhypothese* of the letter, which was, according to W.G. Kümmel, first proposed by J.J. Schmit as early as in 1738. Werner Georg Kümmel, *Einleitung in das Neue Testament* (Heidelberg: Quelle & Meyer, 21st edn, 1983), p. 258.
27. Karl Kautsky, *Der Ursprung des Christentums: Eine historische Untersuchung* (Stuttgart: JNM Dietz Nachfolger, 12th edn, 1922), pp. 338–73. Kautsky describes the beginning of the church, in which the proletariat, who found little attraction to Essenes and Zealots, found their home in the congregation of Messiah (under 'Die Anfänge des Christentums', p. 338). Cf. Bengt Holmberg, *Sociology and the New Testament: An Appraisal*

communities) shifted over the years from 'mostly lower (and some include middle) classes'[28] to a broad 'cross section' of society.[29]

A resurgence of interest in social setting, after an interval of some decades,[30] is observed in the historical investigation of the social world of the early Christian communities, which offers helpful insights into the understanding of early Christian community life, especially the social level of such communities.[31] However, full-scale social-scientific criticism applied to the New Testament interpretations begins with Gager's *Kingdom and Community*, in which the social-scientific study shifts

---

(Minneapolis: Fortress, 1990), pp. 29–31; Luise Schottroff, '"Not Many Powerful": Approaches to a Sociology of Early Christianity', in David G. Horrell (ed.), *Social-Scientific Approaches to New Testament Interpretation* (Edinburgh: T. and T. Clark, 1999), pp. 275–87 (esp. 277–79).

28. Kautsky, *Der Ursprung*, p. 339. Deissmann, *Licht vom Osten*, pp. 6–7. In the 4th edition, Deissmann explains in the note that he uses the plural 'Überschichten' (upper classes) and 'Unterschichten' (lower classes) to avoid the appearance of a simplistic mechanical division. He admits that Pauline communities are different from the earlier Palestinian communities, but on the whole the writings portray non-artistic features and belong to the creative non-literary period (Deissmann, pp. 209–10). Cf. John G. Gager, *Kingdom and Community: The Social World of Early Christianity* (New Jersey: Prentice-Hall, 1975), pp. 23–27; Meggitt, which may turn our prosopographic understanding of Paul's community back to the old consensus. Justin J. Meggitt, *Paul, Poverty and Survival* (SNTW; Edinburgh: T. and T. Clark, 1998).

29. Edwin A. Judge, *The Social Pattern of the Christian Groups in the First Century: Some Prolegomena to the Study of New Testament Ideas of Social Obligation* (London: Tyndale, 1960), p. 61; Wayne A. Meeks, *The First Urban Christians: The Social World of the Apostle Paul* (New Haven: Yale University Press, 1983), pp. 54, 73. For a US counterpart view of social sensitivity in the New Testament interpretations, we have the 'Chicago School' represented by S.J. Case and S. Mathews. Shirley Jackson Case, *The Social Origins of Christianity* (Chicago: University of Chicago Press, 1923), and *The Social Triumph of the Ancient Church* (Chicago: University of Chicago Press, 1934); Shailer Mathews, *The Social Teaching of Jesus: An Essay in Christian Sociology* (New York: Hodder and Stoughton, 1897).

30. According to some scholars, this is due to the influence of the existentialist approach to the text. So Theißen, for example, criticizes Bultmann for turning *Sitz im Leben* into *Gemeindetheologie/Gemeindeglauben*, which drove a wedge between sociology and theology. Gerd Theißen, *Studien zur Soziologie des Urchristentums* (WUNT, 19.2.; Tübingen: Mohr, rev. edn, 1983), p. 6. Cf. Watson, *Paul*, pp. 1–22. Malina criticizes the tendency as a 'systematic theological reductionism'. Bruce Malina, 'The Social Sciences and Biblical Interpretation', *Interpretation* 36 (1982), pp. 229–42 (237).

31. Judge, *The Social Pattern*; Martin Hengel, *Judentum und Hellenismus: Studien zu ihrer Begegnung unter besonderer Berücksichtigung Palästinas bis zur Mitte des 2. Jh. v. Chr.* (WUNT, 101; Tübingen: Mohr, 1969). And more recently, Meeks, *The First Urban Christians*.

from 'social sensitivity' to 'sociological research'.[32] He applies a social-scientific model of the Millenarian movement,[33] whose apocalyptic character offers the community members relief from 'cognitive dissonance', and particularly for the Galatian communities, helps to justify the innovative character of Paul's community formation against the traditional values of Judaism.[34] Since Gager's original attempt to understand the New Testament communities, the communities of the Pauline mission have been interpreted according to a 'sectarian model',[35] which was originally developed by Weber and Troeltsch as a comparative typology of 'Church-Sect'and refined by Wilson in his articulation of various sect types.[36]

The early attempts at sectarian interpretation of the Pauline communities most pertinent to the study of Galatians are those of Watson and

---

32.   Gager, *Kingdom and Community*. The editorial of *Zygon* notes, '. . . successful or not, it is one of the most ambitious attempts available to give a systematic, social-scientific interpretation of early Church', *Zygon* 13.2 (1978), p. 108. The model is taken from P. Worsley, *The Trumpet Shall Sound: A Study of 'Cargo' Cults in Melanesia* (New York: Schlocken, 1968).

33.   Cf. Philip J. Richter, 'Recent Sociological Approaches to the Study of the New Testament', *Religion* 14 (1984), pp. 77–90; Gerd Theißen, 'Die soziologische Auswertung religiöser Überlieferungen: Ihre methodologischen Probleme am Beispiel des Urchristentums', *Kairos* 17 (1975), pp. 284–99.

34.   Gager, *Kingdom and Community*, pp. 23–27; cf. Meeks, *The First Urban Christians*, pp. 173–75, see also 54–55 and note 24 (p. 215). This early attempt at the application of a sociological model was criticized by many, which in itself is a contribution to the refinement of the future works of social-scientific criticism. For the criticism of Gager, see David L. Bartlett, 'John G. Gager's "Kingdom and Community": A Summary and Response', *Zygon* 13.2 (1978), pp. 109–22; Jonathan Z. Smith, 'Too Much Kingdom, Too Little Community', *Zygon* 13.2 (1978), pp. 123–30.

35.   An early application of this model is found in Wayne A. Meeks, 'The Man from Heaven in Johannine Sectarianism', *JBL* 91 (1972), pp. 44–73; Robin Scroggs, 'The Earliest Christian Communities as Sectarian Movement', in Jacob Neusner (ed.), *Christianity, Judaism and Other Greco-Roman Cults: Studies for Morton Smith at Sixty* (4 vols.; Leiden: E.J. Brill, 1975), II, pp. 164–79.

36.   Max Weber, *The Methodology of the Social Sciences* (trans. and ed. E.A. Shils and H.A. Finch; Glencoe: Free Press, 1949), p. 93. Ernst Troeltsch, *The Social Teaching of the Christian Churches* (trans. Olive Wyon; 2 vols.; London and New York: Macmillan, 1931). Bryan R. Wilson, *Magic and the Millennium: A Sociological Study of Religious Movements of Protest among Tribal and Third-World Peoples* (London: Heinemann, 1973); *idem, Religion in Sociological Perspective* (Oxford: Oxford University Press, 1982).

MacDonald.[37] Watson applies to his interpretation the sectarian tactics of 'denunciation/antithesis/reinterpretation' in order to create a rationale for the defence of his sectarian communities. In his view, sectarianism clearly comes to the fore in Paul's peculiar exposition of the Torah and salvation history in Galatians 3–4. Here, the Pauline polemic is not so much concerned with legalism or the righteousness of a person, as it is with the necessity to protect the sectarian nature of his community, which is under pressure from other factions of Judaism.[38] While Watson's historical reconstruction of the inauguration of Paul's Gentile mission, caused by failure in his original mission to the Jews, may rightly be criticized,[39] his sociological interpretation of Paul's polemic against the Torah adds a helpful dimension to the ongoing theological discussion of Paul's understanding of the Torah.

MacDonald, based upon Berger and Luckmann's concept of institutionalization and Weber's 'routinization of charisma' attempts to interpret the development of Pauline and deutero-Pauline communities as various phases of institutionalization, i.e. 'community-building ("genuine Pauline")/community-stabilizing (Col. & Eph.)/community-protecting (Pastorals)' institutionalizations.[40] This bold attempt to synthesize the Pauline and deutero-Pauline writings inevitably faces the problem of material selection to suit one category over and against other categories. For instance, one may wonder how the *Haustafeln* in the 'community-stabilizing' stage of Colossians and Ephesians are more socially accommodating than those in Rom. 13.1–7.[41] Her work, however, helps the reader understand that the development toward institutionalization

37. Watson, *Paul*; Margaret Y. MacDonald, *The Pauline Churches: A Socio-Historical Study of Institutionalization in the Pauline and Deutero-Pauline Writings* (SNTSMS, 60; Cambridge: Cambridge University Press, 1988). One other major work to note, though not a particularly Pauline study, is the work of Jack Sanders. Jack T. Sanders, *Schismatics, Sectarians, Dissidents, Deviants: The First One Hundred Years of Jewish-Christian Relations* (London: SCM, 1993).

38. Watson, *Paul*, pp. 70–72. Cf. Chapter 6 for the further discussion.

39. Cf. A.T. Kraabel, 'Review: Paul, Judaism and the Gentiles, *etc.*', *JBL* 108 (Spring 1989), pp. 160–63; Martin Hengel and Anna Maria Schwemer, *Paulus zwischen Damascus und Antiochien: Die unbekannten Jahre des Apostels* (WUNT, 108; Tübingen: Mohr, 1998), p. 155, note 627. Kraabel questions whether it is necessary to suppose that Paul failed in his Jewish mission, for which we do not have the evidence. Hengel's complaint is basically on the arbitrariness of the use of the evidence found in the Acts of the Apostles. However, cf. Klaus Berger, *Theologiegeschichte des Urchristentums: Theologie des Neuen Testaments* (Tübingen: Francke, 1994), p. 236.

40. Peter L. Berger and Thomas Luckmann, *The Social Construction of Reality: A Treatise in the Sociology of Knowledge* (New York: Penguin, 1966), p. 72; Max Weber, *Economy and Society: An Outline of Interpretive Sociology* (trans. Günther Roth and Claus Wittich; 3 vols.; New York: Bedminster, 1968), I, pp. 243–44.

41. MacDonald, *The Pauline Churches*, pp. 42, 106–22.

(commencing immediately from Paul himself) is a necessary and natural process and that it is a social reality for any community.[42] This perspective highlights the error of earlier scholarship in depreciating the tendency toward institutionalization found within the early Church.[43] Her attempt to interpret community development *via* descriptions of ethics, authority, rituals and belief provides a helpful tool for evaluating the developmental process of each letter.

Another significant sectarian interpretation is Esler's on Luke–Acts,[44] in which he articulately uses analogical comparative cases to provide interpretation of the Lukan community.[45] The refinement observed in the methodology, particularly the analogical comparative analysis,[46] provides the solid foundation for future works of social-scientific criticism of the New Testament. Pertinent to the Galatians study is his interpretation of the issue of mixed meal fellowship, which he bases upon Barth's concept of 'transactional' identity construction,[47] as elucidated further in his commentary on Galatians.[48]

---

42.   Douglas argues that the move from internal to external religious life is vital if a religion seeks to endure 'even a decade after its first revolutionary fervour'. Mary Douglas, *Purity and Danger: An Analysis of Concepts of Pollution and Taboo* (London and New York: Routledge, 1966), pp. 61–63.

43.   Ernst Käsemann, *Exegetische Versuche und Besinnungen* (2 vols.; Vandenhoeck & Ruprecht, 1960), I, pp. 133–34; Emil Brunner, *Das Mißverständnis der Kirche* (Zürich: Zwingli-Verlag, 1951); Günther Klein, *Die zwölf Apostel: Ursprung und Gehalt einer Idee* (FRLANT, 77; Göttingen: Vandenhoeck & Ruprecht, 1961). Cf. Luke T. Johnson, 'Review: The Pauline Churches', *JAAR* 58 (Winter 1990), pp. 716–19. For a more balanced view, refer to Jean Daniélou, *L'Église des Apôtres* (Paris: Edition du Seuil, 1970).

44.   Philip F. Esler, *Community and Gospel in Luke-Acts: The Social and Political Motivations of Lukan Theology* (SNTSMS, 57; Cambridge: Cambridge University Press, 1987).

45.   Esler, *Community* pp. 47–53. Cf. David Barrett, *Schism and Renewal in Africa: An Analysis of Six Thousand Contemporary Religious Movements* (Nairobi: Oxford University Press, 1968).

46.   We will come back to this issue later in this section, as the book depends heavily on such analogical comparative analyses. Cf. Chapter 1 (3.b).

47.   Fredrik Barth, 'Introduction', in F. Barth (ed.), *Ethnic Groups and Boundaries: The Social Organization of Culture Difference* (Oslo: Universitetsforlaget, 1969), pp. 9–38.

48.   Esler, *Community*, pp. 71–109; *idem*, *Galatians*, pp. 93–116. His conclusion on the 'table-fellowship' invited a debate over the Jewish understanding and treatment of the purity issue. Cf. E.P. Sanders, 'Jewish Association with Gentiles and Galatians 2.11–14', in R.T. Fortna and B.R. Gaventa (eds.), *The Conversation Continues: Studies in Paul and John in Honor of J. Louis Martyn* (Nashville: Abingdon, 1990), pp. 170–88; Craig C. Hill, *Hellenists and Hebrews: Reappraising Division within the Earliest Church* (Minneapolis: Fortress, 1992), pp. 118–25; Markus Bockmuehl, *Jewish Law in Gentile Churches: Halakhah and the Beginning of Christian Public Ethics* (Edinburgh: T. & T. Clark, 2000), pp. 49–83. Cf. Christine E. Hayes, *Gentile Impurities and Jewish Identities: Intermarriage and Conversion from the Bible to the Talmud* (Oxford: Oxford University Press, 2002), especially Chapter 3, 'The Impurity of Gentiles in Second Temple Sources', pp. 45–67.

On the Continental side, the most prolific scholar on social-scientific criticism is Theißen, whose most recent attempt to synthesize the development of the first two centuries of Christianity employs eclectically various sociological theories.[49] Theißen paints the picture of a 'semiotic cathedral' (Christian religion) that is constructed by such materials as myth, ethics and rituals. According to his theory, after the initial failure of the universalizing renewal effort within Judaism, the religion sought its autonomy by overcoming its crisis through transformation of religious experiences in the mother religion, as the result of which such central themes as monotheism and the sacrificial system are symbolically intensified in myth and rituals.[50] A pertinent analysis to the present study is on the function of ritual, employing Turner's theory of liminality,[51] to which we will return in our discussion of the rite of baptism.[52]

Particularly under the inspiration of Theißen, a number of sociological and psychological analyses have been attempted on the development of New Testament communities and on Paul as a person. Feldtkeller, for example, attempts to synthesize the development of the identity of the early Antiochean community.[53] In the process, he identifies a number of helpful patterns to interpret the development of a religious community,[54] taking into consideration the distinction between intentional and unintentional missions. The Gentile mission in Antioch is primarily understood as an unintentional spill-over of the intentional Jewish mission. Hence, justification by faith is understood to be Paul's later system-

49. Gerd Theißen, *Die Religion der ersten Christen: Eine Theorie des Urchristentums* (Gütersloh: Chr. Kaiser/Gütersloher Verlagshaus, 2000).

50. Cf. also G. Theißen, 'Judentum und Christentum bei Paulus: Sozialgeschichtliche Überlegungen zu einem beginnenden Schisma', in M. Hengel and U. Heckel (eds.), *Paulus und das antike Judentum* (WUNT, 58; Tübingen: Mohr, 1991), pp. 331–56. Here, Theißen regards Paul's understanding of the relation between the ways of Jews and Christians as independent from each other from the beginning, as it is expressed in the frequent presentation of antithesis between the two in Paul's theology. Rom. 9–11 reflects Paul's later effort and struggle to unite the two (cf. p. 331).

51. Victor Turner, *The Ritual Process: Structure and Anti-Structure* (New York: Cornell University Press, 1969).

52. Theißen, *Die Religion*, pp. 186–94. Cf. Chapter 7.

53. Andreas Feldtkeller, *Identitätssuche des syrischen Urchristentum: Mission, Inkulturation und Pluralität im älten Heidenchristentum* (NTOA, 25; Freiburg: Universitätsverlag/Göttingen: Vandenhoeck & Ruprecht, 1993).

54. Feldtkeller, *Identitätssuche*, pp. 35–39. The individual's shift in religious affiliation is understood in terms of varying degrees of attachment, i.e. rejection, sympathy, full membership and exclusive devotion. Cf. Chapter 4 (2.b) for the discussion of the Gentile incorporation into Judaism.

atization of the unintentional mission, which was gradually becoming the norm in Antioch.[55] Of special significance is his approach to the phenomenon of religious 'syncretism', the basis of which is partially an analogical comparison to the modern missionary phenomena.[56]

A social-scientific attempt has been made recently to understand the person of Paul and consequently his communities by Mödritzer, who interprets the behavioural patterns of such early figures as John the Baptizer, Jesus, Paul and Justin Martyr through application of Lipp's deviance theory.[57] Paul's behaviour of self-stigmatization, especially that of *Exhibitionismus* and *Ekstase*, legitimizes and grants him authority as an apostle and gospel carrier among the Galatian members (cf. Gal. 6.17).[58] According to Mödritzer's categorization, Paul's description of pre-/post-revelation behaviours may be plausibly understood as *Provokation* (as a former enemy) and *Askese* (the idea of ἀφορίζω in Gal. 1.15). This view may contribute to the ongoing debate on Paul's call/conversion issue, which inevitably invited various psychological analyses. Segal, therefore, surveys the phenomena of religious conversion with the help of psychological theories and concludes that Paul should be rightly understood as a convert from a sect of Pharisaism.[59]

Strecker makes an anthropological synthesis of Paul's theology as

---

55.   Feldtkeller, *Identitätssuche*, p. 138; also Chapter 1, 'Entscheidung für gezielte Heidenmission'.

56.   Feldtkeller, *Identitätssuche*, pp. 116–20. Feldtkeller rightly understands that the stigma put on the term 'syncretism' is a subjective evaluation. This concept will be visited in an analysis of Gal. 3–4 with the analogical comparative case of Mukyokai. Cf. Chapter 6 (2. a.-b).

57.   Helmut Mödritzer, *Stigma und Charisma im Neuen Testament und seiner Umwelt: Zur Soziologie des Urchristentums* (NTOA, 28; Freiburg: Universitätsverlag/Göttingen: Vandenhoeck & Ruprecht, 1994), particularly based upon works of Wolfgang Lipp, 'Selbststigmatisierung', in M. Brusten and J. Hohmeier (eds.), *Stigmatisierung 1: Zur Produktion geselleschaftlicher Randgruppen* (Neuwied und Darmstadt: Hermann Luchterhand Verlag, 1975), pp. 25–53; *idem*, 'Charisma – Social Deviation, Leadership and Cultural Change', *The Annual Review of the Social Sciences of Religion* 1 (1997), pp. 59–77. Mödritzer identifies the four types of self-stigmatization as interpretive tools, i.e. (1) *Provokation* (active provocation, drawing punishment on oneself), (2) *Exhibitionismus* (exhibitionistic showing of one's defects), (3) *Askese* (self-denying asceticism), and (4) *Ekstase* (forensic self-stigmatization, martyrdom) (Mödritzer, *Stigma und Charisma*, pp. 24–25).

58.   Mödritzer, *Stigma und Charisma*, pp. 213–14.

59.   Alan Segal, *Paul the Convert: The Apostolate and Apostasy of Saul the Pharisee* (New Haven and London: Yale University Press, 1990), p. 6 and Appendix (pp. 285–300): 'Paul's Conversion: Psychological Study'. His understanding of Paul's conversion particularly depends on the work (among many others) of David Snow and Richard Machalek, 'The Convert as a Social Type', in R. Collins (ed.), *Sociological Theory* (San Francisco: Jossey-Bass, 1983), pp. 259–89. Cf. also Gerd Theißen, *Psychologische Aspekte paulinischer Theologie* (FRLANT, 131; Göttingen: Vandenhoeck & Ruprecht, 1983), especially Theißen's interpretation of Rom. 7.7–23 (pp. 181–268); Paula Fredriksen, 'Paul and Augustine:

'liminal theology', on the basis of Turner's theory of ritual process via van Gennep.[60] In it, Paul is viewed as *Schwellenperson* (a liminal person) and his theology accordingly reflects his attempt to create a state of *communitas* (permanent liminality).[61] Strecker takes Galatians' 'universal' baptism formula as a structure for his thesis and analyses in Paul's letters various teachings on ethnic, social and gender differences.[62] While the concept of liminality has proven helpful, [63] it is rather a challenging task to prove that liminality covers all of Paul's thinking as Schröter rightly critiques.[64] In this sense, the present study of Galatians on the basis of the concept of liminality faces less difficulty as its focus is limited to a section in one of the earliest letters written by Paul, i.e. Paul's exposition of salvation history and the rite of baptism (Gal. 3–4).

The most thorough investigation thus far of Galatians from a social-scientific perspective is done by Esler, who uses social-scientific theories eclectically to understand various important pericopae in the social context of the community. Therefore, for example, the concept of 'honour/shame' and 'limited goods' in the Mediterranean peasant society is employed to articulate the contention at the Jerusalem meeting;[65] the social identity theory of Tajfel and Turner is employed to interpret Paul's polemical exposition of righteousness or salvation history in general;[66]

Conversion Narratives, Orthodox Traditions, and the Retrospective Self', *JTS* 37 (1986), pp. 3–34.

60. Christian Strecker, *Die liminale Theologie des Paulus: Zugänge zu paulinischen Theologie aus kulturanthropologischen Perspektive* (FRLANT, 185; Göttingen: Vandenhoeck & Ruprecht, 1999); Arnold van Gennep, *Les rites de passage: études systématique des rites* (Paris: Librairie Critique, 1909); Turner, *The Ritual Process*.

61. Strecker, *Die liminale Theologie*, p. 111. For others who apply Turner's liminality to understanding Paul, cf. Theißen, *Die Religion*; H. Moxnes, 'Social Integration and the Problem of Gender in St. Paul's Letters', *ST* 43 (1989), pp. 99–113; A.J.M. Wedderburn, *Baptism and Resurrection: Studies in Pauline Theology against its Graeco-Roman Background* (WUNT, 44; Tübingen: Mohr, 1987).

62. Strecker, *Die liminale Theologie*, pp. 349–407.

63. Cf. Moxnes, 'Social Integration', p. 113.

64. Jens Schröter, 'Review: *Die liminale Theologie des Paulus*', *JBL* 120.4 (Winter 2001), pp. 777–80.

65. Esler, *Galatians*, pp. 126–40. J.G. Peristiany (ed.), *Honour and Shame: The Values of Mediterranean Society* (London: Weidenfeld & Nicolson, 1965); J.G. Peristiany and J. Pitt-Rivers (eds.), *Honour and Grace in Anthropology* (Cambridge: Cambridge University Press, 1992); Pierre Bourdieu, 'The Sentiment of Honour in Kabyle Society' (trans. Philip Sherrard), in J.G. Peristiany (ed.), *Honour and Shame: The Values of Mediterranean Society* (London: Weidenfeld & Nicolson, 1965), pp. 191–241; Bruce J. Malina, *The New Testament World: Insights from Cultural Anthropology* (Louisville, KY: W/JKP, rev. edn, 1993); B.J. Malina and Jerome H. Neyrey, *Portraits of Paul: An Anthropology of Ancient Personality* (Louisville, KY: W/JKP, 1996).

66. Esler, *Galatians*, pp. 209–15. Henri Tajfel (ed.), *Differentiation between Social Groups: Studies in the Social Psychology of Intergroup Relations* (London and New York: Academic, 1978); H. Tajfel and J.C. Turner, 'An Integrative Theory of Intergroup Conflict', in W.G.

and the concept of symbolic reversal is suggested for the understanding of the Sarah-Hagar story.[67] These theories, employed by Esler in his work on Galatians, together with the more popular sectarian model, are useful tools to interpret the letter, especially with regard to the aspect of social contention. As demonstrated above, social-scientific criticism has been a legitimate contributor to the study of the New Testament by identifying and ploughing through new dimensions of scholarship.

The present volume is considered to be an extension of these social-scientific studies, with particular interest in the issue of community–identity construction. Mission involves at least partially founding a community of faith. Providing a positive and therefore attractive identity is crucial, especially when the newly emerging community is experiencing the danger of disintegration. In such a situation, we may be able to assume that a founder is mindful of how such an identity might effectively or convincingly be offered to the community members at least as much as he or she is mindful of articulating some important theological ideas. Therefore, the question as to how the identity of the Galatian community might be constructed seems to be a fruitful approach to interpreting the letter. In this sense, Esler's work is helpful in setting the letter to the Galatians in the wider social context of a community identifying itself over against the others. He analyses this letter with a highly confrontational nature from the perspectives of social-psychology and cultural-anthropology in order to show the strategies for hegemony between the Jerusalem leaders and Paul.[68] A contribution that the present work may offer to the Galatians studies is its focus on the issue of how the identity of the Galatian community might be constructed. By it, one may advance the understanding of the letter and of the earliest church movement through articulation of the *motivation* for power struggle within the church. In this book, on the topic of community–identity construction, one other particular contribution for pursuing ongoing social-scientific investigations of the letter to the Galatians is a special focus on the materiality of religion and its physical embodiments in artefacts, rites and lives lived as sources of community–identity (Chapters 7, 8), while not neglecting ideological (cognitive) features that likewise help members to find cohesion in a given community (Chapter 6). A comment on the peculiarity of the theoretical framework of identity construction employed in this study should be added as well. For the discussion of community–identity

---

Austin and S. Worchel (eds.), *The Social Psychology of Intergroup Relations* (Monterey, CA: Brooks-Cole, 1979), pp. 33–47; Michael A. Hogg and Dominic Abrams, *Social Identifications: A Social Psychology of Intergroup Relations and Group Processes* (London and New York: Routledge, 1988).

67.   Tajfel and Turner, 'An Integrative Theory'.

68.   Esler, *Galatians*, especially pp. 86–92.

construction, Brett's suggestion of community identity will be modified and developed. He compares Ezra's community reform to Paul's Gentile mission on the basis of two different ethnic theories, in which he identifies Ezra as 'transactional mode' and Paul as 'instrumental mode'.[69] My modification to this perspective of Brett is based upon a critical evaluation of representative theories of community–identity construction (Chapter 1). Another peculiarity of this social-scientific study of the letter to the Galatians is a comparative study with an analogical case of an emergent Christian community (Mukyokai in modern Japan), which experienced a form of marginalization in its emergence. At present, I will clarify and explain these characteristic features of the present essay.

3. *Characteristic Features of the Book*

Three peculiar features of this book will be explained here. First is the employment of social-anthropological theories. As one seeks to employ social-scientific theories, the relationship between social science and religion must be clarified in order to suggest a justification for this particular approach to interpreting the text. Second is the issue of the employment of analogical comparative study. The meaning of the comparative study in this book will be clearly explained and its usefulness in the particular study of the Galatian community delineated. Third is the interest in the materiality of religion. Explanation will be given of what is meant by 'materiality' of religion and why it is a focus for this study.

a. *Employment of Social-Scientific Theories*
The first characteristic feature in this book to note is the employment of social-scientific theories and concepts. As these theories and concepts are employed, the relationship between sociology and religion must be clarified. Part of the resistance among biblical scholars to applying social-scientific principles to biblical interpretation has its root in the very occasion of the emergence of the discipline of 'sociology', which was earlier perceived as a replacement for the worldview of the church.[70] The early reductionist approach to sociology sought to explain away religious

69. Mark G. Brett, 'Interpreting Ethnicity: Method, Hermeneutics, Ethics', in M.G. Brett (ed.), *Ethnicity and the Bible* (Leiden: E.J. Brill, 1996), pp. 3–22.

70. Wilson argues that Auguste Comte and Henri Sant-Simon viewed sociology as the replacement of theology or religion. 'Before the new science arose, theology, or at a more popular level, religion, had been the inevitable, albeit erroneous, basis for man's comprehension of society'. Cf. Wilson, *Religion*, p. 1. Therefore, application of social-scientific principles to the interpretation of New Testament texts (and for that matter any religious texts) may appear to some a hindrance to doing theology or religious studies by 'explaining away sociologically' important issues of theology or religious studies.

phenomena in purely sociological terms. This perspective persisted, as observed in the Durkheimian notion that religion is grasped as a 'social fact' or society's idealized image of itself.[71] In this reductionist view of religion (i.e. subsuming the discipline of theology under another discipline of sociology), sociological analysis of the New Testament texts seems to ignore any divine or transcendent dimension and runs the danger of reducing apparently theological statements to a purely social schematic.[72] Watson can thus explain away Paul's polemic against the Torah as an 'essentially non-theological decision' under the guise of theological discussion (Gal. 2.15–5.11).[73] However, such an extreme view of religion as 'social fact' is not the only option.[74] The possibility of dynamic exchange between social process and behaviours based on the realization of the transcendent is implied in the dialectical definition of religion by Berger, which says, '. . . it is just as possible that, in a particular historical development, a social process is the effect of religious ideation [conceptualization], while in another development the reverse may be the case'.[75] If a dynamic exchange between society and religion is rightly argued for, then in the analytical process a religious community can be meaningfully considered both from sociological and religious (or theological) perspectives. The dynamic exchange between religion and society is observed well, for instance, in Paul's instruction on the problem concerning table-fellowship in 1 Cor. 11.17–24. Here, the problem is not solved by offering a long list of table manners,[76] but by portraying for the

---

71.   Malina, 'The Social Sciences', p. 237; Peter L. Berger, *The Sacred Canopy: Elements of a Sociological Theory of Religion* (New York: Anchor Books, 1967), pp. 175–77.

72.   For example, Watson's criticism of the conventional approach seems to have moved him to the other end in the theology-sociology continuum. Cf. Watson, *Paul*, Chapter 1, 'Paul, the Reformation and Modern Scholarship' (esp. pp. 1–18). We also note the recent shift in his perspective. Cf. Francis Watson, *Text, Church and World: Biblical Interpretation in Theological Perspective* (Edinburgh: T. & T. Clark, 1994).

73.   Watson, *Paul*, pp. 34–36, 47. Watson argues that Paul's primary concern was to get rid of the targets of ridicule (Sabbath and circumcision) to make his community gentile-friendly (cf. Phil. 3.2; Gal. 5.12). A contrary approach or *Leitgedanke* is suggested by Theißen, who says, 'die bei Paulus vorliegenden theologischen Interpretationen des Verhältnisses von Juden und Christen ein Plausibilitätsbasis in der sozialen Realität haben' [the theological interpretations of the relationship between Jews and Christians suggested here by Paul show the basis of a plausibility in the social reality]. Gerd Theißen, 'Judentum und Christentum', p. 332.

74.   Cf. Wilson, *Religion*, pp. 3–5.

75.   Berger, *The Sacred Canopy*, pp. 47–48 (parentheses added). Cf. Clifford Geertz, *The Interpretation of Cultures: Selected Essays by Clifford Geertz* (New York: Basic Books, 1973), pp. 90–91.

76.   However, considerable information can be found on the commensality in this passage as opposed to a very passing remark on it in Galatians (cf. Gal 2.11–14). This difference may be a sign of transition from a less structured to a more structured community concept in Paul. This matter will be discussed in Chapter 7.

community members the eschatological drama of how unity may be finally experienced in the age to come. This example demonstrates that religious belief has a function of constructing or validating social norms.[77] Thus, the literature which describes the life of a religious community needs both sociological and theological perspectives in order to fully appreciate the meaning of the text.

While sociological reductionism should be rightly avoided, so should the danger of 'theological reductionism', which neglects social factors in the interpretation of biblical texts and reduces social situations into dogma.[78] In this sense, Theißen's criticism of an existentialist approach to the biblical texts seems legitimate. He complains that such a focus shifts the helpful sociological perspective of *Sitz im Leben* from those of human or earthly religiosity to the interests of the 'faith situation' (*Gemeindetheologie/-glauben*).[79] Reductionism in either direction distorts the overall picture of the community. If one seeks to approach a religious text objectively, both the social situation and religious significance behind its socio-religious experiences need to be taken into account. In this analysis of Galatians, the series of events it reports which seem to have caused the emergence of the community (for example, Paul's Damascus-bound religious experience, various social situations necessitated by the Gentile missions, and the possible impact of theological instruction upon the community) should not be reduced to either exclusively theological or sociological discussion. Therefore, this analysis of the letter to the Galatians, which makes a conscious effort to consider the social situation, particularly issues concerning community–identity construction, has a place in the study of Galatians and other Pauline letters in particular and the New Testament in general, because it takes note of the social situation, while not undermining concurrent theological concerns in the text.[80]

It has been argued that the application of social-scientific perspectives to the biblical text can be meaningfully done so long as balance is maintained between social-scientific and religious (or theological) foci. Another concern might be the manner in which social-scientific models

77. Malherbe, *Social Aspects*, p. 78. Cf. Gerd Theißen, 'Die Starken und Schwachen in Korinth: Soziologische Analyse eines theologischen Streites', *EvT* 35 (1975), pp. 155–72 (171–72). Cf. also Theißen, *Die Religion*, pp. 17, 31. Theißen points out theology's function of normative validating power (*die normativ-gültige Kraft*).

78. Malina, 'The Social Sciences', p. 237. Thomas F. Best, 'The Sociological Study of the New Testament: Promise and Peril of a New Discipline', *SJT* 36 (1983), pp. 181–94 (182).

79. Theißen, *Studien zur Soziologie*, p. 6.

80. Esler, in his social-scientific study of the letter to the Galatians, takes this holistic approach to the text. He says that his approach '... does not seek fully to explain the theological in terms of the social but rather aims *holistically* to do justice to both aspects [sociology and theology] of the work's complex meaning'. Esler, *Galatians*, p. 40 (italics and parenthesis added).

and theories are utilized in such a biblical study. Elliott makes a suggestion in light of this concern. He says,

> An abstract selective representation of the relationships among social phenomena is used to conceptualize, analyze, and interpret patterns of social relations. Models are *heuristic constructs* that operationalize particular theories and that *range in scope and complexity* according to the phenomena to be analyzed.[81]

Elliott contends that a model should be applied 'heuristically'. It is often criticized that a social-scientific model is set as a presupposition for interpreting the text, and that the process of interpretation degenerates into mere fact-finding or substantiation of a previously applied model. However, if a model is employed carefully, it is theoretically helpful in leading the interpreter to ask new questions otherwise not available by causing the researcher to look at the evidence from a different perspective. Heuristic model employment incorporates a process of 'working from evidence to hypothesis, involving a back-and-forth movement of suggestion checking'.[82]

During the formative period of sociology as a discipline, theoreticians sought to construct an all-encompassing model and apply it universally. This practice is known as sociological functionalism, in which all of human reality is understood as dwelling beneath universal, iron laws of sociology.[83] This approach runs the risk of following an 'epistemological imperialism of models', leading one to obscure the richness and diversity of the world rather than explaining them.[84] However, it should be noted that recent models are by design limited in scope to suit particular social situations and constraints, therefore offering 'range in scope and complexity'. With various sociological models and theories now available, the best heuristic model employment seems to be an eclectic one, in which the exegete uses whichever model is most suitable for each social situation. When heuristically and eclectically used, therefore, models and theories can provide a helpful interpretive perspective for a given text, and this approach will be adopted for this study of the text.

In addition to the clarification on the relationship between social science and religion just considered above, one qualification needs to be made on theory employment. Chapter 1 will make reference to a modification of Brett's suggestion, which was briefly introduced earlier as suggesting employment of the ethnic theories of Geertz and Barth. The qualification required here concerns the employment of ethnic theories in

---

81. John Elliott, *Social-Scientific Criticism of the New Testament: An Introduction* (London: SPCK, 1993), p. 132 (emphases added).
82. Elliott, *Social-Scientific Criticism*, p. 132.
83. Holmberg, *Sociology and the New Testament*, pp. 13–14.
84. Best, 'The Sociological Study', p. 190.

understanding Galatians. Brett suggests that the difference between Ezran religious reform and Paul's Gentile mission may be understood as variant approaches to (ethnic) community–identity construction; namely, a primordial mode for Ezra and a transactional mode for Paul.[85] Especially as Paul sought to form communities based upon the notion of dissolution of ethnic differences (Gal. 3.28), is it plausible to employ ethnic theories to study such a text? The focus here is on one reason for the plausibility. As we will see in Chapter 1, identity construction is primarily a dialectical process between external categorization and internal identification, the former being the influence of the significant others. The significant others for Paul, the founder of the Galatian community, are the ethnic commonwealth of Israel, Jewish members of the Jerusalem Church and his primary competitors in Galatia, i.e. the circumcisers, with their approaches to community construction, which are influenced by their core ethnic sentiment.[86] One expects Paul's approach to community construction to be in a sense conditioned by or rather a response to the influence and pressure of ethno-centred approaches to community construction exerted by his significant others. In other words, Paul's Gentile mission was challenged in terms of ethnicity; therefore, his response to the challenge can be understood in ethnic terms. It is easily observed in Gal. 2.1–14 that the conflicts Paul experiences with his significant others revolve around the issue of inter-ethnic relatedness. The particular ethnicity of the Galatian members may be taken into consideration as well;[87] however, Paul's concerns for the community, observed in the letter, relate primarily to the influence of one particular group of 'significant others', i.e. circumcisers. This is due to what Paul perceives as the exigence for the community. Therefore, as the context or conditions in which Paul sought to construct the community–identity are considered (Part II), the insight gained from ethnic identity theories will be especially helpful.

b. *Analogical Comparative Study*
i. *Explanation and justification*
Now that the employment of social-scientific theories has been justified, the validity of the comparative study of the Galatian community to an

85. Brett, 'Interpreting Ethnicity', pp. 3–22.
86. Thus, I use the term 'ethno-centred' approach to community-identity construction in this book.
87. Though the peculiar features of the Galatian ethnicity are not discussed in the letter itself, the insight of ethnic theories may prove beneficial in our comparative analysis of Paul's relation to the Galatian community and Uchimura's relation to Mukyokai. Refer to the discussion on the issue of indigenization and its implication to the understanding of Paul's warning against the observation of festivals (Gal. 4.9–11) in Chapter 6 (2.b).

analogical case of a religious community can be argued and explained. Ashton, in his recent book *The Religion of Paul the Apostle*, outlines the difference between genealogical and analogical comparisons and argues for the explanatory value of the latter, particularly in the interpretation of the biblical text. He argues that the usual approach to comparative studies (i.e. genealogical comparative study) in New Testament interpretation has been to seek an explanation of why and how early Christianity emerged out of Judaism. Christianity can be historically traced back in the genealogical line to its mother religion, which is Judaism. In this comparison, an assumption is made that there are some familial similarities between the subject matter (early Christianity) and its genealogical forerunner (Judaism).[88] It is this genealogical approach to the interpretation of the biblical text that has dominated the study of Christian origins. Therefore, a genealogical comparison is beneficial in asking questions regarding how and why the new community fulfils or betrays expectations based upon familial similarities with the mother community.[89]

Analogical comparison, on the other hand, refers to a comparison between groups without 'genetic' connections. Analogical comparison plays an important part in the evolutionary model of biology. Apart from self-evident genealogical resemblances, biologists are aware of a different kind of resemblance, due to what is called 'convergent evolution'.[90] Resemblances on the basis of this convergent evolution force one to consider plausible explanations for a phenomenon, rather than simply describing it. Ashton notes the benefits of considering the similar kind of convergent resemblance displayed in the disciplines of comparative literature and anthropology in order to show 'analogical' evidence of how such a study can be beneficial not only in natural science but also social science and the humanities.[91] Therefore, the assumption is that a tool with such explanatory value can be appropriated in the study of biblical literature.

Indeed, the explanatory value of analogical comparative studies has been recognized in the realm of biblical studies. Bultmann, for example, sought to analyse the history of the formation of the synoptic tradition on the basis of not only the sources of Rabbinic and Hellenistic literatures, but also on the analogical case observed in the history of the collection of

---

88.   John Ashton, *The Religion of Paul the Apostle* (London: Yale University Press, 2000), p. 11.

89.   The discussion on the patterns of Gentile incorporation into 'Judaism' and its implication in the conflicts in Gal. 2 in Chapters 5 and 6 will employ this genealogical analysis.

90.   Ashton, *The Religion*, pp. 15–16.

91.   Ibid., pp. 16–22.

the Buddhist canon in Jakarta.[92] More recently, Fredriksen studied Paul's experience of conversion/call both on the basis of the socio-psychological theory constructed from the investigations of modern religious phenomena of conversion and on a comparative study with an analogy of St Augustine's conversion experience.[93] Sanders, in his survey of the Jewish-Christian relationship of the first hundred years, applied the analogical case of Soka-Gakkai, a newly emerging Buddhist sect originated in Japan, in order to illumine his argument on the success of the early Christian expansion.[94] These examples show that analogical comparison can be utilized as a helpful heuristic tool, which enables us to approach the text with new and different questions and ways to answer those questions.

By drawing an analogy from the Japanese group, it is not meant that the group in modern Japan has an exactly parallel culture with the ancient Mediterranean world, as some analogical analyses have been wrongly criticized.[95] Wedderburn explains a more careful approach that should be involved in such an analogical comparison. He says,

> It is possible to generalize from such individual pieces of evidence; the best that we can do is to say that this was true in one particular instance and it may have been true in some others also. However, we have no reason either for setting any such piece of evidence aside as only an isolated case; it might also be typical of many others.[96]

This study will use the religious group of Mukyokai (literally 'non-church' movement)[97] as a primary analogical comparative case, which has its emergence in the late nineteenth and early twentieth centuries through the work of its founder, Kanzo Uchimura.[98] In what follows, I will place the descriptions of Paul's Galatian community and Uchimura's Mukyokai side by side in order to show that this comparative study is feasible and fruitful.

---

92. Bultmann, *Die Geschichte*, pp. 7–8.

93. Fredriksen, 'Paul and Augustine', pp. 3–34 (particularly, 20–26). For the criticism of the approach to the issue, cf. Larry W. Hurtado, 'Convert, Apostate or Apostle to the Nations: The "Conversion" of Paul in Recent Scholarship', *SR* 22.3 (1993), pp. 273–84 (280–81). Esler's sectarian model is another example, which relies on a sectarian perspective of an African denomination, based upon Weber's church-sect model.

94. J. Sanders, *Schismatics*, pp. 229–57.

95. R.S. Sugirtharajah, *Asian Biblical Hermeneutics and Postcolonialism: Contesting the Interpretation* (Sheffield: Sheffield Academic, 1999), pp. 106–07.

96. Wedderburn, *Baptism and Resurrection*, p. 162.

97. Emil Brunner, 'Die christliche Nicht-Kirche-Bewegung in Japan', in *Gottlob Schrenk, dem Mann der Mission zum 80 Geburtstag* (Festschrift G. Schrenk, 4; Heft; Evangelische Theologie, 1959).

98. Mukyokai will be introduced in detail in Chapter 2. The underground religious movement called Kakure Kirishitan will also be introduced later in Chapter 8 (1.b.).

ii. *Community descriptions*

Paul's Galatian community. Galati or Celts settled in the northern part of
central Anatolia in the middle of the third century BCE, dividing the area
according to their three tribal groups of Tolistoboii, Tectosages and
Trogmi (Strabo, *Geog.* 12.5.1–4; Dio Cassius, *Hist.* 41.63; 42.46–49; Pliny
Elder, *Nat. Hist.* 5.42 [146]). Owing much to the ambitious diplomatic and
military skills of the chieftain of the Tolistoboii, Deïotaros, the three
tribes were united under his kingship and with Roman support in the
middle of the first century BCE. After the deaths of Deïotaros and his
grandson, Amyntas (Deïotaros' secretary) received much of Lycaonia and
Pamphylia from Octavianus in 31 BCE, who, after the death of Amyntas,
annexed the Celt-owned territory as the Roman province of Galatia, ruled
by the emperor's agent of a provincial governor in 25 BCE. The province
continued to annex its neighbouring territories as their own dynasts
diseased.[99] It is in this large provincial area of Galatia that Paul's
community is to be found.

When reference is made to the 'Galatian community' and the like, that
does not imply that there was only one local gathering, as Paul refers to
the original readers and audience of the letter as ἀδελφοὶ ταῖς ἐκκλησίαις
τῆς Γαλατίας (Gal. 1.2). Rather, it can safely be assumed that several
local gatherings formed as a result of Paul's mission in 'Galatia'.[100] What
is meant, then, by the term 'community', is the entire collectivity of these
local religious gatherings that Paul denotes as ἐκκλησίαι, the original
recipients of his letter. It is, of course, difficult to determine the historical
location of Paul's community in Galatia. The majority of scholars assume
that the founding of the community happened during Paul's so-called
'second missionary journey'.[101] The northern area of the Galatian
province is where the original Celts settled (one may call it 'Galatia
proper'),[102] and it is in this area that the population of ethnic Celts was
concentrated, unlike the southern regions of Pamphylia and Lycaonia
which were later additions to Amyntas' Galatia. The problem which

99.   So were added Paphlagonia, Comana Pontica and Pontus Plemoniacus. Galatia was
a model of 'provincial annexation'. Stephen Mitchell, *Anatolia* (2 vols.; Oxford: Clarendon,
1993), I, p. 63. See also the comment of Greg Horsley, 'Anatolia, from the Celts to the
Christians', *Buried History* 36.1–2 (2000), pp. 49–55 (54).
100.   James D.G. Dunn, *The Epistle to the Galatians* (BNTC; Peabody: Hendrickson,
1995), p. 30; J. Louis Martyn, *Galatians: A New Translation with Introduction and
Commentary* (AB, 33a; New York: Doubleday, 1997), pp. 85–86.
101.   Kümmel, *Einleitung*, pp. 265–66. It is the assumption for this book that Paul wrote
the letter to the community he founded in the northern part of the Galatian province during
what is termed as 'the second missionary journey', penned while he was in Corinth.
102.   Murphy-O'Connor locates the recipients of Paul's letter in Pessinus of the original
settlement of Tolistoboii. Jerome Murphy-O'Connor, *Paul: A Critical Life* (Oxford: Oxford
University Press, 1996), p. 192.

occasioned Paul to send this rather harsh letter took place not too long after the founding of the community, at least from Paul's perspective, as Gal. 1.6 (οὕτως ταχέως) seems to indicate.[103] Therefore, the letter to the Galatians can arguably be located in the early developmental stages of the community, during Paul's initial efforts at community construction among the Gentiles.[104]

In identifying the problem that the community was facing, interpreters often employ a scheme called 'mirror-reading', in which the opponents' beliefs and behaviours are inferred through Paul's antitheses against them.[105] Such a rhetorical consideration may be helpful in the further analysis of the life situation of the community,[106] but the present description of the community requires what is obvious from the surface level of the text, with which even those who are skeptical toward the 'mirror-reading' technique would agree as well.[107] Paul identifies certain individuals who visited 'his' community to instruct the members contrary to what Paul had previously taught (Gal. 1.6–8). Later, he reminds the reader of the 'danger' of those people, who are called here 'circumcisers' (Gal. 4.17).[108]

Paul's narration of the conflicts in Jerusalem and in Antioch (Gal. 2.1–14) and his peculiar teaching on salvation history against the possible

103. Although one should take into consideration Paul's possible rhetorical scheme in this expression (οὕτως ταχέως) so as to determine exactly 'how quickly' they turned, it must have been 'quick' from Paul's perspective and reflects some degree of truth in order to prove convincing to the original readers. Cf. Richard N. Longenecker, *Galatians* (WBC, 41; Dallas: WBP, 1990), p. 14; Martyn, *Galatians*, p. 107.

104. The provenance of the letter is arguably either Corinth or Ephesus in the early part of 50s CE during Paul's mission that corresponds with the '2nd missionary journey' in Acts. Cf. Hans D. Betz, *A Commentary on Paul's Letter to the Churches in Galatia* (Hermeneia; Philadelphia: Fortress, 1979), pp. 11–12; Kümmel, *Einleitung*, pp. 265–66. In this book, because of the considerable development in Paul's thought between Gal. and 1 Cor., the time of writing for Galatians is placed during Paul's stay in Corinth (cf. Acts 18.11), which makes the interval between the writing of Galatians and of 1 Corinthians (probably written from Ephesus) at least two to three years.

105. Note the debate on the usefulness of the interpretive scheme. Reference may be made to the guideline for applying the 'mirror-reading' approach to the text suggested by Barclay. John M.G. Barclay, *Obeying the Truth: A Study of Paul's Ethics in Galatians* (Edinburgh: T. and T. Clark, 1988), pp. 36–41. Cf. Esler, *Galatians*, p. 67.

106. The balance between the hermeneutical scheme of 'mirror-reading' and Paul's possible active recreation of the worldview will be discussed in Chapter 6 (1.b).

107. George Lyons, *Pauline Autobiography: Toward a New Understanding* (SBLDS, 73; Atlanta: Scholars, 1985), pp. 170–76.

108. In other words, the ones who pressured the Galatian members to be circumcised in order to become fully incorporated into the Church. They are otherwise known as 'Judaizers' or 'Opponents'. J. Louis Martyn in his commentary introduces them as 'Teachers' in order to treat them neutrally—without Paul's negative value-judgement—and to identify them as distinct missionaries to Gentiles independent of Paul. Cf. Martyn, *Galatians*, pp. 117–26. The highly ambiguous description of circumcisers (1.7, 9; 3.1; 4.17; 5.7, 12; 6.12) causes the debate

persuasion of the circumcisers (Gal. 3, 4) point to the assumption that there was a conflict in the idea of community construction between Paul and those whom he was against. The conflicts in Jerusalem (Gal. 2.1–10) and in Antioch (Gal. 2.11–14) both entail the problems of incorporation of and status for Gentiles.[109] The conflicts and the temporary solution of 'two missions' (Gal. 2.7–9) reflect that there was no hard and fast rule of Gentile incorporation.[110] The situations in Jerusalem and in Antioch correspond with the background of the problem in the Galatian community, or at least Paul narrates the conflicts in Jerusalem and Antioch in a way that is meaningful or convincing for the Galatian members. Paul's interpretation of the Torah and the salvation history, thereby, authenticate the status of Gentile members in the community, who may have felt marginalized by teachings other than Paul's (esp. Gal. 4.21–31). In the middle of the confusion caused by the circumcisers, Paul strives to provide cohesion for the community members, i.e. to secure the identity of the community as an independent and authentic entity over against the disintegrating pressures from without. On the practical level, Paul's defence is against those who seek to enforce circumcision upon members of his community (Gal. 6.12; cf. 5.11–12). It almost goes without saying that circumcision was closely related to the issue of Gentile incorporation into Jewish communities (*Ant.* 20.34–48).[111] 'Another gospel' (Gal. 1.6), therefore, is the message which represents those who oppose Paul's way of community building. These external forces upon the

---

on their identification. For example, J.B. Lightfoot, *Saint Paul's Epistle to the Galatians* (London: Macmillan, 10th edn, 1890), pp. 68, 253; F.J.A. Hort, *Judaistic Christianity* (London: Macmillan, 1904), pp. 80–81; Wilhelm Lütgert, *Gesetz und Geist: Eine Untersuchung zur Vorgeschichte des Galaterbriefes* (Gütersloh: C. Bertelsmann, 1919), pp. 59–60; Johannes Munck, *Paul and the Salvation of Mankind* (London: SCM Press, 1959), p. 112; John Muddiman, 'An Anatomy of Galatians', in S.E. Porter, *et al.* (eds.), *Crossing the Boundaries: Essays in Biblical Interpretation in Honour of Michael D. Goulder* (Leiden: E.J. Brill, 1994), pp. 257–70. One finds a survey of 'opponents' in the recent study of Mark D. Nanos, *The Irony of Galatians: Paul's Letter in First-Century Context* (Minneapolis: Fortress Press, 2002). On the basis of two points, it is assumed in this book that they were Jewish believers of Judaean origin. One is that they are described with the third person plural as outsiders to the Galatians, and the other is that Paul relates the problem in Galatia with circumcisers to the incidents in Jerusalem and Antioch with Jewish Christians. Cf. J. Louis Martyn, 'A Law-Observant Mission to Gentiles: The Background of Galatians', *SJT* 38 (1985), pp. 307–24 (313); Joseph B. Tyson, 'Paul's Opponents in Galatia', *NovT* 10 (1968), pp. 241–54 (252).

    109. Further discussion of this point is found in Chapter 5 (1.a).

    110. Hans Conzelmann, *Geschichte des Urchristentums* (GNT, 5; Göttingen: Vandenhoeck & Ruprecht, 1969), p. 68.

    111. John M.G. Barclay, *Jews in the Mediterranean Diaspora from Alexander to Trajan, 323 BCE–117 CE* (Edinburgh: T. & T. Clark, 1995), pp. 438–39. This issue is further discussed in Chapter 4 (2.d).

Galatian community seem to endanger Paul's very vision of what his community should be like, i.e. the very sense of the community–identity.

Another peculiarity of the epistle is Paul's usage of phraseology that connotes a sense of belonging. Therefore, the negative influence of the outsiders is described as ἐκκλεῖσαι ὑμᾶς θέλουσιν ('they seek to exclude you', Gal. 4.17) and κατηργήθητε ἀπὸ Χριστοῦ ('. . . cut yourself off from Christ', Gal. 5.4). The members are invited to choose their allegiance to either Paul or the outsiders (Gal. 4.12–20). Even in what is considered to be a 'theological' section in Gal. 3, such phrases as τοῦ Ἀβραὰμ σπέρμα ('Abraham's offspring', Gal. 3.29) and κληρονόμοι ('heirs', Gal. 3.29; cf. 4.7) seem to serve as instruction for the original readers as to with whom they were to identify themselves and where they belonged.[112]

The epistle could arguably have been written as Paul's defence of his young community in their struggle to survive as a distinct group with a peculiar sense of identity, conditioned by Paul's vision of community construction and by the historical and social situations in which the community members found themselves. Thus the study of Galatians benefits from employing a social-scientific approach that is sensitive to the concept of community–identity formation, and likewise benefits from the comparison with an emerging minority religious group struggling to define itself under disintegrating pressure from outside.

This book's primary focus is Paul's approach to community–identity construction in relation to that of others, using his letter to the Galatians as the primary source. Therefore, in the course of discussion, explanations often follow along the line of Paul's arguments with his peculiar rhetoric being understood as representative of his own perspective. However, this does not mean that I simply accept Paul's value-judgement. Therefore, for example, while Paul may well have considered circumcisers' pressure as marginalization of the Galatian community, from the perspective of circumcisers it was probably a necessary correction for the benefit of the Galatian community members. While the letter reflects Paul's genuine concern for the welfare of the Gentile members in the Galatian community on the basis of a revelatory experience (Gal. 1.14–15), his highly confrontational narration in Gal. 2.1–14 may be thought of in terms of a power struggle with the Jerusalem leaders as well. Moreover, even Paul's genuine concern for the Gentile members may not have been easily accepted by the recipients. For instance, Paul's remark in Gal. 2.15, 'we are by nature Jews and not Gentile sinners' (Ἡμεῖς φύσει Ἰουδαῖοι καὶ οὐκ ἐξ ἐθνῶν ἁμαρτωλοί), may have caused the Gentile audience to experience perplexity in their identity (cf. 1 Thess. 4.5). Paul's warning against participation in the calendrical observance in Gal. 4.9–11 may have been a refusal of the natives' creative indigenization of the religion

---

112. On this point, further discussion is given in Chapter 6 (1.a).

recently brought by Paul himself.[113] Therefore, the reader will be reminded at times in the course of this study where it is helpful to point out that an argument belongs to Paul's perspective and does not reflect the objective value-judgement of the present analysis.

Uchimura's Mukyokai. A full description of Uchimura and his Mukyokai is found in Chapter 2. Here, I will give the reasons for selecting Mukyokai from among other religious groups and why it is plausible to use Mukyokai as an analogical case. The reason for choosing Uchimura and his Mukyokai as the primary analogical case from among others is three-fold. First, it is a religious movement in the recent history of Japan. A considerable number of first-hand sources about the community (Uchimura himself and the first-generation members of the community) and historical information of the country are readily available, which makes a historical reconstruction of the emergence of this community fairly easy. Second, the emerging period of the community is known, which renders possible the comparison with the emergence of Paul's Gentile mission and the Galatian community. Third, the peculiar emergence experience of Uchimura out of the denominational church resembles Paul's emergence experience closely enough to satisfy a comparison of the two founding figures as a meaningful one. For these reasons, Uchimura and his Mukyokai seem to be the most plausible comparative case for this study amongst other religious communities whose information is also available to me.[114]

Mukyokai's peculiar character is introduced to the western world through the writings of Brunner, a Swiss theologian, who comments, 'A particularly notable example of such a non-church-like *Ecclesia* movement was made known to me in Japan. There exists a whole series of groups, which were called into existence by the strong personality of the early Japanese evangelist, Kanzo Uchimura, mostly consisting of university professors and student ...'[115] Brunner's phrase of 'non-church-like *Ecclesia*' refers to the anti-institutional and anti-sacramental ideologies of Mukyokai. In their teaching, they make a clear distinction between the original *Ecclesia* and the later church. According to Mukyokai, the former

---

113. Refer to Chapter 6 (2.b).

114. My acquaintance with this religious group was occasioned by my friendship with Prof. Chiba of International Christian University (ICU), one of the present leading figures of Mukyokai. I was kindly allowed to conduct two months of research at ICU, in whose library is housed the Uchimura Memorial Collection.

115. Brunner, *Das Mißverständnis*, p. 154 (author's translation). Recent studies on Uchimura and Mukyokai in English are: Hiroshi Miura, *The Life and Thought of Kanzo Uchimura, 1861–1930* (Grand Rapids: Eerdmans, 1996) and Carlo Caldarola, *Christianity: The Japanese Way* (Leiden: E.J. Brill, 1979). For our study, the latter work is extremely helpful as it conducts a critical sociological analysis of the subject matter.

is a fellowship of individuals who seek a union or *koinonia* with God through Jesus Christ. This idea of religious existence is understood by the group as originating with the historical Jesus ('Shiso Kondaku no Gensen' [Origin of Misunderstanding], in *Seisho no Kenkyu* 104 [November 1908]).[116] The Reformation was God's way of bringing his people back to *Ecclesia*. For Mukyokai, the present church shows a similar pattern of institutionalism and perceives itself as God's instrument of reformation ('Mukyokai ni Tsuite' [On Mukyokai], in *Seisho no Kenkyu* 327 [October 1927]).[117] Mukyokai sees itself as holding to the original vision of *Ecclesia*, and therefore is against the institutionalism and sacramentalism of the Church, thus consequently against denominationalism ('Mukyokai no Zenshin' [Advance of Mukyokai], in *Seisho no Kenkyu* 85 [March 1907]).[118]

This peculiar understanding of ecclesiology reflects the social situation of the emerging community. As Uchimura sought to form his religious group, he was reactive in his criticism of denominational churches and the western missionaries behind the denominationalism. Therefore, a part of Uchimura's effort to construct and maintain the positive identity of Mukyokai is done through severe criticism against the mother 'religion' of the denominational church, its western missionaries in particular and cultural traditions in general.[119] One should also take note of the larger social and political context of the modernization of Japan during this period. Uchimura was torn between people's attraction to the church as naïve fascination toward the West and the growing anti-Christian sentiment that attended a rising imperial nationalism. Therefore, Uchimura's effort to present a positive identity of his community was also through redefinition of faith in Christ apart from the western cultural elements and through indigenization of the religion with his nuanced criticism of the imperial nationalism.[120] In the process of founding the community, Uchimura was criticized by the church as a heretic and stigmatized by the secular public as a national traitor.[121]

The writings of both Paul and Uchimura reflect the periods during

116. Kanzo Uchimura, *Uchimura Kanzo Zenshu* [*All Works of Kanzo Uchimura*] (41 vols.; Tokyo: Iwanami Shotcn, 1982), XVI, pp. 82–83.

117. Uchimura, *Zenshu*, XXX, pp. 37–38.

118. Uchimura, *Zenshu*, IX, p. 216.

119. Kanzo Uchimura, 'American Christianity', *The Japanese Christian Intelligencer* 2.5 (July 1927), in *Zenshu*, XXX, p. 368; *idem*, 'On Protestantism', *Seisho no Kenkyu* [*Bible Study*] 190 (May, 1916), in *Zenshu* XXII, p. 259.

120. Kanzo Uchimura, 'Enemies of Christianity', *Seisho no Kenkyu* 199 (October 1917), in *Zenshu*, XXIII, pp. 167–68; *idem*, 'Bushido and Christianity', *Seisho no Kenkyu* 186 (January 1916), in *Zenshu*, XXII, pp. 161–62.

121. Kanzo Uchimura, *Letter to Bell* (March 6, 1891)/*Letter to Miyabe* (January 8, 1891), in *Zenshu* XXXVI, pp. 329–31, 334.

which the communities emerged and became marginalized under outside pressure of disintegration. Both religious groups respectively have their 'mother religion' of Judaism and denominational churches. Both founders felt pressured from the 'orthodoxy' of Jewish churches and Christian denominations (at least parts of these constituents). Therefore, the analogical comparative study between the two communities of Galatians and Mukyokai seems both feasible and fruitful.

c. *Materiality of Religion*

The third characteristic feature of this book to note is its focus on the materiality of religion. As we clarified earlier, 'identity' in the sociological sense (not in the psychological sense here, though these two may be rather inseparably related) relates to features that distinguish a particular group from other groups, and these features are generally ideological (or cognitive) and more concrete, relating to the materiality of religion through elements, such as rituals and artefacts. However, neglect of this non-cognitive materiality of religion has been pointed out.[122] Smart gives the important reminder that the study of religion should not confine itself to the investigation of ideas, failing to take note of the practical, aesthetic and emotional dimensions of religion (including the material dimension).[123] The importance of concrete materiality for the identity of a religious community is stressed by Graham, who says,

> ... seeing, hearing, and touching in particular are essential elements in religious life as we can observe it.... they deserve greater attention than our bias in favor of the mental and emotional aspects of religion (in case of scripture, toward the 'original message' or 'theological meaning' of the text) typically allows.[124]

Objects and actions that can be seen, heard and touched may be important locators, in which can be found the identity of a religious community.

In his study of Galatians, Esler takes into consideration the issues of community–identity.[125] In his study, ideological concepts such as 'righteousness' and 'freedom' are explained as the identity of the community.[126] We note that Esler takes note of such a concrete materiality of religion as

---

122. John Barton, *Holy Writings, Sacred Text: The Canon in Early Christianity* (Louisville, KY: W/JKP, 1997), p. 107. Barton shares the same conviction, particularly on the function of the holy writings apart from their 'semantic contents'.

123. Ninian Smart, *Dimensions of the Sacred: An Anatomy of the World's Beliefs* (London: Harper Collins, 1996), pp. 10–11.

124. W.A. Graham, *Beyond the Written Word: Oral Aspects of Scripture in the History of Religion* (Cambridge: Cambridge University Press, 1987), p. 6.

125. Esler, *Galatians*, particularly pp. 40–57, 69–92, and chapter 4 .

126. Ibid., chapter 6 on 'righteousness' and chapter 8 on 'freedom'.

the issue of commensality at the same time, which is argued to be a significant issue in defining the identity of the communities in Jerusalem and in Antioch (Gal. 2.1–14).[127] In order to join the discussion of the identity of the Galatian community in a constructive way, this study of community–identity construction will focus largely on the area of concrete objects or actions, through which the community members may have communally gained cohesion and distinctiveness. Therefore, the last two chapters (Chapters 7 and 8) will investigate the function of the rite of baptism (Gal. 3.28) and the formal significance of the letter (Gal. 6.11) as sources of community–identity.

4. *Scope and Structure of the Book*

To conclude the Introduction, I will present the scope and structure of the book. It consists of three parts. Part I will outline the theoretical framework of community–identity construction in Chapter 1, and introduce the analogical comparative case of Uchimura and his Mukyokai in Chapter 2. Chapter 1 will outline a theoretical framework of identity-construction, in which both the nature and mechanism of identity construction are discussed. On the nature of community–identity, two particular features will be of note. One is that identity is constructed in the dialectic process between external categorization and internal identification (or internalization). Therefore, one needs to be aware of the influence of Paul's significant others in analysing his effort to effect identity construction. The second feature relates to the flexibility of community–identity. Members perceive identity symbolically, i.e. they gather with variously nuanced understandings of the same symbol. This idea will help in understanding the social reality of unity and diversity in one larger community, like the Jewish commonwealth. The mechanism of ethnic identity will include a review of what is known variously as Primordialism, Instrumentalism and Transactionalism, in order to suggest the benefits and limitations of each theory. Then, an eclectic approach drawing on the three theories will be suggested in which instrumental and primordial modes of identity construction are seen as extreme cases of a transactional mechanism of identity construction in general. These considerations on the theories of identity construction will be applied primarily in the study of the context (or conditions) of community–identity construction in Part II. In addition to these theories of identity construction, a theory of social process based upon van Gennep's 'rites of passage' will also be introduced, which will then be elaborated and employed in an interpretation of Galatians 3 and 4 in Chapters 6 and 7.

127. Ibid., pp. 93–116.

Chapter 2 will give a historical description of Mukyokai as the primary analogical case. An evaluation of the group and its founder will also be given, from political and sociological perspectives, in order to draw out some ways by which the group constructed and maintained its identity. The analogical comparative study will be employed primarily in the study of the patterns (or practical ways) of community–identity construction in Part III.

Part II will analyse the context, which Paul's effort of community–identity construction may be shaped by and derive from. Chapter 3 will seek to establish the case that Paul can be conceived as a community constructor of what is called the 'instrumental mode', free from a core ethnic sentiment in constructing the community–identity. For this suggestion, a part of Paul's biographical account will be considered (Gal. 1.13–2.10). Chapter 4 will study the patterns of Gentile incorporation of the Jewish commonwealth, primarily in the Second Temple period. This is because assumptions are made that the leaders of the Jerusalem Church, being Jews, would follow the genealogical patterns of community–identity construction, which is shaped by the concern of a core ethnic sentiment. This chapter will prepare for the following investigation on Paul's conflicts with the Jerusalem apostles (Gal. 2.1–14) in Chapter 5. Chapter 5 will argue that Paul's accounts of the conflicts in Jerusalem and Antioch are to persuade the Galatian community members that community construction on the basis of Jewish ethnic sentiment results in marginalization and subjugation of non-Jews in the community. This delineation of Paul's style of community–identity construction and the conflicts which it inevitably caused will establish the context, in which consideration of the patterns of Paul's community–identity construction will be made in the following part (Part III).

Part III will suggest three ways of community–identity construction for the Galatian community that are observed in the letter. If Paul is understood as being free from the restraints of a core ethnic sentiment in his approach to community–identity construction, the assumption is that he is free to either recreate or abandon altogether the features that manifest such ethnic sentiment in accordance with (what Paul may have perceived as) the welfare of the community members from his perspective. Chapter 6 seeks to understand Paul's exposition of salvation history in Galatians 3 and 4 (particularly Gal. 4.21–31) as his recreation of a worldview in order to offer cohesion (and therefore a new identity) to community members in the marginalized status of being non-Jews. In it, the status of Gentile members is affirmed as authentic and Jewish believers in Christ who enforce Torah obedience are made unauthentic and outsiders of the community. It is noted that this sense of identity is 'ideological' and not 'material'. This essay is also interested in the materiality of identity construction. Therefore, I suggest that this 'ideological' identity finds its way to physical manifestation in the rite of baptism, which is the focus of Chapter 7. Chapter 7 argues that the rite of baptism, with its egalitarian motif (Gal. 3.28) in the liturgical saying, is an occasion for the community members to act out the recreated worldview, in order to physically (ritually) affirm the newly reconstructed identity. Chapter 8 will consider the function of the letter as a physical object, which the community members may have held as a replacement for the apostle in his absence from the community. With such an understanding, the letter may have functioned as a locus of identity that they could see, hear and touch.

Community–identity construction concerns the *raison d'être* of a community and the individuals cooperatively living in it. To consider the context and patterns of community–identity construction in the letter to the Galatians, therefore, inevitably brings one closer to the reality of the religious experience of the individuals of the recipient group. It is hoped that the book offers this dimension called 'the reality of religious experience' to the ongoing discussion of the letter to the Galatians in particular and the life of the early Christian community in general.

Part I

COMMUNITY–IDENTITY CONSTRUCTION:
A THEORETICAL FRAMEWORK AND ANALOGICAL CASE

If they ask: what is Yamato's soul?
Say: it is the blossom of the wild cherry,
Radiant in the morning sun.[1]

The cherry blossom was certainly considered the 'national' flower as early as the oldest collection of poetries called *Manyoshu* (c. 400–750 CE). Even now most Japanese school children learn to sing the *Cherry Song* at an early age. Yet, one may wonder what it means that cherry blossoms represent the very 'soul' of *Yamato*.[2] Moto-ori Norinaga (1730–1801), one of the four major Japanese philologists in the Middle Ages, sought the ethos of Japan void of the foreign influences of both Buddhism and Confucianism. He did so on the basis of ancient mythologies, and the cherry blossom may have been a convenient symbol that conjures up the 'memory' of ancient Japan. However, is there any didactic value rather than poetic value in the attempt to make a mere flower symbolize the identity of a people or a nation when the author sought to resist foreign ideologies to shape the nation's ethos? Further, is it plausible to assume that all Japanese possess either the same or a very similar sense of attachment toward the pink-coloured petals? For the islanders of the southernmost Okinawan archipelago, which was conquered by one of the Japanese clans in the early eighteenth century, the choice of the cherry blossom over *Erythrina Indica* (or coral tree) as an identity marker of the islanders was a highly political identity construction and it must have been a humiliating decision for the newly added members of the nation.

The concept of identity, whether it is of an ethnic or a religious community (or both for that matter), is, on one hand, rather abstract. It is, on the other hand, loaded with emotion and spoken of in terms of material objects and manners of life. Like the cherry blossom, the abstract

---

1. A *tanka*-poem composed by Motori, Norinaga. Author's translation of the text, which reads, 'Shikishima no Yamato no Kokoro Hito towaba/Asahi ni niou Yama-Zakura Bana.'
2. Yamato is the appelation for ancient and pre-modern Japan. It was considered as the centre of eight Japanese islands.

sense of ethnic and religious sentiment of the Jewish commonwealth manifests itself often in the emotional dispute over foreskin. To begin to understand and appreciate the sensibility and complexity, particularly for this study, of Paul's community–identity construction, one must become familiar with both the *nature* of identity and the *mechanism* of community–identity construction, which are delineated in the first chapter.

The *tanka* represents the effort to create the myth of the ancient origin of the nation in order to establish its strong identity, which became increasingly necessary as the dawn of modern Japan commenced with the new era of Meiji. It was in this time of identity construction of the new nation-state that Mukyokai came into being and sought to find its place in the society. Therefore, the social context of the national-identity construction consequently shaped at least partly the course of Mukyokai's identity construction. In order to interpret the letter to the Galatians from the perspective of community–identity construction especially in relation to its wider social context, insights gained from Mukyokai's struggle for identity construction as an analogy will be instructive. The second chapter, therefore, introduces and analyses the emergence and development of the Mukyokai movement.

Chapter 1

FRAMEWORK OF IDENTITY CONSTRUCTION

The first chapter relates to methodological issues relevant to this book. In it will be a discussion of the nature of identity construction, followed by a discourse on the mechanism of ethnic identity construction and, third, an introduction to the theory of social process. It is suggested that the eclectic use of these theories and concepts will help in analysing the identity construction of the Galatian community.

First, I would like to begin with a discussion of the nature of 'identity' in the sociological sense of the term. This discussion will focus on two issues, i.e. (1) the dialectic nature of community–identity, and (2) the flexible nature of community–identity. The discussion of the dialectic nature of community–identity will explain that identity is formed by both internal 'identification' and external 'categorization' (or 'labelling'). This issue leads to an appropriate perspective on community–identity construction whereby the analysis of construction involves an evaluation of the life-situation of the community in relation to its significant, yet outside, others. This perspective will lead the interpreter to an awareness of the need to consider the influence or pressure of its significant others, namely the general populations of Jews and Galatians and the particular community of Jewish churches (especially the Jerusalem church). Another issue is the flexible nature of community–identity. Community members 'aggregate' around an identity-marker with various nuances in meaning and significance of identity, rather than being homogeneously integrated by a singular and exclusive meaning and application of identity. Discussion of this issue helps to elucidate why Jewish groups or sects with different inclinations and peculiarities exist under an overall identity of 'Jews', yet at the same time distinguish themselves from others outside. This perspective will help explain why there were varying expectations in the Jerusalem church about Gentile believers (or 'sympathizers' from their perspectives) and how to understand the existence of varying attitudes among the Jewish groups concerning important ethnic identity-markers or 'physio-cultural features' (for example, circumcision, commensality, and land) as it is termed in this book, which reflect their core ethnic sentiment.

Second, I will introduce an eclectic approach to three perspectives on ethnic identity construction involving (1) Primordialism, (2)

Instrumentalism, and (3) Transactionalism. The Introduction discussed the reasons for employing ethnic identity theories in the analysis of the Galatian community.[1] In this eclectic view, it is suggested that the transactional perspective generally reflects the reality of identity construction, while understanding that the other two perspectives describe groups with highly distinct characters (extremes). The eclectic approach to the theories will be employed mostly to understand the context of community–identity construction in Part II, while it will continue to be the foundation for our understanding of the contention between Paul and other Jewish Christians (particularly in Jerusalem) in Part III, which discusses the actual practice of community–identity construction.

Third, I would like also to consider a theory of social process developed by Turner on the basis of van Gennep's perspective on 'ritual process'. This social process theory will be employed because it aids understanding of peculiar behaviours of a newly emerging group out of the background context of a larger social structure, and it is particularly helpful in appreciating the function of rituals in such an emerging community. Therefore, Turner's theory will be employed in studying actual practices (behaviours) of community–identity construction in Part III, which discusses the concept and effect of a 'recreation of worldview' in Chapter 6 and the rite of baptism as the concrete demonstration (acting out) of the recreated worldview in Chapter 7. To conclude, a schematic framework of community–identity construction, as outlined above, will be applied to the subsequent chapters.

1. *Nature of Community–Identity*

a. *Identity as Interaction with Outgroups*
The concept of 'identity' has widely been recognized as a natural, dialectic relation between the subjective and the objective in the process of identity formation.[2] The application of this aspect into a sociological and social-anthropological framework of identity construction has been articulated both by Cohen and more recently by Jenkins.[3] These theoreticians of social anthropology inform the present discussion because both are articulate in describing the nature of identity, especially in relation to the

---

1. For the employment of ethnic theories for interpreting Galatians, see Introduction (3.a).

2. Reginald Byron, *ESCA*, s.v. 'identity'.

3. Anthony P. Cohen, *The Symbolic Construction of Community* (London and New York: Routledge, 1989); Richard Jenkins, *Social Identity* (London and New York: Routledge, 1996). One of their contributions is their effort to make Barth's constructive or transactional theory of ethnic identity widely applicable to other social phenomena. Barth's theory is introduced in the following discussion.

issue of the construction of community–identity. Jenkins' main point is to emphasize the dialectic process as crucial to social identity construction. Beginning with the identity (or rather identification, implying the active process of identity construction) of an individual,[4] he argues that individual identity is constructed in a continual process of dialectic between self-hood (internal identification of 'who I am') and human-ness (external categorization of 'who they say that I am').[5] He then applies this 'internal-external dialectic of identification' to describe the construction of collectivities in general. The identity of an individual cannot be discussed in isolation from the opinion of 'others'.[6] The process of 'identity' can thus be understood as located both in the core of the individual and within his or her greater communal culture, emphasizing the relationship between the individual and society for understanding one's own identity.[7] Collective identity is still one step further from this understanding. The process of this type of identification is found both in the core of communal culture (the particular collectivity) and in the aggregate society at large in which the group is located.

Sustaining focus on this mode of internal–external dialectic, Jenkins introduces the distinction between 'group' and 'category'. The former is described as the identity of a collectivity by the ingroup members. The latter is the categorization of the same collectivity by the outgroups.[8] While categorization of 'us' by 'others' does not have to be real, it is a resource upon which 'we' draw in the construction of 'our' own identities.[9] Therefore, Jenkins's 'categorization' is another nomenclature for the concept of 'labelling' in deviance theory, because in categorization one does not simply decide the name of the object of interaction, but also how to respond to or treat it.[10] The consequence of such an act of categorization has enormous influence upon the one being categorized. In

---

4. Jenkins, *Social Identity*, p. 20. By using the term 'identification' instead of 'identity', Jenkins clarifies the initiative sense of 'identification' (something constantly being constructed). By saying 'identity', Jenkins fears that the concept may imply to many something that is given *a priori* (primordially).

5. Ibid.

6. Ibid.

7. Gordon Marshall (ed.), *Dictionary of Sociology* (Oxford and New York: Oxford University Press, 2nd edn, 1998), s.v. 'identity'. The dictionary introduces the psycho-historical analysis of E. Erikson in defining the concept of identity.

8. Jenkins, *Social Identity*, p. 82.

9. Ibid., pp. 86–87.

10. Ibid., p. 77. Jenkins's suggestion here is based upon such works as A.V. Cicourel and J. Kitsuse, *The Educational Decision Makers* (Indianapolis: Bobbs Merrill, 1963); J.R. Mercer, *Labeling the Mentally Retarded: Clinical and Social System Perspectives on Mental Retardation* (Berkeley: University of California Press, 1973); H. Mehan, A. Hertweck and J.L. Meihls, *Handicapping the Handicapped: Decision Making in Students' Educational Careers* (Stanford: Stanford University Press, 1986).

the social reaction perspective or deviance theory, the action of labelling as 'deviant' has a sociological consequence upon the ones labelled as such. Lemert makes a distinction between primary deviance and secondary deviance. While primary deviance is the basic act of 'deviance' which all perform sometime in life, secondary deviance is the resulting deviant actions due to the categorization as 'deviant'. Here, we are referring to the secondary deviance.[11] Jenkins incorporates this theory into his thesis and understands that external categorization has a significant impact on internal identification.[12] In this sense, Jenkins understands the boundary line that distinguishes one group from others as the locus of the dialectic process of identity construction. Cohen describes this dialectic process as a symbolic recreation or syncretism, 'a process in which new and old were synthesized into an idiom more consonant with indigenous culture'.[13] Therefore, one should take note of the influence of the significant outgroups in order to understand the behaviour of the ingroup in their identity construction.

The concept of external categorization mentioned above helps us to make the assumption that Paul's approach to community–identity construction is shaped by the ways in which the community felt pressured from outgroups, i.e. the general population of Israel and particular groups of Jewish Christians (Jerusalem apostles, ψευδαδέλφοι and circumcisers) that exerted various pressures upon Paul and his community. Also of note is the inevitable pressure from the larger population of Galatians outside of Paul's community. Therefore, when Paul speaks against the 'pagan' practices (Gal. 4.8–11; 5.20), one should be aware of the social pressure of the general Galatian population, as well as the general propensity of the members to sin, and also to consider possible behaviours of those Galatians deracinated from the larger population in terms of religious indigenization or syncretism.[14]

---

11. E.M. Lemert, *Human Deviant: Social Problem and Social Controls* (Englewood Cliffs: Prentice-Hall, 2nd edn, 1972), pp. 62–92.

12. Jenkins, *Social Identity*, p. 77.

13. A.P. Cohen, *The Symbolic Construction*, p. 37. A peculiar feature of categorization is 'stereotype'. It is based upon a viewpoint, in this case of others. It is an extremely condensed symbol(s) of collective identification. In the context of inter-group contention, it is the symbol created to stigmatize others based upon an intentional generalization and simplification of their characteristic qualities. Jenkins, *Social Identity*, pp. 119–25. Cf. Esler, *Galatians*, pp. 55–57. By the term 'stereotypical criticism' is meant, therefore, a strategy of identity construction (pp. 77–78).

14. For the possibility of indigenization in Gal. 4.8–10, refer to the first two pages of Chapter 6.

b. *Community as Commonality*

Cohen notes that a community reflects two rather seemingly opposing aspects of identity, i.e. *fluidity* in cultural features and a rather *stable* sense of identity. He describes this function of community–identity as offering a locus for people to aggregate.[15] When he uses the term 'aggregation', he is making a comparison with the functionalist's view of community as integrating individuals; that is, to make the community members dependent upon the community and to perform the function of fulfilling the need of the society.[16] In order to articulate the distinction between integrating nature of society and aggregating nature of society (i.e. between integration and 'commonality'), Cohen introduces the concept of 'symbolic construction'. He explains the symbol and its function as follows: 'Symbols, then do more than merely stand for or represent something else. Indeed, if that was all they did, they would be redundant. They also allow those who employ them to supply part of their meaning'.[17] In other words, it is not so much that the symbol gives meaning as it offers the capacity for the members to create various meanings. If exactly the same meaning to a symbol is given and understood by community members, it would be 'integration'. However, community is commonality and aggregation of individuals, i.e. community members congregate under the same symbol (or a feature that distinguishes the community from others) with varying interpretations or understandings of the same symbol. However, he qualifies at the same time that, while allowing flexibility, there is enough common understanding of a symbol that those who do not share the same understanding would be identified as outsiders and deviants.[18]

For example, Josephus describes the Jews as having unity as a people, while articulating the differences between the three 'philosophies' (φιλοσοφεῖται), i.e. Pharisees, Sadducees, and Essenes (*Apion* 2.179–81; *War* 2.118–19).[19] While seeing the commonality (or unity) in these distinct groups, Josephus still describes the 'fourth philosophy' as something quite foreign from the rest of the 'united' people (*Ant.* 18.1.1).[20] This

---

15. Cohen, *The Symbolic Construction*, p. 20.
16. Ibid., pp. 24–28.
17. Ibid., p. 14.
18. Ibid., p. 16.
19. Martin Goodman, 'Identity and Authority', *Judaism* 39 (1990), pp. 192–201.
20. It should be noted that his description of the 'fourth philosophy' may well reflect Josephus' polemic based upon his political motivation for writing the work, that is to make a distinction between the general population of Jews and rebels against the Roman authority. Cf. Steve Mason, *Josephus and the New Testament* (Peabody: Hendrickson, 2nd edn, 2003), pp. 183–96; E.P. Sanders, *Judaism: Practice and Belief 63 BCE–66 CE* (London: SCM, 1992), pp. 280–84; Christopher Rowland, *Christian Origins: An Account of the Setting and Character of the Most Important Messianic Sect of Judaism* (London: SPCK, 1985), p. 72.

understanding of the nature of community helps us to avoid viewing such entities as Judaism and the church monolithically in the discussion of their respective 'identities'.

This is an important perspective in this study as we seek to understand the coexistence of internal flexibility of the larger Jewish commonwealth and their sense of distinction *vis-à-vis* non-Jews.[21] There are disparate views among the larger Jewish commonwealth, for example, on issues of inter-ethnic intercourse such as Gentile proselytism, marriage and mixed dining, while groups (sects) with various peculiarities aggregate under one name 'Israel'. This concept of aggregation is helpful in understanding the situation of the Jerusalem church, in which can be found members who seem to hold different approaches to the issue of Gentile incorporation, a key cause of the contention found in the Jerusalem meeting (Gal. 2.1–10; cf. Acts 15.1, 5).

Two issues have been considered that relate to the nature of community–identity, namely dialectic identification and aggregation. The mechanism of ethnic identity construction will now be considered.

2. *Mechanism of Ethnic Identity Construction*

In the discussion on the mechanism of ethnic identity, there are primarily three theories suggested, which are Primordialism, Instrumentalism and Transactionalism.[22] It is generally understood that there is a core of ethnic sentiment within each group, manifesting itself in various physical and cultural (denoted from this point 'physio-cultural') features such as geographic location, assumed blood ties, religion and language. The theories primarily differ in their view on the flexibility or intentionality in maintaining and abandoning these physio-cultural features and on the relationship between the physio-cultural features and the core ethnic sentiment of a group. Primordialism, as the term 'primordial' suggests, tends to consider the physio-cultural features as *a priori* (thus primordially) given. Instrumentalism tends to view physio-cultural features 'instrumentally', i.e. as something that a group uses as an instrument to gain benefit (usually political and economic) of the group, sometimes to the point that the core ethnic sentiment seems to be undermined in the process.[23] Transactionalism, while maintaining that some physio-cultural

---

21. Cf. Chapter 5 (2.b.ii).

22. Sergey Sokolovskii, *ESCA*, s.v. 'ethnicity'.

23. We should not understand the economically and politically motivated construction of identity negatively as opposed to the less pragmatic identity construction, for it is one of the manifestations of the concern for community–identity construction and maintenance. Both the instrumental mode and the primordial mode concern community construction, maintenance and at times survival.

features are non-negotiable, understands that an ethnic identity cannot be appropriately understood by looking at the physio-cultural features. Rather, the core ethnic sentiment of a group manifests itself in the group's behavioural patterns regarding its boundary negotiation with groups outside.

The phrase 'identity construction' has been used frequently so far in the discussion. This term implies some level of intentionality, as the word 'construction' connotes. In order to understand how the element of intentionality is appropriated into the construction of identity, a survey of all three theories and the relation between them will be undertaken. This theoretical survey will primarily rely on the works of Geertz (Primordialism), Cohen (Instrumentalism) and Barth (Transactionalism). They are considered as the major proponents of their respective theories and their works articulate the differences between these theories. In the end, an eclectic approach to these theories will be attempted.

a. *Primordialism*

Observing the persistent nature of ethnic identity when faced with the homogenizing political influence of the larger society or new state, Geertz argues for the primordial nature of cultural features, as well as shared biological and geographical features existing within an ethnic group.[24] Geertz's list of these physio-cultural features as foci of natural, sentimental affinity includes assumed blood ties, language, region, religion and custom.[25] This primordial perspective of ethnic identity should be understood in the relational context of conflict between 'old societies and new states'; that is, between ethnic groups and the post-colonial new state that encompasses those groups. Geertz says that there are two motives existing in a new state. One is the desire of smaller, local groups within the new state to have their identity publicly acknowledged, i.e. having the sense of 'being somebody in the world'. The other is the demand of the state for progress as a whole, resulting in the desire to have considerable political and economic influence among the nations.[26] The former is easily manifested in local parochialism and communalism, and the latter is in the state's desire for modernization. In his review of the process of modernization of the post-colonial new states in Asia and Africa, Geertz was impressed by the persistence of the sense of attachment to

24. Clifford Geertz, 'The Integrative Revolution: Primordial Sentiments and Civil Politics in the New States', in *idem* (ed.), *Old Societies and New States: The Quest for Modernity in Asia and Africa* (New York: The Free Press, 1963), pp. 108–13 (109).

25. Ibid., pp. 112–13. The possible importance of having Abraham as the common ancestry and of the concept of *Eretz Israel* (Land of Israel) for constructing and maintaining the community–identity will be discussed in Chapter 5.

26. Ibid., p. 108.

the local ethnic ties, reflected in the persistence of the physio-cultural features. He describes how he understands primordiality:

> By a primordial attachment is meant one that stems from the 'givens' ...
> of social existence: immediate contiguity and kin connection mainly, but
> beyond them the givenness that stems from being born into a particular
> religious community, speaking a particular language, or even a dialect
> of a language, and following particular social practices. These
> congruities of blood, speech, custom, and so on, are seen to have an
> *ineffable*, and at times *overpowering, coerciveness in and of themselves.*[27]

It should be noted that Geertz understands both the core ethnic sentiment and the physio-cultural features (as the expression of the former) to be absolute and given, hence Primordialism.[28] Then he emphasizes the significance of primordiality by negating the possibility of a dialectic (interactive) view of identity construction. He says, '... for virtually every person, in every society, at almost all times, some attachments seem to flow more from a sense of natural – some would say spiritual – affinity than from social interaction'.[29] This negation of a dialectic (interactive) identity construction, which will be considered in the study of the following theories of Instrumentalism and Transactionalism, is the foundation of Geertz's warning that the direct conflict between primordial (local ethnic) and civil (integrative) sentiments is the most threatening problem which the new states face.[30]

This primordial theory has been criticized by many. Eller and Coughlan criticize that the assumption of primordiality abandons the empirical investigation as to how 'cultural-symbolic practices ... produce and reproduce identity and attachment' by assigning the identity markers *a priori* status.[31] The primary problem with the theory is that the highly fixed system does not explain the frequent cultural changes observed within ethnic groups, nor does it explain the emergence of new ethnic groups.[32] Geertz's primordial theory gives the impression that ethnic identity is formed in isolation, if not exemption, from the influence of outgroups, which is exactly the criticism of Barth.[33] Indeed, Geertz gives the overall appearance of underestimating the dialectic (interactive) aspect

---

27.   Ibid., p. 109 (emphases added).
28.   Ibid.
29.   Ibid., p. 110.
30.   Ibid., p. 111.
31.   Jack Eller and Reed Coughlan, 'The Poverty of Primordialism: The Demystification of Ethnic Attachments', *Ethnic and Racial Studies* 16.2 (1993), pp. 183–202 (199).
32.   John Hutchinson and Anthony D. Smith, 'Ethnicity, Religion, and Language', in J. Hutchinson and A.D. Smith (eds.), *Ethnicity* (Oxford and New York: Oxford University Press, 1996), pp. 32–34 (34).
33.   Barth, *Ethnic Groups*, p. 10.

of identity construction as previously noted.[34] While Geertz is rightly criticized for undermining the dialectic feature of identity-construction, it should be noted that his criticism of the dialectic process reflects his warning against the integrating pressure of the colonial power. He points out the reason for the difficulty the old societies face in integrating the policy of their new state. The problem, according to him, is that upon ethnic identities which have gone through the 'centuries of gradual crystallization' is superimposed the unfamiliar civil state, 'born yesterday from the meager remains of an exhausted colonial regime'.[35]

b. *Instrumentalism*
Cohen argues that ethnic identity is asserted and maintained as an instrument to achieve political and/or economic gains of a collectivity. The conclusion he draws here is based upon his observation of the Hausa people in Ibadan in how they construct their identity.[36] For instance, Ibadan Hausa sought to maintain its solidarity in order to achieve an economic advantage in nuts and cattle trades.[37] They also quickly changed their religious affiliations in order to preserve their distinctiveness as a religious community when Yoruba people were collectively converted into the old religion of Hausa as the result of a restructuring process imposed on the whole society following the period of colonialism.[38] Especially in this latter example, the physio-cultural feature of religion was used as an 'instrument' and was exchanged in order to preserve their political benefit as a distinctive collectivity. Cohen stresses this instrumental nature of identity construction over against what is called 'psychological ethnicity', which locates the sense of identity within one's mind, therefore making it primordial. Cohen says, '. . . [ethnicity] is a live political and economic issue and is not just a method of categorization to help the African migrant to deal with the bewildering complexity of urban society'.[39] Though Cohen must assume that some kind of pre-existing form of cultural congruity is necessary as a core of ethnic identity, the construction is entirely motivated by political and economic gain.[40]

---

34. Geertz, 'The Integrative Revolution', p. 110.
35. Ibid., p. 119.
36. Abner Cohen, *Custom and Politics in Urban Africa* (Berkeley: University of California Press, 1969), p. 13.
37. Ibid., p. 131.
38. Ibid., p. 24. Ibadan Hausa changed their religious affiliations to the Tijaniyya order when the group conversion of Yoruba people into Islam took place.
39. Ibid., p. 193.
40. Cf. Marcus Banks, *Ethnicity: Anthropological Constructions* (London and New York: Routledge, 1996), pp. 35–36.

Cohen's instrumental view is challenged by Epstein, who holds to a psychological approach to identity. His thesis is that identity is a life-long developmental process within the context of external influence and internal (psychological) factors.[41] Epstein's main criticism of Cohen is that his theory only explains the ethnic construction of particular cases and is not sufficient to comprehensively understand identity construction. Hutchinson and Smith point out that Primordialism by Geertz is problematic because it is unable to explain why new ethnic groups are constantly emerging. At the same time, they criticize the instrumental approach on two accounts. One is that it does not properly explain the reason why inordinate sentiment of attachment to ethnic ties and cultural symbols are sometimes observed. The other is that the perspective does not take into consideration the relative stability of ethnic identity.[42] We are aware of the concern expressed by Epstein, especially against Cohen, that his theory may not apply to every case of identity construction. Therefore, Hutchinson and Smith's comment is correct that Primordialism must answer why new ethnic groups are being formed and the outlook of some ethnic groups is changing, while Instrumentalism must answer why some ethnic groups persist through centuries with very similar features.[43]

c. *Transactionalism*

While the preceding theories of ethnic identity, and especially Primordialism, tend to focus on the inventory of physio-cultural features, Barth notes in his theory that ethnicity manifests itself in the exchange or negotiation of those features at the boundaries, which divide ethnic groups. From this transactional perspective, he offers a framework that covers the varying phenomena of identity construction observed both by Geertz and Cohen. Barth explains the main theme of his transactional theory in relation to the conventional primordial approach to ethnic identity. He says,

> Ethnic distinctions do not depend on an absence of social interaction and acceptance, but are quite to the contrary often the very foundations on which embracing social systems are built. Interaction in such a social system does not lead to its liquidation through change and accultura-tion; cultural differences can persist despite inter-ethnic contact and interdependence.[44]

---

41. A.L. Epstein, *Ethos and Identity: Three Studies in Ethnicity* (London: Tavistock, 1978), p. 7.

42. Hutchinson and Smith, 'Ethnicity, Religion, and Language', p. 34.

43. Ibid., pp. 32–34.

44. Barth, *Ethnic Groups*, p. 10.

We may recall from the review of Geertz's primordial theory that he emphasizes primordiality of both the core ethnic sentiment and the physio-cultural features that are the expression of the former. On the other hand, Barth emphasizes the persistence of cultural distinction, despite the fluidity of those features. Elsewhere he says explicitly that 'the constraints on a person's behaviour which spring from ethnic identity [i.e. ethnic sentiment] ... tend to be absolute'.[45] Thus it is important to note that Barth considers the core ethnic sentiment to be *a priori* given, while the expressions of the ethnic sentiment may change in the process of social interaction. Barth admits that the ideal type of ethnic group with its physio-cultural features is at times helpful, but gives a falsely preconceived idea that groups develop independently of one another. Obviously, this emphasis of transaction is a reaction against Geertz's Primordialism.

Barth then clarifies the relationship between the core ethnic sentiment and the physio-cultural features. He says that these features are the result of identity construction, but certainly not the cause. He says, 'In my view, much can be gained by regarding this very important feature [physio-cultural features] as an implication or result, rather than a primary and definitional characteristic of ethnic group organization'.[46] Therefore, he suggests that the focus of investigation should be on the ethnic boundary line which defines the group, rather than the 'cultural stuff (features)' in which ethnicity is manifested.[47] Then he articulates how groups behave at the boundary line in relation to the influence of outgroups. Boundaries in stable condition provide a selective structuring of interaction, therefore the pattern of osmosis, at its boundary, gives us a picture of what the identity looks like. He says,

> Stable inter-ethnic relations presuppose such a structuring of inter-action: a set of prescriptions governing situations of contact, and allowing for articulation in some sectors or domains of activity, and a set of proscriptions on social situations preventing inter-ethnic inter-action in other sectors, and thus insulating parts of the cultures from confrontation and modification.[48]

Barth's theory is sometimes criticized for paying insufficient attention to the external pressure that influences the behaviour of ingroups at the boundary line. Therefore, Jenkins points out that the influence of external categorization needs to be taken into account in a group's behaviour at the boundary line.[49] Even though Barth speaks of permeability at the

45. Ibid., p. 17 (parentheses added).
46. Ibid. (parentheses added).
47. Ibid., p. 15.
48. Ibid., p. 16.
49. Jenkins, *Social Identity*, pp. 95–96.

boundary line, he is focusing on the nature of that line and not so much on how the external forces affect the level of permeability or what constitutes 'a set of prescriptions/of proscriptions'. Therefore, Banks's criticism seems valid when he says that Barth appears to give a rather 'democratic' picture of boundary behaviour. Banks notes that Barth, disregarding the political power imbalance between two tribal groups (Pathan and Baluchi groups) in his analysis of their identity construction, portrays Pathans as having a free choice in changing and exchanging identities free from external political pressure from the Baluchi group.[50] Such a qualification by Jenkins and Banks is helpful in an employment of Barthian theory to understand the boundary behaviour of various groups under pressure from outgroups.[51]

d. *Eclectic Approach to the Theories*
The reason that an eclectic approach to these theories is better than choosing only one out of the three is rooted upon the criticism of these theories represented by Epstein, Hutchinson and Smith, and Banks. Epstein suggests that Instrumentalism (and Primordialism for that matter) is not a comprehensive theory to explain all the cases of identity construction of ethnic groups.[52] It is rather that some groups reflect the pattern of identity construction akin to what Geertz proposes and other groups which Cohen proposes. As noted earlier, Hutchinson and Smith point out that Primordialism does not explain why some groups change their outlooks and other new groups constantly emerge, and Instrumentalism has to explain why some groups persist over centuries.[53] Banks also warns that theories need to be understood in view of the objects of research upon which they are built.[54] In this sense, the insight of Brett is helpful as he proposes that one may consider the Ezra-Nehemiah community to represent a primordial mode of community construction, while Paul's mission represents a constructive (i.e. transactional) mode of community construction.[55] It will be noted, however, that Brett's view of Paul's approach to community–identity construction is different from the one this book suggests, i.e. 'instrumental mode' instead of 'Transactionalism'.

    In observation of the three theories and their critiques, one may note

50. Banks, *Ethnicity*, p. 16.
51. We will discuss this issue in detail in Chapter 5.
52. Epstein, *Ethnos and Identity*, p. 7.
53. Hutchinson and Smith, 'Ethnicity, Religion, and Language', pp. 32–34.
54. Banks, *Ethnicity*, pp. 47–48.
55. Brett, 'Interpreting Ethnicity', p. 13.

that Barth's theory of Transactionalism seems to describe best the reality of the mechanism of ethnic identity construction while the other two describe the character of particular ethnic groups. Therefore, the suggested eclectic approach is as follows. Ethnic identity or core ethnic sentiment is reflected in the group's behaviour at the boundary line, where it faces pressure from other outgroups. In the interaction with these groups, an ethnic group decides (not always assuming a democratic atmosphere and sometimes 'behaviour at the boundary line' might be forced) which physio-cultural features to maintain and which to abandon or broaden the definitions regarding a particular feature. This negotiation at the boundary reflects the distinct identity or portrayal of an ethnic group. Then, where do the theories of Cohen and Geertz come in? They are the articulation of a peculiar behavioural tendency of some particular groups. Therefore, their theories describe how each ethnic group behaves differently in its identity construction at its boundary line. Some groups are more resistant to change and exchange in the boundary negotiation. These groups tend to preserve not only the core ethnic sentiment, but also much of the physio-cultural features (primordial mode). Others are more fluid and flexible in the boundary negotiation even to the point that the core ethnic sentiment is undermined. These groups either preserve their ethnicity through changing cultural features (thus the outlook of some ethnic groups change), or in some cases their high fluidity may cause the disintegration of a particular ethnicity (thus we observe the disappearance and creation of ethnic groups; instrumental mode).

How is this eclectic view applied to the general understanding of Jewish ethnicity and its relation to Paul's Gentile mission? The larger ethnic collectivity or commonwealth of the Jews living among non-Jews had to regulate the influence of the Gentile physio-cultural features at the boundary line. In Chapter 4, the issue of Gentile incorporation (proselytism) into Jewish communities will be discussed, in order to point out that the Jewish approach to the issue of identity may be described in terms of Barth's Transactionalism in that their identity is reflected in the ethno-centred negotiation of various physio-cultural features around the boundary that separates them from other groups. The degree of flexibility of each physio-cultural feature might vary between different sects within the Jewish commonwealth. Considering the emergence of the earliest church from its mother religion of Judaism, we may be able to find the same tendency within the Jerusalem church, i.e. the above-mentioned diversity is observed microcosmically within the Jerusalem church (cf. Chapter 4). On the other hand, Paul's effort in his Gentile mission may be understood as an 'instrumental mode' of community construction, as Paul considered himself an autonomous apostle for the Gentile mission and free from the constraints of a core

ethnic sentiment (cf. Chapter 3).[56] Then, it will be suggested that the
conflict between Paul and the Jerusalem apostles (and other members of
the church of Jerusalem, ψευδαδέλφοι) may be due to the various
opposing expectations of behaviour at the boundary line (cf. Chapter 5).
These theories are particularly pertinent to the discussion of the context
(or conditions) of Paul's identity construction, which is the focus of Part
II. There is need to introduce yet another theory of social process by
Turner, which will be employed particularly in Chapters 6 and 7.

3. *Theory of Emergence: Rites of Passage*

The reason for employing this theory by Turner for our interpretation is
that it is helpful in understanding the kind of emergence that we observe
in the Galatian community. For the study of group emergence, the
sectarian model is the one that has often been applied for understanding
the development of the earliest church movement, as reviewed in the
Introduction.[57] The sectarian model has been developed and finely
categorized to suit the sociological analyses of religious groups,[58] and
helpful modifications have been made.[59] Such a model may well be a
helpful tool to understand the development of Pauline communities, as
derivatives of Paul's mission to Gentiles reflect features of 'sects'.
However, the Galatian community can be understood with the help of a
theory of social process by Turner, not only because the emergent
situation of the Galatian community resembles what Turner calls
'permanent liminality' (some correlation between the Galatian situation
and 'permanent liminality' will be suggested later in this section), but also

---

56. Although Abner Cohen uses Instrumentalism to refer to the phenomenon of ethnic
identity construction among various collectives, the focus here is on Paul's (individual)
approach to community–identity construction as reflected in his letter. This means that some
of Paul's co-workers may have approached the Gentile mission in much the same way, but at
the same time this does not mean that Galatian community members were free from ethnic or
cultural constraints (cf. indigenization of Gal. 4.8–10 in Chapter 6). Also of note is that his
'instrumental' approach to community–identity construction in Galatians may be his most
idealistic stage of Gentile mission, and a shift in his approach to mission may be observed in 1
Corinthians. Refer to Chapter 7.

57. Watson, *Paul*; M.Y. MacDonald, *The Pauline Churches*; Meeks, 'The Man from
Heaven'.

58. Wilson, *Magic and the Millennium*; *idem*, 'An Analysis of Sect Development', in B.R.
Wilson (ed.), *Patterns of Sectarianism: Organization and Ideology in Social and Religious
Movements* (London: Heinemann, 1967), pp. 22–45.

59. For example, Rodney Stark and William Sims Bainbridge, 'Of Churches, Sects, and
Cults: Preliminary Concepts for a Theory of Religious Movements', *JSSR* 18.2 (1979), pp.
117–33. Stark and Bainbridge suggest a rather narrow definition of 'sect', which is
distinguished from 'cult', as opposed to Wilson's rather broad idea of 'sect', which moves
toward 'denomination'.

because the theory, which is based upon van Gennep's ritual process theory, is particularly helpful in understanding the functions of religious rituals (or rites) in the construction and maintenance of community–identity; particularly for this essay, the function of the rite of baptism.[60] This section introduces only a brief summary of the theory, but I will further elaborate the theory in Chapter 7, where it is applied specifically to this cultic rite.

Turner develops van Gennep's ritual process theory, known as 'rites of passage' (*rites de passage*), into his own concept of social process. Van Gennep explains the process of rituals, which 'is to transfer an individual from one well-defined life situation to another equally quite well-defined life situation'.[61] 'Rites of passage' refers to the whole process, which involves the three phases of preliminal ('a well-defined life situation'), liminal (very ritual experience), and post-liminal ('another well-defined life situation').[62] In the phase of transition or liminal stage (*limen* meaning 'threshold' in Latin), initiands are in an ambiguous state, passing from one structure to another. In this 'betwixt and between', Turner says, 'they [initiand] may be disguised as monsters, wearing only a strip of clothing, or even go naked, to demonstrate that as liminal [transitional] beings they have no status, property, insignia ...'[63]

Turner observes this pattern of 'preliminal → liminal → postliminal' in the broader scope of social process, correspondingly 'structure → anti-structure (or liminality/*communitas*) → structure'.[64] Therefore, the social process is, like the ritual process, viewed as the repetition of structure and anti-structure, pervading one another in a type of teleological process.[65] The characteristic features of both states can be located in the opposite columns of 'structural' inequality over against 'anti-structural' equality, stability over against transience, complexity over against simplicity, and so on.[66] The emergence situation of the Galatian community shows this type of anti-structure over against the structure of the (mother) religion of

---

60. The usefulness of the theory has been recognized by some scholars. For example, Theißen, *Die Religion*, p. 187: Wedderburn, *Baptism and Resurrection*, pp. 386–87; Moxnes, 'Social Integration', p. 113; Strecker, *Die liminale Theologie*, p. 449.

61. Van Gennep, *Les Rites de Passage*, p. 4 (author's translation).

62. Ibid., p. 14. Also any ritual can be divided into three phases of separation, transition and incorporation. At the same time each ritual can be categorized by its primary function either as the rite of separation (e.g. funeral ceremonies), the rite of incorporation (e.g. marriages) or the rite of transition (e.g. betrothal, initiation).

63. Turner, *The Ritual Process*, p. 95 (parentheses added).

64. Ibid., pp. 96–97.

65. Ibid., pp. 96–97, 127–29.

66. Ibid., pp. 106–107.

Judaism in general.[67] As will be closely observed in Chapter 7, Paul's baptismal liturgical saying includes a claim to dissolve ethnic, social and gender distinctions (Gal. 3.28), which were the conventional hierarchical structural distinctions in Judaism (*t. Ber.* 7.18) and in an even wider social context (Diogenes Laertius, *Vit.* 1.33).

Since Turner tends to understand the social process as a continual alteration of two phases (structure and anti-structure), he is careful to avoid the misconception that the two phases are somehow independently originated and entirely incompatible entities, confronting one another until one overcomes the other once and for all.[68] In seeking to interpret the life situation of the Galatian community as being in tension with the Jewish mission and the wider Jewish structural context, it is crucial to clarify Turner's 'continual process' so that the Galatian community in 'tension with outgroups' may be compatible with Turner's teleological process of society. While he clarifies the social process not so much as 'ingroup/outgroup' tension, but as a teleological transition from one phase to another, he himself still assumes a tension between the liminal state and the previous structure.[69] Therefore, Turner maintains, 'Exaggeration of structure may well lead to pathological manifestations of *communitas* [anti-structure] *outside or against* "the law",' or 'Maximization of *communitas* provokes maximization of structure, which in its turn produces *revolutionary strivings* for renewed *communitas*'.[70] This inevitable antithesis in the structure/anti-structure relationship is even amplified in the state of so-called 'permanent liminality', in which the peculiar emergent situation of the Galatian community is found. By 'permanent liminality' is meant a case of (usually) religious groups that seek to maintain liminality indefinitely outside the wider structural context as in the case of the early Franciscan movement, which was somehow maintained by the Spirituals.[71] To qualify Turner's term of 'permanent liminality', one can say that in the case of the Franciscan movement the liminal state eventually turns into another structural

---

67.   It is not that Judaism is the 'mother religion' in relation to the Galatian members, but rather the relation between Judaism and what Paul envisioned as a new community of faith.

68.   Turner, *The Ritual Process*, p. 132.

69.   Turner's description of the social process is correctly understood as a type of teleological process, though he himself uses the term 'dialectic'. However, it is important that there is still a tension either in the transition from one phase to another or a tension between the liminal state and the larger structural social background as in the case of the relation between the early period of the Franciscan movement and the larger Catholic social context.

70.   Turner, *The Ritual Process*, p. 129 emphases added. We may well compare this teleological process with Mary Douglas's conceptions of 'formal power of control' and 'formless power of danger'. Douglas, *Purity and Danger*, pp. 95–114.

71.   Turner, *The Ritual Process*, p. 145; Fiona Bowie, *The Anthropology of Religion* (Oxford: Blackwell, 2000), p. 167.

state.[72] Therefore, 'permanent' here actually means 'extended period'. This is compared with the ritual process, in which a temporary liminal state is artificially created for the duration of a set of rituals (whether ten minutes, half a day or a week). Here, there is a correlation between this type of 'permanent' (extended period of) liminality and Pauline communities. As will be seen in Chapter 7, Paul's approach to community–identity gradually shifts from liminality toward structure. In the Introduction, I pointed out that MacDonald hints at this structural transition,[73] but in Chapter 7 this transition in Paul's idea of community–identity construction will be elaborated. It should also be noted in advance that we find the same pattern in the structural transition of a former liminal state in the social process of Mukyokai.[74]

Turner's theory helps to see rituals' function in the identity construction of an emerging community. When a ritual is performed, an individual moves out of the mundane life pattern to enter the liminal state, then he or she re-enters the mundane life after the ritual is completed. In the ritual itself, he or she acts out either in a symbolic manner or in a more concrete way a world outside or at the edges of the mundane. Therefore, the features of the liminal state, whether it is temporary liminality of a ritual or permanent liminality of community life, are anti-structural equality (contra inequality), simplicity (contra complexity), transience (contra stability), foolishness (contra sagacity) and un-convention (contra convention).

In the liminal state, again whether it is a temporary ritual or a permanent liminal community, status and value are often reversed as an anti-structural response to the structural state. This recreation of worldview (or 'recreated worldview' which is the term used in this book to refer to the antithetical response to the world outside) is symbolically acted out in rituals, and in the case of the permanent liminal state the recreated worldview is actually lived out in the community as a new 'norm'. The phenomenon of a 'recreated worldview' is widely observed. For example, Cohen identifies at least three patterns of this recreated worldview, introducing them as 'symbolic reversal'.[75] Schwimmer studies a version of recreated worldview in religious communities, which he calls 'symbolic competition'.[76] Elsewhere in the study of the Galatian letter,

72. For the history of the early Franciscan movement and 'Spirituals', Turner relies on the description of Lambert. Malcolm Lambert, *Franciscan Poverty: The Doctrine of the Absolute Poverty of Christ and the Apostles in the Franciscan Order 1210–1323* (London: SPCK, 1961). Cf. David Burr, *The Spiritual Franciscans: From Protest to Persecution in the Century after Saint Francis* (University Park: Penn State University Press, 2001).
73. M.Y. MacDonald, *The Pauline Churches*, p. 71.
74. Refer to Chapter 7 (2.a, note 40).
75. A.P. Cohen, *The Symbolic Construction*, pp. 58–60.
76. E.G. Schwimmer, 'Symbolic Competition', *Anthropologica* XIV.2 (1972), pp. 117–55.

Esler applies the concept of 'social creativity' by Tajfel and Turner to interpret the pericope of 4.21–5.1, in which is observed a type of recreated worldview.[77] Application of this response pattern will be found in Chapters 6 and 7 where Paul's persuasion in Galatians 3 and 4 is considered as his effort to construct a positive identity for the Galatians.

4. *Scheme of Theory Employment*

Consideration has been given to the nature of community–identity, the mechanism of ethnic identity construction and a theory of social process. In conclusion, I will outline a detailed plan of how these theories will be employed to the interpretation of the text in the following chapters. First, concerning the nature of community–identity, identity construction can be seen as a dialectic process between external categorization and internal identification at the boundary line. This concept is particularly helpful as a guiding principle for an analysis of the context of Paul's community–identity construction (Part II).[78] By 'context' is meant both personal condition (Paul's self-understanding in Chapter 3) and social condition (Paul's interaction with significant outgroups in Chapters 4 and 5) that shape the way Paul seeks to construct the identity of the Galatian community. The view that identity construction is a dialectic process leads one to look at how the significant outgroups (particularly Jews in general and Jewish Christians in the Jerusalem Church) might have sought to construct the identity of their communities, because this question concerns the external pressure (categorization) that Paul felt from his significant outgroup. Special note will also be taken of the effect of the possible external categorization from the general population of Galatians upon the members in Paul's community in Galatia. While there is very little evidence of how Galatian believers may have internalized the external categorization from their compatriots, a consideration of Gal. 4.9–10 suggests that they may have made an attempt to appropriate and indigenize the Jewish customs in order to alleviate the pressure from their compatriots in the wider Galatian society. This interpretation will be considered in Chapter 6, where the close comparison between the Galatian community and Mukyokai begins to be made.

Second, also concerning the nature of community–identity, it was suggested that within a symbolic construction coexist flexibility of cultural features and considerable stability of a sense of identity. This perspective

77. Esler, *Galatians*, pp. 52–53, 213–14. Cf. Tajfel and Turner, 'Integrative Theory', p. 43.

78. As explained further in Chapter 5, the main focus, particularly in the 'historical' section of Gal. 1 and 2, is not so much to reconstruct what exactly took place as to articulate the function and intention of Paul's retrospective interpretation of those historical events for constructing the community-identity in the Galatian community.

allows the existence of varying (at times conflicting) approaches to issues of inter-ethnic relatedness, which are represented by different groups and sects under the larger commonwealth of Israel. Awareness of the nature of community introduced in this chapter will guide the survey of Jewish literature for the purpose of understanding issues of proselytism in Chapter 4 and inter-ethnic dining in Chapter 5.

Third, the mechanism of ethnic identity closely relates to the study in Part II concerning the context of Paul's community–identity construction. In this segment it is suggested that Paul may have approached the issue of community–identity construction in Galatians in 'instrumental mode', while other Jews, including Jewish Christians in the Jerusalem church, approached the same issue with strong ethno-centred concern. Chapter 3 will substantiate the suggestion on Paul's approach to community–identity construction by considering his self-awareness as an apostle to the Gentiles. Chapter 4 will consider the issue of Gentile incorporation, in order to substantiate the suggestion that Jews in general approached the issue of identity with a strong concern for their core ethnic sentiment. Chapter 5 will combine the conclusions of the previous two chapters in order to show that the conflicts in Jerusalem and Antioch were closely related to the conflicting approaches to community–identity construction suggested in Chapters 3 and 4.

Turner's social process theory will relate closely to an attempt to find actual ways to construct the community–identity in Part III. Chapter 6 views the Galatian community as being in a permanent (or extended period of) liminal state and suggests that Paul's exposition of salvation history in Galatians 3 and 4 is his way of remaking the tradition and offering a 'recreated (anti-structural) worldview' for community members to find a justification and *raison d'être* of the marginalized community under pressure from a wider structural context. Chapter 7 will understand the rite of baptism with the peculiar baptismal saying in Gal. 3.28 as the community's physical demonstration of the 'recreated worldview'. Therefore, the rite of baptism is seen as a ritual which affirms the new norm of the liminal group over against the oppressing structural convention of the wider structural context. Either as an observer or as an initiand, the baptismal rite is therefore a significant identity-marking event for members of the fledgling and marginalized community.

Apart from these concepts and theories discussed above, the analogical comparative case of Uchimura and his Mukyokai will be brought in as yet another heuristic tool to aid the interpretation of the text. In the following chapter are found a description of this religious group and its effort to construct and maintain a positive identity of its own.

Chapter 2

KANZO UCHIMURA AND HIS MUKYOKAI:
AN EXAMINATION OF ITS COMMUNITY–IDENTITY CONSTRUCTION

One of the distinctive aspects of this book is to provide a novel analogical case rather than to depend solely on the abstract theories of the social-sciences. In order to use Mukyokai effectively as an analogical case for the interpretation of Galatians, one should become familiar with the emerging period of the community. Therefore, this chapter concerns a historical description of Mukyokai. The scholarship on Mukyokai with Japan's modernization as its background has a long history, and a detailed outline of it is constricted here by space. However, sufficient information can be given of the emergence of the community by way of a biographical introduction to Uchimura up to the time of founding Mukyokai, so as not to run the risk of giving a colourless and distorted picture of the community by over-simplifying the data.

The latter part of this historical description will critically evaluate Mukyokai's emergence and maintenance from (1) political and (2) sociological perspectives. This is in order to articulate particular ways of community–identity construction. First, in the political evaluation, Uchimura's response to the significant outgroups as he formulated his own religious community will be explained, pointing out his effort to recreate a worldview, which involves (a) stereotypical criticism of the West and (b) idealization of Japanese tradition, to offer Mukyokai members a positive identity of their community. Second, in the sociological evaluation, how Mukyokai sought to maintain cohesion despite its anti-institutional ideology will be explained, pointing out the important role local leaders play (*sensei* [teacher]–pupil relation) for the cohesion of the community, which has a loose structural organization.

In summary, each way of community–identity construction drawn from the study in this chapter will be clearly defined in reference to where it may be employed to the interpretation of Galatians found in the later chapters.

1. *A Short History of the Emergence of Mukyokai*

This section will look at the historical background of the foundation of Mukyokai. Kanzo Uchimura being the founder of this unique Christian community in Japan, this historical analysis will inevitably mostly be his biographical account. As it will be made clear, the identity of the community was at least partially shaped by the founder's relation and response to the church in general and society at large during a particular period of Japanese history. The historical analysis is divided into the following periods: (a) End of *Pax Tokugawa* and Dawn of Meiji Era, (b) Upbringing and Conversion, (c) Days in the USA, (d) *Fukei-Jiken* (*Lèse-Majesté*) and Isolation, and (e) Founding of Mukyokai. This description depends much upon Uchimura's own autobiographical work entitled *Yo wa Ikani shite Kirisuto-Shinto to Narishi ka [How I Became a Christian]*, his numerous correspondences with Bell, Miyabe and with Nitobe, and his countless number of magazine articles, found particularly in *Seisho no Kenkyu [Study of the Bible]*, as well as the first-hand eye-witness accounts of Uchimura's followers.

a. *End of* Pax Tokugawa *and Dawn of Meiji Era (1868)*
The arrival of US Commodore Perry in 1853 at Uraga Bay with his squadron of four steamships shook the island-chain, which had been under the relatively successful control of Tokugawa Shogunate. What is called *Pax Tokugawa*, a relatively peaceful reign of the islands by the Tokugawa government for 260 years, was partially due to a policy of seclusion, which Perry demanded to abolish by overwhelming military pressure in order to bring 'democracy' and economic 'benefits' to Japan. In 1639, the third Shogun, Tokugawa Iemitsu had banned transaction between Japan and foreign countries with the exception of limited exchange of goods at the special district of Dejima (literally, 'island off-shore'). All expatriates were forced out and the Japanese living abroad were not allowed to return. This extreme policy was largely due to the increasing fear of intrusion by Christianity on the islands of Japan. This point will be further explained later with the idea of so-called *Wakon-Yosai* ('Japanese Soul and Western Skill'), a foreign policy taken by the Meiji government. This diplomatic pressure coincided with a *coup d'état* plotted by dissatisfied warlords, particularly the *samurai*s belonging to the feifas of Satsuma, Choshu, Tosa and Hizen. They sought to set up a government with the long-forgotten emperor as its head and with it to replace the long-established Shogunate of Tokugawa, which they successfully accomplished. Therefore, the reopening of the nation of Japan was due both to internal and external pressures. In November of 1867, the fifteenth Shogun, Tokugawa Yoshinobu, resigned from his

position and the rule of Japan was officially restored to the emperor in January of 1868. Meiji Emperor, Mutsuhito, then 16 years of age, moved from Kyoto to Edo, which was subsequently renamed Tokyo ('eastern capital'), to sit on the throne and reign over the nation in turmoil.

b. *Upbringing and Conversion (1861–77)*

Kanzo Uchimura was born in 1861 as the eldest son of Kin-no-Jo Noriyuki, a *samurai* stationed in Edo to serve Lord Matsudaira. Six years after the birth of Kanzo Uchimura, the historic revolt overturned the Tokugawa Shogunate and the new era of Meiji started. The privileged *samurai* class was dissolved at the occasion of the wholesale restructuring of the nation, which followed the transition from the Edo era to the Meiji era. Uchimura's family lost not only the social status of *samurai*-hood, but also the hope of a smooth transition into a new social status of importance, because Uchimura's father had served a master on the side of the Shogun at the time of the revolt. Uchimura was one of many descendants of the dissolved *samurai* class who were marginalized, serving the wrong side of the power game. Therefore, they turned quickly and eagerly to western education in order to regain social status and a means to support their families.

In the transition period, the last Shogun Yoshinobu was forced to sign a treaty of inequality with the western nations.[1] Therefore, an urgent need of the newly established government was to unshackle these diplomatic fetters. The government determined to avoid any military conflict with the western nations, which would only give them an excuse to move toward colonizing the islands. Therefore, the immediate concern was how to raise the level of the country to be counted as one of the 'civilized' nations, so that the unequal treaties be lifted. This meant that Japan was to equip itself with the technology of the West.[2] Thus, the westernizing policy of the Meiji government was at least partially motivated by the obvious desire for economic advance through the introduction of western technology.[3] Educational institutions were founded to host western instructors to educate the Japanese youth in western technology. This abrupt rise in the demand of western educators coincided with the missionary zeal fuelled by what is called in ecclesiastical history 'the

---

1. They are: (1) Extra-Territoriality (or consular jurisdiction), (2) Limited Autonomy on Tariffs, and (3) Granting of the Most Favoured Nation Status, as were the customary conditions demanded by the western powers on the Asian nations.

2. Ann Waswo, *Modern Japanese Society* (Oxford: Oxford University Press, 1996), p. 43. It is of note that the intention of this simple description is not to put the blame of Japan's expansionism fully on western imperialism.

3. The peculiar features and the implications of the westernizing policy will be analysed later in the section on political and psychological considerations.

Second Spiritual Awakening', especially in the USA and UK. Therefore, many of the early western educators were lay Christian academicians who had a desire to engage in mission work in Japan. Among these was William Clark, who was invited to preside over the Sapporo College of Agriculture. Uchimura later entered this college and was converted to Christianity in 1877 through the persuasion of Clark's first converts at the college.[4] Uchimura enters in his diary: 'Dec. 1, 1877. Entered the gate of the "Jesus Religion" '.[5]

The students at the college gathered together weekly, on their own, to express their newly found faith. Uchimura describes this student meeting as full of optimism, creativity and experiments.[6] A number of unconventional features of Uchimura's community formation may have originated in this early, experimental religious practice during his Sapporo days. The strong sense of camaraderie among members of these meetings was formed in relation to groups outside. Uchimura recalls the frustration of the members who were so united in this meeting but so divided by the liturgies of two local churches (Episcopalian and Methodist), to which the members respectively belonged.[7] Uchimura enters in his diary: 'April 30, 1881. The independence of the church is spoken of for the first time'.[8] The group of young believers did become independent of other local churches, and they formed the foundation of what later became Sapporo Independent Church. Uchimura qualifies that the independence of this time was non-rebellious, only 'to remove obstacles in the ways of others seeking God's Truth for the salvation of their souls'.[9] The rhetoric against denominations and western missionaries became more apparent after his days in the USA, but his distrust and dislike of denominations and western missionaries behind them probably originated during his days in Sapporo.

c. *Days in the USA (1885–88)*
Upon graduating from the college,[10] Uchimura worked as an ichthyologist for two and a half years, then he moved to the USA in 1885. While

---

4.   Kanzo Uchimura, *How I Became a Christian: Out of My Diary* (originally published in May 1895), in *Zenshu*, III, pp. 14–15.

5.   Ibid., III, p. 18.

6.   Ibid., III, pp. 34, 36–37.

7.   Ibid., III, pp. 40–41.

8.   Ibid., III, p. 46.

9.   Cf. ibid., III, p. 65.

10.   Sapporo Nogakko, *Second Annual Report of Sapporo Agricultural College*, 1878 (Tokei: Kaitakusha, 1878), p. 124.

he made some long-lasting friendships with such people as David C. Bell[11] and Julius H. Seelye,[12] the most notable encounter was the reality of the 'Christian nation'. Prior to his move, Uchimura's exposure to western civilization was primarily through literature and encounters with Christian missionaries. Though he had distrust in denominations and missionaries earlier in the days of Sapporo, he nevertheless had a fascination for the West, and America seemed to him an ideal Christian nation. However, he records in *How I Became a Christian*, 'It was only gradually, very gradually, that I unlearnt this childish notion'.[13] The fascination was unlearnt in his daily exposure to the reality in the western land, and disillusionment set in. He writes,

> O Heaven, I am undone! I was deceived! ...To go back to my old faith I am now too overgrown; to acquiesce in my new faith is impossible. O for Blessed Ignorance that might have kept me from the knowledge of faith other than that which satisfied my good grandma! One thing I shall never do in future: I shall never defend Christianity upon its being the religion of Europe and America.[14]

This disillusionment partially caused Uchimura to redefine his Christian faith apart from western civilization. At the same time, he began to re-evaluate his own culture and traditions.

> But looking at a distance from the land of my exile, my country ceased to be a 'good-for-nothing'. It began to appear superbly beautiful ... Its existence as a nation was decreed by Heaven Itself, and its mission to the world and human race was, and is being, distinctly announced. It was seen to be a sacred reality, with purpose high and ambition noble, to be for the world and mankind.[15]

This paradigm shift will be analysed in detail later, for the foundation of the distinct Christian community arguably owes much to this paradigm shift Uchimura experienced during his days in the USA.

d. Fukei-Jiken *(Lèse-Majesté) and Isolation (1888–1899)*
In the early stage of the formation of modern Japan, the country was swinging widely between extreme westernization and imperialistic nation-

11.   Bell was a banker from Minneapolis, with whom Uchimura became acquainted in Washington DC. Uchimura's prolific correspondence with Bell is a highly valuable source of our knowledge on the life of Uchimura. Letters to Bell are all contained in Uchimura's *Zenshu*.

12.   Seelye is the principal of Amherst College, through whom Uchimura experiences a 'second conversion'. Uchimura, *Zenshu*, III, pp. 114, 129.

13.   Ibid., III, pp. 78–80.

14.   Ibid., III, p. 90.

15.   Ibid., III, p. 92.

alism enforced by the enactment of the Meiji Imperial Constitution and of the Imperial Rescript of Education. The Japan to which Uchimura returned from the USA was in the midst of a storm of nationalistic fervour. Uchimura welcomed the patriotic atmosphere of the country, for he had by this time regarded extreme westernization as the cause of people's lack of love and pride for their own nation.[16] However, his patriotism was peculiarly nuanced by his Christian faith, and for this very reason he was caught between the imperialistic nationalism of the government and what Uchimura perceived to be the 'anti-patriotic' Christianity of denominational churches. His criticism of denomination-alism and the western missionaries behind it is clearly evidenced in a letter to one of his friends. He says, 'Either missionaries must go, or I must go. The American missionaries and Uchimura Kanzo seem to be impossible to work together. The two are as distinct from each other as oil from water' (*Letter to Nijima*, Oct. 20, 1888).[17] This complaint was occasioned by conflict with missionary teachers because of differing perspectives on education and operation at the Christian school where he took a position immediately after his return from the USA. The result of the conflict is that Uchimura was severely criticized by the missionaries and other Christian instructors and forced to resign from his position after serving only for four months. He was then accused of being a 'Unitarian and devil'.[18]

The incident that most clearly reflects Uchimura's struggle with the imperialism of the State is *Fukei-Jiken* (Incident of *Lèse-Majesté*). In September of 1890, Uchimura was hired by Ikko High Middle School, where *Fukei-Jiken* took place, through which Uchimura was made known nationwide as a traitor and outlaw. Uchimura's time at the high middle school coincided with the production and enactment of the *Kyoiku Chokugo*, or the Imperial Rescript of Education. This rescript was enacted to consolidate the new system of the Imperial Meiji government in connection with the state religion of National Shinto.[19] The rescript emphasizes loyalty to the Emperor, and was devised to prevent Japan from becoming overly westernized and Christianized.[20] Matsuzawa argues

16. Hiroaki Matsuzawa, 'Kindai Nihon to Uchimura Kanzo [Modern Japan and Kanzo Uchimura]', in Hiroaki Matsuzawa (ed.), *Uchimura Kanzo* (Tokyo: Chuo Koron, 1971), pp. 7–78.

17. Uchimura, *Zenshu*, XXXVI, p. 303.

18. Hiroshi Masaike, *Uchimura Kanzo Den [Life of Kanzo Uchimura]* (Tokyo: Kyobun-Kan, 1977), pp. 164–72.

19. The English translation of the rescript is found in; Ryusaku Tsunoda, *et al.* (eds.), *Sources of Japanese Tradition* (Records of Civilization: Sources and Studies, 54; New York and London: Columbia University Press, 1958), pp. 646–47.

20. Miura, *The Life and Thought*, p. 37. Yasuo Furuya and Hideo Oki, *Nihon no Shingaku [Japan's Theology]* (Tokyo: Yorudan-sha, 1989), p. 98.

that the distribution of a copy of the rescript to all imperial educational institutions was a form of 'witch-hunting', a censorship to protect the national interest and orthodoxy.[21]

The ceremony of reception of the rescript was held at each educational institution, and at Ikko Middle High School in January 1891. Two Christian colleagues of Uchimura considered the ceremonial reception of the rescript as idol worship, so they did not attend the ceremony. Uchimura did not take the matter so strictly and attended the ceremony. As a 'Christian patriot' in his own terms, Uchimura had a 'sincere' respect for the Emperor and was pleased to hear that the Emperor had announced such a moral standard for his subjects. He said to his disciples later, 'There was perhaps no one at that time who expressed more enthusiasm over it' (the enactment of the rescript).[22] At the time of the ceremony, the principal of the school spontaneously decided that the faculty members and students were all to proceed to the copy of the rescript on the auditorium stage and to give the signature of the emperor Mutsuhito the most respectful bow. This Uchimura considered as a questionable act and he was not able to do it. This gesture was regarded as a treason against the emperor, and upset the whole school and eventually the whole nation. He writes to Bell about the event:

> ... I took my stand and did not bow! It was an awful moment for me ...
> The anti-Christian sentiment ... found a just cause (as they suppose) for
> bringing forth against me accusations of insult against the nation and its
> Head, and through me against the Christians in general ... (*Letter to
> Bell*, March 6, 1891).[23]

Fukei Jiken was indeed used by the media (56 newspapers and magazines covered the incident) to fuel the nationalistic sentiment of the country, and Uchimura was caricatured as an outlaw and traitor of the nation.

Later, the principal urged Uchimura to pay respect to the rescript, arguing that the bow had no religious implication. This Uchimura agreed to do. However, Uchimura fell critically ill before fulfilling the promise, so he asked one of his Christian colleagues to take his place. Instead of soothing the emotion of the hostile multitude, this gesture in turn upset the Christian churches for retracting the original commitment to his faith and cowardly asking someone else to do it. Uchimura shares his frustration in the same letter to Bell:

> I also found a set of Christians turning their weapons against me ...
> finding blame in my consenting to bow. They are mostly Presbyterians.
> Not only myself, but my whole family were and are in infamy. The

21. Matsuzawa, *Uchimura*, p. 26.
22. Masaike, *Uchimura*, p. 182 (author's translation).
23. Uchimura, *Zenshu*, XXXVI, pp. 331–32.

Public does not examine into the fact of my finally consenting to bow,
but takes my first hesitation as a determined refusal; while the
Presbyterians ... put forth words of contempt upon my succumbing
... to the authority of the Government' (*Letter to Bell*, March 6,
1891).[24]

Perhaps due to his premature amalgamation of patriotism and Christian
faith, Uchimura was accused nationwide of being a traitor to the country,
so much so that he had to give a false identification when he travelled.
Because of his nuanced patriotism and various misunderstandings, he was
accused by the churches of being a devil, a coward and a sycophant, and
in the end he was refused membership to a local church.[25] Meanwhile, he
lost other significant support. Uchimura's wife, Kazuko, took on the same
illness as Uchimura in the aftermath of *Fukei-Jiken*, for whom she was
attending, and died in April 1891 during the severe attack from both the
government and the churches. Later, in his book, *Consolation of a
Christian Believer*,[26] he refers to six hardships of a believer, four of which
are: death of the loved one, desertion by one's countrymen, desertion by
the church and incurable illness. He went through all of these hardships at
this time. Two other hardships he adds to this list are poverty and failure
of enterprise, which he would experience in the following years as he had
difficulty in finding and keeping a teaching position. This was at least
partly due to the disgrace which was put on his name due to the incident.

In the same book, he used the term *mukyokai* or 'non-church' for the
first time. The term was originally used not to refer to a particular group,
but to describe an extreme sense of loneliness and marginalization. He
writes about how he perceived his experience: 'I have become *mukyokai*.
No church have I that man made, no hymn do I hear that consoles my
soul, nor a minister do I know who prays for me a blessing. I am denied
the sanctuary where I worship and come near to God'.[27]

This trying time for Uchimura was also a period when he was rather
prolific and his prominent books were all written during this period. They
are: *Kirisuto Shinto no Nagusame* [*Consolation of a Christian Believer*] in
1893; *Kyu-an Roku* [*Pursuit of Peace*][28] in 1893; *Daikyo-teki Nihon-jin*

24.　Ibid., XXXVI, p. 334.

25.　Miura, *The Life and Thought*, p. 35. Cf. Uchimura, *Letter to Miyabe*, Jan. 8, 1891, in
Zenshu, XXXVI, pp. 329–31. Cf. Masaike, *Uchimura*, pp. 191–94.

26.　This work, originally published in 1893, is contained in *Zenshu*, vol. II.

27.　Uchimura, *Consolation of a Christian Believer*, in *Zenshu*, II, p. 36 (author's
translation).

28.　If *How I Became a Christian* is a narrative description of his conversion experience,
Pursuit of Peace is a theological reflection on conversion in a systematic manner.

[*Representative Japanese*] (originally titled *Japan and Japanese* in 1894);[29] and *Yo wa Ikani shite Kirisuto-shinto to Narishi ka* [*How I Became a Christian*] in 1895. During this time he also became active in social criticism and reform through secular journalism (*Yorozu Choho* in 1897).[30] Finally, he left journalism and devoted himself to founding his own religious group.

e. *Founding of Mukyokai (1900–30)*
The teachings of Uchimura during this period are found primarily in *Seisho no Kenkyu* [*Bible Study*], which aids in understanding his patterns of identity construction. Here, the general outline of the founding of Mukyokai is given.

Between 1901 and 1902, he published one other magazine called *Mukyokai*. In this short-lived publication, Uchimura attempted to describe what Mukyokai is about by way of introducing the magazine. He says:

> Mukyokai is the church for those who do not have a church. It is, therefore, like an inn for those who have no home ... Because there are many pastor-less sheep who do not have a church, here I am led to publish this humble booklet ... The real church is in fact Mukyokai ... Those who do not have a church in fact have the best church ... ('Mukyokai-Ron' [On Mukyokai], in *Mukyokai* 1 [March, 1901]).[31]

This paradoxical statement, though historically significant for the emergence of the community, is rather an ambiguous one. Later Uchimura clarified the nature of Mukyokai. The statements of Uchimura include two notable features of the group. One is anti-denominationalism and anti-institutionalism, and the other is anti-westernization and Christian patriotism. He says in *Seisho no Kenkyu* concerning anti-denominationalism/institutionalism: 'The natural consequence of the spirit of Protestantism leads to the spirit of Mukyokai. Protestant church is a self-contradiction. It is the same as saying Mukyokai (Non-Church) church' ('Kyokai Mondai' [Problems with the

29.   The purpose of this book is to introduce representative Japanese historical figures to alleviate the 'misunderstanding' among the westerners about Japan's aggression in Asia, as the conflict between Japan and China was expected to turn into a war.
30.   He also founded Tokyo Dokuritsu Zashi in 1898 and became vocal in social criticism from a Christian perspective. He was at the same time very skeptical about the church's affirmation of the government engaging in a war (apparently he changed his stance after the Sino-Japanese war). He did not trust their reform vision which sought to abolish prostitution but to affirm killing, and to help orphans but to create thousands of them through wars. Cf. Matsuzawa, *Uchimura*, pp. 49–50.
31.   Uchimura, *Zenshu*, IX, pp. 71–73 (author's translation).

Church], *Seisho no Kenkyu* 357 [April 1930]).[32] Elsewhere in *Seisho no Kenkyu*, Uchimura says concerning anti-westernization and Christian patriotism:

> Bushido [Way of *samurai*] is the finest product of Japan. But Bushido by itself cannot save Japan. Christianity grafted upon Bushido will be the finest product of the world. It will save, not only Japan, but the whole world. Now that Christianity is dying in Europe, and America by its materialism cannot revive it, God is calling upon Japan to contribute its best to His service. There was a meaning in the history of Japan. For twenty centuries God has been perfecting Bushido with this very moment in view. Christianity grafted upon Bushido will yet save the world ('Bushido and Christianity', *Seisho no Kenkyu* 186 [Jan., 1916]).[33]

The journal *Seisho no Kenkyu* gained a wide readership around the country and readers gathered locally to discuss the content and to share comments. These groups started to be formed under the name, Kyoyu-kai, or 'Fellowship of the Teaching'. Uchimura considered the journal *Seisho no Kenkyu* to be crucial for forming his community.[34] Besides local spontaneous gatherings outside Tokyo, Tokyo Kyoyu-kai was formed in 1905. This was one of several gatherings which Uchimura was directly instructing in Tokyo.[35] His regular meetings consisted of prayer, the singing of hymns and instruction on the Scripture, much akin to a Protestant churches except that Uchimura did not perform the rites of baptism and the Lord's supper.[36]

Uchimura's anti-institutional stance forced him to disorganize *Seisho no Kenkyu* and disband his gathering in 1930 at the time of his death for fear that Mukyokai might become one of the denominations ('Mukyokai no Zenshin' [Advancement of Mukyokai], *Seisho no Kenkyu* 85 [March 1907]).[37] The end of Uchimura's meetings is recorded:

> Discontinuation of Uchimura's Bible Study was announced in the morning of April 6, 1930 with the agreement among Uchimura's wife, Shizuko, his son, Yushi and his disciples. Hyoei Ishihara represented

32. Uchimura, *Zenshu*, XXXII, p. 330 (author's translation and parentheses). Cf. 'Katorikku ni Narazu' [Not Becoming a Catholic], *Seisho no Kenkyu* 333 (April 1928) in *Zenshu*, XXXI, pp. 134–35.

33. Ibid., XXII, pp. 161–62.

34. Uchimura, 'Waga Kyokai' [My Church], *Seisho no Kenkyu* 149 (Dec. 1912) in *Zenshu*, XIX, p. 296 (author's translation).

35. Besides Tokyo Kyoyu-kai, formed in 1905, there were Kashiwa-kai in 1909, Shirosame-kai in 1911, Emao-kai in 1917 and finally Kashiwagi Kyodai-dan in 1918.

36. Uchimura, 'Senrei Bansan Haishi-Ron' [On Abolition of Baptism and Eucharist], *Seisho no Kenkyu* 6 (Feb., 1901) in *Zenshu*, IX, pp. 52–56.

37. Uchimura, *Zenshu*, XIV, p. 489 (translation by Miura).

them and greeted the followers, and announced, 'As of today, the
meetings of Uchimura's Bible Study has been forever unequivocally
disorganized'.[38]

Though Uchimura's personal meetings were disorganized, Mukyokai
established itself as a unique religious community in Japan. Due to the
group's polemic against institutionalism, thus against the idea of counting
membership, the exact number of members of the community has never
been registered. Caldarola gives an estimate of about 35,000 members in
nearly 400 individual groups all around Japan and other parts of Asia.[39]

2. *Critical Analyses of Uchimura and Mukyokai*

a. *Political Context (*Wakon-Yosai*) of Mukyokai*
The focus so far has been on the historical description of Uchimura and
the emergence of Mukyokai. Moving on to a critical analysis of
Mukyokai, two foci emerge, one political and the other sociological.
The first analysis will locate Uchimura and Mukyokai in the political
framework of *Wakon-Yosai*. Furuta and Oki seek to understand
Uchimura in the political context of the period.[40] *Wakon-Yosai*, or
literally 'Japanese Soul and Western Skill', is a term which describes the
westernizing policy of the Meiji government, in which they welcomed
western technology and resisted the influence of spirituality or foundational ideology of western civilization, in order to preserve Japanese 'Soul'
(i.e. culture/traditions to preserve the sense of Japanese identity).[41] A
parodic poem (*kyoka*) of the earlier-mentioned *tanka* of Moto-ori (see
Part I's introduction) depicts the sensibility of *Wakon-Yosai*. It says,
'With the soul of Yamato as the seed/Read the tales brought from beyond
the sea'.[42] It was a highly pragmatic strategy to realize industrial
development while preserving (or rather recreating and affirming) what
the authority believed to be the ethos of Japan. It was at the same time an
unstable strategy because of the difficulty in finding a fine balance between
'soul' and 'skill'. A similar policy had been taken earlier in the long history
of the diplomatic relationship between Japan and China. The struggle had
always been a matter of degree as to how much foreignness to accept.

---

38. Mukyokai-shi Kenkyu Henshu-sha (ed.), *Mukyokai-shi* [*History of Mukyokai*] (4
vols.; Tokyo: Shinkyo Press, 1991), I, p. 100 (author's translation).
    39. Caldarola, *Christianity*, pp. 67–68.
    40. Furuya and Oki, *Nihon no Shingaku*.
    41. Donald H. Shively, 'The Japanization of the Middle Meiji', in Donald H. Shively
(ed.), *Tradition and Modernization in Japanese Culture* (Studies in the Modernization of
Japan; Princeton, NJ: Princeton University Press, 1971), pp. 77–119 (77).
    42. Poet unknown. Author's translation of the text, which reads, 'Shikishima no Yamato
no Kokoro wo Tane to shite, Yomeya Hitobito Kotokuni no Fumi'.

When the foreign elements of western civilization arrived in Japan with the Jesuits' mission, led by Francisco Xavier in 1549, the governments of the time faced the same struggle. Both Oda and Toyotomi regimes, and Tokugawa Shogunate tolerated the 'western soul' of Christianity in order to introduce western goods and technology. Time and again Christianity was banned as the reaction against too much 'western soul' on Japanese soil, and finally the third *Shogun* Iemitsu ended the struggle by both executing a severe persecution of existing Christians, in which around 40,000 believers were martyred, and by enacting the nation-wide seclusion policy (*Sakoku*) in 1639.[43] Western goods and technology continued to be brought to Japan, but with a strict censorship against Christian elements. When the political structure of the Edo era was shattered and the Meiji era was inaugurated, the new government had to decide again where to find the balance between the preservation of Japanese culture/traditions (*Wakon*), therefore resisting western ideology, and the introduction of western technology (*Yosai*). Because resisting Christian influence was a major issue in the diplomatic policy of the previous era, even in the new era Christianity was regarded as the primary 'western soul' to be resisted, among other cultural features of western civilization.[44]

i. *Westernization policy*

In the process of this balance-making in the new era of Meiji, the pendulum swung widely between the two ends of extreme westernizing policy and imperial nationalism. The extreme westernizing policy can be represented in a statement by the Minister of Foreign Affairs, Kaoru Inoue. He proposed that the Empire and her people must be like those of Europe and only then, '... can our Empire achieve a position equal to that of the Western countries with respect to treaties. Only thus can our Empire be independent, prosperous, and powerful'.[45] One of the primary motives of this proposal was to free the nation from unfair treaties with western powers. This diplomatic concern was turned into a promotion of western civilization in all strata of society, and a naïve fascination for the West permeated deeply into society to the point that sober western

43. This seclusion policy caused the surviving Christians to go underground in various parts of Japan. They are called *Kakure Kirishitan* (literally, hide-out Christians). This group will be visited in Chapter 8 (1.b) to consider the function of the scripture for identity construction.

44. Furuya and Oki, *Nihon no Shingaku*, pp. 80–81. Cf. Shively, 'The Japanization of the Middle Meiji', p. 98.

45. *Segai Inoue Ko-den* 3 (1934), pp. 913–29, its translation found in Shively, 'The Japanization of the Middle Meiji', p. 91. Refer also to Yoshio Takahashi's 'Jinshu Kaizo-ron' [On Transformation of the Race], in Ikujiro Watanabe (ed.), *Kyoiku Chokugo no Hongi to Kampatsu no Yurai* (Tokyo: Fukumura Shoten, 1931), p. 206; Shively, 'The Japanization of the Middle Meiji', p. 94.

observers at this period were concerned about the course on which Japan was headed.[46] This fascination turned into an inferiority complex of a 'good-for-nothing' Japanese mentality, which was previously noted in Uchimura's experience of a cultural paradigm shift.[47]

With such a cultural ethos, even Christianity, much resisted in the earlier historical period, was accepted and mimicked as a part of western civilization.[48] In this context of the westernization of Japan, one should understand what appears to be a culturally insensitive approach to mission by the western missionaries. Powles evaluates the early Protestant mission as viewing Japanese tradition as 'pagan and corrupt ... archaic and outmoded', and the implication of the mission was 'the destruction of the old cults'.[49] The overt criticism and debasement of Japanese culture fuelled the nationalistic sentiment which was at that time gradually rising. Christian mission was viewed as closely related to this westernization policy. Together with the persistent scepticism of Christian mission due to the persecution against Christians in the earlier centuries, this overt westernization caused Christianity to become a target of the anti-western rhetoric of nationalism.

ii. *Nationalism*
Anti-western sentiment grew, especially in the 1880s as a reaction to overt and excessive westernization. It was also due to the fact that despite the westernizing efforts, the process of improving the diplomatic status of Japan was very slow with regard to the treaties made with the western nations. This increased frustration among the people. The establishment of the Imperial Constitution was a natural reaction to such overt westernization.[50] This Constitution was enacted in 1889 and it made the

---

46.   Erwin Bälz, *Das Leben eines deutschen Arztes im erwachenden Japan, Tagebücher, Briefe, Berichte herausgegeben von Toku Bälz* (Stuttgart: J. Engelhorns Nachf, 1931), p. 89. Bälz is a German physiologist who was teaching at the Imperial Medical Academy in Tokyo at this period. He describes the ethos of the time in his article on a Japanese martial art, titled 'Aus dem Vorwort zu Kano, "Jiu-jitsu"' ['From the Preface to Kano's *Jujutsu*]. See also, Basil Hall Chamberlain, *Things Japanese: Being Notes on Various Subjects Connected with Japan for the Use of Travelers and Others* (London: Kelly and Walsh, 5th edn, 1905), pp. 135–36, under the entry: 'Dress'. Chamberlain was a pioneer Japanologue instructing at the Imperial University of Tokyo.

47.   Uchimura, *Zenshu* III, p. 92. Refer to Chapter 2 (1.c, note 15).

48.   Toson Shimazaki, *Sakura no Mi no Jukusuru Toki* [*When Cherry Fruits Ripen*] (Tokyo: Shincho-Sha, 1955).

49.   Cyril H. Powles, 'Foreign Missionaries and Japanese Culture in the Late 19th Century: Four Patterns of Approach', *The Northeast Journal of Theology* (Sept. 1969), pp. 14–28 (17–18).

50.   Donald. H. Shively, 'Motoda Eifu: Confucian Lecturer to the Meiji Emperor', in D.S. Nivison and A.F. Wright (eds.), *Confucianism in Action* (Stanford: Stanford University Press, 1959), pp. 302–33 (327–28).

Emperor, who was the head of Shinto, the godhead (*Ara-hito-gami*, literally 'deity manifested in a person') of the nation. In it, two articles became foundational for the imperial cult. Those are: (1) the Empire of Japan shall be reigned over and governed by a line of Emperors for ages eternal (*Bansei-ikkei*), and (2) the Emperor is sacred and inviolable. The constitution was regarded as the ancestral traditions and therefore the canon. As the canon, rather than regulating the authority of the nation-state or the power of the Emperor as the head of the nation, it affirmed the absolute power of the Emperor.[51] Once the legal foundation of the imperial cult was secured, the Imperial Rescript of Education was issued in 1890. It established the ethical foundation of the nation based upon the imperial cult of National Shinto. In the historical description above, the rescript was introduced as a measure against overt westernization and Christianization. Furuya and Oki suggest that the intention of issuing the rescript was above all to regulate and subjugate the influence of Christianity, therefore containing a clear anti-Christian agenda.[52]

iii. *Nationwide identity crisis*
At the transition from the Edo to the Meiji era, Japan was deprived of the armour of *Sakoku* (the seclusion policy) and became aware of the need for a new *kimono* of identity. As the pendulum of identity swung between overt westernization and imperial nationalism, citizens were greatly affected by courses that the government took. Shively observes the situation of the Middle Meiji:

> This was the first time the Japanese had paused ... to consider ... what was it about the Japanese that made them distinct from other peoples?... Would they then become second-rate Westerners?... They began to discuss those features of Japan which set her off from other traditions: the unbroken succession in the Imperial line and the sacred land unsullied by foreign invasions.[53]

We find Uchimura historically located right in the middle of this national identity crisis. Therefore, Kamei is right when he comments on Uchimura: 'The spirit of Meiji era as a whole continued swinging between Japan and the West, in which Uchimura was shaken more violently than any

---

51. Yoshiya Soeda, *Kyoiku-Chokugo no Shakai-shi* [*Social-History of the Rescript of Education*] (Tokyo: Yushindo-Kobunsha, 1997), p. 56.

52. Furuya and Oki, *Nihon no Shingaku*, p. 98.

53. Shively, 'The Japanization of the Middle Meiji', p. 79. Of course, the unbroken succession of the royal line and the unsullied land are myths, which were created as suitable for binding the nation. Cf. Kang Sang-Jung, *Nashonarizumu* [*Nationalism*] (Tokyo: Iwanami, 2001), pp. 54–73; Benedict Anderson, *Imagined Communities: Reflections on the Origin and Spread of Nationalism* (London: Verso Editions, 1983).

other.'[54] In other words, the identity struggle of the nation affected the sense of identity of Uchimura as an individual. However, the political analysis does not stop at the psychological question of how the person of Uchimura was made and conditioned. Uchimura's identity is much to do with his religious identity, and his personal struggle for identity inevitably affected the identity formation of his own Christian community.

iv. *Construction of positive identity*

In this process of finding coherence as a Japanese and a Christian in the experience of marginalization both from the imperialistic nationalism and the churches of the western denominationalism, Uchimura redefined the world around him. The West was redefined and, as a result, disinherited from Christianity, i.e. the West was symbolically denied (deracinated from) its direct and authentic connection to Christianity. In the process of disinheriting the West, Christianity is also redefined. For example, Uchimura says, 'There is a great difference between Christianity and American Christianity. The latter is essentially materialistic, which in the Biblical language is mammonistic; and we know that Mammonistic Christianity is a contradiction in terms' (*The Japanese Christian Intelligencer* 2.5 [July 1927]).[55] With the effort to disinherit or discredit the West, Uchimura also idealizes Japanese traditions. In the political context of *Wakon-Yosai*, Japan and the West were incompatible with each other, therefore in Uchimura's mind they were also set antithetical to each other. In the process of nationalism, the Meiji government attacked Christianity as the representation of the West. Because the political formula of *Wakon-Yosai* had an anti-Christian agenda, when Japan and the West were set antithetically in the political formula, the commitment to Christ and to the nation were made incompatible. However, Uchimura could not live with the incompatibility. He shares this dilemma as follows:

> ... [the] struggle was brought by the fact that I believed in Christianity. If I had not believed in it, the grand ideology could never have occurred to me and I would have merely been satisfied with the world by promoting [imperialistic]) patriotism ('Kon-nichi no Kon-nan' [Today's Struggles], *Tokyo Independent Magazine* [July 1898]).[56]

In order to find balance in his own identity formation, Uchimura needed to redefine both Christianity and nationalism. Redefinition of Christianity

---

54. Shunsuke Kamei, *Uchimura Kanzo: Meiji Seishin no Dohyo* [*Kanzo Uchimura: A Milestone of Meiji Spirit*] (Tokyo: Chuo-Koronsha, 1977), p. 222 (author's translation).

55. Uchimura, *Zenshu*, XXX, p. 368.

56. Ibid., VI, p. 64 (author's translation and parentheses). Here, Uchimura says 'Chu-Kun Aikoku-Shugi', or loyal patriotism. He is most probably referring to nationalism based upon National Shinto. See also 'Katorikku ni Narazu' [Not Becoming a Catholic], in *Seisho no Kenkyu* 333 (April 1928), in *Zenshu*, IX, pp. 134–35.

involved getting rid of western features from it, therefore disinheriting the West from Christianity. Redefinition of nationalism was based upon the process of idealization of Japanese traditions, in which Uchimura amalgamated Christianity and *Bushido*, i.e. 'the way of *samurai*' ('Bushido and Christianity', *Seisho no Kenkyu* 186 [Jan. 1916]),[57] an idealization of *samurai* ethics that was popularized at this time in the history of Japan to support the interests of the imperial nationalism.[58] The idealized nationalism made it possible for Uchimura to begin redefining the *Beruf* of Japan at the time of the Sino-Japanese and Russo-Japanese wars.[59] In this *Beruf*, imperialism was in principle denied and Japan was

57.   Uchimura, *Zenshu*, XXII, pp. 161–62. The quotation can be found in Section 1.e, note 33, above.

58.   As I point out Uchimura's reference to *Bushido*, a qualification should be in order. The ideology of Bushido was introduced widely outside Japan through the work of Inazo Nitobe, who was a classmate of Uchimura at Sapporo Agricultural College and later served as the Under-Secretary of the League of Nations. I. Nitobe, *Bushido, the Soul of Japan: An Exposition of Japanese Thought* (Tokyo: Shokwabo, 1901). While the work was received favourably especially before the Second World War and the Japanese translation of the work has lately been widely publicized again, the work has always been faced with careful critics since its original publication. Cyril H. Powles, 'Bushido: Its Admirers and Critics', in John F. Howes (ed.), *Nitobe Inazo: Japan's Bridge across the Pacific* (Oxford: Westview Press, 1995), p. 113. Note especially the comment of the earlier mentioned Japanologists, B.H. Chamberlain in his *Things Japanese*, p. 72. The criticism can be summarized by saying that it is the idealized presentation of the ethos of the ruling class of the past, based upon Nitobe's superficial knowledge of the subject matter and the desire to affirm the unique and proud identity of the nation that was going through the process of rapid westernization. Yuzo Ota, 'Mediation between Cultures', in John F. Howes (ed.), *Nitobe Inazo: Japan's Bridge across the Pacific* (Oxford: Westview Press, 1995), p. 248. The idealized picture of Bushido was indeed utilized by nationalists to support the new polity of Meiji by strengthening the subjects' loyalty to the Emperor. Tetsufumi Furukawa, 'Bushido', in *Nihon Rekishi Dai-Jiten* [*Grand Dictionary of Japanese History*], VIII 22 vols.; Tokyo: Kawade Shobo, 1970); cf. B.H. Chamberlain, *The Invention of a New Religion* (Canton: Pan-Pacific Cultural Association, 1933), p. 6. Uchimura used this idealized notion of *samurai*-hood to redefine nationalism to make Christian patriotism possible. However, like Nitobe, Uchimura was not aware of the nationalistic implication that the ideology of Bushido had already carried. Their naïve fascination toward *samurai*-hood that led them to accept the ideal memory of the class is due to the fact that they were both descendants of the last *samurais*, whose class had already been dissolved, and also due to their special education in English in their youth, which limited their knowledge of the Japanese antiquities and therefore made a critical approach to such an ideology difficult. Cf. Yuzo Ota, *Uchimura Kanzo: Sono Sekai-Shugi to Nihon-Shugi wo Megutte* [*Kanzo Uchimura: On His Globalism and Nationalism*] (Tokyo: Kenkyusha Shuppan, 1977), p. 23; Masao Maruyama, *Thought and Behaviour in Modern Japanese Politics* (Oxford: Oxford University Press, 1963), p. xii.

59.   On the basis of his understanding of *Beruf* of Japan, Uchimura earlier supported the Sino-Japanese war, but the reality of Japan's expansionism made him retract this view. Cf. Uchimura, 'Justification of the Korean War', *The Japan Weekly Mail* (Aug. 1894) in *Zenshu*, III, p. 39, and *Letter to Bell*, May 22, 1895, in *Zenshu*, XI, pp. 296–97.

called to be a peace-making servant among the nations.[60] In this way he could finally secure an identity between the two poles of Japan and Christianity, which were once pulling him apart. His resolution is described in the idea of 'two J's'. He says:

> There are for us only two names which we are to love, one is the name of *Iesu* [Jesus] and the other is of *Nippon* [Japan]. In English they are first Jesus, and second Japan. Since the two words both start with 'J', I call them 'two J's'. It is for Jesus Christ and it is for Japan. We are to commit our lives for the service of these two beloved names ('Shinko to Kibo, [Faith and Hope], *Seisho no Kenkyu* 33 [February 1903]).[61]

Uchimura reached this state of identity through the process of redefinitions and idealizations of the world around him. This process of redefinition and idealization not only formed the identity of a Japanese Christian Uchimura, but also helped him to construct and consolidate the identity of his religious community as he committed this recreation of the worldview (redefinition and idealization) in the teachings for his community.

b. *Sociological Analysis*

Caldarola's *Christianity: The Japanese Way*[62] is so far the most thorough sociological study of Mukyokai. The notable contribution of this work is two-fold. One is that it attempts the comprehensive study of the movement from its stage of emergence to the present time (c. 1977). The other is that it is one of the few critical works which attempt an in-depth sociological investigation of the movement and its founder. What has not yet been considered in this historical and political evaluation of Mukyokai is the means by which Mukyokai maintains its identity in the current daily religious life. This aspect of Mukyokai will depend on Caldarola's research conclusions.

This section will first summarize Caldarola's conclusion and make some modifications to his perspective on the formation and development of Mukyokai. Then, special note will be taken of a particular way Caldarola suggests, by which Mukyokai maintains its cohesion, namely the *sensei* [teacher]–pupil relationship. The reason that attention is given to this way of maintaining the distinction of the community is because it provides an

60. Uchimura, 'Justification for the Korean War', *The Japan Weekly Mail* (Aug. 1894), included in Uchimura's *Zenshu*, III, pp. 38–48.
61. Uchimura, *Zenshu*, XI, p. 49 (author's translation and parentheses).
62. Caldarola, *Christianity*.

analogy for how the materiality of religion plays a significant role in maintaining the identity of a religious group.[63]

According to Caldarola, Mukyokai is a rather peculiar entity. He warns against the danger of reductionistic categorization to force the community into a conventional process of formalization.[64] This apprehension toward a reductionist approach in a social theory has validity. For in such an approach the unique features of the movement might be neglected or underestimated. Therefore, Caldarola goes on to point out the unique features of the movement, which resist the process of formalization.[65] Those features are summarized as follows:

a) *Common values*: Some of the most notable ones in the case of Mukyokai are its polemic against the institutional churches and independence of individual members which makes a professional minister unnecessary.

b) *Diffused leadership*: The widely dispersed charismatic leaders, as opposed to a centralized single charismatic figure, prevents the process of routinization and bureaucratization.[66]

c) *Warm informal interaction*: This kind of interaction prevents depersonalization which is consequential upon rules and regulations.

d) *Tension with the secular society*: This kind of tension helps to evoke among the individual members a strong sense of commitment to the original ideology, which may otherwise be enforced by a strong centralized leadership.[67]

Two modifications to Caldarola's suggestion can be made. One is a minor point and the other relates to a rather essential point of his thesis. To begin with the minor point, it is immediately noticeable that points (c) and (d) are not necessarily unique features of Mukyokai. Institutional churches use 'warm informal interaction' to add a personal dimension to their corporate religious life. Christianity being such a minority religion in Japan (around 1 per cent of the population), 'tension with the secular society' is felt by any institutional church. It is therefore the peculiar 'common value' of anti-institutionalism (a) that distinguishes Mukyokai from institutional churches in its course of development and maintenance of its cohesion. This leads to the next modification.

---

63. We should note that, while the analogy from Mukyokai is a helpful interpretive tool, such a tendency toward the materiality of religion is widely observable in various religious experiences and therefore I do not claim that the materiality of religion is a unique feature of Mukyokai as I introduce the *sensei*–pupil relationship.

64. Caldarola, *Christianity*, pp. 141–44.

65. Ibid., p. 142.

66. Ibid., p. 146. Cf. Geoffrey Nelson, *Spiritualism and Society* (London: Routledge & Kegan Paul, 1969) for the validation of the argument.

67. Caldarola, *Christianity*, p. 191.

Mukyokai follows a peculiar course of development. Those four features, though not particularly unique to Mukyokai, nevertheless helped and are helping the community to be distinct in its development as a community because of its unique ideology of anti-institutionalism. However, this does not mean that the community reflects no sign of formalization. In fact, Uchimura himself shares his fear that the tendency of formalization might reside in the community ('Mukyokai ni Tsuite' [On Mukyokai], *Seisho no Kenkyu* 327 [Oct. 1927]).[68] One of his followers, Iso'o Yamagata, also admits such a tendency when he says: 'In *Sensei* [Teacher] there was contradiction. While promoting Mukyokai, his gathering in Kashiwagi was little different from a church ...'[69] One of the current leaders of Mukyokai admits the need for 'organization' if not 'institution' in order to maintain the cohesion of the community.[70] Therefore, the modification to Caldarola's perspective is that Mukyokai is unique in its ways of formalization or concretization of their religious life. This does not mean that the community shows no sign of formalization. It only means that the anti-institutional ideology of Mukyokai slows down and diversifies the process of formalization.[71]

Now, a special note should be taken of one particular way by which Mukyokai maintains its cohesion, relating to point (b) of Caldarola's suggestion. As he explains, 'diffusion of leadership' keeps the community from taking an expected course of institutionalization in terms of

68. Uchimura, *Zenshu*, XXX, pp. 437–38.

69. Iso'o Yamagata, 'Byo taru Uchimura Kanzo' [Squint-Eyed Kanzo Uchimura], in Toshiro Suzuki (ed.), *Kaiso no Uchimura Kanzo* [*Memories of Kanzo Uchimura*] (Tokyo: Iwanami Shoten, 1956), p. 207 (author's translation).

70. This was pointed out to me in my conversation with Prof. Chiba. For outsiders of Mukyokai, the difference between 'institution' and 'organization' is subtle, but the difference may be significant for those who struggle between the community's need to maintain itself and the anti-institutional ideology that makes Mukyokai distinct from others.

71. Karuro Karudarora, *Uchimura Kanzo to Mukyokai* (trans. Mitsuzo Tamura, *et al.*; Tokyo: Shinkyo Shuppan, 1978), p. 369. [Translation of Caldarola's *Christianity: The Japanese Way*]. Their evaluation of Caldarola's work is that it is more positive than necessary – 'positive' in the sense here of Caldarola's overemphasis of Mukyokai's uniqueness and significance in the sociological study of social process. Cf. also Mark R. Mullins, *Christianity Made in Japan: A Study of Indigenous Movements* (Honolulu: University of Hawai'i Press, 1998), p. 56.

The emergence situation of Mukyokai from the institutional church may also be understood in Turner's language of permanent (extended period of) liminality. Its anti-institutionalism and the 'paradox' of non-church 'church' lead us to see the community's resemblance to Turner's description of liminal state. The unique process of formalization seen in Mukyokai may be understood as the process of a liminal state moving toward a structural state, which is different from the previous structural state, from which it has emerged. The similar tendency of a shift from liminality toward structure is observed in Paul's idea of community between Gal. and 1 Cor. For the discussion of this matter, refer to the conclusion of Chapter 7 (§3).

organization of the community. Indeed, in the case of Mukyokai, local leadership and members are tightly and personally bonded to form a local unit. It is in this closely bonded relationship between *sensei* [teacher] and pupils, we find a peculiar expression of their religiosity, i.e. materiality of religion. Caldarola describes how 'the intense and lingering interest in the *sensei*' often moves the pupils to collect and preserve their deceased *sensei*'s letters and relics, and publish a number of biographies and *Zenshu* [collected works].[72] This veneration of *sensei* is, therefore, inevitably a target of criticism by the church for placing too much authority on a person.[73] Takahashi, a second-generation Mukyokai leader, admits the problem and shares his concern that this tight *sensei*–pupil relationship is a type of blood-related institution and it opposes 'Mukyokai's vision of earthly demonstration of the universal body of Christ'.[74] It is notable that, despite the 'danger' of formalization, such tangible objects as relics and letters of a deceased *sensei* help to maintain the cohesion of a local group. Or rather, because of the anti-institutional ideology of the community, concretization of the members' religious life takes this particular form. In this loosely structured community, such an object that evokes the memory of their leader and replaces his or her presence helps to concretize their religious life and provide cohesion of the community.

3. *Patterns of Mukyokai's Community–Identity Construction*

As the result of critical analysis of Uchimura and Mukyokai from the political and sociological perspectives, ways by which the identity of Mukyokai was constructed and maintained were pointed out. As a conclusion, each way of identity construction will be defined and pointed out with reference to where it will be employed in the interpretation of the text in later chapters.[75]

72. Caldarola, *Christianity*, p. 127.

73. A number of Mukyokai members sought to justify such a peculiar bond between *sensei* and pupils or the veneration of *sensei* to create cohesion of the community. Yanaihara contends that the veneration is to the word of God behind the teachers, and that succession of the teacher in Mukyokai is rather spontaneous. Tadao Yanaihara, *Mukyokai-Shugi Kirisuto-Kyo Ron* [*On Mukyokai Christianity*] (Tokyo: Iwanami Shoten, 1982), pp. 191–92. Sekine argues that the strong tie of the *sensei*–pupil relationship is evidence of the mutual love among the existential community of individuals. Masao Sekine, *Sekine Masao Chosakushu* [*All Works of Masao Sekine*] (20 vols.; Tokyo: Shin-chi Shobo, 1981), II, p. 452.

74. Saburo Takahashi, *Mukyokai towa Nani ka* [*What is Mukyokai*] (Tokyo: Kyobun-kan, 1994), pp. 12–13.

75. Therefore, what follows is a sort of inventory of Mukyokai's patterns of identity construction that were referred to in the preceding discussion. The list is not comprehensive, but consists of those patterns that are pertinent to the scope of discussion in this book.

a. *Recreation of the Worldview*
Recreation of the worldview is a pattern of response to pressures and expectations from outgroups.[76] It is on the one hand negatively criticizing the outgroups' values in order to make the ingroup seem more attractive, and it is on the other hand positively constructing the new worldview for the purpose of authenticating the ingroup. In the political evaluation were pointed out the two responses, namely, a criticism of the West (and the church) and redefinition of Japanese traditions. Here, these two responses are further categorized. The critical response to the West and the church are subdivided as (1) disinheriting of the West, (2) stereotypical criticism of the West, (3) disinheriting of the church and (4) stereotypical criticism of the church. Then, the idea of redefinition of Japanese traditions is subdivided as (1) inheriting (or ownership of) the tradition and (2) a recreated worldview. These responses are compared with Paul's reinterpretation of salvation history in Galatians 3 and 4 (Chapter 6) and with Paul's use of the baptismal liturgical saying in Gal. 3.28 (Chapter 7).

i. *Disinheriting the West*
The outgroup's validity is denied by the ingroup members' criticism, thus its competitiveness is decreased. When the ingroup is related to the outgroup in origin, the right of inheritance of truth and traditions is removed from the outgroup, thus disinherited or disqualified, and transplanted to the ingroup. For Uchimura, one of the primary outgroups that he contended against was the West in general. References are as follows:

> 'How I Became a Christian'.[77] / 'Enemies of Christianity', *Seisho no Kenkyu* 199 (Oct. 1917).[78] / 'Exclusion Again', *Seisho no Kenkyu* 287 (June 1924).[79]

ii. *Stereotypical criticism of the West*
The outgroup's authenticity is challenged and as the result its competitiveness decreases because of the criticism from the ingroup members. While some of the criticisms are based on historical reality, they often rely on exaggerated features of the outgroups. Again, one of the primary outgroups of Uchimura was the West in general. References are as follows:

---

76. Cf. Jenkins, *Social Identity*, p. 77; Cohen, *The Symbolic Construction*, pp. 58–60.
77. Uchimura, *Zenshu* III, p. 90.
78. Ibid., XXIII, pp. 167–68.
79. Ibid., XXVIII, pp. 231–32.

'American Money and Gospel', *Seisho no Kenkyu* 228 (July 1919).[80] / 'American Christianity', *The Japanese Christian Intelligencer* 2.5 (July 1927).[81] / 'Quantitative Christianity', *Seisho no Kenkyu* 191 (June 1916).[82] / 'Churches and Missionaries', *Seisho no Kenkyu* 189 (April 1916).[83] / 'Japanese Christianity', *The Japanese Christian Intelligencer* 1.3 (May 1926).[84] / 'Again about Sectarianism', *The Japanese Christian Intelligencer* 2.9 (Nov. 1927).[85]

iii. *Disinheriting the church*
As we noted above, 'disinheriting' also applies to the significant outgroup of the denominational churches, especially because of their tie with the western denominations. References are as follows:

'Warera no Purotestanto-Sugi' [Our Protestantism], *Seisho no Kenkyu* (July 1904).[86] / 'Kyokai to Shinko' [Church and Faith], *Seisho no Kenkyu* (Feb. 1908).[87] / 'Churchless Christianity', *Seisho no Kenkyu* 344 (March 1929).[88]

iv. *Stereotypical criticism of the church*
As we noted above, 'stereotype criticism' was also directed to another significant outgroup of the denominational churches, especially because of their connection with the western denominations. References are as follows:

'On Protestantism', *Seisho no Kenkyu* 190 (May 1916).[89] / 'Mukyokai ni Tsuite' [On Mukyokai], *Seisho no Kenkyu* 327 (Oct. 1927).[90] / 'Shino no Kyodotai-Teki Igi' [Significance of Communal Faith], *Seisho no Kenkyu* 206 (Sept. 1907).[91] / 'Mukyokai wo Sutezu' [Not Forsaking Mukyokai], *Seisho no Kenkyu* 141 (April 1912).[92]

v. *Inheriting (or ownership of) the traditions*
As noted earlier in the explanation of 'disinheriting', when the ingroup is somehow related to the outgroup in origin, the right of inheritance of truth and traditions is removed from the outgroup, who are thus

80. Ibid., XXV, pp. 46–47.
81. Ibid., XXX, p. 368.
82. Ibid., XXII, pp. 368–69.
83. Ibid., XXII, pp. 233–234.
84. Ibid., XXIX, pp. 476–80.
85. Ibid., XXX, pp. 477–79.
86. Ibid., XII, p. 241.
87. Ibid., XV, p. 386.
88. Ibid., XXXII, pp. 51–52.
89. Ibid., XXII, pp. 259–60.
90. Ibid., XXX, pp. 437–38.
91. Ibid., XXIII, pp. 331–34.
92. Ibid., XIX, p. 92.

disinherited or disqualified, and the ingroup inherits the traditions instead. References are as follows:

> '*Bushido* and Christianity', *Seisho no Kenkyu* 186 (Jan. 1916).[93] / 'Paul a Samurai', *Seisho no Kenkyu* 239 (June 1920).[94] / 'Hebrews and Japanese', *Seisho no Kenkyu* 350 (Sept. 1929).[95] / 'Spirits and Forms', *The Japanese Christian Intelligencer* 1.11 (Jan. 1927).[96]

vi. *Recreated worldview*
The term 'recreated worldview' denotes a shift in value and status concerning powerless ingroup members in relation to powerful outgroups. It is a reversal of status, because in this process the minority group somehow overpowers the majority, or the marginalized themselves marginalize the majority in their newly constructed worldview. Though this point is not fully articulated in this political analysis, Uchimura's whole effort to justify his group's existence over against the powerful outgroups can be identified by this concept. With this response, Uchimura also seeks to deal with the stigma placed on him as 'outlaw' and 'heretic'. This tendency will be particularly clear in the analysis of the function of the rite of baptism in Chapter 7.[97] References are as follows:

> 'Meiyo ka Fu-Meiyo ka' [Ashamed or Not], *Tokyo Dokuritsu Zasshi* 32 (May 1899).[98] / 'Hazukashiki Na' [Shameful Names], *Tokyo Dokuritsu Zasshi* 31 (May 1899).[99] / 'Itan' [Heretic], *Seisho no Kenkyu* 102 (Sept. 1908).[100] / 'Seikyo to Itan' [Orthodoxy and Heretic], *Seisho no Kenkyu* 103/104 (Oct. and Nov. 1908).[101] / 'Bushido and Christianity', *Seisho no Kenkyu* 186 (Jan. 1916).[102]

b. *Materiality of Religion and Sensei–Pupil Relationship*
As has been observed, the members' veneration for the leaders (*sensei*) leads to the collection of relics and letters, and publication of leaders' biographies and works.[103] These objects, in which the memories of *sensei* remain, act as a surrogate for the presence of *sensei*, and thus help to maintain communal cohesion. This particular expression of religiosity will

93.   Ibid., XXII, pp. 161–62.
94.   Ibid., XXV, pp. 362–63.
95.   Ibid., XXXII, pp. 186–87.
96.   Ibid., XXX, pp. 191–95.
97.   See Chapter 6 (2.e).
98.   Uchimura, *Zenshu*, VII, pp. 94–95.
99.   Ibid., VII, p. 76.
100. Ibid., XVI, p. 73.
101. Ibid., XVI, p. 82
102. Ibid., XXII, pp. 161–62.
103. Caldarola, *Christianity*, p. 146.

be discussed in reference to the importance of scripture for constructing community–identity in Chapter 8.[104]

Part I introduced the theoretical framework of community–identity construction (Chapter 1) and the primary analogical comparative case of Mukyokai and its founder Uchimura (Chapter 2). The conclusion of each chapter contained a summary of the main points and suggested exactly where they will be applied for the interpretation of Galatians, in terms of the context (or conditions) of community–identity construction (Part II) and the patterns (or practical ways) thereof (Part III). The social-scientific theories and particularly the history of Mukyokai and of the modernization of Japan are not necessarily subjects widely known to those in the field of biblical studies. Therefore, they will be resummarized from time to time for the sake of clarity of discussion. Where Uchimura's sayings are referred to without being quoted, the page where the quotation is found will be provided. This format may lead one to a sense of repetition at times, but it has been chosen to present the following discussion as clearly as possible.

---

104. See Chapter 8 (1.a). Chapter 8 also refers to a similar way of maintaining the cohesion of a religious community–identity which is found in the underground religious community of Kakure. The description of Kakure is deferred until Chapter 8.

Part II

THE CONTEXT OF IDENTITY CONSTRUCTION IN THE GALATIAN COMMUNITY

> But Antiogonus in answer to Herod's proclamation told Silo and the Roman army that it would be contrary to their own notion of right if they gave the kingship to Herod who was a commoner and an Idumaean, that is, a *half-Jew* [ἡμιιουδαίῳ], when they ought to offer it to those who were of the (royal) family, as was their custom (*Ant.* 14.403).

In 129 BCE, John Hyrcanus I conquered Idumaea and forced the non-Jewish residents to observe the rite of circumcision (1 Macc. 4.36–59; 2 Macc. 10.1–8), which is generally considered as a final step of Gentile incorporation into Judaism. Josephus comments that Idumaeans '... continued to be Jews since then' (... ὥστε εἶναι τὸ λοιπὸν Ἰουδαίους, *Ant.* 13.257). Yet, ethnic incorporation is not so simple. Herod's identity as a 'half-Jew' raised a question as to whether he would be given the kingship. Even though the term is used here pejoratively as a rhetoric of resistance, the possibility of such an intermediate identity is significant to grasp the complexity and importance of a question: how did Jews view themselves in relation to those outsiders who were either approaching or crossing their ethnic boundary in various ways? In other words, the question concerns the Jewish identity and their ideas of Gentile incorporation.

The analysis in subsequent chapters shows that there were various understandings of this issue of Jewish identity expressed in their ideas of Gentile incorporation. One can make an assumption, therefore, that the conflicts reported in Gal. 2.1–14 may relate directly to the different expectations of how Gentiles may be incorporated into the larger Jewish commonwealth. In other words, the intricate relation between varying approaches to community–identity is the context in which Paul's effort to build his community should be located. Paul's persuasion in his letter to the Galatians arguably reflects the interaction of these varying approaches (or expectations) observed among Paul himself, the Jewish leaders and Judaism in general. Therefore, it is important to take into consideration both personal (Paul's approach to community–identity based upon his self-understanding) and social (Jewish approaches to community–identity) conditions that contribute to Paul's actual constructive efforts in forging a community–identity.

First, I will consider Paul's personal condition on the basis of his self-understanding (Chapter 3). In it, I will argue that Paul approaches the issue of community–identity in the 'instrumental mode' on the basis of the framework of identity-construction. Then consideration will be given to how Jews in general approach the issue of community–identity, particularly in the area of Gentile incorporation. As the Jerusalem church is closely linked genealogically with the Jewish commonwealth, I will assume that the Jerusalem church reflects similar (ethno-centred) modes of community–identity construction (Chapter 4). Following this identification, an interpretation will be offered regarding the conflicts in Jerusalem and in Antioch as stemming from different and opposing approaches to community–identity construction (Chapter 5). By recounting the events, Paul demonstrates for the Galatians that the ethno-centred mode of mission marginalizes the Gentile members and that this awareness ought to lead the Galatians to be convinced by Paul's persuasion and efforts to build and maintain the community. It is within this context, I suggest, that the identity of the Galatian community is constructed (see Part III).

Chapter 3

PAUL AND INSTRUMENTAL MODE OF COMMUNITY–IDENTITY CONSTRUCTION

The purpose of this chapter is to establish the case that Paul is, on the basis of the framework of identity construction, following an 'instrumental mode' in his approach to community–identity construction, one that is free from core ethnic sentiment or traditional issues important to the Jewish structure of religion. If he is properly identified as such, then the features of the instrumental mode of community–identity construction can be used as a hermeneutical tool for our interpretation of Galations 2 (Chapter 5) and for studying the ways of community–identity construction in the later chapters. Therefore, in this chapter, I will argue for the case of the 'instrumental Paul' by looking at two aspects of Paul's self-understanding. First, we will look at Paul's perspective on his relationship to what he calls 'Judaism' (Gal. 1.14). In it, he portrays himself as standing clearly outside of 'Judaism'. This is to claim that he is an apostle ordained by God through a personal revelation free from traditions and human authority. Second is consideration of Paul's relationship to the leadership of the Jerusalem church, i.e. James, Peter and John, referred to in this discussion as the 'Jerusalem apostles'. In it, while acknowledging the authority of the Jerusalem apostles among the Jewish believers, he emphasizes the divine provenance of his calling to the Gentile mission as opposed to the Jewish mission of the Jerusalem apostles. All these observations will lead one to conclude that Paul understood himself as an authentic apostle, autonomous from traditions and authorities of human institutions.[1] In this sense, Paul can be identified as being of an

---

1. The definition of apostleship in the New Testament has long been debated, and it requires a separate essay fully to cover the debate and come to some form of conclusion. Cf. Hengel and Schwemer, *Paulus*, p. 156. For further discussion on this matter, cf. Johannes Munck, 'Paul, the Apostles, and the Twelve', *ST* 3 (1949), pp. 96–110; Walter Schmithals, *Das kirchliche Apostelamt: Eine historische Untersuchung* (FRLANT, 79; Göttingen: Vandenhoeck & Ruprecht, 1961), pp. 56–76, especially p. 72 on the interpretation of Gal. 1.17, 19 under 'Paulus kennt die Zwölf nicht als Apostel'; K.H. Rengstorf, 'ἀπόστολος', in Gerhard F. Kittel (ed.), *Theological Dictionary of the New Testament* (trans. Geoffrey W. Bromiley; 10 vols.; Grand Rapids: Eerdmans, 1964), I, pp. 398–447; J. Andrew Kirk, 'Apostleship since Rengstorf: Toward a Synthesis', *NTS* 21 (1975), pp. 249–64. In this

'instrumental mode' in his community–identity construction. On the basis of this understanding of Paul, he is expected to take innovative approaches in his community construction, which inevitably face challenges peculiar to the very nature of innovation.

1. *Paul's Relationship to 'Judaism'*

The argument that Paul is an instrumental mode of community constructor is substantiated by his own self-perception in relation to his former affiliation (i.e. 'Judaism')[2] and present affiliation (i.e. the church as a whole). Particularly in this section, the focus will be on the former, i.e. Paul's relationship to what he calls 'Judaism', primarily in the biographical section of the letter. This survey of Paul's relation to 'Judaism' (ʼΙουδαϊσμός as he calls it in Gal. 1.14) will observe how he perceives and portrays the relationship between his pre-revelation life and post-revelation life. For this purpose, two issues will be of primary importance, i.e. (a) Zeal and Violence (Gal. 1.13–14) and (b) Call/Conversion and Peculiar Process of Emergence (Gal. 1.15–16).

a. *Zeal and Violence*
In the beginning of Paul's biographical account, a drastic shift in his life is reported to have happened at the occasion of direct revelation, illustrated in Gal. 1.15–16. The two verses in question here are retrospective of Paul's former life in Judaism (τὴν ἐμὴν ἀναστροφήν ποτε ἐν τῷ Ἰουδαϊσμῷ). In vv. 13–14, Paul's affiliation to Judaism and his being a very zealous member (περισσοτέρως ζηλωτὴς) of it are placed alongside his extremity (καθ' ὑπερβολὴν) in persecution and destruction of the church of God

---

discussion, the term 'apostle' is used according to Paul's own claims in his letters. It seems evident from the fact that Paul introduces himself as an apostle (Gal. 1.1; 1 Cor. 1.1; 2 Cor. 1.1; Rom. 1.1) that he uses the term ἀπόστολος as a title given to a person with specific functions and rights. Some of the functions are specified: (1) proclamation of the gospel (Rom. 1.5) and (2) forming the community of believers as the result of the proclamation (1 Cor. 9.2). The ground, on which Paul introduces himself as an apostle, is his conviction that his experience of the Damascus road christophany is parallel to Jesus' calling and commissioning of the twelve disciples for apostleship (cf. 1 Cor. 9.1–3; 15.1–10). Because Paul understands his commissioning for apostleship as equal to that of the twelve disciples, he claims to possess the authority and rights of apostleship equal to those of the Jerusalem apostles (1 Cor. 9.4–7; cf. 7.17). At the same time, Paul elsewhere specifies his apostleship as being for the Gentiles (Rom. 1.5; 11.8; cf. Gal. 2.7–8) and his commissioning was given through the revelation of the risen Christ (Gal. 1.16).

2. Paul uses the term 'Judaism' (ʼΙουδαϊσμός) as a general designation for the 'Jewish' people as a whole with the thoughts and customs within their religious life. This matter will be discussed later in the section on 'Zeal and Violence'. Cf. *inter alia* of this chapter.

(ἐδίωκον τὴν ἐκκλησίαν τοῦ θεοῦ καὶ ἐπόρθουν αὐτήν).[3] The term 'zealous' (ζηλωτής) is used to depict the Jewish reactive attitude toward those who are disobedient to the Torah (apostasy) under foreign oppression (1 Macc. 2.23–28, 49–50; 2 Macc. 4.1–2).[4] The manner of his destructive actions described primarily by πορθεῖν (and διώκειν) is unclear,[5] yet the term seems to imply some level of violence.[6] Together with the Acts' account of Paul's persecution of the Jewish Christians in mind (Acts 9.21), it may be assumed in the term πορθεῖν here that at least some level of physical violence was present and served to intensify the level of persecution, which he was reported to have performed.[7] It gives the impression to the reader that the more zealous one is in Judaism, the more harmful the person is to the welfare of the church. Therefore, Paul's earlier life in Judaism and the church are depicted as disjunctive, or rather, incompatible with each other. If this is the case, the disjunctive connective δέ in Gal. 1.15 indicates a shift in Paul's life, occasioned by the revelatory experience. The aftermath of this experience is that 'the church in Christ' glorifies God because of Paul (Gal. 1.22–24). The revelatory experience places Paul in an incompatible relation to Judaism, as is clearly summarized in the report of the Judaean churches: 'the one who once persecuted us is now proclaiming the faith, which he once was destroying' (ὁ διώκων ἡμᾶς ποτε νῦν εὐαγγελίζεται τὴν πίστιν ἥν ποτε ἐπόρθει, Gal. 1.23).[8]

3. Conzelmann suggests that Paul's persecution was in Syria and more specifically in Antioch, because (1) the Law-observant Jewish churches in Judaea would not have motivated other Jews to persecute them and (2) Paul says in Gal. 1.22 that he was not known to the Judaean churches. Conzelmann, *Geschichte des Urchristentums*, pp. 51–52, 64. However, cf. Hengel and Schwemer, *Paulus*, pp. 60–61, note 216.

4. Beverly R. Gaventa, *From Darkness to Light: Aspects of Conversion in the New Testament* (Philadelphia: Fortress, 1986), p. 26. However, she seems to see too much of a correlation between Paul and the Maccabean resistance when she argues that Paul portrays himself in the tradition of the zealotic forerunners on the basis that Paul in Gal. 1.13–14 and the description of the Maccabean revolt share such terms as ζηλωτής, ἀναστροφή and Ἰουδαῖος (2 Macc. 2.21; 6.23; 8.1; *4 Macc.* 4.26).

5. According to Menoud, πορθεῖν was to destroy the faith of the church but not physical violence for such a persecution was not legally accepted. Luke's description here is influenced by the recent memory of the violence of Zealots. Philippe-Henri Menoud, 'Le sense du verbe πορθεῖν', in Franz H. Kettler (ed.), *Apophoreta* (Festschrift E. Haenchen; BZNWKAK, 30; Berlin: Töpelmann, 1964), pp. 178–86 (179, 184–85).

6. So 'plundering' of Jerusalem by Antiochus IV (*4 Macc.* 4.23) and 'ravaging' of Jerusalem by the Babylonian king (*Ant.* 10.135).

7. Martin Hengel, 'Der vorchristliche Paulus', in M. Hengel and U. Heckel (eds.), *Paulus und das antike Judentum* (WUNT, 58; Tübingen: Mohr, 1991), pp. 177–293 (274–75). Contra: Gaventa, *From Darkness to Light*, p. 25. Even though she denies physical violence, she sees some kind of excessive action. See especially p. 23.

8. The possible relationship between Judaean churches and the early mission of Paul suggested in vv. 22–24 will later be discussed in Chapter 5 (section 1).

Also of note is the peculiarity of the expression, 'Judaism'. In the New Testament, the term, 'Jew' (᾿Ιουδαῖος) usually points to the ethnic identity of the people (cf. Rom. 1.16; 2.9–10, 17, 28–29; Gal. 2.14; 3.28; Col. 3.11).[9] The term 'Judaism' (as in ἐν τῷ ᾿Ιουδαϊσμῷ) is used only twice in the New Testament, both of which are found here, in the account of Paul's former life (Gal. 1.13–14). The term is usually understood in a general sense that describes Jewish religion and life as a whole.[10] For example, in the Second Temple Jewish literature, the term is used in 2 and 4 Maccabees as the object of liquidation in the Hellenizing campaign of Antiochus IV (2 Macc. 2.21; 14.38; *4 Macc.* 4.26). It is the general designation for the practices and systems of the religion of the Jewish people.[11] Ignatius contrasts Judaism and Christianity in a general sense as ᾿Ιουδαϊσμὸν and Χριστιανισμὸν (Ignatius, *Phld.* 6.1). In Paul's experience of revelation, he portrays himself as standing outside this general boundary of 'Judaism', therefore as autonomous from the authority of the religious institution.

b. *Call/Conversion and Peculiar Process of Emergence*
The connective δε (Gal. 1.15) makes the reader anticipate in the revelatory experience and its aftermath a development antithetical to Paul's former life in Judaism. As the account of the revelatory experience is examined, a question arises as to whether Paul's experience was a 'call' or a 'conversion', a concern related to the discussion of Paul's autonomy from 'Judaism'.

While Paul himself describes his experience partly with the term καλεῖν, his usage of the term is so diverse that one cannot determine on the basis of the term the character of the revelatory experience (whether it is inter-religious transfer of affiliations ['conversion'] or intra-religious vocational assignment ['call']). For example, when Betz denies the possibility of 'conversion' on the basis of the use of the term καλεῖν in Gal. 1.15, his examples are from LXX Isaiah (41.9; 42.6, 11; 43.1; 45.3; 48.12, 15; 49.1; 50.2; 51.2, plus Paul's 'self'-designation as an apostle in Rom. 1.1; 1 Cor. 1.1), in which the context favourably connotes 'designation'.[12] However, in Gal. 1.6, καλεῖν seems to refer to the phenomenon of the Gentile Galatians coming into the community that Paul was building (so also Gal.

9.   The ethnic connotation is clear, especially as the term is compared with the Gentiles (Acts 14.1b; 18.4; 1 Cor. 1.24; 10.32; 12.32) and with the Gentile proselytes (Acts 2.10).

10.   *BAGD*, 379. Cf. also Ignatius, *Magn.* 8.1; 10.3.

11.   Hengel, *Judentum und Hellenismus*, pp. 1–2. He gives a definition of ᾿Ιουδαϊσμός: 'it connotes both political and genealogical associations with the Jewish people as the exclusive faith in one God of Israel and the strict observance of the Torah given to them by their God' (p. 2, author's translation).

12.   Betz, *Galatians*, pp. 64, 70, note 137.

5.8, 13). In this sense, the term καλεῖν in Gal. 1.6 better suits the category of inter-religious transfer generally termed 'conversion'. In other Pauline letters, Paul mixes Jews and Gentiles in the act of the same 'calling' (Rom. 9.24; 1 Cor. 7.18, 20).[13] In the context of καλεῖν in Gal. 1.15, Paul portrays himself as standing outside and antithetical to 'Judaism'. In order to clarify (and qualify) the issue of Paul's independence from the human authority of 'Judaism', one should consider Paul's account of revelatory experience.

Stendahl raises the issue of Paul's 'conversion' experience in his work, *Paul among Jews and Gentiles*, in which he rejects the modern concept of conversion as applicable to Paul's experience.[14] Conversion in this sense is inter-religious transfer, caused by the desire to resolve some kind of psychological dissonance in one's life, i.e. guilt-feeling and restlessness. Rather, he finds in the experience of Paul a vocational 'call', parallel to what we find in Jeremiah 1 and Isaiah 6 (cf. Gal. 1.15).[15] Segal qualifies this argument. While he accepts Stendahl's rejection of the psychologically-motivated conversion, he still duly notes Paul's radical shift in life. He concludes that the radical nature of the transfer even between sects or denominations can rightly be called 'conversion'.[16] He maintains that Paul's experience was such a 'conversion', while allowing for the resulting awareness of a 'call', in the sense of 'being commissioned for a task'. Most recently, Hurtado, while supporting the stance of Segal on conversion, substantiated Stendahl's suggestion of 'call' by positing the view that Paul never renounced his people or the God of his ancestors.[17]

Even if consensus is generally made that Paul's experience was not based upon his vulnerable conscience over sin and guilt, a tension still remains between call and conversion.[18] On one hand, there is some level of commonality in motifs, symbols and theological themes between Paul and 'Judaism', and on the other, a considerable degree of radicalness in his shift is also observed in Paul's experience. Hurtado's conclusion that it is both call and conversion, fails to explain or reconcile this tension.[19]

---

13. C.E.B. Cranfield, *A Critical and Exegetical Commentary on the Epistle to the Romans* (ICC; 2 vols.; Edinburgh: T. & T. Clark, 1979), II, p. 498; C.K. Barrett, *A Commentary on the Epistle to the Romans* (BNTC; London: A. & C. Black, 2nd edn, 1991), p. 176; Raymond F. Collins, *First Corinthians* (SP; Collegeville: The Liturgical Press, 1999), p. 285.

14. Krister Stendahl, *Paul among Jews and Gentiles* (Philadelphia: Fortress, 1976).

15. Ibid., pp. 80–81. See, in the following argument, the correlation between Paul's revelation and the 'call' experiences of Jeremiah and Isaiah.

16. Segal, *Paul*, p. 6.

17. Hurtado, 'Convert', p. 284.

18. Stendahl's rejection of Paul's psychological dissonance is questioned by some scholars. Theißen, *Die Religion*, p. 296, note 7; Hengel and Schwemer, *Paulus*, pp. 160–61.

19. Segal, *Paul*, p. 6; Hurtado, 'Convert', p. 283. For Hurtado, it is all three: convert, apostate and apostle.

It is suggested here that the tension is due to the peculiar process of emergence of primitive Christianity as a whole and Paul as the founder of the Gentile wing within it. This peculiar process of emergence from the mother religion involves, by definition, both continuity and discontinuity. It is discontinuous as it emerges *out of* the mother religion, but it is also continuous as it makes sense *in relation to* the mother religion.[20] Segal is right to take note of the radicalness of shift in Paul's experience, and this discontinuous feature of Paul's experience reflects the peculiar process of emergence. However, when he terms this radical shift a 'conversion', he has to redefine the term 'conversion'. Commonality also reflects the peculiar process of emergence. The prophetic vocational motif suggested to be shared between Jer. 1.15 and Gal. 1.15 may be such an example.[21] Whether or not the original Gentile audience heard the possible echo of the Scripture aside, it is possible that Paul himself conceptually related his experience to that of Jeremiah because of the parallel ideas of (1) commissioning to the Gentiles (εἰς ἔθνη/ἐν τοῖς ἔθνεσιν), (2) setting apart (ἁγιάζειν/ἀφορίζειν), and (3) in the mother's womb (κοιλία).[22] However, one should take note of the manner in which motifs, symbols and even God are 'shared'.[23] For example, in the conclusion of Paul's interpretation of salvation history in general and on the Sarah/Hagar conflict in particular, we find Jews under the Torah 'enslaved' (Gal. 4.24–25) and 'driven out' (Gal. 4.30). Rather than sharing the motifs and symbols, what one encounters is reinterpretation of salvation history or, if we borrow a term used in the sectarian model, 'monopolizing the truth' in the religious phenomena of emergence.[24] Hurtado is right that Paul never renounces

20. Indeed, accepting Strecker's thesis of liminality to explain Paul's revelatory experience and the outcome of it, one is able to integrate the two phenomena of conversion and call (*Bekehrungs-/Berufungsthese*). Strecker, *Die liminale Theologie*, pp. 155–56.

21. Jeremiah's experience of commissioning as a prophet is described as follows. Πρὸ τοῦ με πλάσαι σε ἐν κοιλίᾳ ἐπισταμαί σε καὶ πρὸ τοῦ σε ἐξελθεῖν ἐκ μήτρας ἡγίακά σε, προφήτην εἰς ἔθνη τέθεικά σε (LXX Jer. 1.15). Rengstorf argues that Paul's understanding of apostleship partly derives from prophetic figures such as Jeremiah and Isaiah. Rengstorf, *TDNT*, I, s. v., 'ἀπόστολος'.

22. Strecker sees the parallelism between Paul and the 'peripheral prophets' in this verse to support his argument for Paul being a liminal person (*Schwellenperson*). Strecker, *Die liminale Theologie*, pp. 96–112 (especially, 111).

23. Hurtado, 'Convert', p. 284. He bases his argument for 'call' on the supposition that: 'He did not renounce his people or the God of his ancestors'.

24. It was primarily the study of Troeltsch that finds correlations between this peculiar process of emergence with the emergence of separatist groups at the time of the Reformation. Ernst Troeltsch, *The Social Teaching of the Christian Churches* (trans. Olive Wyon; 2 vols.; London: Macmillan, 1931), I, p. 331, II, 691–94. Later sociologists developed comprehensive theories of 'sectarianism', which widely deal with religions in general. Cf. Bryan Wilson (ed.), *Patterns of Sectarianism: Organization and Ideology in Social and Religious Movements* (London: Heinemann, 1967). 'Monopolizing the truth' is related to the concept of 'reversal of status' in Turner's *The Ritual Process*. See Chapter 1 (section 3).

his people and the God of his ancestors, but he reinterprets and shapes even the way his own people may approach his God.[25] In the letter to the Romans, for example, which adopts a less polemical tone against Judaism, Paul gives a redefinition of 'Jews' and 'Judaism' (2.27–29), then he describes both Jews and Gentiles as equally 'called' into the 'heirship' of God (9.24; cf. 9.6–8). The manner of 'sharing' then is somewhat akin to what we observe in Justin Martyr's *Dialogue with Trypho*, in which Christians own the Hebrew Bible because they understand it, and the Jews do not because they do not understand it (*Dial. Tryph.* 29).[26] Drawing as an analogy an example from the emergence of Mukyokai, one of the founder's immediate disciples, Tsukamoto, reinterpreted salvation history and reshaped the very motif favoured since the Reformation among the Protestant churches. Therefore, he claimed a salvation history outside the church (*Extra Ecclesiam Salus* [Salvation outside the Church]), i.e. within Mukyokai, instead of *Extra Ecclesiam Non Salus* [No Salvation outside the Church].[27] One of the ways to emphasize the justification and authenticity of a newly emerging group out of its mother religion is to claim the monopoly of the truth found in the mother religion. This often happens, as seen in the analogical case of Mukyokai and in the general theory of sect emergence, by reinterpreting and reshaping the motifs found in the previous affiliation. When understanding Paul in the peculiar process of emergence from the mother religion of 'Judaism', one can explain both apparent commonality with and a radical shift from 'Judaism'.

To refer to this experience as a 'call' or a 'conversion' is at least partially a definitional matter. Part of the problem in responding to the question of call/conversion is that while the *etic* expression of 'conversion' and the *emic* expression of καλεῖν considerably overlap with each other, they should not be equated.[28] Therefore, the conventional connotation of 'conversion' may not fit precisely the revelatory experience of Paul, in which one transfers his or her affiliation from one religion to another

---

25.   Cf. Theißen, *Die Religion*, pp. 227–28, note 17. He says about Rom. 11.25ff, 'So wie er [Paulus] ein Feind des Evangeliums war, so sind die ungläubigen Israeliten Feinde des Evangeliums' [Just as he (Paul) was an enemy of the gospel, so were the unbelieving Israeliten] (author's parentheses and translation).

26.   The examples of 'monopolizing truth' in the context of religious contest is observed in many groups. For example, Kanzo Uchimura, 'Bushido and Christianity', *Seisho no Kenkyu* 186 (Jan. 1916), in *Zenshu*, XXII, pp. 161–62. Or the Buddhist version of 'monopolizing the truth' by a sect is readily observed in Nichiren's 'Vision of the Holy See'; cf; Masaharu Anesaki, *Nichiren: The Buddhist Prophet* (Cambridge: Harvard University Press, 1916), p. 98.

27.   Toraji Tsukamoto, 'Mukyokai towa Nanzoya' [What is Mukyokai?], in *Tsukamoto Toraji Chosakushu Zoku* [*Works of Toraji Tsukamoto, II*] (8 vols.; Tokyo: Seisho Chishikisha, 1927), I, pp. 221–22.

28.   Cf. Strecker, *Die liminale Theologie*, pp. 155–56; Akira Satake, 'Apostolat und Gnade bei Paulus', *NTS* 15 (1968–69), pp. 96–107 (106).

religion that is usually genealogically independent from the former. However, the term 'call' in the sense of 'commission' or 'assignment' does not explain Paul's radical departure from the mother religion of 'Judaism' as Paul himself describes it. Therefore, while admitting the limitation of the *etic* expression of 'conversion', one may well prefer 'conversion' to 'call' in order not to undermine the radical departure in Paul's experience of emergence from the mother religion of Judaism as the result of the revelatory experience.[29] Also of note is that the *etic* expression of 'call' does not adequately express Paul's nuanced attitude toward the shared motifs with his former life in Judaism. The term 'conversion' is not undermined by the existence of commonality between Judaism and Paul, because the common features are reinterpreted, or Paul claims monopoly of them. Therefore, in this context of peculiar process of emergence, which one may describe as 'conversion', Paul is rightly understood as an autonomous apostle, even with regard to some elements he 'shares' with the mother religion he calls Ἰουδαϊσμός (Gal. 1.13).

Paul's experience of transition ('conversion') can also be understood in light of Jenkins's concept of identification, in which identity is constructed in the dialectic process of 'external categorization' and 'internal identification'.[30] Generally speaking, Paul's former relatedness with the church (i.e. persecution and destruction) is a form of external categorization against 'apostasy' placed by Judaism upon the church. Then, the justification of Paul's transfer to the state of 'apostasy' requires a rather radical shift in his understanding of his religion or salvation history. Paul's rather peculiar exposition of the Torah or salvation history in relation to Abraham (Gal. 3–4) may be thought of as his redefinition, or in Jenkins's term 'internal identification', in response to the 'external categorization' of Jewish persecution of the church, in order that Paul may make sense of his experience and may offer cohesion for his community members in Galatia.[31]

Two aspects of Paul's experience of transfer in Galatians 1 have been considered, in order to understand Paul's relation to 'Judaism'. In Gal. 1.13–14, Paul's former life in 'Judaism' was seen as antithetical to his life after the revelatory experience. Therefore, by portraying himself as antithetical to and outside of the general boundary of 'Judaism', Paul shows that he is independent from the human authority of the religious institution of 'Judaism'. Then, in the discussion of conversion/call, Paul's

---

29. Thus, the argument follows that of Segal on this definitional matter. Segal, *Paul*, p. 6.

30. For the detailed consideration of this concept, see Chapter 1 (1.a).

31. An attempt to interpret Paul's understanding of the salvation history in Gal. 3–4 in Chapter 6 will be made. The conflicts Paul experienced in Jerusalem and Antioch may be understood as an 'external categorization' to shape his ways to construct his community and its identity, which can be observed in the following chapters.

radical experience of emergence out of 'Judaism' leads to the conclusion that such an experience could be described as 'conversion', in a qualified sense (i.e. conversion in the context of sect emergence). The shared motifs found in Paul and Judaism can be explained as this peculiar process of emergence, and therefore it does not negate Paul's autonomy from the mother religion of Judaism.[32] Paul's self-awareness of being apart from the religious/ethnic institution of Judaism is, therefore, evidence for the suggestion that Paul's mode of identity construction is 'instrumental'.

2. *Paul's Relationship to the Jerusalem Apostles*

Paul's relation to 'Judaism' has thus far been considered in order to argue for his self-understanding as an autonomous apostle. In this section, I wish to take into account part of the biographical section of the letter, in order to better understand Paul's relationship primarily to the Jerusalem apostles. In the biographical account in Galatians, we immediately note Paul's nuanced stance toward the leadership in Jerusalem, who are called here 'the Jerusalem apostles'.[33] Even on the surface level, Paul's recognition of their authority is to some degree reserved (Gal. 2.2, 6, 9) and his stance of distance and independence from the 'Jerusalem apostles' is also observed (Gal. 1.16–20; 2.7–9).[34] This nuanced relationship between Paul the apostle and the Jerusalem apostles seems to help establish the case that Paul's approach to community–identity construction was 'instrumental mode'. Therefore, the following features of Paul's relation to the Jerusalem apostles in the biographical account are to be considered: (1) Paul's emphatic denial of the connection with the Jerusalem authority in Gal. 1.16b–20, (2) Ἀποκάλυψις and the occasion of the Jerusalem visit (Gal. 2.1–2) and (3) Δοκέω and the nuanced acknowledgement of the Jerusalem leaders (Gal. 2.2, 6a, 6b, 9).[35]

The appellation 'Jerusalem apostles' requires an explanation. Cephas/Peter is explicitly introduced as an apostle (Gal. 1.19; 2.8). While John's

---

32. Perhaps, Theißen's nuanced description is closer to the conclusion that two religions developed upon (or share at times) the same traditional foundation with different authoritative structures. Gerd Theißen, 'Judentum und Christentum', p. 254.

33. Refer to footnote 37 of the present chapter.

34. Cf. Günther Bornkamm, *Paulus* (Stuttgart: Verlag W. Kohlhammer, 2nd edn, 1969), p. 59. The tension between Paul's mission and the mission of the Jerusalem church (or of Peter) can hardly be missed in the historical description of the letter (esp. Gal. 2.1–14). Probably the work which emphasizes the tension the most in recent study of the early Church is by Goulder. Michael Goulder, *A Tale of Two Missions* (London: SCM Press, 1994), pp. 1–7. The issue of division between the two missions will be dealt with in detail in Chapter 5.

35. An important remaining concern in the visit to Jerusalem is the issue of the relationship between the two missions (Gal. 2.7–9). There will follow an extended discussion on this issue in Chapter 5 (1.b).

status is not specified in the letter, the assumption from the gospels and Acts that he is one of the original twelve disciples and fulfils the role of apostleship together with Peter (Mk 3.14–19; Acts 3.1; 8.14–25) has not been disputed very much.[36] Paul seems to include James the brother of Jesus to the list of apostles, but the qualification Paul makes in Gal. 1.19 is slightly ambiguous. The sense of exception in 'I did not see any other apostle except James' (εἰ μή as in ἕτερον δὲ τῶν ἀποστόλων οὐκ εἶδον εἰ μὴ Ἰάκωβον) is more accurately brought out in the interpretation (a) 'only other apostle I saw was James' rather than (b) 'I did not see any other apostle. I did see James nevertheless'. The exceptive force of εἰ μή can certainly influence either ἕτερον in the case of (a) or εἶδον in the case of (b). However, the connection between εἰ μὴ and ἕτερον is stronger, for both εἰ μὴ and ἕτερον carry the nuance of limitation or qualification.[37] Therefore, the 'Jerusalem apostles', in this discussion, are those apostles in Jerusalem represented by James, Cephas and John. In contrast to 'those who were already apostles before me' (Gal. 1.17), Paul has a clear self-awareness that he is an apostle (Gal. 1.1) and somewhat distant and independent from them.[38]

a. *Emphatic Denial of the Jerusalem Connection (Galatians 1.16b-20)*
Paul denies, after the revelatory experience, his immediate contact (προσανεθέμην) with any human (σαρκὶ καὶ αἵματι) in Gal. 1.16. Προσανατίθημι generally means 'to add/contribute something to someone' or 'to consult someone for something'.[39] The revelation to Paul was direct, and therefore he was in no need of an interpreter, even such a qualified one as an apostle, to act as an intermediary between God and Paul. After three years, Paul visits (ἱστορῆσαι) Cephas (Gal. 1.18). The nuance of the term ἱστορέω is more general than προσανατίθημι, and it

---

36. As noted earlier, there is a debate as to whether they had an agreement on who bore the title 'apostle'. Hengel and Schwemer, *Paulus*, p. 156.

37. F.F. Bruce, *Commentary on Galatians* (NIGTC; Grand Rapids: Eerdmans, 1982), pp. 100–101. Cf. Schmithals, *Das kirchliche Apostelamt*, pp. 54–55. Schmithals suggests that the ambiguity of James' status (apostleship) is intentional on Paul's side, due to the ambiguous nature of the formal title at that time.

38. Lüdemann suggests that the lack of the title 'apostle' for him in Gal. 2.7–8, where one may expect it, is due to the concern that Paul did not want the reader to connect his apostleship with Jerusalem and its leaders. Gerd Lüdemann, *Paulus, der Heidenapostel: Studien zur Chronologie* (FRLANT, 123.1; 2 vols.; Göttingen: Vandenhoeck & Ruprecht, 1980), I, p. 103.

39. BAGD, p. 711. Dunn finds in the classical usage of the term a more technical sense of consulting a qualified interpreter for the meaning or significance of some sign. Cf. J.D.G. Dunn, 'The Relationship between Paul and Jerusalem according to Galatians 1 and 2', *NTS* 28 (1982), pp. 461–78 (462).

means 'to visit for the purpose of acquainting with someone or something'.[40] Paul's choice of the word seems to imply that the visit was not to have his revelation authenticated or validated by the Jerusalem apostles. A suggestion has been made on the basis of the connotation of ἱστορέω that Paul gained from the teaching of the earthly life of Jesus,[41] but this seems to contradict the insistence on the divine provenance of the message asserted in Gal. 1.12. The emphatic denial of seeing other apostles seems to show that Paul stresses the private nature of the visit, i.e. no official meeting with the authorizing body was convened to validate his message and status as an apostle to the Gentiles.

The emphatic negation in v. 20 is peculiar. The manner of emphasis is almost like an oath (ἰδοὺ ἐνώπιον τοῦ θεοῦ ὅτι οὐ ψεύδομαι), as is the custom for Paul elsewhere when such an emphasis is felt necessary (cf. Rom. 1.9; 9.1; 2 Cor. 1.23; 11.31; Phil. 1.8; 1 Thess. 2.5, 10).[42] Earlier in his defence against the false gospel (or 'another gospel', ἕτερον εὐαγγέλιον in v.6), Paul even put himself to an oath-like test, which involves a curse (Gal. 1.8).[43] Paul's seriousness in preservation of the authenticity of the gospel is assumed by the severity of the test. Paul's seriousness now peculiarly falls on the denial of his connection with the Jerusalem apostles. There is a debate as to what Paul is denying in the statement in v. 20. To be sure, Paul's assertion that he is not lying applies to the entire historical account preceding the denial.[44] However, the primary concern seems to be about the fact that Paul did not see any other apostles except for Cephas and James. The chronological development in the larger context is indicated by sign-posts such as ὅτι (Gal. 1.15; 2.11) and ἔπειτα (Gal. 1.18, 21; 2.1). Therefore, the content in vv. 18–20, demarcated by two ἔπειτα in v. 18 and v. 21, consists in an independent thought. Thus, the immediate context of this oath-like denial (v. 20) is best understood to relate to his connection with the Jerusalem apostles (vv. 19–20).

Through the peculiarly emphatic denial of connection, Paul, therefore, wants to distance himself from the authority of the Jerusalem apostles. This seems to suggest that Paul understands and wants the Galatian members to understand that he is an apostle standing autonomously from the Jerusalem authority.

40. BAGD, p. 383.
41. Dunn, 'Relationship', p. 465. Cf. Bruce, *Galatians*, 98; Longenecker, *Galatians*, p. 38.
42. Esler, 'Making and Breaking', p. 303.
43. Though perhaps he was most certainly sure that he would pass the test.
44. Betz, *Galatians*, p. 79, especially n. 216.

b. *Occasion of and Apprehensiveness about the Jerusalem Visit (Galatians 2.1–2)*

Another chronological signpost (ἔπειτα) shifts attention to the next visit to Jerusalem (Gal. 2.1). There are two points, particularly in v. 2, which relate to the present consideration. One is the occasion of the visit to Jerusalem, and the other is Paul's apprehensiveness about visiting Jerusalem.

Paul reports that his visit to Jerusalem was 'according to a revelation' (κατὰ ἀποκάλυψιν). He is ambiguous as to what this 'revelation' might mean. Some understand this revelation to be the prophecy of Agabus concerning famine.[45] In Acts 11.27–30, Paul and Barnabas are sent to Judaea to bring the financial aid from Antioch, and are reported to have subsequently stayed in Jerusalem.[46] Others understand the revelation to be the occasion of the commissioning of Paul and Barnabas by the Antiochean elders (Acts 13.1–3).[47] However, it is admittedly difficult to determine what historical occasion might be implied by the anarthrous ἀποκάλυψις.[48] Paul's intention was, therefore, not to point the Galatian audience to a specific historical event, but rather to emphasize that the visit was occasioned by his own response to God's revelation and that it was not a response to a summons from the Jerusalem apostles. Paul elsewhere refers to ἀποκάλυψις in order to deny his human connection (Gal. 1.12; cf. 1.16).[49]

Paul's apprehensiveness is observed when he describes a purpose for presenting his gospel to those reputed ones in Jerusalem. He says, 'lest somehow I may run or may have run in vain' (μή πως εἰς κενὸν τρέχω ἢ

---

45. Bruce, *Galatians*, pp. 21–22. Many who hold to *Provinzhypothese* seek to connect Gal. 2.1 and Acts 11.27–30. While the expression ἔπειτα διὰ δεκατεσσάρων ἐτῶν gives some confines of historical reconstruction, there is again a debate as to the point in time from which Paul counts 14 years. Cf. Murphy-O'Connor, *Paul*, pp. 7–8.

46. However, one may understand with Schneider that the description of Herod's persecution (Acts 12.1–24) was inserted in the middle of Paul and Barnabas' brief visit to bring the contribution from Antioch to Jerusalem. Gerhard Schneider, *Apostelgeschichte: Kommentar* (HTKNT, 5; 2 vols.; Freiburg im Breisgau: Herder, 1982), II, p. 102. The insertion of the account of persecution here may be because the author of Acts wanted to imply why Peter was away when the delegation came to Jerusalem. Hengel and Schwemer, *Paulus*, pp. 371–72.

47. Thomas W. Manson, *Studies in the Gospels and Epistles* (Manchester: Manchester University Press, 1962), pp. 176–77. However, as Manson himself warns, we may not fall into the danger of correlating between Acts and Pauline letters too easily.

48. Note that Bornkamm disregards κατὰ ἀποκάλυψιν altogether and suggests that Paul's visit to Jerusalem was caused by the circumcisers' earlier visit to Antioch (Acts 15.1). Bornkamm, *Paulus*, p. 54. See also Lüdemann for a similar view, except that Lüdemann sees the problem of the circumcisers and the Antioch incident as the same and argues that the Antioch incident happened before the Jerusalem meeting. Lüdemann, *Paulus*, pp. 104–105.

49. Betz, *Galatians*, p. 85; Dunn, *Epistle to the Galatians*, p. 91.

ἔδραμον, Gal. 2.2). Paul is certainly convinced that the gospel and his entire mission have been validated by the divine revelation personally received (Gal. 1.1, 12, 16), and that his gospel needs no human validation.[50] However, the present apprehensiveness gives an impression that Paul may be concerned with the possible outcome of disagreement with the Jerusalem apostles. Paul's apprehensiveness needs to be elaborated in order to understand his autonomy in relation to the Jerusalem apostles. What is Paul's apprehensiveness about 'running empty' (εἰς κενὸν τρέχω ἢ ἔδραμον)? In order to reach a plausible answer to this question, we need to speculate an outcome of their disagreement on the gospel. Even if the Jerusalem apostles had disagreed with Paul and not affirmed his version of the gospel, it seems plausible to assume that Paul would not have given in to the decision of the Jerusalem authority and changed his gospel.[51] Based upon Paul's strong conviction about the divine provenance of the gospel and his own apostleship, the apprehended outcome would be that the body of Christ, the church of God, would be divided.[52] Paul would continue building Gentile churches, and the Jerusalem apostles would not approve churches with a gospel other than theirs. Paul and the Jewish churches would then go in different directions. Thus, their unity as one religion would be at stake. Even though Paul does not see himself under the human authority of the Jerusalem apostles and their church, it is clear that he still saw a continuity between churches in Judaea and himself. In Gal. 1.13, Paul contrasts 'Judaism' and 'the church of God' as a whole without any division between Paul and the Jerusalem church in the subsequent verses (Gal. 1.17–21). The aftermath of the revelatory experience is that the churches in Judaea praised God on account of Paul's ministry in Syria and Cilicia (Gal. 1.21–24). Therefore, the apprehensiveness of Paul concerns the breach in this continuity.[53]

A question remains as to why this breach of continuity is described as εἰς κενόν. The natural sense of εἰς κενὸν τρέχω ... is that something is proven fruitless. Paul uses the phrase elsewhere to mean that effort and energy put into his ministry would be wasted, without questioning the effectiveness and truthfulness of the gospel itself (1 Thess. 3.5; Phil.

---

50. Contra Heinrich Schlier, *Der Brief an die Galater* (Göttingen: Vandenhoeck & Ruprecht, 1949), pp. 36–37. Schlier argues that the revelation experience, though undeniable for Paul, is not sufficient without the affirmation of the authority in Jerusalem.

51. Some Western witnesses (D*, it^d, etc.) omit οὐδέ in Gal. 2.5 to have us read, 'Because of the false brothers...I yielded for a brief time'. Metzger suggests that it is due to the scribes' adjustment in line with 1 Cor. 9.20–23, Acts 16.3. Bruce M. Metzger, *A Textual Commentary on the Greek New Testament* (Stuttgart: United Bible Society, 1975), p. 591.

52. Bruce, *Galatians*, p. 111.

53. Segal, *Paul*, p. 198.

2.16a).[54] Therefore, the phrase εἰς κενὸν points to the loss of his past and current effort and energy in the proclamation of his gospel because of the hindrance Paul expects to face in his mission by those who do not agree with his gospel. The apprehensiveness of Paul in 2.2 may be a forecast of the harmful development of his relation to the Jerusalem apostles, which results in Paul's public accusation of Peter (Gal. 2.14) and in a strained relationship with the Jewish Christians, possibly including those in the church of Antioch.[55] From Paul's perspective, the apprehensiveness is also substantiated by his present experience of the problem among the Galatian members (Gal. 4.11), and thus the report of a conflict in the cities far away is meaningful for the recipients of the letter.

To summarize, Paul's second visit to Jerusalem was not in response to a summons from the Jerusalem authority, i.e. Paul portrays himself as not answerable to the Jerusalem apostles. The apprehensiveness of Paul at the meeting with the Jerusalem apostles was not that he would discover his gospel was wrong, but that he anticipated the inevitable loss in his ministry due to the breach in continuity between his mission and the Jerusalem church. Paul's stance to the Jerusalem apostles is that of distant allies. While being independent of the Jerusalem authority, he desires to maintain a degree of continuity with them.

c. Δοκεῖν *and Nuanced Acknowledgement*
The term δοκεῖν in various participial forms is used four times in the description of Paul's second visit to Jerusalem.

v. 2: τοῖς δοκοῦσιν – to those who are reputed ...
v. 6a: τῶν δοκούντων εἶναί τι – the ones who appear to be someone ...
v. 6c: οἱ δοκοῦντες – those who are acknowledged ...
v. 9: οἱ δοκοῦντες στῦλοι εἶναι – who appear to be pillars ...

The referents of δοκεῖν are unclear until the fourth usage in v. 9. The last phrase is placed as an appositive to the three names of the Jerusalem apostles, namely, Ἰάκωβος καὶ Κηφᾶς καὶ Ἰωάννης. It is widely assumed that δοκεῖν refers each time to this group of the Jerusalem apostles.[56] It would be difficult to suppose that a different group is meant each time δοκεῖν is used within eight verses without a clear indication. False brothers (ψευδαδέλφους) in v. 4 are not included within the list of the reputed ones because their intention to 'enslave' Paul and his company under the Torah

54. However, Paul seems to have confidence in success in the end because of the content of the gospel. Cf. Albrecht Oepke, 'κενός', in Gerhard Friedrich (ed.), *Theological Dictionary of the New Testament* (10 vols.; trans. Geoffrey W. Bromiley; Grand Rapids: Eerdmans, 1965), III, pp. 659–62, especially 660.

55. Cf. Murphy-O'Connor, *Paul*, p. 158.

56. For example, Betz, *Galatians*, p. 86; Martyn, *Galatians*, p. 191; Dunn, *Epistle to the Galatians*, p. 92.

is contrasted with the reaction of those who are acknowledged – who, by the way, added nothing to Paul's message (Gal. 2.6).[57]

Whether the term itself contains some level of sarcasm or irony is difficult to determine.[58] Betz identifies 'ironic usage' of δοκεῖν in the writing of Plato, in which while acknowledging a claim he distances himself from the claim itself.[59] He then suggests that a similar distant stance toward the Jerusalem apostles is observed in Paul's use of δοκεῖν here. On the other hand, Bruce sees no insinuation of negativity in the term and points to examples such as the one in Josephus' *Jewish War*, where Josephus does not seem to question the reputation of the leaders in authority.[60] Therefore, evidence exists for both ironical and affirmative uses of the term. In other words, the nuance of δοκεῖν itself is neutral and whether the term is used ironically or affirmatively is determined by the context. Bruce, in order to argue for the affirmative sense of the term, compares δοκεῖν in Galatians 2 and the use of the term in Gal. 6.3, for in the latter δοκεῖν is certainly used with an ironic or negative nuance: 'if someone supposes to be something (important) though he is nothing, he deceives himself' (εἰ γὰρ δοκεῖ τις εἶναί τι μηδὲν ὤν, φρεναπατᾷ ἑαυτόν). Bruce argues that in Gal. 6.3 Paul points out the wrong self-perception of the person who thinks himself someone important. On the contrary, he maintains, the Jerusalem apostles are acknowledged and accepted as leaders by the community. Therefore, δοκεῖν is used affirmatively.[61] However, what is in focus primarily is Paul's perception of the claim, and whether the claim is widely accepted or privately cherished is a secondary matter. Therefore, the context of δοκεῖν to note is the general attitude of the observer toward the claim. Gal. 2.6 contains Paul's attitude toward the claim, which is acknowledged and accepted by the community. Here, Paul is clearly detached from such a claim of the Jerusalem apostles. He says, 'whoever they were once does not matter to me' (ὁποῖοί ποτε ἦσαν οὐδέν

---

57. However, Hengel and Schwemer think that the identity of δοκεῖν in v. 2 and v. 6 are different from v. 9. The first two refer to the elders of the Jerusalem church who are also James' delegates to Antioch. Hengel and Schwemer, *Paulus*, p. 371.

58. Kittel suggests the possibility that Paul's use of δοκεῖν here may be his response to the circumcisers' slogan. Cf. Gerhard Kittel 'δοκέω', in *idem* (ed.), *Theological Dictionary of the New Testament* (trans. Geoffrey W. Bromiley; 10 vols.; Grand Rapids: Eerdmans, 1964), II, pp. 242–55; cf. 233).

59. Betz, *Galatians*, pp. 86–87. Cf. *Apol.* 21B, C, D, E; 22A, B; 29A; 36D; 41E.

60. Bruce, *Galatians*, p. 109. Cf. *War* 3.453; 4.141, 159. However, we find in *Apion* 1.67 that the same author uses the term to discredit those who are 'reputed to be the most exact of historians' (οἱ δοκοῦντες ἀκριβέστατοι συγγραφεῖς).

61. Bruce, *Galatians*, p. 117.

μοι διαφέρει).[62] Paul justifies this detached stance by reminding the Galatians of God's fairness in dealing with humans (cf. Rom. 2.11). His stance to the leadership of the Jerusalem apostles is clear – while acknowledging that they are regarded as such, it does not matter to him (οὐδέν μοι διαφέρει).

In such a context of detachment from authority, Paul's use of δοκεῖν is indeed in line with what Betz suggests as 'ironic usage'. Therefore, v. 6 should read, 'but from those who were supposed to be someone (important) – whatever they once were does not matter to me, God does not show partiality – for those who were supposed (to be important) did not add anything for me'. Since Paul repeats δοκεῖν four times in this short description of the Jerusalem visit, it is plausible to assume that he maintains the same nuance throughout. Paul uses the term δοκεῖν in order to emphasize his attitude of distance and detachment from the Jerusalem apostles. Therefore, Paul's self-portrait for the Galatians is: while he is aware that their authority is acknowledged by the Jerusalem church, he himself does not submit to it.

While Paul admits that the Jerusalem apostles are acknowledged pillars in the community and probably in a wider circle of Jewish churches, he distances himself from the centralized system based upon the authority of the Jerusalem apostles. When Paul visits Jerusalem for the first time, he emphatically denies his contact with anyone but Peter and James. When Paul visits Jerusalem for the second time, he frequently refers to the leaders with the adjectival participle δοκεῖν. The pattern seems to be that when Paul is physically close to the Jerusalem authority, he takes care to depict himself as keeping a distance from them. Therefore, Paul clearly portrays himself as independent of those who are acknowledged as authoritative within the Jerusalem church.[63]

Three issues in Paul's biographical account have been surveyed, in order to understand his relation to the Jerusalem apostles. His emphatic denial of any formal connection with the Jerusalem apostles shows that he understands himself as independent of their authority. In his description of the second visit to Jerusalem, the phrase 'according to a revelation' can

62.   The past tense and the chronological adjective seem to point to their special relation to Jesus in his earthly ministry, upon which their apostleship and leadership at Jerusalem are based. Cf. Ernst DeWitt Burton, *A Critical and Exegetical Commentary on the Epistle to the Galatians* (ICC; Edinburgh: T. & T. Clark, 1921), p. 87. Cf. Barrett for his eschatological interpretation. C.K. Barrett, 'Paul and the "Pillar" Apostles', in J.N. Sevenster and W.C. van Unnik (eds.), *Studia Paulina* (Festschrift J. de Zwaan; Haarlem: Bohn, 1953), pp. 1–19 (16).

63.   This portrayal is of course independent of how the Jerusalem apostles viewed Paul. I will discuss this matter in Chapter 5. 'Pillar' is used for humans only here in the NT. 1 Tim. 3.15 and Rev. 3.12 use the term to refer to a church. A similar usage is found in *1 Clem.* 5.2, where it says of Peter and Paul, 'the greatest and the most righteous pillars' (οἱ μεγίστοι καὶ δικαιότατοι στῦλοι).

mean that the visit was Paul's own response to God's summoning rather than a summons from the Jerusalem authority. This description shows Paul's self-understanding as independent of the Jerusalem authority as well. He introduces the Jerusalem apostles with the term δοκεῖν. It is understood that Paul uses the term to detach himself from the claim of authority for the Jerusalem leaders. This detachment shows that Paul understands himself as autonomous from the Jerusalem authority. Paul also seems to place the two missions (one for the circumcised by the Jerusalem apostles, particularly Cephas, and the other for the uncircumcised by Paul and his companions) in parallel (Gal. 2.7–9), in order to emphasize that Paul stands apart from and yet equal to the Jerusalem authority. While Paul's apprehensiveness over the breach of religious unitarity shows that he sees himself and his mission contiguous with the Jerusalem apostles and their mission, he never subordinates himself to the latter.[64] Paul's strong sense of autonomy and authenticity is yet further evidence for the suggestion that Paul's mode of community–identity construction is 'instrumental'.

3. *Paul's Mission as an Instrumental Mode of Community–Identity Construction*

The survey of Paul's relationship to 'Judaism', and his relationship to the Jerusalem apostles, both lead to the conclusion that Paul understood himself as an independent apostle of God, and particularly an autonomous apostle in comparison to the assumed centre of authorization, the Jerusalem church and its apostles. That the Jerusalem church and particularly the Jerusalem apostles are the assumed locus of authority is observed from Paul's biographical account in the letter. Therefore, the conventional thought pattern is expected to be: connection with and dependence upon the Jerusalem apostles imply authenticity.[65] On the other hand, independence and distance from the Jerusalem church and its apostles would make the status of the new community somewhat ambiguous and perhaps unauthentic.[66] It is, therefore, peculiar that

64. Hengel and Schwemer, *Paulus*, p. 317, note 1315.
65. Cf. Goulder, *Two Missions*, p. 24.
66. This understanding would not be affected whether one espouses the traditional view on the formation of the office of the Twelve apostles through Jesus' commissioning the inner circle of his followers (Mk 3.14) or the view, as Munck suggests, that the centralization of authority in the Jerusalem church with the new concept of 'Twelve apostles' was developed as a response of the Jewish churches against the successful Gentile mission, in order to increase and maintain the authority of the original Jewish church in Jerusalem. Either way, one would have to deal with Paul's acknowledgement of the authority of the leadership in Jerusalem and his equal and independent authority, with which he continues to struggle in his

Paul, instead of seeking to establish a strong connection with the
Jerusalem apostles, emphasizes autonomy from them. He emphasizes the
divine provenance of his apostleship on one hand, and on the other hand
he denies emphatically his connection with and appearance of submission
to the Jerusalem apostles. Paul's departure from Judaism and his self-
understanding of autonomy and authenticity are sufficiently strong
arguments for the suggestion that Paul's approach to community–identity
construction is what is known as the 'instrumental mode', since in the
'instrumental mode' of community–identity construction the welfare of
the community and/or the ideology of its founder is sought apart from the
constraints of the traditional values (i.e. physio-cultural features and even
core ethnic sentiment).[67] His firm conviction in his connection with God
rather than human institutions and traditions (Gal. 1.1, 15–16) causes him
to approach the ethno-centred traditions and institutions in a critical and
flexible manner (Gal. 1.7–9), at the same time defending the divine
revelation out of his revelatory experience from being culturally adapted
('syncretized') by the host environment (Gal. 4.8–9).[68] In this chapter, I
have elaborated Paul's approach to community–identity construction on
the basis of his self-understanding. The following chapter will analyse the
genealogical background of the ethno-centred mode of community
construction of the Jerusalem church by looking at the patterns of
Gentile incorporation by Judaism in general (Chapter 4). Then, the
frictions or conflicts in Jerusalem and Antioch will be considered on the
basis of these differing and opposing modes of community–identity
construction in Chapter 5.

---

letters. For the suggestion of the alternative view on the office of Twelve apostles; cf. Munck,
'Paul, the Apostles, and the Twelve', pp. 96–110; Schmithals, *Das kirchliche Apostelamt*, pp.
56–76.

    67. In the 'primordial mode', it is not that the welfare of the community is neglected, but
it is sought within the constraint of traditional values.

    68. The idea of 'indigenization/syncretism' will be discussed in Chapter 6, pp. 165–66,
note 579.

Chapter 4

JEWISH IDEAS OF GENTILE INCORPORATION IN THE SECOND TEMPLE PERIOD

I concluded in the last chapter that Paul had a self-understanding as an independently authorized apostle of Christ for the mission among the Gentiles, and that consequently his approach to community–identity construction is in accordance with what has been described as the 'instrumental mode'. This instrumental approach of Paul to community–identity construction may have been a point of contention with the constituents of the Jerusalem church and their approaches to community–identity construction. The letter to the Galatians contains certain facts that enable us to determine how they approached the issue of identity.

The Jerusalem visit and the incident in Antioch, depicted by Paul, show a strong interest among the Jerusalem apostles and members of the Jerusalem church in the physio-cultural features based upon their core ethnic sentiment. For example, ψευδαδέλφοι in Gal. 2.4 pressured the non-Jewish delegate Titus to receive circumcision, the physical mark that was perceived to distinguish a Jewish male from other ethnic groups. The Jerusalem apostles regarded themselves as ones who were called specifically to the Jews as an ethnic people (Gal. 2.7–8).[1] James' pressure upon the believers' community in Antioch caused an ethnic division between ethnic groups of Jews and non-Jews (Gal. 2.11–14). Moreover, the division was occasioned by Peter's fear of 'those of circumcision' (Gal. 2.12), which seems to suggest that there was an ethnically related fear involved.[2] These evidences seem to show that the Jerusalem church members' approach to community–identity construction, evidenced here in their association with and incorporation of Gentiles, is constrained by certain physio-cultural features that reflect their core ethnic sentiment. If we take into consideration the evidence from the accounts in Acts, this view is made even clearer. The account of Peter's early mission outside Jerusalem (Acts 10.1–11.18) shows that the early assumption of the

---

1. The meaning of τὸ εὐαγγέλιον τῆς ἀκροβυστίας will be discussed in Chapter 5.
2. For the details of the Jerusalem meeting and the Antioch incident, refer to Chapter 5.

Jerusalem church seems to be that the new religious enterprise was rather limited to Jews (cf. Acts 11.18).[3] That this attitude was maintained at least by a segment of the church at the time of the Jerusalem Council is evident in their insistence on circumcising the Gentile constituents of the church in Antioch (Acts 15.1, 5). In Paul's last visit to Jerusalem, a part of the membership of the Jerusalem church was concerned that the Gentile mission might result in neglect of the Jewish tradition (Acts 21.21). In these data, such physio-cultural features as commensality (Acts 10), circumcision (Acts 15), and other customs based upon the Torah (Acts 21) are crucial issues in their group identity. This confirms the understanding on the basis of Galatians of how the Jerusalem church members approached the issue of community–identity.

More about their perspective on community–identity construction can be found by conducting a genealogical comparative study on the issue of Gentile incorporation among the Jews in general. As seen above, the Jerusalem church seems to be operating within the larger ethnic population of Jews. Paul's apprehensiveness as to whether the Jerusalem church would identify itself with him through the acceptance of his gift (Rom. 15.31) could be evidence for the church's further continuity with the larger Jewish commonwealth over against Paul, who was a distant partner of the church. Haenchen highlights Paul's apprehensiveness that the church may have distanced itself from him in order not to harm their relationship with the larger Jewish community.[4] Because of this close proximity between the Jerusalem church and the general population of Jews, the genealogical study of Gentile incorporation among Jews in the Second Temple period may deepen the understanding of the approach to the community–identity construction of the Jerusalem church and illumine the conflict both in Jerusalem and Antioch that Paul describes in Galatians 2. This is the context of Paul's community–identity construction, which is the primary interest of this present section, Part II. This chapter will look at how this issue of Gentile incorporation is described primarily in the literature of the Second Temple period by considering primarily, (1) Jewish concepts of Gentile incorporation and (2) the modes of Gentile incorporation.

---

3. One may find here a background experience that explains Peter's lenient view on the application of the Torah for Gentile incorporation observed in Gal. 2 as opposed to the strict view of the 'ψευδαδέλφοι'. We will compare these two views in detail in Chapter 5.

4. Ernst Haenchen, *Die Apostelgeschichte* (Göttingen: Vandenhoeck & Ruprecht, 13th edn, 1961), p. 544. Cf. Walter Schmithals, *Paulus und Jakobus* (FRLANT, 85; Göttingen: Vandenhoeck & Ruprecht, 1963), p. 82.

1. *Jewish Concepts of Gentile Incorporation*

The understanding of Jewish proselytism has shifted from one perspective
to another over the centuries. Jewish studies within Christian scholarship
up until the end of the nineteenth century took a customary polemical
assertion against Judaism, saying that Jews were largely unconcerned
with the idea of proselytism. This assumption implies that Judaism was
inferior to Christianity, which was known for its missionary zeal.[5] In the
early part of the last century, this understanding was challenged by
scholars such as Jeremias, Kuhn and others, and countered with the
widely accepted idea that Second Temple Judaism was a missionary
religion.[6] Consequently, it was suggested that missionary activities of the
early church should be understood as derivative of active Jewish
missionary efforts. A considerable Jewish influence in the surrounding
cultures and their ideology behind this success have been regarded as
evidence for the assumption that there were active missionary efforts in
which Jews took the initiative in 'winning souls' among the non-Jews. In
the literature of the Second Temple period, confidence and faith in God's
triumph over pagan gods and in the Torah are substantiated by such
accounts as the conversion of a Babylonian king (Bel 28, 41), a king of the
Seleucid Dynasty (2 Macc. 9.17), and by the report of wider Jewish
influence in Egypt and in Antioch (Philo, *Vit. Mos.* 2.17; Josephus, *War*
7.3.3).[7] While there is the possibility of overstatement in the above literary
accounts,[8] the considerable influence of Jews and Judaism in the

5. Cf. Scott McKnight, *A Light among the Gentiles: Jewish Missionary Activity in the Second Temple Period* (Minneapolis: Fortress, 1990), p. 2.

6. Among the above-mentioned scholars, consulted here are the following: Joachim Jeremias, *Jesus' Promise to the Nations* (trans. S.H. Hooke; SBT; London: SCM, 1958), pp. 11–19. Jeremias suggests that post-exilic Judaism was an active missionary religion, especially with the rise and development of Diaspora Jewish communities (p. 11). He finds Mt. 23.15 as evidence of Pharisaic missionary activity (p. 19). Schürer, *The History of the Jewish People*, III, pp. 150–77; Karl G. Kuhn, 'προσήλυτος', in Gerhard Friedrich (ed.), *Theological Dictionary of the New Testament* (trans. Geoffrey W. Bromiley; 10 vols.; Grand Rapids: Eerdmans, 1968), VI, pp. 727–44). Active Jewish proselytism is assumed throughout Kuhn's etymological treatment in *TDNT*, VI, pp. 730, 735 and 742. BAGD, p. 714.

7. Louis H. Feldman, *Jew and Gentile in the Ancient World* (Princeton: Princeton University Press, 1993), esp. chs. 9–10; *idem*, 'Jewish Proselytism', in Harold W. Attridge and Gohei Hata (eds.), *Eusebius, Christianity, and Judaism* (Detroit: Wayne State University Press, 1992), pp. 372–407 (373).

8. Cf. John J. Collins, 'A Symbol of Otherness: Circumcision and Salvation in the First Century', in Jacob Neusner and Ernest S. Frerichs (eds.), *'To See Ourselves as Others See Us': Christians, Jews, 'Others' in Late Antiquity* (Chico: Scholars, 1985), pp. 163–86 (170).

surrounding cultures is substantiated by accounts in non-Jewish sources. Seneca, a Roman historian hostile to the Jews, says, 'The customs of this accursed race have gained such influence that they are now received throughout all the world. The vanquished have given their laws to the victors.'[9] The historical expulsion of Jews from Rome, such as those in 139 BCE and 19 CE are best explained as owing to the threat of considerable Jewish influence in the city.[10] However, this assumption of an active/initiating kind of Jewish mission has recently been challenged by scholars such as McKnight and Goodman.[11] While some sources imply the existence of proselytes, this does not automatically justify the assumption that there was a proselytizing movement among Jews of the active/initiating kind akin to the one observed in the history of Christian mission.

Feldman finds evidence of an active/initiative kind of Jewish proselytism in descriptions of universal penetration of Torah by Philo and Josephus (*Vit. Mos.* 2.36, 41, 44; *Dec.* 81; *Apion* 2.279–95).[12] According to *De Vita Mosis*, a festival was held on the anniversary of the completion of the LXX where the translation was made (*Vit. Mos.* 2.41). Not only Jews but other multitudes as well gathered for the occasion. However, it may only reflect a Jewish veneration of the Torah. Feldman strongly argues that the translation of the Torah into Greek is an extension of the active Jewish proselytizing movement, so as to make the Scripture easily accessible to their targeted audience.[13] While it may be true that the LXX enabled Gentiles to read and understand the Torah,[14] there is no direct

9.   Seneca, in Augustine, *De Civitate Dei* 6.11. Cf. a corresponding report found in Josephus's *Apion* 2.10.123. M. Stern, *Greek and Latin Authors on Jews and Judaism* (3 vols.; Jerusalem: The Israel Academy of Sciences and Humanities, 1974), I, p. 431.

10.   Valerius Maximus, *Fact. ac. Dict.* 1.3.3; Dio Cassius, *Hist.* 57.18.5a. Cf. Feldman, *Jew & Gentile*, p. 94; Collins, 'A Symbol of Otherness', pp. 170–71.

11.   McKnight, *Light*; Martin Goodman, *Mission and Conversion: Proselytizing in the Religious History of the Roman Empire* (Oxford: Clarendon, 1994).

12.   Feldman, 'Jewish Proselytism', pp. 381–82. Further, Feldman argues that *2 En.* 48.6–9 is clear evidence of such an active proselytism: '... you must hand over the books to your children ... and among all nations who are discerning so that they may fear God, and so that they may accept them'. McKnight argues that this passage may suggest an occasional Jewish propaganda through literature, except that the textual problem and the problem of the dating of the writing cause him to be cautious in making a decision. Cf. McKnight, *Light*, p. 59.

13.   Feldman, 'Jewish Proselytism', pp. 380–81.

14.   Alan F. Segal, 'The Costs of Proselytism and Conversion', in David J. Lull (ed.), *SBLSP 1988* (Atlanta: Scholars, 1988), pp. 336–69 (345). Refer also to: McKnight, *Light*, p. 60; Goodman, *Mission*, p. 79.

evidence that the LXX was distributed among Gentiles as propagandistic literature.[15]

The historicity of the Jewish annexation of Idumaeans in the second century BCE seems to be well-attested. It is known that Josephus was critical of forced proselytism (*Life* 112–13; *War* 2.454), therefore to report such an activity by his direct ancestors would fail to make sense, if it were not for the actual proselytism of the Idumaeans, evidence for an active/ initiating mode of Jewish proselytism.[16] However, it may not be tenable to treat such colonizing activity as evidence for active proselytizing efforts. Those who were forced to convert were given a choice to decide whether they would stay on the land alive as proselytes or their plea for Jewish protection would be rejected. This forced 'persuasion' may reflect the milieu of military tension between Jews and Idumaeans. The imposition of circumcision on the Idumaeans may simply reflect the importance of ceremonial purity for those residing in the land.[17] Therefore, while they are actively maintaining the purity of the nation of Israel, they are not necessarily actively 'winning the souls' of many through enforcing the rite of circumcision. This Jewish concern for religious purity amidst the Gentile presence should be distinguished from a proselytizing zeal.

While the presence and influence of Judaism and Jewish culture among the surrounding cultures is recognized, one is cautioned against reading into the above-mentioned references a Christian concept of active/ initiative mission, i.e. Jews sending out missionaries among surrounding societies to win converts to their religion (cf. Mt. 23.15).[18] Nor is there

15. McKnight, *Light*, p. 60. It should be noted that Feldman argues for the great influence of the LXX among the Gentiles through the usage of Gen. 1.3 and chs. 9–10 by Longinus, a Gentile literary critic. This usage may suggest that the LXX (at least partly) was widely known among the Gentiles. Cf. Feldman, 'Jewish Proselytism', p. 382. Hata recently argued for an apologetic reason for the initial production of the LXX. Gohei Hata, 'The Origin of the Greek Bible: Another Explanation', Paper presented at the Jewish Studies Seminar at Wolfson College, Oxford, March 4, 2003.

16. Feldman, 'Jewish Proselytism', pp. 374–75. Refer also to Segal, 'The Costs of Proselytism', p. 357. For the argument against the existence of forced proselytism, refer to Aryeh Kasher, *Jews, Idumaeans, and Ancient Arabs: Relations of the Jews in* Eretz Israel *with the Nations of the Frontier and the Desert during the Hellenistic and Roman Era (332 BCE – 70 CE)* (Tübingen: Mohr, 1988), pp. 46–85.

17. Goodman, *Mission*, p. 50. In his argument, God's command is to root out, not the Gentiles, but pagan worship from the nation of Israel (Deut. 12.1–3). Personal attack on the evilness of Gentiles is rarely found. As Goodman points out, pagans were considered evil only in so far as they brought defilement to the nation of Israel. See Hayes for a further qualification that it was not the issue of ritual impurity but moral impurity of the Gentiles that was the issue. Hayes, *Gentile Impurities*, p. 55. Cf. Jonathan Klawans, *Impurity and Sin in Ancient Israel* (Oxford: Oxford University Press, 2000).

18. McKnight, *Light*, p. 48. Goodman interprets Mt. 23.15 as the Pharisees' effort to win followers among the Jews for their own teachings rather than as their missionary effort among non-Jews. Goodman, *Mission*, pp. 69–72.

evidence of an active/initiative kind of proselytism in the teaching found in *Letter of Aristeas* on successful persuasion (*Ep. Arist.* 226; cf. Philo, *Spec. Leg.* 1.320–33), for it is not clear whether the context of this persuasion is proselytism or simple debate among Jews.[19] Contrary to the earlier assumption that the later churches' active/initiative kind of mission follows the pattern of Jewish proselytism, there is little evidence of such practice as is found in the Gentile mission of Paul.[20] Instead, there is some evidence of Jewish confidence in their God and their concern for purity in relation to the Gentiles. The active/initiative mission, found in Paul's activity, seems to be an innovative enterprise, different from the Jewish approach to the issue of Gentile incorporation. This innovation may be understood as the result of his instrumental approach to community–identity construction. Though the approaches to Gentile incorporation by the general Jewish commonwealth did not take the initiative form of mission, they did have to face the issue of encounter and association with non-Jews. The following section will demonstrate various ways Gentiles came closer to the Jewish community.

2. *Modes of Gentile Incorporation*

a. *Concept of Boundaries*
In this section, I will first consider the concept of ethnic boundaries by evaluating such terms as נכרים, גרים and προσήλυτοι, which are used in the Hebrew Bible and Second Temple literature. This will be followed by an outline of the various modes of Gentile incorporation. How did Jews understand the boundary between themselves and outsiders? In the Hebrew Bible, the Jewish concept of Gentile incorporation into the Jewish community can generally be understood in terms of two categories of humanity. The Jews are separated from the rest of humanity, who are נכרים ('outsiders'). נכרי denotes one who is outside the ethnic and religious fellowship of Israel (Deut. 14.21; 15.3; 23.21; 29.21–23). Those Gentiles who are affiliated with Jews are called גרים (generally translated as 'resident aliens'). They are strangers, but remain in the land and place themselves under the protection of God and his people.[21] They have

19. Cf. McKnight, *Light*, p. 52.
20. J.J. Collins, *Between Athens and Jerusalem: Jewish Identity in the Hellenistic Diaspora* (Grand Rapids: Eerdmans, 2nd edn, 2000), pp. 262–63; Goodman, *Mission*, p. 90. Collins concludes that though there were some proselytizing activities from time to time, Judaism cannot be understood as a 'missionary' movement. Also cf. Alan le Grys, *Preaching to the Nations: The Origins of Mission in the Early Church* (London: SPCK, 1998), pp. 20–51.
21. Kuhn, *TDNT*, VI, s.v. 'προσήλυτος'.

attendant responsibilities and privileges upon attaching themselves to the
Jews.[22] גרים observe the Sabbath rest (Exod. 20.10; 23.12; Deut. 5.14),
fast on the Day of Atonement (Lev. 16.29), observe laws of purity (Lev.
17.8–13), offer sacrifices (Lev. 17.8–13), participate in the festivals (Deut.
16.14), and celebrate the Passover (Exod. 12.48–49; only upon the
condition of adhering to the rite of circumcision). Inclusion of גרים into
the community of Israel can be observed in Deut. 29.10–12, which says,
'You stand assembled today, all of you, before the Lord your God – the
leaders of your tribes, your elders, and your officials ... and the aliens
(גרים) who are in your camp ...'[23] This conception of incorporation is
carried over into the Second Temple period in a rather loose way because
of the expansion of Jewish presence among surrounding cultures and
because they are not bound by the land.

The Greek word προσήλυτοι is generally the translation of גרים in the
LXX, but with a qualification.[24] Sometimes a rather simplistic classification
is made, in that προσήλυτοι are 'converts' by going through the rite of
circumcision and σεβόμενοι τόν θεόν are those who revere God but fall
short of the final commitment of circumcision.[25] However, this classification does not apply to many passages. גרים (and LXX προσήλυτοι) are
not necessarily circumcised to begin with (Exod. 12.48; 20.10; Lev. 16.29).
The few references to προσήλυτοι in the literature of the Second Temple
period do not specify the requirement of circumcision for προσήλυτοι (cf.
Tob. 1.8; *Quaest. in Exod.* 2.2; *Spec. Leg.* 1.51).[26] The term σεβόμενοι
seems to be a non-technical word, which means 'worshippers', and it is
used for Jews (*Jos. Asen.* 8.8), Gentile sympathizers as a whole over
against Jews (*Ant.* 14.110), and even for pagan worshippers (Wis. 15.6;
Jos. Asen. 11.7). Both terms are, therefore, used for Gentile sympathizers

22. Neil J. McEleney, 'Conversion, Circumcision and the Law', *NTS* 20 (1974), pp. 319–41 (320).

23. Kuhn, *TDNT*, VI, s.v. 'προσήλυτος'. Paul F. Stuehrenberg, *ABD*, V, s.v. 'proselyte'. Here the reaffirmation of the covenant relationship and the declaration of the entrance into the legacy of the covenant relationship seem to be in view. Cf. Peter C. Craigie, *The Book of Deuteronomy* (NICOT; Grand Rapids: Eerdmans, 1976), p. 357.

24. One should note the change in the meaning of גרים/προσήλυτοι between pre- and post-exilic periods. While in the former they are aliens who observe prohibitive commands (cf. Judg. 4.10–11; ch. 5) under the protection of the Jews, in the latter they live in their own lands and join the minority communities of Jews. Cf. Hayes, *Gentile Impurities*, p. 57.

25. Ulrich Becker, 'προσήλυτος', in *NIDNTT*, I, s.v. 'conversion'. Bauer also accords with their conclusion: '... a designation for a Gentile won for Judaism by Jewish missionary efforts, who became a Jew by undergoing circumcision' (BAGD, p. 715).

26. Cf. the debate over *Quaest. in Exod.* of Philo in the following pages. J.J. Collins, 'A Symbol of Otherness', p. 173; Peder Borgen, 'The Early Church and the Hellenistic Synagogue', *ST* 37.1 (1983), pp. 55–78 (67). However, see also Goodman, *Mission*, p. 81; John Nolland, 'Uncircumcised Proselytes?', *JSJ* 12 (1981), pp. 173–94 for a slightly varied conclusion.

in general. This broad conception of προσήλυτοι may reflect the broad range of modes of Gentile attachment to Judaism in this period. McKnight views this broad range of Gentile incorporation as a 'wall between Judaism and paganism ... made from steps and there were Gentiles at each level'.[27]

b. Modes of Gentile Incorporation
i. Admiration of aspects of Judaism
Observing the issue of Gentile incorporation in the Second Temple literature, one notes that Gentiles had various ways to associate themselves with Judaism. This section will modify Cohen's detailed description of the issue, in which he classifies the modes of Gentile incorporation into seven categories,[28] and consider the modes of Gentile incorporation into the Jewish community.

It has been attested that Jewish benevolence was well received among Gentiles and that they patterned themselves after this Jewish custom. Josephus reports, 'Moreover, they attempt to imitate our unanimity, our liberal charities ...' (Apion 2.283). A simple imitation of the Jewish philanthropical practice by the Gentiles may sometimes have appeared to other unrelated Gentiles (πάροικοι/גרים) as getting closer to the people or their religion.

ii. Acknowledgement of and reverence for God
Foreign kings and dignitaries are reported to have venerated God when they witnessed his power. Heliodorus was faced with God's power in his attempt to seize the Temple treasure and 'bore testimony to all concerning the deeds of the supreme God, which he had seen with his own eyes' (2 Macc. 3.36). The Persian king, Cyrus, after witnessing Daniel's triumph over idols, confessed the supremacy of Israel's God (Bel 40–41). However, the Gentiles' acknowledgement of the power of God may be distinguished from devotion to God. Cohen argues that many Gentiles incorporated the 'God' of the Jews into the pagan pantheon,[29] a practice of polytheism from the Jewish point of view.

The inscription of Aphrodisias presents rather definitive evidence for the widespread existence of Gentile sympathizers to Judaism, generally

27. McKnight, Light, p. 100.
28. Shaye J.D. Cohen, 'Crossing the Boundary and Becoming a Jew', HTR 82 (1989), pp. 13–33. See also the varying degrees of religious attachment suggested by Feldtkeller under 'Intensitäten der Beziehung zu einem Religionssystem'. Feldtkeller, Identitätssuche, pp. 35–39.
29. S.J.D. Cohen, 'Crossing the Boundary', pp. 16–17.

known as 'God-fearers'.[30] Nine out of the fifty-four θεοσεβείς listed on the inscription of Aphrodisias, who funded the construction of a building attaching to the local synagogue, were members of the city council. As such, they were expected to participate in the worship of Aphrodite.[31] They may have contributed to the building project in Aphrodisias out of reverence to Israel's God and admiration for Jewish benevolence, though they were still involved in a polytheistic practice, which was unacceptable from the Jewish perspective. A joint building project as in Aphrodisias and a sacrifice to Israel's God at the pantheon may have been regarded as the result of Gentile admiration and veneration. Such descriptions as Ἰουδαῖος (Bel 28) and θεοσεβής (Aphrodisias' inscription) seem to reveal the Gentiles' positive association with Judaism.

iii. *Selective practice of Jewish rituals*
A sincere interest in the religion can be observed in Josephus' accounts of Gentiles following Jewish customs, which says, '... and there is not one city, Greek or barbarian, nor a single nation, to which our custom of abstaining from work on the seventh day has not spread, and where the fasts and lighting of lamps and many of our prohibitions in the matter of food are not observed' (*Apion* 2.282). Cohen observes that there were certain customs which required closer contact with Jews (attendance at synagogues and public ceremonies), and some which did not (fasting, lighting lamps, food laws and Sabbath rest).[32] Therefore, there were different levels of Gentile closeness to Judaism according to Josephus' report. Though a finely developed systematic procedure of incorporation is not attested in the literature, Gentile sympathizers expressed varying commitments through selective Torah adherence.

iv. *Distancing from pagan gods*
In *Joseph and Asenath*, rejection of pagan gods seems to be the chief concern (*Jos. Asen.* 12–13). Philo also emphasizes the importance of turning away from pagan gods: 'But what is the mind of the sojourner (προσήλυτος) if not alienation from belief in many gods and familiarity with honouring the one God and Father of all?' (*Quaest. in Exod.* 2.2). The same exhortation for the Gentiles against pagan worship is elsewhere observed (*Sib. Or.* 3.547–50, 716–23; 4.162–69; *Ep. Arist.* 128–38, 148).

---

30. Robert F. Tannenbaum, 'Jews and God-Fearers in the Holy City of Aphrodite', *BARev* 12.5 (September–October 1986), pp. 54–57 (55); J. Andrew Overman, 'The God-Fearers: Some Neglected Features', *JSNT* 32 (1988), pp. 17–26 (21); P.W. van der Horst, 'Juden und Christen in Aphrodisias im Licht ihrer Beziehungen in anderen Städten Kleinasiens', in J. van Amersfoort and J. van Oort (eds.), *Juden und Christen in der Antike* (Kampe: Kok, 1990), pp. 125–43 (128–31).
31. Tannenbaum, 'Jews and God-Fearers', p. 57.
32. Cohen, 'Crossing the Boundary', p. 20.

Scholars argue that this emphasis on monotheism and the additional ethical emphases in the Second Temple period were developed during the rabbinic period, in a midrash on the flood narrative in which God made a covenant with all humanity, into what is known as the Noachide regulations (cf. *t. 'Abod. Zar.* 8.4).[33] Cohen observes that turning to monotheism from polytheism may be one of the key features in coming closer to Judaism.[34]

c. *Righteousness of the Gentile Sympathizers*

A wide range of patterns has been observed by which Gentile sympathizers were coming closer to Jews and Judaism. Jewish and some non-Jewish sources attest to this multifaceted phenomenon ranging from a mere surface level of attraction, admiration of the people and their religion, to selective practice of Jewish customs and beliefs. A more conscious level of Gentile incorporation is found in teachings on monotheism and other moral regulations for Gentiles. The codification of these regulations for the Gentile sympathizers is found in the Noachide Laws. They function, according to Segal, as 'natural laws' of righteousness, the purpose of which is to allow Gentiles to attain the status of 'righteous Gentiles'.[35] However, the regulations introduced in the previous note (cf. footnote 33) were already present in the Second Temple Jewish literature.[36] While such regulations in *Jub.* 7.20–21 may be rightly argued as grounds for condemning the Gentiles,[37] other passages seem to be in the context of bringing the Gentiles closer to Judaism (cf. *Sib. Or.* 3.547–49; *Ep. Arist.* 128–38). Later rabbis discuss the state of Gentiles, upholding two opposite stances; one which states that it is impossible for Gentiles to be saved (rabbi Eliezer b. Hyrcanus) and the other which contends that some righteous Gentiles will have a portion in the world to come (rabbi Joshua b. Hanahyah) (*t. Sanh.* 13.2). The

---

33.   Simon R. Schwarzfuchs, 'Noachide Laws', in Cecil Roth (eds.), *EncJud*, XII (18 vols.; New York: Macmillan, 1971). The Noachide (or Noahide/Noachic/Noachian) regulations usually include prohibitions against idolatry, blasphemy, bloodshed, sexual sins, theft, and eating from a living animal, as well as the injunction to establish a legal system. Cf. Segal, 'The Costs of Proselytism', p. 363; Bockmuehl, *Jewish Law*, pp. 145–62.

34.   Cohen, 'Crossing the Boundary', p. 22. He also argues that 'coming closer' through the monotheistic belief does not automatically mean one is becoming a member of the Jewish community. J.J. Collins agrees with this conclusion. Cf. Collins, 'A Symbol of Otherness', p. 169.

35.   Segal, 'The Costs of Proselytism', p. 363: Cohen, 'Crossing the Boundary', p. 22. A distinction should be made between the state of being saved (or becoming 'righteous') and full incorporation into the Jewish community. Segal, *Paul*, pp. 191, 198; cf. Goodman, *Mission*, p. 63.

36.   Bockmuehl, *Jewish Law*, pp. 172–73.

37.   Segal, 'The Costs of Proselytism', p. 364.

Noachide regulations were used by both stances either as a base to condemn the Gentiles or as a criterion for righteousness.[38] So it seems, at least for some Jews, the purpose of the regulations in these writings is, '... to convince pagans of the inherent morality of Judaism and bring them to (but apparently no closer than) the status of God-fearers, in the first instance. If they later choose to join Judaism [further integration into Judaism], that was their own decision'.[39] The means of this further 'integration' seems to be the rite of circumcision.[40]

d. *Full Integration into the Jewish Commonwealth*

The question here is what place circumcision has in the process of Gentile incorporation. The Hebrew Bible frequently refers to the circumcision of Jews (Gen. 17.9–14; 21.4; Exod. 4.25; Josh. 4.2–7), and more importantly to the state of Gentiles as 'uncircumcised' (Judg. 14.3; 15.18; 1 Sam. 17.26, 36; 1 Chron. 10.4; Ezek. 32). Therefore, the physical rite is regarded as a special physio-cultural feature to define the boundary of the Jewish community against the non-Jews outside. For Gentiles, the rite of circumcision is seen as a step of religious or ethnic integration (Gen. 34; Exod. 12.44, 48–49).

In literature of the Second Temple period, references to circumcision are mostly found in reacting context against the Hellenization of the Jewish people. The banning of circumcision is a part of a Hellenizing policy (1 Macc. 1.48, 60–61; *3 Macc.* 2.6). Mattathias' reaction against Hellenization is depicted in his forced circumcision of those children who were uncircumcised (1 Macc. 2.46). A clear account of circumcision at the time of conversion to Judaism is seen in the case of Achior: 'he believed firmly in God. So he was circumcised ...' (Jdt. 14.10b, ἐπίστευσε τῷ θεῷ σφόδρα καὶ περιετέμετο τὴν σάρκα τῆς ἀκροβυστίας αὐτοῦ). The specific description of the result of the circumcision is that '... [he] joined the house of Israel' (Jdt. 14.10c, καὶ προσετέθη εἰς τὸν οἶκον Ἰσραηλ). The emphasis on physical circumcision in Maccabees may reflect the primacy of ethnic and religious survival during a very adverse time.[41] Judith clearly relates the rite of circumcision to belief in God and Gentile incorporation into the Jewish community even of Achior the Ammonite (cf. Deut. 23.3–

---

38. Bockmuehl, *Jewish Law*, p. 159; Segal, *Paul*, p. 197.

39. Segal, 'The Costs of Proselytism', p. 367 (parentheses added).

40. In the discussions of later rabbis, some argue for the righteousness of uncircumcised Gentiles (*b. Pesaḥ* 96a). Goodman suggests that Paul's mode of Gentile incorporation apart from circumcision may reflect this lenient view of proselytism. Goodman, *Mission*, pp. 67, 169. Also cf. Segal, *Paul*, pp. 192–93; Bockmuehl, *Jewish Law*, p. 159.

41. Shaye J.D. Cohen, *From the Maccabees to the Mishnah* (Philadelphia: Westminster, 1987), p. 53.

5).[42] The scarcity of the evidence of conversion through circumcision may simply be the very scarcity of conversion accounts. The observation here is simply that circumcision is positively related to proselytism.

In *De Migratione Abrahami*, Philo introduces an allegorical interpretation of the rite of circumcision (*Migr. Abr.* 89–93). The context is that Philo criticizes those who are so extreme in their allegorical interpretation that they turn away from the actual physical rite.[43] He says, 'It is true that receiving circumcision does indeed portray the excision of pleasure and all passion ... but let us not on this account repeal the law laid down for circumcision' (*Migr. Abr.* 92). Philo makes it clear in this passage that he believes the spiritual significance of circumcision should not undermine the physical practice of the circumcision rite. Philo, in his emphasis both on the physical and spiritual senses of circumcision, does not denounce the extreme allegorists as apostates, yet he does criticize the abandonment of the physical rite.[44]

Philo's teaching in *Quaestiones in Exodum* has been debated. The problematic statement in the Greek fragment reads, ὅτι προσήλυτός ἐστιν, οὐχ ὁ περιτμηθεὶς τὴν ἀκροβυστίαν ἀλλ' ὁ τὰς ἡδονὰς καὶ τὰς ἐπιθυμίας καὶ τὰ ἄλλα πάθη τῆς ψυχῆς (*Quaest. in Exod.* 2.2).[45] The most literal interpretation of the statement is that physical circumcision is not an essential prerequisite for being a προσήλυτος.[46] Note that Kuhn adds 'merely' to the text and translates it, 'that the proselyte is one who is circumcised not *merely* in the foreskin but in lusts and desires and other passions of the soul'. Based upon his narrow definition of προσήλυτος, Kuhn decides to add 'merely' to underscore the rite of circumcision as a requirement for προσήλυτοι.[47] Nolland argues that, though the treatment of Kuhn is not tenable, the whole discussion here seems to presume physical circumcision.[48]

However, a distinction should be made between the statement in *De Migratione Abrahami* and that of *Quaestiones in Exodum*. The former relates to the Jews while the latter relates to προσήλυτοι. In *Quaestiones in Exodum*, Jews were afflicted because of their devotion to God even without circumcision during the time of Exodus (*Quaest. in Exod.* 2.2).

42. Ibid., pp. 52–53. Cf. Carey A. Moore, *Judith* (AB, 40; New York: Doubleday, 1985), p. 235.

43.Gary Gilbert, 'The Making of a Jew: "God-Fearer" or Convert in the Story of Izates', *Union Seminary Quarterly Review* 44.3–4 (1991), p. 304; Nolland, 'Uncircumcised Proselytes?' p. 175.

44. Gilbert, 'The Making of a Jew', p. 304; Segal, 'The Costs of Proselytism', p. 347.

45. Philo, *Questions and Answers on Exodus* (trans. Ralph Marcus; LCL; Sup. 2; Cambridge: Harvard University Press, 1953), p. 36, note d.

46. Collins, 'A Symbol of Otherness', p. 173. Borgen, 'The Early Church', p. 67.

47. Kuhn, *TDNT*, VI, s.v. 'προσήλυτος' (emphasis added).

48. Nolland, 'Uncircumcised Proselytes?', pp. 174–75, 78.

Προσήλυτοι are uncircumcised yet devote themselves to God. Knowing that devotion to God sometimes causes affliction, Jews should act favourably to προσήλυτοι. Later in the same passage, they are called 'newcomers' who are coming into the new lifestyle of 'laws and customs'. It seems clear that Philo does not intend to undermine the rite of circumcision in this passage. Philo's definition of προσήλυτοι in *De Specialibus Legibus* is those who only adhere to unalloyed truth and reject the fabulousness of pagan cults (*Spec. Leg.* 1.51).[49] While Philo deplores the fact that some Jews abandon circumcision altogether by signifying only the spiritual sense of the rite, the evidence does not lead one to the assumption that Philo requires circumcision of προσήλυτοι.

Josephus' account of the conversion of Izates raises a question on the role of circumcision (*Ant.* 20.34–48). Ananias and Eleazer have two different approaches to the Gentile king who desired to adhere to the religion of the Jews. The former does not require circumcision, but the latter does. Josephus speculates on the motivations for the treatment of each person. While Ananias's dissuasion of circumcision seems to be motivated by his own safety,[50] Eleazer is reported to 'have a reputation for being extremely strict when it came to the ancestral laws' (*Ant.* 20.43). We note in this account that Josephus has both Izates and his mother connecting the rite of circumcision with 'becoming a Jew' (*Ant.* 20.38, 39). The two treatments seem to reflect the broad range of Gentile incorporation into Judaism, in that a Jew with a strict view of Torah required of Gentile sympathizers a further and fuller integration in 'becoming a Jew'. The story concludes with Izates' circumcision and God's blessing on the nation of the circumcised king. Therefore, Josephus himself seems to favour the treatment of Eleazer, while recognizing that there is different treatment of the circumcision issue or the issue of Gentile incorporation. *Life* 113 is sometimes used against this conclusion. It is argued that Josephus strongly opposes forced circumcision of two men from Trachonitis (*Life* 113).[51] Josephus's criticism, however, seems to be focused here on the forced demand of the Jews, not on the rite of circumcision as a requirement for proselytism.

Extant literature from the Second Temple period suggests that the rite of circumcision is a significant physio-cultural feature that reflects core Jewish ethnic sentiment, and consequently the circumcision of Gentile sympathizers was considered the step for full integration into the Jewish community, as the phrase 'becoming a Jew' (*Ant.* 20.38, 39) and 'entering

49. Cf. Philo, *On the Decalogues, On the Special Laws Books I–III* (trans. F.H. Colson; LCL; 10 vols.; Cambridge: Harvard University Press, 1937), VII, pp. 128–29, note a.
50. Nolland, 'Uncircumcised Proselytes?', p. 193.
51. Segal, 'The Costs of Proselytism', p. 357.

the house of Israel' (Jdt. 14.10) seem to suggest.[52] However, strictly speaking, those who are fully incorporated into the Jewish community through the rite of circumcision seem to be differentiated from native-born Jews whose ancestry goes back to Jacob, at least in some communities of Jews.[53]

3. *Jewish Modes of Gentile Incorporation as Transactional Boundary Negotiations*

There is little evidence from the literature of the Second Temple period to suggest that Judaism was a 'missionary religion', actively sending out missionaries to recruit new members for its community. In this sense, one can already assume that Paul's approach to Gentiles is quite innovative and different from the ways in which most Jews understood the issue of Gentile incorporation. For Jews, the concept of Gentile incorporation encompassed a wide range of acculturation phenomena of Gentile sympathizers around and toward the boundary line. Gentile sympathizers demonstrate their varying levels of attachment to Jews and their religion, such as mere admiration of the culture, selective practice of customs and beliefs, and distancing from their original lifestyle. Some finally choose to integrate fully into the Jewish community through the rite of circumcision. Such terms of classification as προσήλυτος and θεοσεβής cover this wide range of attachment by Gentile sympathizers to Judaism. From the perspective of the Jews looking out at the boundary line, the positive attraction and attachment of Gentile sympathizers to Judaism are both a source of pride and confidence in God's supremacy and at the same time cause for concern for the purity of the religion and the coherence of the ethnic community. Already in the Second Temple period, moral regulations, purity regulations, tithing and monotheism became means to secure the purity and coherence of the Jewish community as it faces the close attachment of Gentile sympathizers. These regulations, which were later codified into the Noachide laws, offered the criteria for Gentiles to attain a state of righteousness. However, the state of righteousness does not automatically lead one to membership within the Jewish community. The

---

52. Feldman, *Jew and Gentile*, pp. 155, 157.

53. We are reminded of the intermediate identity of 'half-Jew', as Herod was referred to as such (refer to the opening quotation of Part II). So Goodman says, 'it is significant that the distinct definition of a proselyte [i.e. convert] as a particular sort of Jew was retained throughout antiquity, it was even possible to describe the descendants of the Idumeans who had converted to Judaism as "*half-Jew*"' (*Ant.* 14.403; emphasis and parentheses added). Goodman, *Mission*, pp. 85–86. Cf. Gary G. Porton, *The Stranger within Your Gates: Converts and Conversion in Rabbinic Literature* (Chicago and London: University of Chicago Press, 1994), pp. 7, 19–22, 31; Hayes, *Gentile Impurities*, p. 11.

rite of circumcision was one of the important requirements for this full integration of a sympathizer into the ethnic community. The degree of insistence on this important physio-cultural feature for Jewish ethnic identity seems to vary from one group to another.

For the Jews, the issue of Gentile incorporation is, in a sense, a matter of maintenance of their ethnic identity. The righteousness of Gentiles may be expressed in some general moral ideas we find in Noachide regulations, but as they come closer or deeper in their attachment to Judaism, such a physio-cultural feature as circumcision becomes an important factor for further incorporation. Though the degree of importance that the rite of circumcision possesses in incorporation of Gentiles may differ from one Jewish group to another, one may conclude that the general Jewish approach to the issue of community–identity (particularly here in the issue of Gentile incorporation) differs from the instrumental mode of Paul's community–identity construction. The kind of identity construction we find in the Second Temple literature is typically expressed in an ethno-centred transactional manner, in which Jewish identity-construction is shaped by a strong core ethnic sentiment, expressing itself in various degrees of insistence on such a physio-cultural feature as circumcision.[54] As I suggested earlier, the Jerusalem church's approach to identity construction is constrained by this Jewish core ethnic sentiment and they may have viewed themselves maintaining at least a certain degree of continuity with the larger Jewish commonwealth. Therefore, the Jerusalem church's approach to community–identity construction was similar to what has just been observed in the Second Temple literature. With this assumption, I will continue deliberating within the context of community–identity construction, in which an interpretation of both the Jerusalem meeting and the Antioch incident in Galatians 2 will be sought in the following chapter.

54. There may have been Jewish groups whose inclination on the issue of Gentile incorporation was akin to Eleazer's in *Ant.* 20.34–48, and they may be described as 'primordial' in their approach to physio-cultural features in comparison to others (represented by Ananias, for example).

Chapter 5

CONFLICTS IN JERUSALEM AND IN ANTIOCH AS THE CONTEXT FOR
IDENTITY CONSTRUCTION IN THE GALATIAN COMMUNITY
(GALATIANS 2.1–14)

In the first chapter on the framework of identity construction, it was seen that identity construction is based upon transactional behaviours at boundary lines, which divide groups. The transactional behaviours are shaped by a core ethnic sentiment that is usually primordially given, while physio-cultural features, which are the expressions of the sentiment, are negotiable.[1] Within the construct of 'transactional' identity construction, some groups are more resistant to the change and exchange of the physio-cultural features, while other groups are comparatively flexible and open to such a change. Still other groups are special cases (i.e. instrumental mode), for which even the core ethnic sentiment can be negotiated and therefore the physio-cultural features are freely chosen as instruments to achieve cohesion, provide welfare or secure protection within the community. This construct provides an explanation for the co-existence of ethnic groups that persist throughout centuries and those that are changing their group outlook, and even emerging as new groups.[2]

The survey of Paul's self-understanding in Chapter 3, as expressed in his relation to Judaism and to the Jerusalem apostles, has shown that Paul portrays himself as an apostle of Christ independently authorized for mission among Gentiles, and I suggested that Paul's approach to community–identity construction is according to an 'instrumental mode'. In the work of constructing a new community among Gentiles, therefore, one would expect Paul to be free from concern for the traditional ethnic sentiment, which most Jews would feel to be primordially given and therefore constraining. Once the core ethnic sentiment is disregarded for community construction, Paul is free to choose either to borrow, recreate or create identifying features for the benefit of his new community. This is a part of the context (or personal condition) that shapes Paul's community–identity construction.

---

1. For further explanation of 'physio-cultural features' and their function in identity construction, cf. Chapter 1 (section 2).
2. Cf. Hutchinson and Smith, 'Ethnicity, Religion, and Language', pp. 32–34.

The previous chapter demonstrated that Jews in general approached the issue of identity construction in the transactional ethno-centred mode, by which their ethnic sentiment plays an important role in change and exchange of physio-cultural features. The degree of insistence on physio-cultural features sometimes differs from one group or sect to another, and it is particularly evident in the rite of circumcision. The Jews of the church of Jerusalem, represented by the Jerusalem apostles, who were themselves Jews and primarily concerned with their relation to Jews outside the church, would relate to the issue of Gentile incorporation in much the same way as the rest of the Jews.[3] This is another part of the context (or external condition) which influenced Paul's community–identity construction from without.

Having located Paul and the Jerusalem apostles (plus other Jewish members of the Jerusalem church) within appropriate modes of community–identity construction, I will now attempt to interpret the conflicts in Jerusalem and in Antioch depicted by Paul in Gal. 2.1–14 as conflicts between different approaches to community–identity construction. Then, the narration of Gal. 2.1–14 can be seen as presenting two conflicting modes (sometimes three as he differentiates the Jerusalem apostles from ψευδαδέλφοι) of community–identity construction in a context of contention, in which the dispute in Galatia is projected onto its community members. Paul narrates this to the Galatians so that they could choose between the two, i.e. between the one which marginalizes non-Jews according to ethno-centred values and one which fights against it for the benefit of non-Jews, particularly Galatians.[4] In this way, Paul's narration of historical events can be regarded as a retrospective interpretation of history, shaped by the exigency in the Galatian community, whose members face the choice between Paul and circumcisers, representative of the two conflicting modes of community–identity construction.[5]

The evidence for the retrospective interpretation is found within the description of the Jerusalem visit in the text of Galatians. Paul directly connects his resistance to enslavement (v. 4: καταδουλώσουσιν) and the end result of truth remaining with the Galatians (v. 5: ἡ ἀλήθεια τοῦ εὐαγγελίου διαμείνῃ πρὸς ὑμᾶς). The preaching of the gospel among the Galatians must have taken place after this visit to Jerusalem in Gal. 2.1–10. Therefore, the description of Gal. 2.5 does not concern the effect of

---

3. Cf. Segal, *Paul*, p. 194. Cf. Chapter 4 (section 3).

4. While the argument here seeks to closely follow Paul's logic, the reader should be reminded that the present study does not simply accept Paul's rhetoric and value-judgement to the neglect of those of other parties as was pointed out earlier.

5. Lyons suggests that the retrospective narration convinces the Galatian members to imitate the way Paul fights against the external pressure. Lyons, *Pauline Autobiography*, p. 136. Cf. Beverly R. Gaventa, 'Galatians 1 and 2: Autobiography as Paradigm', *NTS* 28 (1986), pp. 309–26 (313).

Paul's action on the Galatians at the time of his visit to Jerusalem. Rather, Paul's actions in Jerusalem turn out to have significant implications for the future Galatian community, which was yet to be founded.[6] Paul's description of his Jerusalem visit covers two stages; one concerns events at the time of his Jerusalem visit and the other portrays its effect on the future community of Galatia.[7] The significant effect of Paul's action on the Galatian community is that the truth or integrity of the gospel would remain continually, or persist among the Galatians (ὑμᾶς), even through external pressure to go through the rite of circumcision.[8]

In his retrospective historical narration, Paul bypasses historical details at times and focuses instead on contrasting the two conflicting values or modes of community–identity construction.[9] Therefore, the current scheme for interpreting the pericope (Gal. 2.1–14) is to focus on how Paul perceives and narrates the conflict between the two modes of community–identity construction, while attempting some historical reconstruction where possible and helpful.

1. *Paul's Depiction of the Conflict in Jerusalem (Galatians 2.1–10)*

In this section, the conflicts in Jerusalem and in Antioch will be considered with the following special foci in mind. In the Jerusalem conflict, I will

---

6.   Southern Theory basically suggests that the recipient community of the letter is located in the southern part of the Province of Galatia where Paul reportedly evangelized during his 'first missionary journey' according to Acts chs. 13–14. Even if Southern Theory is taken, one may understand Paul's resistance to circumcision as related primarily to Paul's Gentile mission in general and therefore it relates also to the Galatians specifically but secondarily. An argument is also made that the expression in v. 5 is a support of the fact that the mission in Galatia took place prior to the Jerusalem visit. Cf. J. Murphy-O'Connor, 'Pauline Missions before the Jerusalem Conference', *RB* 89 (1982), pp. 71–91 (78–79).

7.   Betz, *Galatians*, p. 92; Martyn, *Galatians*, p. 198; Dunn, *Epistle to the Galatians*, p. 101.

8.   Contra Burton, *Galatians*, p. 86.

9.   Lüdemann, *Paulus*, pp. 77–78. Lüdemann follows Betz's rhetorical perspective and argues that the pericope (*Narratio*) must be convincing as much as or more than credible to those who judge the argument. Cf. Raymond E. Brown, *An Introduction to the New Testament* (New York: Doubleday, 1996), pp. 422–43. Berger argues that Paul narrates the relation between Peter and himself in such a way that gives a reason as to how the division of mission fields resulted. Berger, *Theologiegeschichte*, p. 253. Haenchen explicitly points out that the conflict in Antioch between Paul and Peter was not as severe as Paul emphasizes and has us assume. Ernst Haenchen, 'Petrus-Problem', *NTS* 7 (1960–61), pp. 187–97 (195–96). A brief comment on John Knox's important contribution to the historical reconstruction of the earliest church is in order. There is no doubt that Knox is right in emphasizing that Acts' information should be placed secondary to Paul's testimony in reconstructing the historical situation of his missionary effort. However, the present discussion on retrospective interpretation emphasizes that just as the author of Acts had reason to edit materials available to him, so also Paul had reason to edit his own materials to produce a '(hi)story'. Cf. John Knox, *Chapters in a Life of Paul* (London: SCM Press, rev. edn, 1989), p. 44.

seek to understand the difference between Jerusalem apostles and ψευδαδέλφοι in light of the study on the modes of Gentile incorporation in the previous chapter. Then the distinction between the mission to Gentiles and the mission to Jews will be articulated in the language of community–identity construction.

a. *The Jerusalem Apostles and* Ψευδαδέλφοι
i. *The Jerusalem apostles and* Ψευδαδέλφοι *as insiders of the church*
In the Antioch incident, one should first take note of Paul's clear agendum to paint a negative picture of the Jerusalem apostles. Then, a consideration will be made in reference to two important physio-cultural features, i.e. *Eretz Israel* and commensality, particularly inter-ethnic dining.

There are two groups identified whom Paul, Barnabas and Titus met in their visit to Jerusalem. One is the Jerusalem apostles, consisting of James, Cephas (Peter) and John. The other group is introduced as 'the false believers who are (secretly) brought in' (Gal. 2.4, τοὺς παρ–εισάκτους ψευδαδέλφους). Ψευδαδέλφοι are further modified by the infinitive 'to spy in' (κατασκοπῆσαι) and with the motive of subjugating Paul and his company (ἡμᾶς καταδουλώσουσιν). The relationship between the Jerusalem apostles and ψευδαδέλφοι is debated because of Paul's peculiar depiction of ψευδαδέλφοι. For some, the negative descriptions for ψευδαδέλφοι give the impression that Paul and the Jerusalem apostles are united against them, and it leads them to assume the unity of the church and the finality of orthodoxy between Paul and the Jerusalem apostles.[10] However, while they are very negatively depicted, the expression ψευδαδέλφοι suggests that they are considered as members of the church in Jerusalem (ψευδ- being Paul's evaluation and ἀδέλφοι being their status at the church). Despite Paul's negative description of the ψευδαδέλφοι, they seem to have exerted some influence in Paul's meeting with the Jerusalem apostles as members of the church. This suggests that they functioned as insiders of the church of Jerusalem (cf. Acts 15, especially vv. 5, 24).[11] Paul, as an outsider, visited the church because of the fear that the very unity of the church and the

---

10. For example, Gaston maintains that the relation between Paul and the Jerusalem apostles was sensitive but positive. Lloyd Gaston, 'Paul and Jerusalem', in P. Richardson and J.C. Hurd (eds.), *From Jesus to Paul* (Waterloo: Wilfrid Laurier University Press, 1984), pp. 61–71 (65).

11. Cf. Hans Conzelmann, *Acts of the Apostles* (Hermeneia; Philadelphia: Fortress, 1987), p. 115. Conzelmann argues that the vagueness of the provenance 'Judaea' is to avoid the impression that the problem was caused by the authority of the Jerusalem church.

truthfulness of his gospel might be under suspicion in Jerusalem (Gal. 2.1–2).[12] One should see the Jerusalem scene as the Jerusalem apostles and ψευδαδέλφοι in the church on one side and Paul, Barnabas and Titus standing on the other. The relationship between the Jerusalem apostles and Paul will be dealt with in the subsequent discussion. If the Jerusalem apostles and ψευδαδέλφοι coexist in one church, the distinction needs to be noted between the Jerusalem apostles and ψευδαδέλφοι in their applications of circumcision in relation to the incorporation of Gentile sympathizers. How can one explain their coexistence in one church community?

ii. *Unity and diversity of the Jewish community*
In order to understand the coexistence of and relationship between the Jerusalem apostles and ψευδαδέλφοι within the church of Jerusalem, one should appreciate the symbolic function of the community suggested in the discussion of the framework of community–identity construction.[13] As noted in the theoretical chapter, a community can be viewed more as an 'aggregating mechanism' rather than 'integrating mechanism'. Cohen uses the term of 'aggregating mechanism' in his thesis, noting that communities are symbolically constructed and maintained. A symbol, as an identifier of a community, does not represent one singular meaning or application for community members to be narrowly 'integrated'. Rather, it offers a locus for community members to gather with varying meanings and applications of the symbolic item or concept.[14] Therefore, it is possible in theory that members gather under the same core ethnic sentiment that is viewed as primordial, yet approach the physio-cultural features that represent the sentiment in various ways.[15] There seems to be certain flexibility among the church members in the degree of insistence regarding the physio-cultural feature of circumcision. Though the Jerusalem apostles and ψευδαδέλφοι differ in the application of the symbolic identity of circumcision, i.e. how they understand the role of the rite in relation to the issue of Gentile incorporation, they coexist and form a larger collectivity symbolically, constructed and maintained under the primordial ethnic sentiment. How do the Jerusalem apostles and

---

12. Burton, *Galatians*, p. 79. Lüdemann likewise relates the occasion of Paul's visit to Jerusalem (Gal. 2.1–10) with Acts 15.1, but he also sees Acts 15.1 as identical with the Antioch incident, making the Antioch incident happen before the Jerusalem visit. Lüdemann, *Paulus*, pp. 104–105. However, Joseph A. Fitzmyer, *The Acts of the Apostles* (AB, 31; New York: Doubleday, 1998), p. 541.

13. Refer to Chapter 1 (section 1.b).

14. A.P. Cohen, *The Symbolic Construction*, pp. 14–16. The example of Josephus's view of unity and diversity was pointed out earlier in Chapter 1 (section 1.b; cf. *War* 2.118–19; *Apion* 2.79–81).

15. Barth, 'Introduction', p. 10.

ψευδαδέλφοι differ in their application of circumcision? As Gal. 2.1–10 shows, the former allowed close intercourse (close but secondary attachment) of Gentiles without requiring the rite of circumcision and the latter insisted upon full integration of Gentiles through the rite of circumcision.

iii. *Gentile sympathizers and circumcision*

For this question, it may be helpful to recall how the Jews viewed Gentile incorporation into Judaism, which was discussed in the previous chapter. The Gentiles showed sympathy toward the Jews and their religion in a variety of ways, from mere attraction to their culture to selective practice of their customs and beliefs.[16] The final step of this spectrum of sympathy is full incorporation into Judaism through the rite of circumcision.[17] At the boundary between Jews and Gentiles in general is this collectivity of Gentile sympathizers, some of whom come ever closer in the degree of their incorporation into the Jewish community. If we take into consideration the 'conversion' account of Izates in Josephus (*Ant.* 20.34–48) as a comparative case, it is seen that Jews had different opinions as to how a Gentile could be incorporated into Judaism. While Ananias considered it acceptable to leave Izates as an uncircumcised sympathizer of Judaism, Eleazar felt it necessary to insist on full incorporation by circumcision. The question there is simply put: 'Can one adhere to the Jewish religion without being a Jew (through circumcision)?' Ananias would respond positively, while Eleazar negatively. Josephus's description of Eleazar is that he has 'a reputation for being extremely strict (ἀκριβὴς) when it came to the ancestral laws' (*Ant.* 20.43). The strict application of circumcision reflects a strong concern over the issue of Gentile impurity, which actively seeks the full incorporation of the entity called Gentile sympathizers. This strict view of purity within the community may have been emphasized precisely at the time of imperial threat from the outside world.[18] If we take into consideration the current political situation of Palestine, it is very possible that anti-imperial ethnic fervour at the early stage of the mission of the church led a segment of the Jewish population to a stricter view of

---

16. S.J.D. Cohen, 'Crossing the Boundary', pp. 13–33. Cf. Feldtkeller, *Identitätssuche*, pp. 35–39.

17. Refer to the previous section on Jewish proselytism. Cohen, 'Crossing the Boundary', p. 22; Collins, 'A Symbol of Otherness', p. 169; Segal, 'The Costs of Proselytism', p. 367.

18. Cf. Barclay, *Jews in the Mediterranean Diaspora*, p. 191 on Wis.; p. 194 on *3 Macc.*; p. 207 on *Ant.*. Barclay uses the expression 'cultural antagonism' as a reaction of the Jews in adverse times. Hengel uses the term 'Torah fixation'. Both expressions refer to certain reactions against the outside pressure of the dissolution of a particular identity. Cf. Hengel, *Judentum und Hellenismus*, I, pp. 555–64; cf. 570.

Torah observance.[19] While it is not possible to determine the exact
historical context that led to the existence of such a strict view among the
church in Jerusalem, one may still understand the dissonance between the
Jerusalem apostles and ψευδαδέλφοι as reflecting 'unity and diversity' on
the issue of Gentile sympathizers and circumcision (i.e. Gentile incorporation) which is found in the larger context of Judaism.[20]

At the boundary between the church and Gentiles in general was the
collectivity of Gentile sympathizers who sought allegiance to Christ and
his church. Ψευδαδέλφοι, who were more strict about the purity of the
community in terms of ethnicity, insisted on full incorporation of
sympathizers through circumcision. On the other hand, the Jerusalem
apostles allowed an intermediate state of Gentile sympathizers to be
attached to the church. Thus circumcision was not required of Titus by
the Jerusalem apostles, despite the pressure of ψευδαδέλφοι (Gal. 2.5–6).
The verb προσανατίθημι (Gal. 2.6) seems to mean, from the context, that
apostles did not 'add' anything to the content of Paul's gospel.[21] This is
contrasted with the demand of ψευδαδέλφοι, who insisted on circumcision. Whatever the historical occasion of the meeting, Paul depicts a
difference between ψευδαδέλφοι and the Jerusalem apostles in their
approach to Gentile incorporation.[22] Paul's depiction may be clarified in
the language of identity construction. The Jerusalem apostles and
ψευδαδέλφοι differed in their approach to boundary negotiation, i.e.
incorporation of Gentile sympathizers into the church. The difference is
on the question of how one expresses the same core ethnic sentiment at the
boundary area. Though one is more strict and the other more lenient in
their stance toward the Gentile incorporation, the Jerusalem apostles and

19. Robert Jewett, 'The Agitators and the Galatian Congregation', *NTS* 17 (1970–71),
pp. 198–212. Cf. M. Hengel, *Die Zeloten: Untersuchungen zur Jüdischen Freiheits-Bewegung
in der Zeit von Herodes 1. bis 70 n. Chr.* (Leiden and Köln: E.J. Brill, 1961), p. 231. However,
the present study does not simply accept Jewett's premise that the phrase τοὺς ἐχ περιτομῆς
(Gal. 2.12) points to the Zealots' activities.

20. Also of note is the parallel account in Acts. If Acts 15.1–29 is Luke's depiction of
Paul's visit to Jerusalem in Gal. 2.1–10, Luke either reasoned the strict view as a typical
Pharisaic feature or a now extinct source was available to him to clarify Paul's ambiguous
account in this way.

21. Cf. Betz, *Galatians*, p. 95.

22. The depiction of Paul, implying that there were two groups in Jerusalem, might be his
way of making a scapegoat to lay the blame upon one group and maintain some degree of
association with the other. Paul's depiction is in some way akin to Luke's depiction of
'pharisaic members' within the church in Jerusalem (Acts 15.1, 5, 24). At any rate,
ψευδαδέλφοι and Jerusalem apostles may be closer in their approach to the Gentile
incorporation than some assume. J.B. Lightfoot, *Saint Paul's Epistle to the Galatians*
(London and New York: Macmillan, 9th edn, 1888), p. 106. He comments, 'Pharisees at
heart, these *traitors* [ψευδαδέλφοι] assume the name and garb of believers' (italic and
parentheses added).

ψευδαδέλφοι were still strongly bound together based upon the core ethnic sentiment, which they both considered primordial.[23]

vi. *Secondary attachment or full incorporation*
The suggestion above requires further elaboration. As long as the Jerusalem church consisted of all Torah-observant Jewish followers of Jesus as the Jewish messiah,[24] both the Jerusalem apostles and ψευδαδέλφοι had no special need to be concerned with the idea of preserving Jewish ethnic identity, at least within the church. It is when they were faced with Gentile sympathizers that they were concerned with preserving their ethnic identity. What concerned the Jerusalem church is that something foreign (Gentile sympathizers) was about to attach itself to their group, which had a strong sense of ethnic identity as Jews. Jews responded to Gentiles who adopted religious and cultural aspects of Jewish society in various ways. For example, Josephus reports positively that Gentiles were adopting beliefs and practices of the Jews (*Apion* 2.282). Feldman observes what he calls 'Jewish triumphalism' in these reports of Jewish influence among other cultures (cf. Bel 28, 41; Tob. 14.6–7; 2 Macc. 9.17; Wis. 18.14).[25] However, this does not mean that these Gentile sympathizers were automatically regarded as full members of the Jewish community.[26] As Gentiles came closer into contact with Jews, ethnic purity and preservation started to become issues. This is the process of incorporation into the Jewish community and the direction becomes ever closer to full incorporation through the physio-cultural symbol of circumcision. Generally speaking, by the rite of circumcision, its full incorporation and partial attachment seem to be divided.[27]

When the church of Jerusalem was faced with Gentile sympathizers, this distinction was destined to become a sensitive issue. When the Jerusalem Church members and perhaps the followers of Christ in wider Judea heard the report about Paul's mission presumably in Cilicia and Syria (Gal. 1.21–24), apart from the reason that Paul ceased to persecute

23.　Acts' description of Paul's other visit to Jerusalem (Acts 21.17–26) may reflect this situation. James worries that the presence of Paul, who had been known as encouraging the Diaspora Jews to forsake the Torah (v. 21), would upset the peace of the community. Therefore, James and other believers who welcomed Paul (v. 17) had a reconciliatory function between Paul and those who were zealous for the Torah (v. 20). Cf. Fitzmyer, *Acts*, p. 693.

24.　Cf. Adolf von Harnack, *Die Mission und Ausbreitung des Christentums in der ersten drei Jahrhunderten* (2 vols.; Leipzig: J.C. Hinrichs, 4th edn, 1924), I, p. 51.

25.　Feldman, 'Jewish Proselytism', p. 373.

26.　One example of this may be the 'God-fearers' found in the inscription from Aphrodisias (cf. ch. 4, 2.b.ii).

27.　Segal, 'The Costs of Proselytism', p. 367.

those with faith in Christ, they may have rejoiced over their influence among Gentile cultures without implication of the issue of Gentile incorporation into the larger community of faith in Christ (akin to the case of 'Jewish triumphalism' by Feldman). When Paul presented his gospel to the Jerusalem apostles (Gal. 2.2), the rite of circumcision was not required of the Gentiles because they were thought of as Gentile sympathizers, short of full incorporation into the Jewish community of faith in Christ.[28] Would the Jerusalem apostles then require circumcision for the Gentile sympathizers who desired to join the Jerusalem church? Based upon the belief that Paul and the Jerusalem leaders shared the same gospel, some interpreters resist such a possibility.[29] However, a different view can be suggested as one observes the relationship between the Jerusalem apostles and ψευδαδέλφοι. While Paul in the end defied the influence of the ψευδαδέλφοι, it is nevertheless curious that they seem to have been able to exert some influence upon the Jerusalem meeting, or at least their influence seems to have met no resistance from the Jerusalem apostles (Gal. 2.4–5).[30] There was at least room for negotiation between the Jerusalem leaders and the ψευδαδέλφοι concerning the influence of Gentile sympathizers on the Jerusalem church. Moreover, had an uncircumcised member already existed in the Jerusalem church, the visit of Titus may not have caused the ψευδαδέλφοι to demand a change in their 'standard operation' on Gentile incorporation, which had already been determined.[31]

The ψευδαδέλφοι take a strict stance on this issue of Gentile incorporation. The cause of their stance is uncertain, but they were still operating within the church as ἀδέλφοι. On this point, ψευδαδέλφοι may have been more realistic about the implication of Paul's effort to construct religious communities among Gentiles. They may have been more sensitive to the potential impact of the existence of Gentile sympathizers upon the coherence of their ethno-centred community in Jerusalem (and possibly in wider Judaea). As Gentiles began to congregate as churches in

28. Cf. Feldtkeller, *Identitätssuche*, p. 138. Feldtkeller understands the Gentile mission in Antioch to be such an operation based upon the criteria of God-fearers (*Gottes-Fürchtigen-Kriterium*).

29. Schmithals, *Paulus und Jakobus*, pp. 37–38.

30. The verbal adjective παρεισάκτους can be understood either in a passive sense to suggest the apostles' intention to bring them in or in an active sense to suggest the plot of ψευδαδέλφοι to have their voice heard. For the former, see Theodor von Zahn, *Der Brief des Paulus an die Galater ausgelegt* (Leipzig: Deichertsche, 1905), p. 85; and for the latter, see Franz Mußner, *Der Galaterbrief* (HTKNT, 9; Freiburg: Herder, 5th edn, 1981), pp. 108–109.

31. A historical consideration coincides with and, therefore, enforces the present sociological consideration. Bockmuehl suggests that the political situation in 40s and 50s CE in Palestine would have allowed only a thoroughly Jewish mission. Bockmuehl, *Jewish Law*, p. 172; cf. Schmithals, *Paulus und Jakobus*, p. 75.

Gentile land as the result of Paul preaching his gospel, they may have anticipated that the Gentile sympathizers would not remain an unrelated collectivity of sympathetic bystanders. Therefore, ψευδαδέλφοι insisted that Gentiles be fully incorporated into the Jewish community of faith in Christ through the rite of circumcision. In this sense, both Paul and ψευδαδέλφοι insisted on establishing a unified church of Jews and non-Jews by abandoning the rite on one hand and insisting on the rite on the other.[32] Accompaniment of the uncircumcised delegate, Titus, must have alarmed ψευδαδέλφοι more than the Jerusalem apostles. It is often suggested that Titus was a sort of specimen of uncircumcised believer that Paul brought as evidence of the validity of his ministry (i.e. conversion without circumcision).[33] Το ψευδαδέλφοι, Titus may have been more than an uncircumcised sympathizer. Indeed he may already have been an uncircumcised leader, a fellow worker of Paul who was involved in the affairs of the Gentile assemblies, therefore, more than a sympathetic bystander (cf. 2 Cor. 8.23, κοινωνός/συνεργός).[34] From the perspective of ψευδαδέλφοι, such a person, deeply involved in the affairs of the church in general must be fully (and formally) integrated into the community through the rite of circumcision. The pressure of ψευδαδέλφοι on Titus for circumcision (Gal. 2.3–4) can be understood as being based upon the primordial ethnic sentiment. The Jerusalem apostles may have viewed Titus as belonging to the group of Gentile sympathizers attached in the secondary sense to the religious community represented by the church of Jerusalem. Their ethnic sentiment was not threatened by the visit of a Gentile sympathizer.

Paul's depiction is that there existed within the Jerusalem church different views on Gentile incorporation into the community, namely represented by ψευδαδέλφοι and the Jerusalem apostles. This phenomenon is one of varying behaviours of identity maintenance based upon the Jewish core ethnic sentiment, which can also be observed in the larger Jewish society (as in the case of the conversion of Izates). Ψευδαδέλφοι wanted to see full incorporation of Gentile sympathizers, while the Jerusalem apostles did not see the need for insisting that Gentile sympathizers become fully integrated members through the rite of circumcision. The focus of Paul's response was against those who seek

32. Paul's problem in Gal. 2 is suggested as being due to his vision of creating one community of Jews and non-Jews together. Segal, *Paul*, p. 198; Bockmuehl, *Jewish Law*, p. 35. Ψευδαδέλφοι's vision might be the same in the sense of realizing a united church but with a different approach.

33. Betz, *Galatians*, p. 88; Bruce, *Galatians*, p. 117.

34. See how Paul may be taking care to emphasize the importance of Titus' place in the mission by distinguishing him from two other anonymous ἀπόστολοι and by referring to him as συναγωγός. Margaret E. Thrall, *A Critical and Exegetical Commentary on the Second Epistle to the Corinthians* (ICC; 2 vols.; Edinburgh: T. & T. Clark, 2000), II, p. 553.

to 'subjugate' (καταδουλώσουσιν) the uncircumcised by exerting a 'deceptive' influence (Gal. 2.4). Paul is depicted as the protector of the Gentile members (and the implication is that he is such for the Galatian members, v. 5) against the ill influence of ψευδαδέλφοι who insist on the rite of circumcision. The Galatian audience would probably be able to project Paul's narration to their own situation quite easily. Then the 'historical' description functions favourably for Paul's later persuasion, developed in Galatians 3 and 4.

b. *Mission to Jews and Mission to Gentiles*
i. *Two missions as two general jurisdictions*

Different perspectives on Gentile incorporation between the Jerusalem apostles and ψευδαδέλφοι have been elucidated, considering the subject within the framework of the transactional boundary negotiation for the construction of community–identity. Now the contrast between the Jerusalem apostles and Paul in their perspectives on Gentile incorporation needs to be considered. In the latter part of his account of the Jerusalem visit, Paul focuses on two missions resulting from the meeting (Gal. 2.7–9). But what is the difference between these missions? There has been debate on whether the difference is geographical or ethnic. Those who understand the demarcation to be geographical suggest that the mission (or 'gospel') to Jews (τό εὐαγγέλιον τῆς περιτομῆς in v. 7/ἀποστολὴν τῆς περιτομῆς in v. 8) is primarily the mission located within the geographical confines of Palestine.[35] The mission to Gentiles then covers the rest of the world. However, apart from the fact that περιτομή and ἀκροβυστία themselves denote ethnicity rather than geography, to understand the term simply as a geographical demarcation poses a difficulty, as Jewish colonies existed in most major cities throughout the empire.[36] On the other hand, to understand it as a strictly ethnic term (i.e. people groups) faces a difficulty as well, for Paul may have preached to a mixed audience of Jews and non-Jews (e.g. Acts 13.48–50; 18.4).[37] We are to be reminded, however, that geographic concern is one of the significant physio-cultural features that manifest a given core ethnic sentiment, therefore the very debate as to whether the demarcation is ethnic or geographic is rather irrelevant. The presentation of Paul's gospel and the resultant discussion on the treatment of Gentile sympathizers, represented by Titus, lead to the articulation of two missions. Therefore, in the context of the discussion lies an *ethnic* issue, i.e. Gentile incorporation and Jewish ethnic purity, but it may have been understood and manifested at least partially in terms of *geographic*

35. von Zahn, *Galater*, pp. 106–108; Schlier, *Galater*, p. 46.
36. Burton, *Galatians*, pp. 96–99.
37. Burton, *Galatians*, p. 125. But cf. Sanders, *Judaism: Practice & Belief*, p. 224.

demarcation. That this demarcation does not mean that they came to a new and clear agreement on the standard treatment of what to do when facing a Gentile sympathizer to the church and what to do when facing a Jewish sympathizer to the church is evidenced from the consequence reported in the Antioch incident (Gal. 2.11–14).[38] Rather, it is an acknowledgement of what Paul and perhaps the Antioch Church were already doing and what the Jerusalem apostles were already doing, i.e. the difference between the ministry whose primary focus is Gentiles and the ministry whose primary focus is Jews.[39] The focus of the contrast, therefore, lies in two jurisdictions. This distinction can be elaborated as the difference in modes of community–identity construction.

The Jerusalem apostles regarded Gentile sympathizers in Paul's Gentile mission as a secondary attachment to the religious community of Jews who followed the Jewish messiah, Jesus.[40] The content of belief of the movement may be summarized in the 'gospel of the uncircumcised' (2.7, τό εὐαγγέλιον τῆς ἀκροβυστίας). What then was Paul's perspective on Gentile sympathizers in his mission? While both the Jerusalem apostles and ψευδαδέλφοι were interested in and constrained by the preservation of the core ethnic sentiment, Paul does not see the core sentiment as something fixed, therefore primordially given as noted in the preceding chapters.[41] There, Paul was described as innovative and free from such ethnic constraint, i.e. his approach to community–identity construction is 'instrumental'.[42] Indeed, Paul must have determined that such a sentiment was against his aim of establishing a unified community of believers in Christ, as can be seen in the subsequent section on the Antioch incident. This fundamental difference between Paul and the Jerusalem church is initially caused by the revelatory experience (Gal. 1.15–16) in which Paul was convinced that he was autonomously called by God to the Gentile mission. In the 'instrumental mode' of identity construction, it is the assumption that even the core ethnic sentiment is fluid and negotiable, and therefore the physio-cultural features are freely abandoned, recreated or created for the benefit and cohesion of the new community. For example, recreation of a physio-cultural feature is apparent in Rom. 2.12–29. In this pericope lies a surprising redefinition of the core features of ethnic sentiment. Therefore, Paul gives his 'spiritual' (ἐν πνεύματι οὐ γράμματι) redefinition of 'Jew' and 'circumcision' (Rom. 2.28–29). Through this

38. Conzelmann, *Geschichte des Urchristentums*, p. 70. Conzelmann suggests that the confusion in Antioch (Gal. 2.11–14) derives from the ambiguity concerning the demarcation. See also Dunn, *Epistle to the Galatians*, p. 122.

39. Bornkamm, *Paulus*, p. 60.

40. Cf. Segal, *Paul*, pp. 191, 198.

41. Cf. Chapter 3 (section 3).

42. Cf. Segal, *Paul*, pp. 193–94. Segal suggests that Paul sought the unity of the church through abrogating the ethno-centred regulations.

redefinition, Paul denies those 'Jews' outside the definition (or outside the community) to be authentically 'Jewish'.[43]

ii. *Concession rather than unity*

The Jerusalem apostles separate the two entities (Jews and non-Jews) and consider Paul's work among Gentile sympathizers as a secondary attachment, not equal to Gentiles' full incorporation, so that the purity of the ethnic religion might be preserved. The preservation of a core ethnic sentiment is a significant concern for the Jerusalem apostles. Paul, on the other hand, whose primary interest is to construct the Gentile community of faith, decided that the Jewish ethnic sentiment had no place in constructing the community. The Jerusalem apostles concern themselves primarily with preserving their Jewish identity, while Paul's primary concern is effective execution of his operation, the Gentile mission, in which he portrays himself as defender of the welfare of the Gentile members (cf. Gal. 2.5; 4.17-20). It may have been that Paul's desire for a united community through abandoning a particular ethnic sentiment as foundational was rather difficult to reconcile with the already existing Jewish community of believers in Christ. The concession may have been that the Jerusalem apostles authorized Paul to continue his mission to Gentiles independent of the work of the Jerusalem church.

If such a gap existed between the Jerusalem apostles and Paul, based upon different approaches to the construction of the community with Gentile sympathizers, then the alleged agreement portrayed in the latter part of the Jerusalem visit may have to be reconsidered.[44] Paul reports

43. It is noted, however, that the problem of the effectiveness of such an ethnic motif exists even in such a redefinition of ethnic terms. Would such a motif be helpful for the Gentile audience, while it may have been an effective way to set Paul's religion distinct from 'Judaism'? A similar problem occurs in Gal. 2.15, where Paul says, 'we are Jews by nature and not *Gentile sinners*'. It has been suggested that Paul envisions by it a sort of 'third race', i.e. 'Gentile' in the phrase 'Gentile sinners' are those Gentiles without faith in Christ, distancing Gentile members in the community away from other Gentiles (cf. 1 Thess. 4.5). If it is the case, and certainly creating a new entity seems clear in the case of Rom. 2, Paul may not be perfectly consistent in the case of Galatians, as he refers to the Gentile segment of the Antiochean church (i.e. believing Gentiles) as ἐθνῶν (cf. Gal. 2.12). This arbitrariness on Paul's part may be unconscious due to his background in Judaism, even though he consciously parts himself from it (Gal. 1.13).

44. Haenchen, *Die Apostelgeschichte*, p. 414. Recently Esler employed an anthropological perspective of 'honor and shame/limited goods' to suggest a helpful scenario of power-competition between Paul and the Jerusalem apostles in the pericope. The suggestion that Paul and the Jerusalem apostles came to a pseudo-agreement on the ritual of the Eucharist on the basis of the term κοινωνίας in Gal. 2.9 aside, his anthropological perspective helps to substantiate the context of contention in the meeting at Jerusalem. Esler, *Galatians*, pp. 127-34. Indeed, Paul's ambiguity on the nature of the agreement is noted (for example, Dunn, *Epistle to the Galatians*, p. 122).

that he presented the gospel, which he was preaching among the Gentiles (Gal. 2.2), and that the Jerusalem apostles realized that Paul was entrusted with a gospel for the Gentiles as Peter was with a gospel for the Jews (πεπίστευμαι τὸ εὐαγγέλιον τῆς ἀκροβυστίας καθὼς Πέτρος τῆς περιτομῆς, Gal. 2.7). The Jerusalem apostles may have recognized that Paul's presentation was a sufficient adaptation of the gospel of the Jews for a Gentile audience and that it was good for establishing a secondary group of Gentile sympathizers. This process can be compared with how the halakhic interpretation of the flood narrative (i.e. Noachide regulations) enabled the possibility of righteousness for some Gentiles, but not necessarily their full incorporation into the Jewish community.[45] The Jerusalem apostles are reported to have added nothing to the gospel of the Gentiles (2.6, οὐδὲν προσανέθεντο), because they realized that Paul's focus was already specifically Gentiles.

It may have been for the reason of solving the urgent problem of tension and maintaining temporary unity that the Jerusalem apostles resorted to a 'separation policy', which allowed Paul to continue with his Gentile mission. The Jerusalem apostles continue the mission among Jews, in which they construct the community based upon a core ethnic sentiment. Paul continues his mission among Gentiles, in which he constructs a community free from the Jewish core ethnic sentiment.[46] The division of labour between the Jerusalem apostles and Paul does not necessarily mean that they all agreed that the two communities are autonomous and equal. Indeed some regarded the Gentile mission to be only a secondary attachment to the Jewish church.[47] This unresolved gap helps us to understand the incident faced in Antioch. But before moving to a discussion of the incident in Antioch, an attempt will be made to understand Paul's description in v. 9 that he and Barnabas received the 'right hand of fellowship' from the Jerusalem apostles.

iii. *Right hand of fellowship*
In light of the scenario just given, the expression 'giving the right hand' (Gal. 2.9, δεξιὰς ἔδωκαν) merits further consideration. On a surface level, given the modifying genitive 'of fellowship' (κοινωνίας), the entire phrase

45. Segal maintains that Paul's approach to the Torah is halakhic rather than theological in order to realize the unified community of Jews and non-Jews. Segal, *Paul*, pp. 192–93; cf. 201. 'Halakhic' here means an attitude to the Torah in order to pursue a suitable interpretation for a particular community life situation rather than the pursuit of the only true interpretation ('theological'). Cf. Gary G. Porton, in *ABD*, III, s.v. 'Halakah'.

46. A similar but more general solution is suggested that the agreement at the conference was so ambiguous that the Jerusalem apostles used the agreement for the welfare of Jewish believers while Paul did so for the benefit of his Gentile members. Dunn, *Epistle to the Galatians*, p. 122.

47. Cf. Segal, *Paul*, p. 190.

seems to connote some kind of mutual agreement and acceptance. Indeed, the lexical entries generally suggest a sign of agreement, alliance and friendship.[48] However, Esler has suggested a special connotation of the phrase in the context of competition attested in Second Temple Jewish literature. When one in a militarily superior position 'gives the right hand' to an inferior, the implication is the enforcement of *status quo* in the power balance from the powerful to the powerless (1 Macc. 6.58–59; 11.50, 62, 66; 13.45, 50; 2 Macc. 4.34; 11.26; 12.11; 13.22; 14.19 etc.).[49] The nuance of pressure is probably derived from a war context, and not innate within the phrase itself (δεξιὰς ἔδωκαν). Therefore, the meaning of the symbolic action must be decided by the context. The phrase does not necessarily mean a 'friendly agreement of equals', as it is often interpreted.[50] What is the context in which the phrase is used in our pericope? The demarcation of missions may have been a concession by both the Jerusalem apostles and Paul. For the Jerusalem apostles, while retaining a sense of superiority over the delegates of the Gentile mission represented by Paul, they allowed Paul to continue work among the Gentiles, to gain sympathizers among them.[51] The 'right hand of fellowship' was for the Jerusalem apostles a gesture to permit the ministry of a secondary group of sympathizers attached to the authentic community of faith represented by the Jerusalem church. Paul, on the other hand, may not have been satisfied with the permission to establish groups that are only secondary and not authentic, so he accepted the 'right hand of fellowship' and interpreted and reported it as a gesture of recognition of autonomously authentic mission.[52] It may well have been, as Segal suggests, that Paul originally presented his gospel to help establish one unified community of Jews and non-Jews mixed together by abandoning ethnic issues, especially the rite of circumcision for Gentiles. When he realized that his gospel would not fully persuade the Jerusalem church, he had to abandon hope for total unity with the church as a whole.[53] Paul tells the Galatians about this rather unsatisfactory meeting in reality as an occasion to win the affirmation of the apostles that Paul's mission was autonomously authentic, from which the Galatian community was born.

---

48.   Walter Grundmann, 'δεξιός', in Gerhard Kittel (ed.), *Theological Dictionary of the New Testament* (trans. Geoffrey W. Bromiley; 10 vols.; Grand Rapids: Eerdmans, 1964), II, pp. 37–40; cf. BAGD, p. 174.

49.   Esler, 'Making and Breaking', pp. 299–300.

50.   Betz, *Galatians*, p. 100.

51.   Haenchen, *Die Apostelgeschichte*, p. 414.

52.   Having the authority of mission derived from his revelatory experience, the second best thing next to having the united church of Jews and non-Jews according to Paul's ideas is to secure his mission from interference by the Jerusalem apostles.

53.   Segal, *Paul*, pp. 190–91. However, in 1 Cor. 15 we will see the evidence of *détente* between the Jerusalem apostles and Paul.

In the Jerusalem meeting, the distinction between the mission of Paul and the mission of the Jerusalem apostles was made evident.[54] The difference is one of ways to approach the construction of the community of faith. The Jerusalem apostles operated on a core ethnic sentiment, while Paul was free from such sentiment as a foundation for the community, and thus the demarcation of the mission to Jews and the mission to Gentiles emerged as a sort of concession between the two parties.[55] In this scenario, Paul realized that it was not possible to attain one united community of faith with the Jerusalem church through abandoning a core ethnic sentiment. He went his own way to a Gentile mission, independent from the Jewish mission of the Jerusalem church and possibly churches throughout Judaea. The subsequent persuasions in his letter are, then, his effort to attain and maintain such a united community within his Gentile mission.

2. *Paul's Depiction of the Conflict in Antioch (Galatians 2.11–14)*

The scene shifts now to the community of believers in Antioch-on-Orontes, who are, according to the account in Acts 11.26, called 'Christians' (Χριστιανούς) for the first time. Very little can be said about the historical situation of Jews or 'Christians' of the city from the sources now available.[56] According to Josephus, the original population of the city was gathered from among Macedonians, Athenians and Jews, apart from the native Syrians (*Ant.* 12.119). This may be why there was rather a large community of Jews in this third biggest cosmopolitan area of the empire in the first century CE.[57] While a hypothesis of the birth of Christian churches in Antioch such as given by Taylor, based upon the enmity between Jews and non-Jews, may be insightful albeit highly

---

54. Hans Conzelmann and Andreas Lindemann, *Arbeitsbuch zum Neuen Testament* (UniT, 52; Tübingen: Mohr, 1975), pp. 412–13. They understand the Jerusalem Council as a sort of Pandora's box, which made the participants of the meeting aware of the difficulty of realizing an inter-ethnic community.

55. Ibid.

56. Frank Kolb, 'Antiochia in der frühen Kaiserzeit', in H. Cancik, *et al.* (eds.), *Geschichte Tradition – Reflexion* (Festschrift M. Hengel; 3 vols.; Tübingen: Mohr, 1996), II, pp. 97–118 (99).

57. To give an idea of the scale of the Jewish population, it has been estimated as 20–35,000 out of 300,000 by Hengel and Schwemer. Hengel and Schwemer, *Paulus*, pp. 291–92. Cf. Kolb, 'Antiochia', p. 101; Schürer, *The History of the Jewish People*, III, pp. 126–27. It may also be helpful to note that the Jews seem to have been well-off economically as Josephus reports that there was a large sum contributed by the Antiochean Jews to the Temple in Jerusalem (*War* 7.3.3).

speculative,[58] the increased tension between Jews and non-Jews in the city, especially after the reign of Caligula (37–41 CE), may be worth noting for the situation of the Gentile mission in the city.[59]

When surveying the incident in Antioch, one is immediately faced with the fact that Paul is notoriously ambiguous and brief in the way he recounts the event, which seems to have had a grave influence upon his mission to Gentiles, such as possibly the parting with his mission partner Barnabas (Acts 15.39) and the harm to his relationship with the Antiochean church.[60] However, the ambiguity seems to reflect Paul's retrospective interpretation of events in Judaea and Syria, which he believes to have significant implications for the current urgent concerns of the fledgling and struggling community members in Galatia. The cursory manner in which the events are recounted in the letter seems to give the original audience an impression that the Jewish ethnic sensibility (i.e. core ethnic sentiment) poses a threat to the well-being of Gentile believers. Therefore, this present interpretation deals with two layers of the pericope (Gal. 2.11–14). First, attention is given to the general theme of the message that Paul seems to have desired to communicate to the Galatian members through his retrospective interpretation and recounting of the event. Then, a consideration is made of the two physio-cultural features of locality (the concept of *Eretz Israel*) and of commensality (the issue of mixed dining), which seem to have played a significant role in the conflict in Antioch and, in Paul's mind, have a direct implication for the situation in the Galatia community.

a. *Message to the Galatians*
The Galatian letter is silent about the occasion or purpose of Peter's visit to Antioch, and the parallel account in Acts 15 does not record such a visit by Peter. He may have been, as suggested, already a travelling missionary-apostle at the time of Paul's visit to Jerusalem, and it may have been his custom to visit various locations for preaching the gospel to the

58. His hypothesis, on the basis of the fact that the name 'Christ' or 'Christian' in non-Christian sources in the first century CE are associated with a social disturbance, is that the enmity between the Jews and non-Jews in Antioch is at least partly due to some Jews' Christianizing the non-Jewish population of Antioch. John J. Taylor, 'Why Were the Disciples First Called "Christians" at Antioch?', *RB* 101 (1994), pp. 75–94.

59. Murphy-O'Connor, *Paul*, p. 147. For the life situation of Jews in Syria, cf. also, Barclay, *Jews in the Mediterranean Diaspora*, particularly pp. 252–54.

60. Murphy-O'Connor, *Paul*, p. 158. However, such a break of relationship seems to have lasted only temporarily (cf. 1 Cor. 9.5–6). Cf. Betz, *Galatians*, p. 111; Martyn, *Galatians*, p. 234.

circumcised (Gal. 2.7–8).[61] Due to the high concentration of the Jewish population, the city of Antioch may have been a likely location to visit for the apostle to the Jews.[62] While one cannot be certain as to why Peter visited Antioch,[63] one may infer Paul's intention in recounting Peter's visit to Antioch for the original readers in Galatia. The disjunction (δέ) in v. 11 seems to shift attention not so much on the change of geographical locations as to the outcome of the 'agreement' previously made in vv. 1–10. Therefore, the emphasis of v. 11 is that Peter is in the wrong. Paul says, 'when Cephas came to Antioch, I stood against to his face' (κατὰ πρόσωπον αὐτῷ ἀντέστην), then 'because he stood self-condemned' (ὅτι κατεγνωσμένος ἦν).

In the following verse (v. 12), Paul writes, 'For until certain people came from James (τινας ἀπο Ἰακώβου), he used to eat with Gentiles'. The phrase, τινας ἀπο Ἰακώβου (v. 12), is most naturally understood as the delegates sent by James. It does not seem so convincing when some suggest that ἀπο Ἰακώβου means a more general provenance of Jerusalem, and that the message of the 'delegates' did not necessarily reflect James' intention.[64] If one seeks to generalize euphemistically the provenance or association of delegates, would one not use a geographical location for a person instead of a person for a geographic location? Other attempts have been made to deliver James from the primary cause of the division in Antioch, so some argue that the delegates misrepresented James and others maintain that Peter over-reacted.[65] The most natural reading of the text seems to be that both James and Peter were present when the agreement was made (Gal. 2.7–9) but, nevertheless, both played a role in the alienation of Gentile members (Gal. 2.11–14).

The identification of 'those of circumcision' (τοὺς ἐκ περιτομῆς, Gal. 2.12) has been variously suggested as well. Some argue that the phrase τοὺς ἐκ περιτομῆς refers to ψευδαδέλφοι in Gal. 2.4,[66] yet it is rather difficult to understand why Paul did not simply call them ψευδαδέλφοι and why Peter had to fear them.[67] Therefore, it is not plausible to

61. A suggestion is made that after the deliverance from his arrest in Jerusalem, Peter stayed outside the city to escape the danger. Meanwhile, the leadership in Jerusalem shifted from the original apostles to James and the πρεσβύτεροι (Acts 11.30). Note the order of the Jerusalem leadership begins with James rather than Peter in Gal. 2.8. Hengel and Schwemer, *Paulus*, pp. 370–71. If this suggestion is right, the phrase 'Jerusalem apostles' would require a modification.

62. Conzelmann, *Geschichte des Urchristentum*, p. 70. Note that Conzelmann suggests that the fact that Peter visits Antioch shows that the Jerusalem agreement was not a specific geographical agreement.

63. A suggestion for this will be made in subsequent discussion on *Eretz Israel*.

64. Lightfoot, *Galatians*, p. 112.

65. Hort, *Judaistic Christianity*, pp. 80–81; cf. Bockmuehl, *Jewish Law*, pp. 72–73.

66. Lightfoot, *Galatians*, p. 112.

67. Schmithals, *Paulus und Jakobus*, p. 54.

understand τοὺς ἐκ περιτομῆς as ψευδαδέλφοι. It should be noted that περιτομή is the customary designation of 'Jews' in general (Rom. 4.12; Col. 4.11; cf. Acts 10.45; 11.2), so it seems that the custom applies here as well.[68] Therefore, James related to Peter a concern via his delegates, which caused Peter to 'fear' the Jews (φοβούμενος τοὺς ἐκ περιτομῆς).[69] The members in Galatia are now prepared to hear how the agreement in Jerusalem was broken in Antioch by the Jerusalem apostles, and they are told that there was division between Jews and non-Jews as a result. Therefore, the primary message from Paul to the Galatian audience can be outlined as follows (here including the previous pericope):

a. Titus was pressured to be circumcised by ψευδαδέλφοι (v. 4).
b. Paul, the apostle to the Gentiles (together with Barnabas) resisted the pressure for the sake of the Galatian members (v. 5).
c. Peter, the apostle to the Jews, by the pressure of James, breached the agreement to preserve the truthfulness of the gospel (vv. 7–9, 11–12).
d. Jews (τοὺς ἐκ περιτομῆς) exerted a 'fearful' pressure upon Peter (v. 12).
e. Gentile believers in Antioch were alienated from Jewish constituents as a result (vv. 12–13).

Whatever the historical background may be, there seems to be a clear message by Paul to the Galatian community members, which is that Jewish ethnic sensibility (i.e. core ethnic sentiment) caused a threat to the well-being of Gentile believers and that Paul fought for the Gentiles.[70] The implication is that Paul fights for the Galatians as well as against the evil influence of the circumcisers.

b. *Ethnic Concerns and the Welfare of Gentile Believers*
i. Eretz Israel *(Land of Israel) as a physio-cultural feature of locality*
A brief consideration of the details of the incident at this point seems to aid in understanding why Paul referred to this event for the purpose of constructing community–identity in Galatia. First, I want to consider a physio-cultural feature, which reflects Jewish ethnic sentiment, i.e. geographical boundary, in order to understand at least an aspect of the

---

68. Ibid.
69. The possible reason for 'fear' will be discussed in the subsequent discussion on 'mixed dining' (2.b.ii).
70. Paul's intention for the Galatian members in the retrospective narration is clear, while the historical details remain ambiguous, whether or not one discredits the historicity of Paul's account. Bornkamm, *Paulus*, p. 66. Cf. Haenchen, 'Petrus-Probleme', p. 195.

incident in Antioch.[71] It has been suggested that the traditional Jewish view of the Land of Israel (*Eretz Israel*) may extend beyond Palestine and include Syria and Cilicia.[72] The land that is promised to both Abraham (Gen. 15.16) and Moses (Exod. 23.31), and included in the Davidic census (2 Sam. 24.6–7) borders on the north and east with R. Euphrates and Mt. Amanus. This extended perspective of *Eretz Israel* continues in the Second Temple period, and may explain the Hasmonean effort to extend the Jewish presence in Syria (*Ant.* 13.9.1; 13.15.5).[73] Also notable is the rabbinic debate on the extent of *Eretz Israel* in the setting of the end of the first century CE, in which R. Gamaliel suggests the northern border of Kezib (modern border with Lebanon, *m. Ḥal.* 4.7–8). Having noted the existence of interpretations of both smaller and wider size *Eretz Israel* in Jewish sources, Scott concludes that 'the territorial status of Antioch and its environs may have been ambiguous [as to whether they belonged to the Diaspora or to *Eretz Israel* proper] in Jewish circles'.[74] This indicates, then, that the interpretation of the Torah on the issue of the land may have varied among Jews in the first century CE as well.[75] Based upon this view, Bockmuehl suggests that the Jerusalem apostles may have understood that their jurisdiction would be extended as far as to the Jews in Antioch, and this would explain why Paul's letters are silent about the Apostolic decree in his defence against the circumcising opponents, which was meant only for the churches within *Eretz Israel*.[76] On this point, one might ask why Paul would not use such a strong argument against

71. It has been suggested that the geographical expansions of the missionary movement may be understood better, when one considers the concept of *Eretz Israel*. James M. Scott, *Paul and the Nations: The Old Testament and Jewish Background of Paul's Mission to the Nations with Special Reference to the Destination of Galatians* (WUNT, 84; Tübingen: Mohr, 1995). Scott makes a thorough investigation of the 'Table of the Nations' to consider the destinations of Paul. 'Table of the Nations' refers to the nations populated by the descendants of Noah according to the genealogy in Gen. 10 (cf. J.M. Scott, *Paul*, pp. 5–8). Cf. Hengel and Schwemer, *Paulus*, pp. 270–71.

72. Martin Hengel, "Ἰουδαία in der geographischen Liste Apg 2, 9–11 und Syrien als "Grossjudäa"', *RHPR* 80 (2000), pp. 51–68, especially 64. Ἰουδαία between Mesopotamia and Macedonia in Acts 2.9–11 is explained by the expansion of the border of *Eretz Israel* in the messianic time based upon the promise to Abraham (Gen. 15.18–21) and in view of the great kingdom of David.

73. Bockmuehl, *Jewish Law*, pp. 67–69. See also the references from Palestinian Targum (*Frg. Tg.* and *Tg. Nef. Num.* 34.8; *Tg. Ps.–J. Num.* 13.21), but note the conservative (smaller size of the land) view on the issue in *Ant.* 4.7.3; *Tg. Ps.–J. Num.* 34.

74. J.M. Scott, *Paul*, p. 158 (parentheses added). Cf. Bockmuehl, *Jewish Law*, pp. 68–69.

75. Another evidence that a physio-cultural feature is symbolically understood and interpreted in various ways within the same ethnic group.

76. Bockmuehl, *Jewish Law*, pp. 72, 79 note 131.

the exercise of strict application of the purity regulations by the circumcising opponents in the land outside *Eretz Israel*.[77]

The Jerusalem apostles and Paul may have held different views on this very issue. James may have regarded this physio-cultural feature of geographic boundary as significant and exerted his influence as far as Antioch through his delegates, while Paul understood such an action as an intrusion on his jurisdiction not according to such an understanding of *Eretz Israel*, but according to the contemporary geopolitical distinction, i.e. Antioch being within the provincial boundary of Cilicia and Syria and outside of Judaea and Samaria (Israel). This may well explain why James' interference in the church at Antioch resulted in division (Gal. 2.11–14).[78] It was suggested earlier that the distinction between the mission to Jews and the mission to Gentiles cannot be neatly made and that the mission to Jews may have simply meant the mission that the Jerusalem apostles had been engaged in, largely among the Jews. Therefore, the awareness of extended *Eretz Israel* together with the fact of the existence of a large population of Jews in Antioch and the possible history of the establishment of the Antioch church by the migration of Jewish believers (cf. Acts 11.19, 20), may have caused James to claim his jurisdiction over the church in Antioch.[79] Paul, being free from such a physio-cultural feature, considered *Eretz Israel* on the basis of the current geopolitical boundary. Moreover, if Paul could redefine the 'Israel of God' (Ἰσραὴλ τοῦ θεοῦ) to be primarily Galatian Christians (Gal. 6.16),[80] *Eretz Israel* may have been reinterpreted on the basis of his newly recreated sense of salvation history (i.e. '*Eretz Israel*' being those who have faith in Jesus Christ and are not under the Torah; cf. Gal. 4.21–31). Then the physio-cultural features of locality (*Eretz Israel*) is made inconsequential by Paul. He also seems to portray Syria and Cilicia as a remote land, information about which is difficult to attain in the churches in Judaea (Gal. 1.21–23).[81]

---

77. One should note that the possibility of the widespread influence of the Decree was argued for by F.F. Bruce and most recently by M. Slee, who point out such references as Rev. 2.14, 20 and *Hist. Eccl.* 4.1.26 as evidences. F.F. Bruce, *Paul: Apostle of the Free Spirit* (Exeter: Paternoster Press, 1977), p. 186, note 31; Michelle Slee, *The Church in Antioch in the First Century* CE: *Communion and Conflict* (JSNTSup, 244; London and New York: T. & T. Clark/Continuum, 2003), p. 39. I should point out, however, that these texts most probably refer to the church's negative view on idolatry in general and may not be a direct reference to the Decree.

78. J.M. Scott, *Paul*, p. 158, note 111.

79. Though the agreement was not specifically on geographical demarcation (Gal. 2.7–8), James' understanding of *Eretz Israel* may have influenced his action.

80. Betz, *Galatians*, pp. 322–23.

81. As Bockmuehl understands the difference between James and Paul as 'halakhic' rather than as 'theological' (p. 79), their difference on the issue of *Eretz Israel* may have been 'halakhic', just as is observed in *m. Hal.* 4.7–8.

ii. *Mixed dining as a physio-cultural feature of commensality*
Modes of mixed dining in Jewish literature. Another physio-cultural feature to be considered is the issue of commensality, particularly inter-ethnic dining.[82] This discussion will consider the recent scholarly debate over the issue of the modality and extent of mixed dining.[83] Thanks to this debate, there has been a deepened understanding of the sensitivity surrounding the issue of mixed dining; however, Esler's point, especially on the basis of his social-scientific analysis, has not been carefully evaluated by his critics. A brief summary of the debate is given here which points out the implication for the present study. The fundamental question is whether Jews were able to have a 'mixed dining of the Eucharistic mode', which Esler understands to mean Jews passing around one bread and one cup of wine in a mixed group of Jews and non-Jews (cf. 1 Cor. 11.23–26). Esler differentiates this mode of mixed dining ('Eucharistic mode') from the 'parallel mode', in which Jews and non-Jews use separate vessels and consume separate meals and drink. Esler argues from 1 Corinthians 11 that the Eucharistic mode of mixed dining was being practised in Pauline churches, whereas it was not permissible among the Jews.[84]

Sanders argues on the general issue of Jewish association with Gentiles. In it, what appears to be a negative view toward the issue of Jewish association with Gentiles and of mixed dining both in the sources of the Second Temple and rabbinic periods assumes that Jews were associating with Gentiles (LXX Est. 4.17x; Tob. 1.11; Jdt. 10.5; 12.17–19; 2 Macc. 7.1–2).[85] Sanders understands the debate between Shammaites and Hillelites in *m. Pesah.* as one of degree of Gentile ritual impurity. According to Sanders, Shammaites consider such an association as akin to semen-impurity (impurity of one day, cf. Lev. 15.16–18) and Hillelites to grave-impurity ('like one who separates himself from the grave': impurity of one week) (*m. Pesah.* 8.8). Particularly in the Shammaites' understanding, that this kind of impurity is common in Jewish society is clear and it should not

---

82. As pointed out earlier, one of the most significant factors which bind people together as a distinct group (identity construction and maintenance) is said to be commensality. Cf. Manning Nash, *The Cauldron of Ethnicity in the Modern World* (Chicago and London: University of Chicago Press, 1989), pp. 10–11. Esler takes note of the importance of commensality in the maintenance of Jewish identity. Esler, *Community*, p. 76.

83. Of particular interest is the dialogue between the scholars below: James D.G. Dunn, *Jesus, Paul and the Law: Studies in Mark and Galatians* (Louisville: Westminster/John Knox, 1990), pp. 137–48; Esler, 'Making and Breaking'; idem, *Galatians*; Sanders, 'Jewish Association', pp. 170–88; Bockmuehl, *Jewish Law*.

84. Esler, *Galatians*, pp. 101–102.

85. Sanders, 'Jewish Association', p. 177. Sanders treats some evidence of exclusion as an extremists' approach (cf. *Jub.* 22.16; 'eat not with [Gentiles]', and *Jos. Asen.* 7.1; 'Joseph never ate with the Egyptians').

be understood by this that Jews did not therefore associate with Gentiles (*m. 'Abod. Zar.* 5.5).[86] Sanders concludes, on the issue of mixed dining, that Jews can share the meal table with Gentiles so long as Jews do not eat Gentile meat and drink Gentile wine, as they could be ceremonially impure.[87]

Esler argues that what is suggested by Sanders (and Murphy-O'Connor for that matter, i.e. the assumption of mixed dining) is a superficial mixed dining, or 'parallel meal' as Esler calls it, and that while such a mode of association may have been possible, in which Jews and Gentiles do not share meals and vessels, the Eucharistic mode of dining was not possible.[88] He argues that the references to mixed dining are of the parallel meal type (Jdt. 10.5; *m. 'Abod. Zar.* 5.5), and not the Eucharistic mode of dining, i.e. Jews sharing one bread and one cup of wine with Gentiles. Jdt. 10.5 is an example of how mixed dining may have been possible, but it is a parallel kind at best and cannot be considered a more

---

86. However, it should be noted that Sanders's interpretation of *m. Pesaḥ.* 8.8 should be reconsidered, as it may not refer to the Gentile problem of ritual impurity. In the Jewish literature, there is a development in inter-ethnic association. Büchler and Klawan suggest that the idea of Gentiles as ritually impure was not clearly spelled out until the rabbinic literature, well into the first century, and probably the second century. Cf. Adolf Büchler, 'The Levitical Impurity of the Gentile in Palestine Before the Year 70', *JQR* 17 (1926), pp. 1–81 (80); Jonathan Klawans, 'Notions of Gentile Impurity in Ancient Judaism', *Association for Jewish Studies Review* 20.2 (1995), pp. 285–312 (302). Recently, Hayes argued that the concern in the rabbinic debate is over what to do with a Gentile who is converted between the paschal sacrifice and its consumption, because solutions to such a special case is the larger context of the debate. Cf. Hayes, *Gentile Impurities*, pp. 113–22 for the full treatment of *m. Pesaḥ.* 8.8. Shammaites require only the bath of purification in order for the newly converted to partake of the paschal meal, as all Jews are required to bathe before partaking of the meal. Cf. Sanders, *Judaism: Practice and Belief*, p. 228. On the other hand, Hillelites require the second Passover for such a converted Gentile in the manner of a person whose relative dies (*onen*: mourner) between the paschal sacrifice and its consumption. Therefore, just as a mourner ('one who separates himself from the grave') requires the second Passover, a newly converted Gentile between the paschal sacrifice and its consumption may not partake of the paschal meal but observe the second Passover. The concern for inter-ethnic association is more apparent in *m. 'Abod. Zar.* 5.5 (or *t. 'Abod. Zar.* 4.6), where the issue seems to be the danger of unintended involvement in idolatry through association with Gentiles.

87. Sanders, 'Jewish Association', p. 178. Or more practically, Murphy-O'Connor suggests, 'all they [Gentiles] needed to do was to buy at a Jewish shop when they had Jewish guests and to accept the added expense'. Murphy-O'Connor, *Paul*, p. 151. Even in case of a stricter rule as found in *t. 'Abod. Zar.* 4.6, the debate over mixed dining usually takes for granted such a fellowship and focuses on the degree of association or separation between Jews and non-Jews. Sanders, 'Jewish Association', pp. 175–76. Cf. Bockmuehl, *Jewish Law*, pp. 58–59.

88. Esler, *Galatians*, p. 101.

integrated 'Eucharistic type' of dining.[89] *Mishnah 'Abod. Zar.* 5 warns of the danger of unintended idolatry through sharing a meal with Gentiles. R. Shimon in *t. 'Abod. Zar.* 4.6 even goes so far as to prohibit even the parallel mode of dining.

> R. Shimon ben Elazar says: Israelites outside the land worship idols in purity. How? If a non-Jew prepared a wedding feast for his son and sent out to invite all Jews in his town – even if they have food and drink of their own and have their own servant waiting at them, they worship idols. Thus it is said: '[... Lest you make a covenant ... when they sacrifice to their gods and] when one invites you, you eat of his sacrifice'.

Dunn, on the other hand, argues from a point of general correlation, stating that since Jews were able to associate with Gentiles in other modes of interaction such as sports and theatre, one could assume that Jews associated with Gentiles in 'table fellowship' as well (e.g., *Ant.* 2.39; *Vit. Mos.* 1.5.23–24).[90] Esler counters this logic on the basis of Barth's perspective of behaviours around the boundary line. That Jews were able to interact in sports and theatre does not necessarily mean that they were able to have mixed dining in the Eucharistic mode.[91] Indeed, Barth's transactional theory of ethnic identity prohibits this kind of 'generalization': *if other physio-cultural features are conceded the food issue must also be expected to be conceded.* Barth's description of an ethnic group's behaviour at the boundary line does not appear to concede to such a general (predictable) manner. In order to protect the core ethnic sentiment against the influence of other cultures, a group behaves in such a way as to allow some influences to enter and to reject others.[92] It so happened that for Jews participation in games and theatre was allowed, but intimate mixed dining was not allowed.[93]

Indeed, Barth's view of permeability at the ethnic boundary (Transactionalism) helps to avoid committing a simplistic correlation between different physio-cultural features, as Esler points out. At the same time, however, Barth's view does not guarantee that all Jews (Jewish communities with different peculiarities) approach the issue of mixed dining in exactly the same way. Though one is not to make a simplistic

---

89. On Judith's sensitivity to *kashrut*, see Moore, *Judith*, p. 201. However, she notes how the degree of sensitivity to *kashrut* differs from HB Esther 2.9, in which Esther is given by the king Ahasuerus 'a portion [of food]' (מנות). LXX Esther 4.17x says that she never ate at Haman's table or the king's feast nor drank the wine of libation, and therefore different views on inter-ethnic dining are observed.

90. Dunn, *Jesus, Paul and the Law*, p. 147.

91. Cf. Esler, *Galatians*, p. 100.

92. Barth, 'Introduction', p. 16. Note the coexistence of 'proscription' and 'prescription' in his description of boundary negotiation. Cf. Chapter 1 (section 2.c).

93. Esler, *Galatians*, p. 99.

general correlation as Esler rightly alerts against Dunn, the following comparative analysis may be helpful in understanding the sensitivity of the issue. A practice which probably touches the core ethnic sentiment as deeply, if not deeper, as inter-ethnic dining may rightly be the issue of mixed blood.[94] On this issue, Torah's prohibition of inter-ethnic marriage is limited to the high priest (Lev. 21.14–15) and the prohibition thereof for the ordinary priests was probably of a lesser degree (cf. Lev. 21.7) and even for ordinary Jews the prohibition is limited mostly to the seven Canaanite nations (Deut. 7.3–4; Exod. 34.15; Num. 31.15–17).[95] In the Second Temple period, we see varying views on the issue. On one hand, Ezra, Nehemiah, Jubilees and 4QMMT extend the prohibition to all Israel against all nations (Ezra 9.1–2; Neh. 13.23–27; *Jub.* 22, 30; 4QMMT B 75–82).[96] On the other hand, some groups of Diaspora Jews in Alexandria between the first century BCE and the first century CE are possibly represented by the view *Joseph and Aseneth* presents positively on the issue of inter-ethnic marriage (*Jos. Asen.* 20).[97] The relaxed view compared to the Ezran prohibition on intermarriage is observed in the rabbinic debate in *b. 'Abod. Zar.* 36b.[98] Various groups within Jewish society approach this important physio-cultural feature differently, but they are all bound under the same core ethnic sentiment.

Another issue which reflects Jewish identity is the issue of idolatry. The important point on the observation of the Jewish attitudes to gymnasium and theatre is not so much that they associated with Gentiles in those settings, but that it touches on the issue of idolatry. The Pentateuch clearly prohibits any practice of idolatry (cf. Exod. 34.17; Lev. 16.1; 19.4; Deut. 12.3). However, both Josephus and Philo seem to bypass the

---

94. Hayes seeks to understand Jews' identity in terms of purity, in which she classifies the concept of purity into ritual, moral and genealogical purities. Hayes, *Gentile Impurities*, pp. 7–8.

95. Cf. Shaye J.D. Cohen, 'From the Bible to the Talmud: The Prohibition of Intermarriage', *Hebrew Annual Review* 7 (1983), pp. 23–39; Louis Epstein, *Marriage Laws in the Bible and Talmud* (Cambridge: Harvard University Press, 1942), p. 158; Jacob Milgrom, *Leviticus 17–22* (AB, 3a; New York: Doubleday, 2000), pp. 1819–20.

96. Hayes sees two lines: (1) Priestly Code (*Josephus, Theodorus, Testament of Levi*) and (2) Holiness Code (Ezra, Jdt., *Jub.*, 4QMMT). Hayes, *Gentile Impurities*, p. 81. For the interpretation of 4QMMT, refer to Hayes, *Gentile Impurities*, pp. 82–91. Cf. Martha Himmelfarb, 'Levi, Phinehas, and the Problem of Intermarriage at the Time of the Maccabean Revolt', *Jewish Studies Quarterly* 6 (1999), pp. 17–23.

97. The provenance and date of the work has not been settled, but a rough estimation of Burchard is that it was written between 100 BC–100 CE in Alexandria. C. Burchard, 'Joseph and Aseneth', in *OTP*, II, pp. 187–88. However, see also Ross Shepard Kraemer, *When Aseneth Met Joseph* (Oxford and New York: Oxford University Press, 1998), pp. 3–16 for a considerably different view on the issue.

98. For the detailed interpretation of the debate, see Hayes, *Gentile Impurities*, pp. 148–57.

concern against idolatry when they hold the gymnasium education in a positive light (*Ant.* 2.39; *Vit. Mos.* 1.5.23–24). Jews in Alexandria were eager to receive a gymnasium education, probably because it was a prerequisite for obtaining citizenship (cf. *Leg. Gai.* 44.349).[99] This secular education involved pagan religious practices such as singing hymns to gods and making sacrifices, and the involvement in such a system certainly touches the Pentateuchal prohibition code.[100]

Various groups approach issues (physio-cultural features) which affect the Jews' identity (core ethnic sentiment) in different ways. As a result, they formed various sects, but still under the commonwealth of Israel,[101] or according to Cohen, within a community symbolically constructed.[102] We have already pointed out the examples of this phenomenon. Eleazer and Ananias, both being Jews, had different views on the conversion of Izates. The extent of *Eretz Israel* was understood differently among Jews. We may also add the case of Noachide regulations in that they were regarded by some Jews as a basis for condemning Gentiles while others regarded them as a criterion for acknowledging or affirming their righteous state (cf. *t. Sanh.* 13.2). Might it not then be possible to consider various Jewish groups approaching the issue of mixed dining in various ways, including possibly the intimate mode of mixed dining ('Eucharistic' mode)?

Most Jews were able to associate over a meal with Gentiles with certain restrictions that reflect their concern for purity. Two passages require consideration at this point. One is *Letter of Aristeas*, reference of which to inter-ethnic dining can either be a Eucharistic mode of dining or a parallel mode. The other is *Joseph and Aseneth*, which may refer to a case of Eucharistic mode of mixed dining. The case of *Letter of Aristeas* (181–84) was well defended by Esler as a parallel meal, so only two minor points will be noted. In the account, the chief steward Nicanor summoned Dorotheus to make sure that the meal would be prepared in accordance with Jewish custom. According to Sanders, mixed dining was feasible because the king ate the Jewish meal.[103] One concern is the process of

99. Feldman, *Jew and Gentile*, pp. 57–58.

100. Henri I. Marrou, *Histoire de l'Education dans l'Antiquit* (Paris: Editions du Seuil, 6th edn, 1965), pp. 179–80. Marrou points out that this type of procession was compulsory (by law) for the purpose of ensuring that the youth onform to public expectation with order and dignity. Cf. Edward N. Gardiner, *Athletics of the Ancient World* (Oxford: Oxford University Press, 1930), p. 22. Babylonian Talmud forbids participation in the athletic events at the gymnasium (*b. 'Abod. Zar.* 18b).

101. Hayes, *Gentile Impurities*, pp. 13, 90, 197–98.

102. A.P. Cohen, *The Symbolic Construction*, pp. 14, 20.

103. Sanders, 'Jewish Association', p. 178.

meal production. While Esler suggests that Dorotheus and all the other kitchen staff were Jews,[104] one cannot be definite on this point because the text is not clear whether the kitchen staff may all have been Jews. Another concern is on the mode of dining. Esler points out that the king was reclining on his own couch (183), therefore there was no contiguity between him and Jews.[105] While reclining on a separate couch does not necessarily prohibit sharing the same meal, the implication found in the pericope (vv. 181–84) is that sharing a meal with Jews requires special attention.

One other passage to be considered is found in the description of a feast in *Joseph and Aseneth*. Earlier, in 7.1, it says, 'And Joseph entered the house of Pentephres and sat upon the throne. And they washed his feet and *set a table before him* by itself, because *Joseph never ate with the Egyptians*' (emphases added). Even though the author takes care to point out that Joseph never dined with the Egyptians, he ate the meal prepared at the house of Pentephres. Moreover, later in 20.5–8, the family of Aseneth entered and together with Joseph, '... they ate and drank (and celebrated)' (v. 8). There is no mention of elaborate meal preparation according to Jewish custom, nor is a separate or parallel kind of feast mentioned (cf. also 21.8 for the royal wedding feast). The longer text of the same verse gives the appearance that Aseneth's parents devoted themselves to Joseph's God as they 'glorified God (who gives life to the dead)'.[106] There are two points to be made about this description. One is that there is no way to know whether they became 'Jews', especially Pentephres, through circumcision, or remained sympathizers. Also of note is the general tendency of the longer Text-group (d) to resolve anomalies and clarify ambiguities.[107] It may be that the shorter Text-groups and the longer Text-group represent varying views on the particular point of mixed dining. While the book is inconsistent on the issue of mixed dining, as noted, these passages may describe daily association between Jews and Gentiles, at least as it occurred in some local communities.

From the discussion on the issue of mixed dining outlined above, it seems that some kind of mixed dining was done between most Jews and Gentiles despite such a strict view on mixed dining portrayed in *t. 'Abod. Zar.* 4.6. There is evidence that permits a 'parallel mode' of mixed dining (*m. 'Abod. Zar.* 5.5) and there seems to be some evidence that might suggest at least isolated cases of intimate dining between Jews and

---

104. Esler suggests that Dorotheus may have been a popular name among the Egyptian Jews and it may have been a custom for one in a position to bring in relatives to provide for them a job. Esler, *Galatians*, p. 114; Bockmuehl, *Jewish Law*, p. 58, note 37.

105. Esler, *Galatians*, p. 114.

106. Burchard, 'Joseph and Aseneth', p. 234.

107. Kraemer, *Aseneth*, pp. 50, 76.

Gentiles (equivalent to the Eucharistic mode of dining, *Jos. Asen.* 20.8, cf. HB Est. 2.9). While such a Eucharistic mode of mixed dining was usually avoided among many Jewish groups, this does not exclude the possibility (even as an exceptional case) of some Jewish groups or individuals who considered amongst themselves that such an intimate mixed dining was at one time or another possible without necessarily obliterating their core ethnic sentiment. Therefore, the reality of the Jewish commonwealth may be that different groups of Jews approached the same physio-cultural feature (mixed dining) differently and remained within the same ethnic commonwealth, just as in the other cases of physio-cultural features such as intermarriage and attendance at the gymnasium.[108] However, the group or individuals with a relaxed view on the issue of commensality among others may have expected warning and criticism at times by those other groups who held more strict views on the issue (Tob. 1.11; Jdt. 10.5; 12.17–19; *t. 'Abod. Zar.* 4.5).[109] Therefore, when some Jews in a church in Antioch, for example, entertained the possibility of a Eucharistic type of mixed dining with Gentiles, the sense of deracination that the Jews would feel from the larger Jewish population varied according to one's previous approach to such an issue, but they all would expect some degree of social pressure from the larger Jewish population based upon stricter views on the particular physio-cultural feature, especially when an anti-imperial ethnic fervour was rising among Jews as a reaction to the threat to their identity.[110]

Conflict over mixed dining. The Eucharistic mode of communal dining certainly accords with Paul's instrumental approach to his Gentile mission.[111] However, to conclude that this highly integrated mode of communal dining was the norm of the Antioch Church, one may have to over-emphasize Paul's influence in the community. The available sources on the emergence of the Antiochean church do not support such an assumption. In it, the original focus in founding the church was on the Jewish people and it subsequently extended its mission to the Gentiles (Acts 11.19–26). Paul was not a founding leader in the church, though he might have been a welcome addition to the ministry (Acts 11.25–26). That the Jewish segment of the church finally sided with Peter instead of Paul

108. Note that this is quite different from Dunn's correlation that we observed earlier.

109. When one suggests that impurity through association with Gentiles was not a serious concern for Jews including Pharisees (Sanders, 'Jewish Association', pp. 175–76), that monolithic view may overlook regulations concerning *'am ha'aretz* (m. *Dem.* 2.3; 6.6; b. *Šabb.* 15a; b. *Ḥag.* 22a). Cf. Hayes, *Gentile Impurities*, p. 266, note 95. Sanders's view on this issue may be related to his conclusion that the issue of Gentile purity lacks clarity. Cf. Sanders, *Judaism: Practice & Belief*, pp. 72–76.

110. Murphy-O'Connor, *Paul*, pp. 139–41.

111. Esler, *Galatians*, pp. 101–102.

(Gal. 2.13) may indicate that Paul's ideology did not necessarily represent the whole Antiochean church.[112] Nevertheless, the church in Antioch directly faced the issue of inter-ethnic association because of the undeniable presence of Gentile believers in the community, and the assumption can be made that the ethos of the community was such that it allowed more room for ethnic integration than in Jerusalem.[113] In light of the mode of inter-ethnic dining, therefore, I suggest that a form of parallel dining was being practised in the Antiochean church,[114] and the most separatist mode of communal dining was a foreign idea occasioned by the visit of 'certain people from James' (τινας ἀπὸ Ἰακώβου, Gal. 2.12).

At this point, a correlation of the ongoing discussion of identity construction with available historical data may be helpful. What might be the 'fear' of the Jews (Gal. 2.12), which consequently led to a division in the Antioch church? What was the 'fearful' pressure of the Jews that moved James, Peter and eventually all the Jewish segment of the church in Antioch to isolate its Gentile constituents? Schmithals suggests that the fear of the Jews in v. 12 relates to the recent persecution of the churches in Judaea under the reign of Agrippa I, which led to the killing of James the son of Zebedee, the arrest of Peter (Acts 12.2–3), and eventually the execution of James the Just as well.[115] Paul's own account of the persecution of the churches in Judaea by Ἰουδαίοι (1 Thess. 2.14–16) may refer to this time of adversity that the Jerusalem church experienced.[116] Under the reign of Agrippa I (41–44 CE), who sought to maintain good terms with the ruling class of Judaea (cf. *Ant.* 19.229–334), there may have

112. A suggestion was recently made by Slee, however, that the 'Law-free' approach to Gentile mission originated from the Hellenist church members in Antioch, who migrated from Jerusalem because of the persecution caused by the dispute between them and the Hebraists concerning the rightful mode of communal dining. Slee, *The Church in Antioch*, p. 23. Her attempt to extract the issue of communal dining out of the Acts' accounts of the selection of the seven (Acts 6.1–7), Stephen's martyrdom and the subsequent persecution in Jerusalem (7.54–8.3) and the aftermath of the Petrine mission in Caesarea (11.1–18, 19) is very insightful, yet it begs some questions. Why then did the Jerusalem leaders accept the Antiochean approach to Gentile incorporation presented by Paul and his companions (Gal. 2.1–10) if their stricter view caused the Hellenists to seek refuge in Antioch? One may wonder how extensive Paul's 'success' in mission was, which Slee argues to have caused the Jerusalem leaders to reconsider their earlier position on communal dining (p. 37). Again, if the break between Hebraists and Hellenists had already been so sharp in Jerusalem earlier, one may wonder why the Antiochean church members, who were so integrated as to engage in the Eucharistic mode of communal dining, became persuaded by the Jerusalem delegates against Paul, their own delegate.

113. Feldtkeller, *Identitätssuche*, p. 138.

114. Cf. Sanders, 'Jewish Association', p. 178; Murphy-O'Connor, *Paul*, p. 151.

115. Schmithals, *Paulus und Jakobus*, p. 55.

116. F.F. Bruce, *1 and 2 Thessalonians* (WBC, 45; Waco: WBP, 1982), pp. 45–46; Charles A. Wanamaker, *The Epistles to the Thessalonians* (NIGTC; Grand Rapids: Eerdmans, 1990), p. 113.

been increased pressure upon the Jerusalem church to show allegiance to the national institutions.[117] On the other hand, noting the accounts of Josephus on a series of 'zealotic' activities, it has been suggested that the persecutions (Gal. 5.11; 6.12) and this threat (Gal. 2.12) relate to the activity of 'Zealots' (*Ant.* 20.113–17, 118–20).[118] Whether such isolated incidents of fundamentalists can be directly connected to Paul and his mission is questionable. However, the general anti-imperial ethnic fervour under the reign of Claudius (41–54 CE) should be worth noting as a political background to the incident in Antioch.[119] These ethnic (and political) issues may well be behind the concern related to Peter via James' delegates, and the rather integrated mode of inter-ethnic association, perhaps demonstrated somehow in their mode of communal dining through a parallel mode, may have become problematic.

Again, Paul is ambiguous as to what exactly James communicated to Peter, which caused the division in Antioch. With the general historical and political situation of Palestine suggested above in mind, scholars have suggested a number of scenarios. Schmithals argues that for the fear of Jewish persecution of the Judaean churches, James urged Peter to keep a distance in his fellowship with Gentile believers. Peter went too far to 'judaize' the Gentiles, i.e. 'indirectly compel' Gentiles to observe the Torah.[120] For a similar reason, Bockmuehl recently argued that James urged Peter and other Jews to take care to live the Jewish life, as in the Holy Land. Then, Peter and the rest over-reacted and parted company

---

117. Cf. Hengel and Schwemer, *Paulus*, pp. 387–89; Mason, *Josephus and the New Testament*, p. 163.

118. Jewett, 'The Agitators', pp. 204–206.

119. Murphy-O'Connor, *Paul*, pp. 139–41, 151. Taking up on Klinghardt's analysis of the prohibitions of the Apostolic decrees (Acts 15), the breach of which results in 'extermination' in Lev. 17–18, Theißen suggests that the Jerusalem leaders may have demanded that Gentile members observe the particular ban for fear of the fundamentalistic currents among the Jews. This may be behind the 'fear' (*Ausrottungsandrohung*) of the circumcision (Jews). Theißen, *Die Religion*, p. 348, note 9. Cf. Matthias Klinghardt, *Gesetz und Volk Gottes: Das lukanische Verständnis des Gesetzes nach Herkunft, Funktion und seinem Ort in der Geschichte des Urchristentums* (WUNT, 2.32; Tübingen: Mohr, 1988), pp. 204–206.

120. Schmithals, *Paulus und Jakobus*, pp. 55–57. Schmithals suggests further that the Jerusalem church's close connection with Paul, against whom the legal proceedings might have been taken, would inflict a persecution of the Jews against the church (p. 82). Haenchen's view is closer to this. He argues that Paul's apprehensiveness as to whether the Jerusalem church would receive the contribution may be due to the 'fear' that the acceptance of the contribution would mean to the Jews a close connection of the church with Paul (cf. Rom. 15.31, ἡ διακονία μου ἡ εἰς Ἰερουσαλὴμ εὐπρόσδεκτος τοῖς ἁγίοις γένηται). Haenchen, *Apostelgeschichte*, p. 544.

with the Gentile segment of the church.[121] Murphy-O'Connor argues that for the 'nationalistic' concern in Judaea, James insisted on the observance of dietary regulations for the Jews of the church, which made them doubt whether the food prepared by Gentile believers would meet the purity standard of the Jews.[122] Because of Paul's ambiguity, one cannot be certain as to what exactly James communicated to Peter and how Peter responded to it. All of the above hypotheses are plausible concerns of James and possible reactions of Peter and the rest of the Jewish members of the church. The experience in Antioch made Paul realize, if he had not done so earlier, that so long as the core ethnic sentiment was the foundation of the community–identity, it would manifest itself in ethnic-related problems, such as the division of the community in Antioch. This realization may have caused Paul to resort to a harsher rhetoric against such an approach to community–identity construction. Therefore, Paul's accusation of Peter, 'how can you compel the Gentiles to live like Jews? (ἀναγκάζεις ἰουδαΐζειν;)' (v. 14), while admitting the ambiguity as to what exactly 'compel to live like Jews' might mean,[123] communicates primarily the grave effect of a community construction based upon the core ethnic sentiment. This very concern makes the connection between the conflicts in Jerusalem and Antioch and the current problem in the Galatian community. Therefore, Paul's retrospective interpretation functions favourably for him to persuade the Galatian members to remain with him and in the community, whose identity is constructed free from Jewish ethnic concern.

If the church in Antioch had been practising the parallel mode of communal dining before the incident, the incident itself may have been the very occasion when Paul began to seek a new and highly ethnically-integrated mode of communal dining, the idea of which is reflected in 1

---

121. Bockmuehl, *Jewish Law*, pp. 72–73. He points out that James' concern was for Jewish behaviour and not for Gentile behaviour, and that it was not necessarily about food. However, the concern for Jewish behaviour must have been at least partly in relation to non-Jews.

122. Murphy-O'Connor, *Paul*, p. 151. He assumes here a parallel mode of dining.

123. Robinson notes the coexistence of 'the truth of the gospel' and ἀναγκάζω in both Gal. 2.5 and 2.14. D.W.B. Robinson, 'The Circumcision of Titus, and Paul's "Liberty," ' *Australian Biblical Review* 12 (1964), pp. 24–42. Esler, based upon this correlation, understands the content of Peter's 'judaizing' influence to be the rite of circumcision. Esler, *Galatians*, p. 137. Cf. Schmithals, *Paulus und Jakobus*, pp. 55–57. Gutrod gives basically two definitions to the term ἰουδαΐζειν: (1) to convert to Judaism through circumcision (LXX Est. 8.17) and (2) to adopt Jewish customs. Here again, various stages of Gentile incorporation into the Jewish commonwealth are found. Walter Gutrod, ' ἰουδαΐζειν', in Gerhard Friedrich (ed.), *Theological Dictionary of the New Testament* (trans. Geoffrey W. Bromiley; 10 vols.; Grand Rapids: Eerdmans, 1965), III, pp. 369–391). So also is the accusation that Peter lived like a Gentile (ἐθνικῶς καὶ οὐχὶ ἰουδαϊκῶς ζῇς) ambiguous. Haenchen understands it to be the earlier behaviour of mixed dining. Haenchen, 'Petrus-Problem', p. 196.

Corinthians – Jews and non-Jews sharing one bread and one cup (10.16–17; cf. 11.17–34).[124] This intensification of Paul's instrumental tendency, however, seemed to wane as the intensely instrumental mode of his Gentile mission faced the difficult reality of inter-ethnic 'cohabitation'. Therefore, 1 Corinthians speaks of the difficulty in dealing with inter-ethnic dining (8.4–13) even while pointing out the significance of the eucharistic meal that symbolizes the unity of the community (10.16–17). Furthermore, the instructions concerning a selective diet in the letter to the Romans may imply selective (or the parallel mode of) dining in the context of meal 'fellowship' (Rom. 14.1–3).[125] In it, Paul had to deal with the problem of division on the basis of the injunction against idolatry commonly held but manifested differently between Jewish and Gentile community members. While the discussion on this shift in Paul's instrumental tendency in the latter Pauline letters is beyond the scope of the present study,[126] it appears to be instructive for the present study to refer to the shift briefly for at least two reasons. First, it suggests the general direction of the formation of community–identity that the Pauline mission began to take. Second, it infers how the Jewish ethnic concerns may have contributed to directing the course of community–identity construction in the Pauline churches, thus consequently affecting the identity of the church as a whole in the earliest time of its development.

3. *Conflicts as the Context of Community–Identity Construction*

The difference in the approach to community–identity construction between the Jerusalem apostles and Paul was so great that the demarcation between the mission to Gentiles by Paul and the mission to Jews by the Jerusalem apostles had to finally result. Realizing that it was not possible to attain unity without compromising his approach to community–identity construction (instrumental mode), Paul sought to attain unity within his own mission among the Gentiles.

The account of the Antioch incident according to Paul is paradigmatic for the understanding of the Christian religion in one important respect: community construction on the basis of a core ethnic sentiment would not work because its effect was at best to make Gentile community members

---

124. Cf. Esler, *Galatians*, p. 108.

125. Bockmuehl, *Jewish Law*, p. 58. Probably for the most part, ὁ δὲ ἀσθενῶν λάχανα ἐσθίει implies Jewish Christians and the following ὁ ἐσθίων Gentile Christians in the church (Rom. 14.2–3). Cf. Joseph A. Fitzmyer, *Romans* (AB, 33; New York: Doubleday, 1993), pp. 686–89.

126. Though from a different angle, this 'shift' (or development) in Paul's thought is lucidly explained by Rowland. Christopher Rowland, *Radical Christianity: A Reading of Recovery* (Cambridge: Polity Press, 1988), pp. 34–41.

second-class citizens and to exclude those members who were uncircumcised from the people of God as a secondary attachment of sympathizers. Paul's understanding of the unity of God's people on the basis of his revelatory experience sought abandonment of the community–identity construction based upon a core ethnic sentiment as theologically and ethically inadequate as a way of expressing unity within the church. Negotiations at ethnic boundaries always presupposed a core commitment to cultural values and behaviours which resulted in marginalizing Gentile believers as second-class citizens. The Antioch incident, which resulted in what was believed to be the marginalization of Gentile members of the church, is to Paul an epitome of the incoherence of community–identity construction based upon a core ethnic sentiment. This proves to the Galatian members that Paul's approach to community–identity construction, which is free from such a constraint of a core ethnic sentiment, is the only legitimate mode of mission and that they should remain in a community built on such a mode of mission.

Now that the context of identity construction within the Galatian community has been delineated, I would like to discuss in the remaining chapters the patterns or actual ways in which the identity of the Galatian community was constructed.

Part III

PATTERNS OF COMMUNITY–IDENTITY CONSTRUCTION IN THE GALATIAN COMMUNITY

'And do not keep your fasts with the hypocrites. For they fast on Monday and Thursday; but you should fast on Wednesday and Friday' (Didache 8.1).

For an outside observer, the difference is merely on days of a week when the dietary custom, commonly practised in many religions, should be observed. However, what seems to be a childish grumbling is found in *Didache* as a rhetoric to underscore for the insiders the distinction between Jewish and Christian identities. We have already been reminded that such a mundane aspect of our lives as meal fellowship and such a peripheral sign as circumcision were also foci of a heated disputation on identity. They are manifestations of materiality of religion, i.e. aspects of religious experience that are present in a given community to be seen, heard and/or touched. I suggested in the Introduction that materiality of religion is as important a locus of identity to be studied as ideology or the cognitive aspect of religion. With the understanding of Paul's approach to community–identity construction delineated in the previous chapters in Part II, the focus of Part III will be the patterns or actual practices of community–identity construction. I will start with the cognitive aspect of religion. This aspect is in effect the internal logic for aspects of materiality of religion to function as a locus of identity, which is the focus of the subsequent discussion.

Therefore in the sixth chapter, I will consider Paul's conceptual foundation of the Galatians' identity (recreated worldview) by seeking to understand Paul's exposition of the Abrahamic inheritance and salvation history in Galatians 3 and 4, but particularly 4.21–31. In the seventh chapter, a suggestion will be made that the rite of baptism with its formula (Gal. 3.28) is a significant identity-marking event for the community by materializing or acting out the recreated worldview, which is delineated in the previous chapter. The final chapter will consider the function of the physical form of the letter ('physico–documentary dimension') and postulate that the communal possession of such a religious writing may have helped construct and consolidate the identity of the community in Galatia.

Chapter 6

THE RECREATION OF WORLDVIEW (GALATIANS 4.21–31): REMAKING
THE TRADITION OF ABRAHAMIC INHERITANCE

In this chapter, I will discuss how Paul may have provided for the
Galatian community members a conceptual foundation of their community–identity. It will be suggested that Paul did this by recreating the
worldview or remaking the tradition of Abrahamic inheritance and
offering it to the Galatians as a positive identity of their own,[1] so that they
could remain in the community as the founder envisioned, despite the
pressure and persuasion of circumcisers. Paul's recreation of worldview is
not necessarily confined to this short pericope (Gal. 4.21–31). In fact, this
pericope is a part of the whole recreation outlined in the larger section of
Gal. 3.1–4.31.[2] However, this chapter's focus is on the short pericope,
because it shows the most peculiar and creative presentation of the new
worldview.

   As the concept of 'recreated worldview' is employed in this chapter, it is
to understand the pericope (Gal. 4.21–31) on the basis of Turner's social
process theory. In the Introduction, the basic theory of Turner's liminal
process was outlined. I will review the concept of liminality and the
liminal response of 'recreated worldview' at this point as I apply them to
the text. A feature of a liminality is an antithetical recreation of the world
against structure (in this case the mother religion of 'Judaism'), in which
values and orders are either temporarily or permanently reversed.
Therefore, the newly recreated world manifests anti-structural equality
(contra inequality), simplicity (contra complexity), transience (contra
stability) and un-convention (contra convention).[3] In considering Paul's
mission as a newly emerging entity out of the conventional structure of the

---

1. Cf. Watson, *Paul*, pp. 61–72. Watson takes a social-scientific approach and suggests a
sectarian reactive interpretation (Denunciation – Antithesis – Reinterpretation) of Paul's
teaching on the Torah in Galatians.
   2. With the notable exception of Esler's structural outline, there is a consensus of this
general outline. Refer to the subsequent argument (1.a). Cf. Esler, *Galatians*, p. 204.
   3. Cf. Turner, *The Ritual Process*, pp. 106–107. See Chapter 1 (§3), for further
explanation. As briefly noted earlier, Strecker understands Paul as a 'liminal person'
(*Schwellenperson*) and his theology as a liminal theology. Strecker, *Die liminale Theologie*, p.
111.

mother religion of 'Judaism' in general, one may be able to understand his persuasion in the letter as his recreation of worldview, which challenges the external categorization that uncircumcised Gentile believers as such are a secondary entity or 'second-class citizens' in relation to the authentic believers based upon the physio-cultural features (for example, circumcision) that represent the core ethnic sentiment, in order to offer a positive identity and cohesion to the members in the liminal state.[4]

For this discussion on the patterns of community–identity construction, I will first set the present pericope (Gal. 4.21–31) in the wider context of recreation of worldview observed in the entire 'theoretical section' of Gal. 3.1–4.31. Second, I will evaluate the 'reactive perspective' (i.e. 'mirror-reading'), which is often presupposed in the interpretation of the pericope. It will be argued that, while the thoughts of the circumcisers are reflected in the epistle in general and in the pericope in particular and their thoughts might have somehow influenced the way Paul seeks to make himself understood in his persuasion, Paul has his own purpose for introducing his version of salvation history or 'recreated' tradition of Abrahamic heirship. Third, qualification will be made to the correlation between Paul and Uchimura before seeking to interpret the text with the help of the analogies from Uchimura's Mukyokai. This qualification will point out the difference in cultural positions, i.e. positions in relation to the culture where the religion starts to take root might have affected the way each person recreated the worldview. This discussion will lead to a suggestion on the basis of Gal. 4.8–10 that the Galatian members may have been engaged in a form of indigenization. Finally, I will seek to interpret the pericope (Gal. 4.21–31) on the basis of the interpretive framework of 'recreation of worldview' suggested above. The interpretation of the pericope will actively seek to employ analogical comparative analysis with the case of Mukyokai's emergence situation, which was oulined earlier in the second chapter.

1. *Scheme of Recreation of Worldview*

a. *The Remaking of Abrahamic Tradition in Wider Context (Galatians 3 and 4)*
It was assumed earlier that Gal. 4.21–31 is a part of the whole recreation of tradition that Paul presents in the larger pericope Gal. 3.1–4.31. Betz, in his analysis based upon the rhetorical conventions, places Gal. 4.21–31

---

4. For further explanation of the theoretical framework of community–identity construction, refer to Chapter 1. The following chapter will make a further correlation between the Galatian community and Turner's liminal state for the purpose of understanding the functions of rituals. Cf. also Jenkins, *Social Identity*, p. 77; A.P. Cohen, *The Symbolic Construction*, pp. 37, 44.

as the last of the six arguments or proofs (Gal. 3.1–4.31) for the preceding summary of the arguments (Gal. 2.15–21), which are then followed by the exhortation section (Gal. 5.1–6.10).[5] A short pericope interrupts the flow of thought by departing temporarily from the theme of Abraham's heirship (Gal. 4.12–20). This apparent interruption causes some to suggest that the section of argument ends at Gal. 4.11 and the section of exhortation begins at Gal. 4.12.[6] However, this outline does not explain well what the role of the pericope (Gal. 4.21–31) might be within the section of exhortation. One may well understand that the temporary interruption was caused by a sudden swell of emotion,[7] or rather that such an emotive persuasion may have been consciously inserted by Paul to strengthen his case.[8]

These two chapters will be briefly surveyed, in order to locate Gal 4.21–31 as the finale of Paul's attempt to recreate the tradition.[9] It has been suggested that the theme or question as to who the authentic heirs of Abraham are runs through Galatians 3–4.[10] Terms related to the idea of inheritance are plentiful in this long section (κληρονόμος/κληρονομία/κληρονομέω) in Gal. 3.18, 29; 4.1, 7, 30; σπέρμα in 3.16, 19, 29; υἱοθεσία in 4.5; υἱός in 3.7, 26; 4.6, 7, 22; cf. ἐπαγγελία/ἐπαγγέλλω in 3.14, 16, 17, 18, 19, 21, 22, 29; 4.23).

Particularly in Gal. 3.6–14, the schemes of inheritance are found both for Gentiles and for Jews. Abraham and the Gentiles are found to be related through their faith in God. The blessing of God given to Abraham is inherited by Gentiles who share the same faith with Abraham (Gal. 3.6–9). This is the content of the 'gospel' announced (προευηγγελίσατο) to Abraham (Gal. 3.8). Unlike the Gentiles, the inheritance scheme for the Jews ('those who rely on the works of the law', 3.10) is introduced rather negatively (Gal. 3.10–12). In this exposition, Abraham's personal faith in God becomes the focal point for Paul, and he presents a very

5.   Cf. Betz, *Galatians*, p. 128. In a slightly different manner, both Bruce and Dunn see the cohesion from Gal. 3 to the end of Gal. 4. Bruce, *Galatians*, p. 214; Dunn, *Epistle to the Galatians*, p. 243.

6.   Longenecker, *Galatians*, p. 186. Esler places 4.21–5.1 as a part of the following section of exhortation because of the thematic closeness with the following thought (5.2–6.10). Esler, *Galatians*, p. 204.

7.   Burton, *Galatians*, p. 235.

8.   Betz, *Galatians*, pp. 220–21.

9.   For an extended observation of Paul's remaking (or in his term, 'redefining'), see Barclay, *Obeying the Truth*, pp. 86–96.

10.   Mußner, *Der Galaterbrief*, p. 216; Watson, *Paul*, p. 70; Bernard H. Brinsmead, *Galatians: Dialogical Response to Opponents* (SBLDS, 65; Chico: Scholars, 1982), pp. 83–84.

strict view of Torah obedience in order to argue for its impossibility.[11] In verse 11, Paul quotes from Habakkuk 2.4. The MT is ambiguous as to whose faith(fulness) is meant: וצדיק באמונתו יחיה (the righteous one will live by *his* faith/faithfulness). Manuscripts of the LXX have two different readings: ὁ δίκαιος ἐκ πίστεώς μου ζήσεται (the righteous one will live on the basis of my [God's] faithfulness) or ὁ δίκαιος μου ἐκ πίστεως ζήσεται (in the case of *Codex Alexandrinus*: my [God's] righteous one will live on the basis of faith/faithfulness). In either case, the context of Habakkuk requires a patient trust under the oppression of enemies until God's vindication is brought forth. Thus, one who trusts will be vindicated. Paul's rendition reflects an intention to highlight 'personal faith' as opposed to obedience to the Torah as the requirement for 'righteousness' (δικαιοῦται, v. 11); thus, ὁ δίκαιος ἐκ πίστεως ζήσεται. The plight of the Jews under the Torah is highlighted through the editing of Deut. 27.26 (plus 28.58) on Paul's part. While the MT says דברי התורה הזאת, 'the words of this law' (most probably referring to the Dodecalogue), the LXX translates with an additional emphasis as πᾶσιν τοῖς λόγοις τοῦ νόμου τούτου, '*all* the words of this law'. Paul emphasizes further the extent of obedience by saying πᾶσιν τοῖς γεγραμμένοις ἐν τῷ βιβλίῳ τοῦ νόμου, 'everything written in the book of the Law'. The conclusion is that Jews are under a curse because they are under the obligations of the Torah.

Elsewhere, Paul disregards the context of God's covenant-giving with the people of Israel and focuses on the singular aspect of the noun σπέρμα to make Christ the sole and immediate heir of Abraham (3.16).[12] By making Christ the sole seed (σπέρμα) of Abraham (Gal. 3.16), Paul is able to bypass the period of the Torah (Gal. 3.17–22). The result is a direct connection between Abraham and those who believe (both Gentiles and Jews) through faith in Christ instead of through Torah regulations. Therefore, Paul reconfirms that all who believe in Christ are heirs of

---

11. As observed in the Introduction, the scholarly understanding of the nomistic system of Judaism in general gradually shifted in the last century. Sanders, in his *Paul and Palestinian Judaism*, suggests that in what he calls 'covenantal nomism' the obedience to the Torah is a matter of maintenance of the covenant membership and the covenant restoration is provided in the nomistic system (p. 422). Though minor modifications have been suggested for the last 25 years, this view is widely accepted as the general picture of the nomistic system with which Paul was familiar. Therefore, the nomistic system that Paul presents and criticizes here is a stereotypical description of the Torah system for the purpose of making a clear distinction between it and Paul's approach to the Gentile incorporation based upon faith in Christ. Cf. Esler, *Galatians*, pp. 55–56.

12. Cf. Gen. 13.15–16 where σπέρμα is described as countless (cf. Gen. 17.8). Later, Paul moves from this peculiar interpretation of σπέρμα to a rather conventional understanding of it (cf. Rom. 4.16–17). Cf. G. Quell and S. Schulz, 'σπέρμα', in Gerhard Friedrich (ed.), *Theological Dictionary of the New Testament* (trans. Geoffrey W. Bromiley; 10 vols.; Grand Rapids: Eerdmans, 1971), VII, pp. 536–38.

Abraham (Gal. 3.29). In recreating the worldview, Paul consciously eliminates Torah obedience from the inheritance scheme. Therefore, obedience to the Torah and faith in Christ are repeatedly set in antithetical relation to one another (Gal. 3.1, 5; cf. 2.16, 21). Elsewhere, the Torah is depicted as a secondary insertion between the tight relationship (covenant connection) of Abraham and Christ (3.15–18; cf. 3.19–20). The indirect reception of the Torah is emphasized, as opposed to the direct reception of the promise (Gal. 3.19–20).[13] Though Paul quickly qualifies that the Torah is not opposed to the promise of God, he immediately shifts the audience's attention to its inability to bring righteousness (Gal. 3.21). And finally, the Torah is depicted as being equal to enslaving principles (τὰ στοιχεῖα τοῦ κόσμου, Gal. 4.3; cf. 4.9).[14]

In what is often regarded as the theoretical section, Paul offers the Galatian members a new worldview, in which the understanding of salvation history is recreated. The Torah is given a secondary place at best, and the Gentiles and Abraham, the patriarch, are connected directly on account of faith in God, without the requirements of the Torah. This is again by focusing on Abraham's faith in Genesis 15 and neglecting the covenant regulations in Genesis 17. In this new worldview, the status of those not under the Torah and those under it are reversed and consequently the Galatian members are given the *raison d'être* of their fledgling and marginalized community.

The highly peculiar nature of the exposition of the Sarah-Hagar story in 4.21–31 has been noted by many. It is found 'forced',[15] 'strange and an arbitrary exegesis',[16] or 'strained and distorted in an unconvincing but highly Rabbinic fashion'.[17] While Paul follows the Jewish tendency of interpretation which paints a gravely negative view of Hagar, he departs widely from conventional expectation as he connects Hagar with Mt. Sinai, implying the denunciation of the Torah (Gal. 4.26, 30).[18] It indeed betrays the natural reading of the story concerning the heirship of Abraham in relation to Sarah and Hagar, narrated particularly in Gen. 16–17. By this unique exposition on the narrative of Abraham's heirship, the status of those not under the Torah and those under it are reversed. Therefore, we see that Paul's effort at recreation of worldview is carried on in Gal. 4.21–31. This unique exposition, with the final imperative to

---

13. Betz, *Galatians*, pp. 170–72; Wright, *The Climax of the Covenant*, pp. 169–70.

14. Feldtkeller understands that in Gal. 4.1–7 Paul urges the Gentile members to 'intensify' their commitment to Christ over against the elemental spirits and the Jews against the Torah. Feldtkeller, *Identitätssuche*, p. 46.

15. Dunn, *Galatians*, p. 243.

16. Barclay, *Obeying the Truth*, p. 91.

17. R.P.C. Hanson, *Allegory and Event: A Study of the Sources and Significance of Origen's Interpretation of Scripture* (London: SCM, 1959), p. 82.

18. The interpretation of Hagar and Ishmael will be dealt with later in this chapter.

exclude those under the Torah (Gal. 4.30), may serve as a finale of Paul's presentation of the recreated worldview.

b. *The Remaking of Tradition (Galatians 4.21–31): Active Recreation or Passive Response?*
The unique and seemingly rather artificial exposition on the narrative of Abraham's heirship in Gal. 4.21–31 causes some to conclude that the peculiarity is best understood as a response to the message of the circumcisers based upon the Genesis story, which in this section is called 'reactive approach'.[19] It is evident that Paul assumed the influence of circumcisers among the members of his community in Galatia (cf. Gal. 3.1–5; 4.21). Therefore, it is admittedly helpful at times to apply with caution the mirror-reading technique or reactive approach in interpreting the text.[20] However, the reactive approach sometimes leads to a view that seems to undermine Paul's clear intention in building up the community. Therefore, three examples of a typically reactive approach will be briefly evaluated to conclude that the pericope should be understood as reflecting Paul's clear intention to construct a positive identity of the community rather than simply reacting to circumcisers' claims.

It is argued that the introduction of two covenants (Gal. 4.24) is forced by the message of the circumcisers, for Paul himself sees the covenant to be one (Gal. 3.16).[21] However, Paul is quite capable of saying that there is only one gospel (Gal. 1.6–7), and referring to the gospel for the uncircumcised and the gospel of the circumcised (Gal. 2.7). The introduction of the two covenants may well be the occasion to firmly establish the distinction between the two approaches to Gentile incorporation, which Paul began to introduce in his retrospective interpretation of history in Galatians 2.[22]

It is also suggested that the entire discussion on the Abrahamic inheritance is conditioned by the message of the circumcisers and that Paul is not interested in the subject himself.[23] In fact, in Paul's exposition of the Sarah-Hagar story, Abraham appears only once, at the outset. In

---

19.   Martyn, *Galatians*, pp. 302–306 under 'The Teachers' Sermon'; Barclay, *Obeying the Truth*, p. 89; Longenecker, *Galatians*, p. lxxxix. Brimsmead understands Paul's peculiar exposition as a response to an 'Abraham apology' of opponents. Brimsmead, *Galatians*, p. 107. C.K. Barrett, 'The Allegory of Abraham, Sarah, and Hagar in the Argument of Galatians', in J. Friedrich, *et al.* (eds.), *Rechtfertigung* (Festschrift E. Käsemann; Tübingen: Mohr, 1976), pp. 1–16 (9). G.W. Hansen, *Abraham in Galatians: Epistolary and Rhetorical Contexts* (JSNTSup, 29; Sheffield: JSOT Press, 1989), p. 171.

20.   Moisés Silva, *Interpreting Galatians: Explorations in Exegetical Method* (Grand Rapids: Baker, 2nd edn, 2001), pp. 104–108; Barclay, *Obeying the Truth*, pp. 36–41.

21.   Martyn, *Galatians*, pp. 454–56.

22.   Cf. the previous chapter on the analysis of Gal 2.1–14.

23.   Martyn, *Galatians*, p. 434.

Gal. 1.13–14, Paul says that he departed from the patriarchal tradition (τῶν πατρικῶν μου παραδόσεων). Therefore, Abraham's blessing may seem to some a secondary issue within the salvation scheme of God through faith in Christ.[24] However, it seems odd that Paul spends two chapters (one third of the whole letter) on the theme of Abraham's heirship, if he is not interested in the subject. On the contrary, it is here suggested that Paul may have consciously offered the patriarch to the Galatian members of his community, who may have felt deracinated from the rest of the wider Galatian population. It has been pointed out that 'assumed common ancestry' functions as a significant symbol for the cohesion of an ethnic group.[25] Paul's interest in the heirship of Abraham will be discussed in the section where the concept of 'assumed common ancestry' is further introduced to interpret vv. 22–23.

Another example of a reactive approach is that the circumcisers are said to have persuaded the Galatian members to obey the Torah and be circumcised like Isaac in order to become authentic as descendants of Abraham.[26] However, this line of argument may not be as convincing or convenient as one might think. In persuading the Gentiles to accept circumcision, the contrast between Isaac and Ishmael may cause dissonance. Ishmael was the illegitimate child of Abraham. Even though he had himself circumcised, he was outside the blessing of Abraham because of his birth. In the case of the biblical account and in the later Jewish understanding (e.g. *Ant.* 14.403), birth takes precedence over circumcision. In the story of Isaac and Ishmael over authentic heirship, Paul could make the case of 'circumcised and yet marginalized Ishmael' (indeed secondary status) as material evidence against the circumcisers' persuasion of the Galatians. In the Jewish tradition, Ishmael insisted that he was more righteous than Isaac because he willingly submitted himself to the rite of circumcision at the age of 13 while Isaac made no such conscious decision of obedience. However, Ishmael was after all discredited and marginalized on account of his illegitimate birth (*b. Sanh.* 89b on Gen.

---

24. Ibid., p. 306.
25. Anthony D. Smith, 'Chosen People: Why Ethnic Groups Survive', *Ethnic and Racial Studies* 15.3 (1992), pp. 440–49. This topic will be further considered in the interpretation of Gal. 4.22–23, in section 3.b of this chapter. Recently, Esler applied the social-psychological theory of 'prototype' to interpret the significance of Paul's reference to Abraham for constructing a positive and competitive identity of the inter-ethnic community in Rome. Philip F. Esler, *Conflict and Identity in Romans: The Social Setting of Paul's Letter* (Minneapolis: Fortress Press, 2003), ch. 8 on 'Abraham as a Prototype of Group Identity' (pp. 171–94). An example of assumed common ancestry was earlier introduced that the fictitious 'unbroken royal line' of the emperor (*Bansei-ikkei*) was used by the Meiji government to strengthen the nationalistic ideology.
26. Longenecker, *Galatians*, pp. 207–208. Martyn suggests an entire message of the circumcisers in Martyn, *Galatians*, pp. 303–306 (esp. 304).

22.1; *Tg. Ps. – J. Gen.* 22.1). The story of tension between Isaac and Ishmael, instead of persuading the Gentiles to the rite of circumcision, may impress upon them the secondary status of Gentiles on account of their birth.

Therefore, it is suggested that, while admitting that the reactive perspective is at times helpful, it should not undermine Paul's clear intention in presenting his peculiar exposition of the account of the heirship of Abraham. The intention is to help the community members to construct a positive identity of the community through remaking the tradition.[27]

2. *Paul, Uchimura and Galatian Indigenization*

a. *Paul and Uchimura in their Cultural Positions*

Before conducting an analysis of the pericope of Gal. 4.21–31 with the help of an analogical comparative study, a qualification should be made to the correlation between Uchimura and Paul introduced earlier in the introduction to this chapter. It was noted in the comparison between Paul's Galatian community and Uchimura's Mukyokai that both founders faced the need to construct the identity of their respective communities, which were under external pressure to conform. However, it becomes immediately obvious that while Uchimura sought to indigenize the religion, Paul saw his religion as incompatible with 'paganism'.[28] Uchimura indigenized the religion while Paul did not, or at least his letter does not reveal a clear effort to adapt his message to the host culture.[29] In this consideration, the aim is two-fold. First, it is to clarify that Paul's resistance to the indigenization of his religion to the host culture does not mean that he was confined to a traditional core ethnic sentiment, but rather that he was resistant to altering his religion because of the strong influence of his revelatory experience (Gal. 1.15–16). Second, a consideration will be made as to what Paul might have been resisting in Gal. 4.8–

27. Recently, social-scientific criticism has been applied to the text and the function of Paul's peculiar exposition in chapters 3–4. Esler, *Galatians*, pp. 213–14. Cf. Watson, *Paul*, pp. 69–72.

28. This polemic approach is reflected in Paul's rather odd reference to Gentiles as 'sinners' and 'ignorance' of God even when he writes to the Gentiles themselves (cf. Gal. 2.15; 1 Thess. 4.5).

29. However, the peculiarity in the expression of Paul's baptismal saying (Gal. 3.26–28), which we will discuss further in the following chapter (Chapter 7), may be an example of Paul's 'sensitivity' to the host culture. The language of robing/disrobing or attiring in the manner of deity may well have been a meaningful expression of the significance of baptism for those who were familiar with the mystery religions of the Graeco-Roman world. Cf. Bultmann, *Theologie*, p. 140; Wedderburn, *Baptism and Resurrection*, p. 339; Eduard Lohse, *Umwelt des Neuen Testaments* (GNT, 1; Göttingen: Vandenhoeck & Ruprecht, 1971), p. 178.

10. In it is suggested that Galatians may have been indigenizing Paul's message by way of the circumcisers' teaching on the Jewish calendar in order to achieve a level of cohesion of the community under the pressure of the larger Galatian population.

As suggested, both Uchimura and Paul sought to construct a positive identity for their respective religious communities that were marginalized by various pressures from significant others. The difference between the two figures can be understood as their positional difference, i.e. where they are located in relation to the culture from which the religion was brought and the culture to which the religion was introduced. Paul is from the former and maintains a nuanced relation with the former (ethnically a Jew, but viewing himself detached from 'Judaism', Gal. 1.13), but is generally an outsider to the latter.[30] Uchimura is in the latter, even though he feels a sense of deracination from the wider Japanese population. Observing the two founders, the most creative transformation of a religion seems to happen in the culture from which the messenger (or missionary/ founder) either originates or to which the person belongs. For Paul, the transformation manifests itself most clearly in his criticism of his mother religion based upon his revelation. Therefore, Paul recreates the world-view by remaking the tradition of his mother religion, and therefore it is sometimes regarded as 'religious reformation'.[31] However, he does so apart from the creative adaptation of the 'pagan' cultures. For Uchimura, the transformation manifests itself in the adaptation of a religion foreign to his own culture by connecting the foreign religion with what is perceived to be the best in his indigenous cultural and religious elements. Therefore, Uchimura's recreated worldview is here regarded as 'indigen-ization'.[32] Once Uchimura establishes the new worldview, he protects it from the influence of foreign cultures through sharp criticism of the West as a whole (cf. 'Enemies of Christianity', *Seisho no Kenkyu* 199 [Oct. 1917]).[33] For Paul, too, his new worldview on the basis of his revelatory

30. Cf. 1 Cor. 9.9–23. In this passage, Paul speaks of his approach to interpersonal relations, which sometimes involves inter-cultural considerations. However, this discussion focuses on the idea of adaptation of the religious message in our discussion.

31. Theißen, *Die Religion*, pp. 217–18. Theißen associates Paul's criticism of the Torah with Zimrii's criticism of the Torah (*Gesetzeskritik*, Josephus *Ant.* 4.6.10–12), Ezekiel's doubt about the Torah (*Gesetzeszweifel*, Ezek. 8.20–36), and a radical allegorical dissolution of the Torah (*Gesetzesauflösung*, Philo *Migr. Abr.* 89–90).

32. Cf. Uchimura, 'Bushido and Christianity', *Seisho no Kenkyu* 186 (Jan. 1916), in *Zenshu*, XXII, pp. 161–62. The full quotation is found on p. 63. Feldtkeller understands under the concept of *Extensivierung* that a commitment to a new religion does not necessarily mean abandoning the old culture. Uchimura's effort of indigenization is to solve the problem of the sense of deracination that he and his community members experience in the particular social situation. Feldtkeller, *Identitätssuche*, pp. 54–55.

33. *Zenshu*, XXIII, pp. 167–68. He maintains that the western culture is the primary enemy of Christianity. Cf. Chapter 2 (section 3, note 94).

experience (Gal. 1.15) is protected from the influence of foreign cultures (as well as from the influence of Judaism), especially manifested in his criticism of the host cults (cf. Gal. 4.7–8; 5.20). When the two figures and the corresponding strategies of community–identity construction are compared, one finds in both ways that the identity of the new religious community is sought by recreating the worldview. The lack of evidence of active adaptation of the message to the new culture on Paul's part does not mean that his approach to community–identity relies on a traditional core ethnic sentiment. For Paul, the core sentiment is his personal revelatory experience, and anything that gets in the way of the revelation must expect a divine curse (Gal. 1.8–9).

b. *Indigenization by the Galatians (Galatians 4.8–10)*
It has been suggested that Paul's resistance to cultural adaptation relates to his cultural position. However, this does not mean that there were no such efforts on the part of Galatian members, who are originated in the 'host' culture. Therefore, a consideration will be made as to what might be said about Galatians' response to the missionary messages in their own cultural position. As the dialectic nature of community–identity was introduced in Chapter 1, it was suggested that one should take note of the pressure of the larger population of Galatians as the influence of the significant others for the Galatian members. Consequently, Paul's warning against their 'idolatry' might reflect the existence of such an influence apart from (or rather than) the general propensity to 'sin',[34] which may well lead one to idolatry. There is a possibility behind Gal. 4.8–10 that the Galatians sought to indigenize or make Paul's religion more compatible with their cultural expectations by means of the circumcisers' teaching on observance of the Jewish calendar, for the purpose of alleviating at least a part of the pressure from the larger Galatian population.[35]

---

34. Cf. Stephen Mitchell, *Anatolia* (2 vols.; Oxford: Clarendon, 1993), II, p. 14.

35. Here is a brief consideration of the term, 'syncretism'. The term 'indigenization' is preferred for discussion here in order to avoid the confusion because of the presupposed negative value in the term 'syncretism'. The term has been used in the popular level to condemn disparagingly the adulteration of 'true' and 'pure' Christian belief. However, such a value judgment is usually found in those who possess the power to pressure to conform, often ignorant of or ignoring the life situation of those who resort to a creative adaptation of a religion to their indigenous culture. Cf. Lamont Lindstrom, *ESCA*, s.v. 'syncretism'. Feldtkeller is aware of this problem of the use of the term 'syncretism' in the study of the New Testament. Feldtkeller, *Identitätssuche*, p. 122. Anthropologists have come to doubt the descriptive precision of the concept and it is losing its evaluative value, because it has to presuppose some kind of pure and unique cultural forms. Cf. R. Linton, 'One Hundred Per-Cent American', *The American Mercury* 40 (1937), pp. 427–29. For this discussion, the term 'indigenization' will be used because a reference is made here to a creative effort to adapt a

The interpretation of Gal. 4.10 has primarily focused on the question as to whether the Galatian members returned to 'pagan' practice or adopted the observance of the Jewish calendar through the influence of circumcisers.[36] Due to Paul's customary ambiguity in the letter, a careful speculation is all one can offer on this question. Paul complains to the Galatians for observing 'days, months, seasons and years' (ἡμέρας παρατηρεῖσθε καὶ μῆνας καὶ καιροὺς καὶ ἐνιαυτούς, Gal. 4.10). If the similar complaint in Col. 2.16 is considered, the description there clearly refers to Jewish festivals (ἐν βρώσει καὶ ἐν πόσει ἢ ἐν μέρει ἑορτῆς ἢ νεομηνίας ἢ σαββάτων). Therefore, some assume that Gal. 4.8–10 also refers to Jewish practices.[37] However, it has also been suggested that the Galatians were returning to pagan religious practices.[38] Calendar observance for Galatians may remind one of such a Celtic observance as the harvest festival, which was held on the night of the full moon, therefore 'moon festival' (cf. Strabo, *Geog.* 3.4.16).[39] Calendar observance may reflect an even wider social influence of the imperial cult, as Mitchell suggests for the background of Gal. 4.8–10. When Mitchell says, 'The packed calendar of the ruler cult dragooned the citizens of Antioch into observing the days, months, seasons, and years ...',[40] he describes the situation of Pisidian Antioch. Yet, a similar pressure of the imperial cult

---

new religion meaningful and tolerable to one's 'indigenous' culture. Whether the effort is regarded by the 'decision-maker' (in our case Paul) as acceptable or not is another matter. Whether one regards such an effort as indigenization or syncretism is quite a subjective discussion. It is noted that Mullins's evaluation of Uchimura's strategy of indigenization as 'christianizing the non-Christian past' may be a helpful insight. Mullins, *Christianity Made in Japan*, p. 60. Mullins refers to Uchimura's saying, 'Buddha is the Moon; Christ is the Sun/ Buddha is the Mother; Christ is the Father; Buddha is Mercy; Christ is Righteousness' (*Zenshu*, XXIX, pp. 456).

36. This question relates to the identification of 'circumcisers'. Dieter Lührmann, 'Tage, Monate, Jahreszeiten, Jahre (Gal. 4.10)', in R. Albertz *et al.* (eds.), *Werden und Wirken des Alten Testaments* (Festschrift C. Westermann; Göttingen: Vandenhoeck & Ruprecht, 1980), pp. 428–45 (429); Mußner, *Der Galaterbrief*, pp. 24–25.

37. Dunn suggests the observance of the Jewish calendar, i.e. Sabbath (Exod. 31.16–17; Deut. 5.15; Isa. 56.6; *Ant.* 11.346; *Jub.* 2.17–33), New moon (Num. 10.10; 28.11; 2 Kgs 4.23; Ps. 81.3; Ezek. 46.3), Pilgrim festivals (Exod. 13.10; 23.14, 17; Lev. 23.4; Num. 9.3) and the celebration of New Year. Dunn, *Galatians*, pp. 227–29; *idem*, *The Epistles to the Colossians and to Philemon* (NIGTC; Grand Rapids: Eerdmans, 1996), p. 175. This interpretation may be based too much upon Col. 2.16. Cf. Lührmann, 'Tage', p. 430; Troy Martin, 'Pagan and Judeo-Christian Time-Keeping Schemes in Gal. 4.10 and Col. 2.16', *NTS* 42 (1996), pp. 105–19 (119). Bruce understands v. 10 as the OT festivals of κληταὶ ἅγιαι (Lev. 23.2). Bruce, *Galatians*, p. 205–206. Nanos understands that some are persuaded to adopt Jewish customs and some are returning to the pagan practices. Nanos, *The Irony of Galatians*, pp. 81, 87.

38. Martin, 'Pagan and Judeo-Christian Time-Keeping Schemes', pp. 105–19.

39. While Strabo speaks of the example of the Iberian Celts, Ó Hógáin argues that the festival was commonly held among the ethnic Celts. Dáithí Ó Hógáin, *The Celts: A History* (Woodbridge: Boydell Press, 2002), p. 79.

40. Mitchell, *Anatolia*, II, pp. 9–10.

can also be assumed in northern Galatia, especially in Ancyra, which housed the imperial temple.[41] Therefore, there are those who find Jewish practice in v. 10 and those who find pagan practice in the same verse.[42] However, if one takes into consideration the social reality, in which Galatian members felt pressure from the larger Galatian population as much as or more so than from circumcisers, a different scenario emerges.

Paul's description seems to connect the Galatians' attraction to the observance of the (Jewish) calendar (Gal. 4.10) and their previous 'pagan' attachment to 'weak and beggarly elemental spirits' (Gal. 4.8). This may be describing a situation in which Galatian members adopted some aspects of the observance of the Jewish calendar, which was taught by circumcisers as practised by churches in Judaea. They may have found those feasts compatible with the cultural and cultic practices of their larger Galatian context. In order to alleviate the external pressure from their significant others ('pagan' Galatians), they may have considered it wise to adopt some practices that would give the appearance that they were preserving their loyalty to Galatian ethnic distinctiveness or to imperial governance rather than abandoning the expected customs altogether as something 'evil'. If they found out that by adopting the Jewish calendar they could give an appearance that they feast with the fruits of harvest according to the lunar calendar as their compatriots, there would have been a strong incentive for them to adopt it, especially if it is the kind of celebration the churches in Judaea supposedly held. In the process of adoption and adaptation, the feast may have fallen on the day of the full moon instead of the new moon. Such an act, though genuinely creative indigenization on the part of the Galatians, appeared to Paul as a departure from his gospel by adhering to old 'pagan' practices through adopting Jewish customs.

Three grounds are given for this speculation, i.e. (1) social theories, (2) analogical correlations, and (3) historical and genealogical considerations. Earlier, a certain social-anthropological concept was noted which states that community–identity is constructed in a dialectic process of external categorization and internal identification. In it, Cohen suggested that the ingroup members would often attempt a 'symbolical recreation', or as he says 'syncretism', at the boundary, which explains the coexistence of change in structural and cultural features and persistence of sense of

---

41. Ibid., II, pp. 13–14. Note that Mitchell follows *Provinzhypothese* on the letter's destination, contrary to the current assumption. Cf. S. Mitchell, *ABD*, II, s.v. 'Galatia'.

42. Betz understands the expression, especially παρατηρεῖσθε in v. 10, as a general description of religious observance. Betz, *Galatians*, p. 217. Cf. H. Friedrich, 'παρατηρέω', in Gerhard Friedrich (ed.), *Theological Dictionary of the New Testament* (trans. Geoffrey W. Bromiley; 10 vols.; Grand Rapids: Eerdmans, 1972), VIII, pp. 146–51; Rudolf K. Bultmann, *Der Stil der paulinischen Predigt und die kynisch-stoische Diatribe* (FRLANT, 13; Göttingen: Vandenhoeck & Ruprecht, 1910), p. 103.

belonging. He goes on to suggest the inevitable result of strong pressure upon a group. He says, '... the greater the pressure of communities to modify their structural forms to comply more with those elsewhere, the more are they inclined to reassert their boundaries symbolically by imbuing these modified forms with meaning and significance which belies their appearance'.[43] The description of identity construction above, which Cohen elsewhere calls 'illusory conformity',[44] seems highly germane to the social situation of Paul's Galatian community. One may rightly suspect a form of perfidy in an 'illusory conformity', whether or not it is intended. One may well suppose a sincere attempt by Galatian members to maintain cohesion of the community. However, 'illusory conformity', even with an intended pretence, can be rightly regarded as an appropriate social response, or an 'art of resistance' under domination. Scott, in his social study of resistance under domination, takes note of the subordinate groups' manifold strategies of resistance 'in disguised forms', when they face those who dominate them. Such a resistance is a legitimate art of survival especially for those who are under an inordinate pressure to conform. The Galatian community members may be found in such a social situation.[45]

Similar efforts of adaptation can be found widely in missionary situations, whether they are called 'indigenization' or 'syncretism'. The most extreme case is the practice of Kakure Kirishitan, an underground Christian community during the severe persecution of Christianity in the pre-modern period of Japan. *Nando Gami* (Closet-god; equivalent to a Buddhist altar at home), for example, was a focus and medium of worship under the guise of Buddhist religious practices.[46] In the lesser degree of the pressure of conformity in the modern period of Japan, marginalized Christian communities offer substitute services and feasts on important festal occasions, which have various degrees of local or national religious importance. One of the purposes for this is to give the appearance in public to the general Japanese population that the churches pay respect to traditional values instead of abandoning them as evil pagan practices, while at the same time making a severe criticism in private of certain

43. A.P. Cohen, *The Symbolic Construction*, p. 44.
44. Ibid., p. 37.
45. James C. Scott, *Domination and the Arts of Resistance: Hidden Transcript* (New Haven and London: Yale University Press, 1990), pp. 136–37.
46. Ann M. Harrington, *Japan's Hidden Christians* (Chicago: Loyola University Press, 1993), p. 39.

religious aspects of those traditions.[47] Scott finds in this difference in
message between public and private discourses a dynamic force of
resistance under domination.[48]

When attention turns to the situation in Anatolia in the Graeco-Roman
period, all sorts of religious adaptation to the social and political
influences of outgroups around the Galati or Celts are observed. As
Galatians migrated to the central part of Anatolia during the third
century BCE, they mingled with the native Phrygians. The Galatians were
tolerant of the Phrygian cult of Agdistis (*Geog.* 12.5.3), and indeed they
assimilated it as an expression of their devotion to the Celtic mother-
goddess.[49] The 'syncretic' tendency was not only due to a degree of
compatibility between the two cults of mother-goddess,[50] but probably
also due to the fact that the worship of Agdistis, better known as Cybele,
the Great Mother, was officially recognized by Rome in 204 BCE.[51] The
Galatians' religious expression changed most drastically under the
pressure of the imperial cult, especially in urban areas. In Ancyra, for
example, the divine couple of Agdistis and Men was replaced by the
temple dedicated to Augustus and the goddess Roma. I noted earlier the
pressure of the imperial cult upon the social life in Pisidian Antioch
suggested by Mitchell. In commenting on Gal 4.8–10, he continues to
suggest that under such a pressure . . ., 'it was not a change of heart that
might win a Christian convert back to paganism, but the overwhelming
pressure to conform imposed by the institutions of his city and the
activities of his neighbours'.[52] Under such pressure from the imperial cult,
there is an example of peculiar resistance in disguise among the Celts in
Gaul. They erected columns of Jupiter with explicit homage to the

47. One may well compare this phenomenon with the account of Afro-Brazilian religions
by Bastide. Roger Bastide, *Les religions africaines au Brésil: vers une sociologie des
interpénétrations de civilisations* (Bibliothèque de Sociologie Contempraine; Paris: Presses
universitaires de France, 1960), particularly *Les Problèmes du Syncrétisme religieux* (pp. 362–
421) and *Naissance d'un Religion* (pp. 422–74).

48. See his discussion of 'public transcript' (an open interaction between subordinates
and those who dominate) and 'private transcript' (a discourse taking place 'off stage' beyond
the direct observation of power holders). J.C. Scott, *Domination*, pp. 2, 4.

49. Mitchell, *Anatolia*, I, pp. 48–49.

50. Ó Hógáin, *The Celts*, p. 69.

51. One may find in this cultural/cultic adaptation of the Galati a close correlation with
Abner Cohen's description of the cultural/cultic adaptation of Ibadan Hausa, upon which he
bases his theory of Instrumentalism. Refer to Chapter 1 for the brief explanation of the
theory.

52. Mitchell, *Anatolia*, II, p. 14.

imperial divinity but secretly decorated them with images of their sun-god worship and of the dualistic myth taught by their 'wisemen' (*druids*).[53]

There was among the ethnic group of Celts an effort to preserve their cultural and religious traditions through a careful adaptation to the influence of neighbouring Phrygians and of imperial governance. The influence of the latter was particularly outstanding. Such an adaptation of religion under pressure is observed widely not only in antiquity, but also in pre-modern and modern periods as observed, for instance, among Japanese society. Cohen's theory on identity seems to give an important perspective on both analogical and genealogical comparative cases.

Upon these grounds, the speculation on the situation in Gal. 4.8–10 seems worthy of careful consideration. In Paul's persuasion in Galatians 3 and 4, he seems to present both the Torah and non-Jewish religious practices and regulations as 'enslaving elements' (ὑπὸ τὰ στοιχεῖα τοῦ κόσμου ἤμεθα δεδουλωμένοι, Gal. 4.3; πῶς ἐπιστρέφετε πάλιν ἐπὶ τὰ ἀσθενῆ καὶ πτωχὰ στοιχεῖα οἷς πάλιν ἄνωθεν δουλεύειν θέλετε;, 4.9). Therefore, the phrase στοιχεῖα does not lead one to either Jewish or 'pagan' religious practices. Gal. 4.8–10 is in the context of the circumcisers' pressure to conform (Gal. 4.16, 17), therefore even though Paul speaks of 'turning again' (ἐπιστρέφετε πάλιν) in 4.9, Gal. 4.8–10 does not automatically rule out the effect of the circumcisers' persuasion to conform to the Jewish religious observance. It is known from Col. 2.16 that 'Judaizers' did pressure Gentile believers to observe the Jewish calendar. Indeed the phrase ἡμέρας παρατηρεῖσθε καὶ μῆνας καὶ καιροὺς καὶ ἐνιαυτούς is reminiscent of LXX Gen. 1.14b (ἔστωσαν εἰς σημεῖα καὶ εἰς καιροὺς καὶ εἰς ἡμέρας καὶ εἰς ἐνιαυτούς), which is used as a foundation for observation of the Jewish calendar (Wis. 7.17–19; Sir. 33.7–9; *1 En.* 82.9; *Jub.* 2.8–10). Or rather, both Jewish and pagan elements may be suggested to be indivisible in the practice of the Galatian believers in this particular pericope. It seems plausible to consider a possibility, outlined above, that Galatian members found in Jewish observance of the calendar an 'appropriate' expression to give an appearance of conformity to the significant others, in order to find for themselves a cohesion of the newly emerging community. Instead of the popular understanding that the Galatians were attracted to the Sinai covenant to complete their conversion from 'paganism',[54] they may have found aspects of Jewish practices in the new religion introduced by circumcisers as an attractive and convenient way to adapt the new-found

53. Miranda J. Green, *The Gods of the Celts* (Gloucester: Sutton, 1986), pp. 61–67; *idem*, *Dictionary of Celtic Myth and Legend* (London: Thames and Hudson, 1992), pp. 127–29; also 86–87 on druidism.

54. For example, Betz, *Galatians*, p. 216.

faith more favourably to their own culture.[55] One should not undermine such a creative energy within a religious group in the 'foreign' culture, some of which, however, Paul might have regarded as unacceptable for his community based upon the revelatory experience.

This section was a qualification on the correlation between Paul and Uchimura, and it led to the postulation of the Galatians' effort of indigenization. First, it was suggested that while there is an apparent difference between Paul and Uchimura in their approaches to indigenization due to their different cultural positions, both of them seek to provide coherence for their respective communities through recreating the worldview. Second, it was suggested that a sensitivity to the influence of the significant others may lead to a new interpretation of Gal. 4.8–10, i.e. the possibility of Galatians' effort to indigenize Paul's message for the cohesion of their community. In the following, observation will be made as to how Paul may have sought to provide a positive identity for the community through recreating the worldview.

3. *Recreation of Worldview*

An interpretive framework of 'recreation of worldview' has been suggested for the purpose of interpreting the theoretical section of Galatians (chapters 3 and 4) and particularly Gal. 4.21–31.[56] 'Recreation of worldview' denotes a new interpretation of the world order favourable to a newly emerging group for the very purpose of providing for such a group a sense of cohesion and its reason for existence.[57] An analogical comparative study with the historical case of Uchimura and his Mukyokai will also be given. By drawing an analogy from this Japanese group, it is not meant that this group within post-industrial Japan has a perfectly parallel culture to the ancient Mediterranean world. The point of the analogical comparison is that it offers the biblical exegetes a much-needed heuristic tool by which a different set of questions can be put to the text.[58]

The short pericope has the structure of being an independently complete unit, though the flow of thought in the pericope assumes the preceding discussions in Galatians 3 and 4. First, Paul draws the attention

55.   In his repeated creation of the circumcisers' (Teachers') message, Martyn says, 'the true calendar established by God, and Paul did not convey it to you [Galatians]'. It may be that the circumcisers' version of religious practices was more suitable to the cultural adaptation because of corresponding religious calendrical observances. Martyn, *Galatians*, p. 414.

56.   E.g. Turner, *The Ritual Process*, pp. 189–90; A.P. Cohen, *The Symbolic Construction*, pp. 58–60.

57.   Cf. Watson, *Paul*, pp. 61–72. Cf. Esler, *Galatians*, p. 185.

58.   For the validity and value of analogical comparative analysis, see the Introduction (section 3.b).

of a specific audience (Gal. 4.21). Then the recreation of worldview is outlined (vv. 22–27) in which Paul first prepares the audience with the part of the Abrahamic tradition conventionally accepted (vv. 22–23), then he offers an unexpected typological development in reversal (vv. 24–27).[59] Lastly, an application of the typology is offered. Now that the recreated world is set before the community members, they are to live according to the newly established worldview (vv. 28–31). The study begins with an interpretation of Gal. 4.21.

a. *Audience Analysis (Galatians 4.21)*
Paul calls to attention a specific group of people, οἱ ὑπὸ νόμον θέλοντες εἶναι (v. 21). The description is specific in that these are the people who are being persuaded by circumcisers' pressure.[60] Paul has been showing his concern and frustration with those community members who yield to the pressure (cf. Gal. 4.9–11). While an urgent concern of Paul may be to persuade those who are yielding to the pressure of the circumcisers,[61] his exposition has a significant function and application for all community members (cf. Gal. 4.28, 31).[62] The subsequent rhetorical question, τὸν νόμον οὐκ ἀκούετε;, could be taken to indicate those who have attended the synagogue to hear the Torah.[63] Then an assumption is made that the audience was well-versed in the LXX.[64] Based upon this understanding, one could easily assume that the audience would hear the inter-textual echo of the Jewish literature rather loudly.[65] However, the question itself says nothing about the level of their familiarity with the Torah. Betz may be right at this point that the rhetorical question in v. 21 is rather sarcastic (or 'ironic'), that if they 'correctly' hear the Torah they would not be persuaded by the 'Torah observant' circumcisers.[66] Both those who have some familiarity with the Jewish literature and are able to relate to Paul's

59. Betz is quite right that Paul's typology ends with the quote from Isa. 54.1. Betz, *Galatians*, p. 248.
60. Dunn, *Epistile to the Galatians*, p. 245.
61. Lütgert, *Gesetz und Geist*, pp. 11, 88.
62. Longenecker, *Galatians*, p. 206.
63. The presence of Jews in Asia Minor at this period is well attested. Van der Horst explains that the Jews had a relatively successful expansion in Asia Minor except for occasional pressure from the empire. Van der Horst, 'Juden und Christen in Aphrodisias', pp. 141–42; cf. Marcel Simon, *Verus Israel: Étude sur les Relations entre Chrétiens et Juifs dans l'Empire Romain (135–425)* (Paris: E. de Boccard, 1948), pp. 126–27.
64. Dunn, *Galatians*, p. 245.
65. Ibid., p. 255. So Dunn comments on the quotation from Isa. 54.1 in Gal. 4.27, 'Paul's *claim*, therefore, is that Isaiah's hoped for restoration of Judea/Zion was best understood as fulfilled eschatologically in the amazing fruitfulness of the Christian, including the Gentile mission' (author's emphasis). More on this interpretation later.
66. Betz, *Galatians*, p. 241.

thought world and those who hear the surface level of the story may be borne in mind here.[67] One should assume that there were members who could welcome and accept Paul's exposition as persuasive and those others to whom the exposition sounded too forced, strange or unconvincing to accept easily (Jews and those familiar with the Jewish tradition).[68] Those who are familiar with the Jewish tradition may require an additional degree of commitment to the cause and the mission of Paul if they decide to identify themselves with the newly given worldview, which may at first appear to them as forced or strange. This worldview is different from the one traditionally accepted among the Jews, in which salvation history is depicted as a patriarchal inheritance of Abraham's blood descendants with the covenant expressed in the Torah.[69]

b. *Abraham and Common Ancestry (Galatians 4.22, 23)*
Authentic heirship of Abraham is the theme throughout the third and fourth chapters of the epistle. As the finale, the exposition on the story of Abraham and his descendants (Gal. 4.21–31) clearly shows that those not under the Torah are the authentic heirs of Abraham. Therefore, in Paul's exposition, the Galatian members are given a common ancestry.

Consideration should now be given to the important idea of possessing Abraham as a common ancestry for the Galatian community. Anthropologists are aware of the importance of sharing a presumed common ancestry for providing and securing cohesion of a group, thus constructing a positive identity for a community. Nash and Smith in particular identify key factors that help create or solidify a communal identity, mainly of an ethnic community. They are generally thought of as 'common ancestry', 'cult' and 'commensality'.[70] Forming a new community of people involves an experience of deracination from the old tie of security, therefore, holding a commonly assumed ancestry helps to create a positive identity for the newly emerging community.

In the analogical case, Uchimura had to secure the cohesion of the deracinated group members by providing them with a firm ancestral heritage on which to fall. Therefore, Uchimura provided an interesting exposition of the history of *Bushido* (literally, 'the way of *samurai*'), which Uchimura perceived as a significant symbol of Japanese ethos and the locus of its spirituality. By connecting this Japanese ancestral heritage and God's salvation history, the Japanese ancestry contributes to the positive

67.   Cf. M. McNamara, ' "To de (Hagar) Sina oros estin en te Arabia" (Gal. 4.25a): Paul and Petra', *Milltown Studies* 2 (1978), pp. 24–41 (36).

68.   Dunn, *Galatians*, p. 243; Barclay, *Obeying the Truth*, p. 91; Hanson, *Allegory and Event*, p. 82.

69.   For example, Hanson, *Allegory and Event*, p. 82.

70.   Nash, *Cauldron of Ethnicity*, pp. 10–15.

identity of the group ('*Bushido* and Christianity', *Seisho no Kenkyu* 186 [Jan. 1916]).[71] According to this statement, the convergence of *Bushido* and Christianity is the destined climax of God's salvation history. Uchimura says that *Bushido* had been ordained to inherit Christianity and thus has been prepared to do so for the last 2,000 years.[72] In this rhetoric, one can observe a response to a peculiar social dynamic.[73] It is the response against the country's nationalistic reaction against the overt westernization policy. In that, Christians both of the church and Mukyokai are caught in between their commitment to the state and faith in Christ. Since Christianity represented Western spirituality or ideology, their commitment to the nation was suspect in the arguably anti-Christian nationalism.[74] Consequently, they held the sense of uprootedness in their marginalized state. Therefore, the rhetoric on *Bushido* to connect Japanese ancestral heritage with Christianity gave back to the marginalized community members their ancestral pride as a unique identity-marker of the group. Unlike Paul's teaching in the selected pericope, where a 'foreign' patriarch becomes the ancestor of the Galatian members, Uchimura makes the Japanese ancestral heritage a Christian heritage, in order to establish it as a positive identity-marker for the cohesion of the marginalized community.[75] However, in both cases, possessing or adopting either ancestral heritage or an ancestral figure functions as a positive identity-marker for marginalized and uprooted community members.

For the Galatian community members, entering into the community may mean marginalization and possibly ostracism, uprooted from the

71. *Zenshu*, XXII, pp. 161–62 (cf. Chapter 2, note 33). Both Uchimura and Paul employ the fulfilment theme in order to present the new and recreated worldview. Cf. Gal 4.4, τό πλήρωμα τοῦ χρόνου.

72. In the attempt to amalgamate Christianity and the Japanese ancestral heritage, Uchimura points out the close proximity between Japanese culture and Hebrew culture, in which Paul even becomes a 'true *samurai*'. Cf. Uchimura, 'Paul a Samurai', *Seisho no Kenkyu* 239 (June 1920) in *Zenshu*, XXV, pp. 362–63; 'Hebrews and Japanese', *Seisho no Kenkyu* 350 (Sept. 1929) in *Zenshu*, XXXII, pp. 186–87; 'Spirits and Forms', *Japanese Christian Intelligencer* 1.11 (Jan. 1927) in *Zenshu*, XXX, pp. 191–95.

73. This response is arguably a rather forced one. It was earlier noted that the idealization of Bushido at the time of Uchimura functioned as a fictitious memory of the nation to support and strengthen its nationalistic ideology. See Chapter 2 (Section 2.a.iv, note 58). His amalgamation of Christianity and Bushido could, therefore, be criticized as naïve and superficial, but it reflects Uchimura's upbringing and Mukyokai's unique life situation. Yuzo Ota, *Uchimura Kanzo*, p. 23.

74. Furuya and Oki, *Nihon no Shingaku*, p. 98.

75. Mullins compares this with the concept of 'Christianizing the pre-Christian past' by K. Bediako. Mullins, *Christianity Made in Japan*, p. 61. Cf. Kwame Bediako, *Christianity in Africa: The Renewal of a Non-Western Religion* (Edinburgh: Edinburgh University Press, 1995), pp. 75–87.

previous ties, such as cultic practices (4.8) and other ways of life that are now considered sinful (1.4). Such a social situation may arguably have caused them to long for their old ties or, according to the preceding suggestion on Gal. 4.8–10, it may have motivated them toward an indigenization that was not acceptable for Paul. For such deracinated group members, a sense of belonging may be provided by having a common ancestry for the community. The implausibility of the view that Paul himself was unconcerned with the discussion of Abraham was noted earlier.[76] Such a conclusion seems to neglect the life situation of the newly emerging community and Paul's conscious effort to provide a common ancestry for the deracinated community members for the purpose of constructing a positive community–identity.

c. *Allegory-Typology as a Vehicle of Reversal (Galatians 4.24)*

In vv. 22–23, Paul introduces two lines of inheritance, i.e. 'Abraham/slave woman/a son through the slave woman', and 'Abraham/free woman/a son through the free woman'. The birth situation of the former is described as κατὰ σάρκα and that of the latter as δι' ἐπαγγελίας (Gal. 4.23). One of Paul's key words in the description of salvation history is 'promise' (ἐππαγγελία/ἐπαγγέλλω in Gal. 3.14; cf. 3.18, 29), therefore the line of inheritance 'through the free woman' (ἐκ τῆς ἐλευθέρας) seems to suggest a positive relation with salvation history (Gen. 15.1–5). On the other hand, 'flesh' seems to possess a negative idea in the epistle, especially when it is contrasted with 'spirit' (Gal. 3.3; 4.29; cf. 5.16–21). While 'according to the flesh' (κατὰ σάρκα) may connote a natural birth process,[77] the negativity of the term may imply human intervention against God's plan (cf. Gen. 16.1–3) in the line of inheritance 'through the slave woman' (ἐκ τῆς παιδίσκης). So far, the contrast of the two lines of inheritance is the one that is generally expected and accepted by the Torah observants.

Paul starts to present a recreated worldview as he employs what he calls an 'allegorical' method of interpretation (Gal. 4.24). Paul qualifies that the two things 'are (understood as) allegorized' (ἅτινά ἐστιν ἀλληγορού–μενα). Some make a distinction between allegory and typology and identify Paul's exposition as a typology, in that a typology identifies the scriptural figures and locations as the prototype of figures and locations of the present situation, while an allegory departs from the original meaning

---

76. Martyn, *Galatians*, p. 424.
77. Bruce, *Galatians*, p. 217.

of the passage to identify deeper philosophical or theological principles.[78] Betz rightly suggests that Paul mixes the two.[79] In the course of the exposition, Paul does outline a sequence of parallel antitheses, yet the unexpected correlation depends on his allegory. This 'allegorical typology' enables Paul to reverse the values and statuses of the conventional structure. It will now be observed that the Abrahamic tradition is recreated and presented through the vehicle of allegorical typology in order to construct a positive identity for the Galatian community.

d. *Two Jerusalems (Galatians 4.25–26)*

Paul introduces two covenants (Gal. 4.24).[80] One is identified as Hagar and her descendants, thus the unauthentic line of inheritance (corresponding to slavery). The status is clearly reversed in the pericope as Hagar and Mt. Sinai are connected. This connection betrays entirely the conventional expectation of the salvation-historical line of Abraham, Sarah, Isaac, Moses with the Torah (Mt. Sinai), and the 'present Jerusalem', and the new connection is only understandable as part of the whole recreation of worldview or the Abrahamic tradition in Galatians 3 and 4.

Some commentators give justification for this shifted typological correlation (Hagar and Mt. Sinai) by pointing out the Targumic tradition that Hagar resided in Mt. Sinai and that the location of the recipient of the Torah was called Hagra/Hagar in Arabic (*ḥadjar*).[81] The association between Hagar and Mt. Sinai in the Targumic fashion may well be possible within Paul's thought-world in view of his educational background and his residence in the Nabataean kingdom after the revelatory experience (Gal. 1.17). However, did the primary audience understand such a sophisticated correlation? Suggestion has been made that Paul was

---

78. Hanson, *Allegory and Event*, p. 80. Longenecker compares Philo's allegorical interpretation and Paul's and concludes that Paul's interpretation is more like typology. Longenecker, *Galatians*, pp. 208–11. Lorse may be making too much of a correlation between Paul and Philo in their interpretative schemes. Lohse, *Umwelt des Neuen Testaments*, p. 98.

79. Betz, *Galatians*, p. 239.

80. The two covenants are best understood as in an antithetical relation. Therefore, it is difficult to compare the two covenants in the sense of degree, i.e. one is better than the other as Dunn suggests. Cf. Dunn, *Galatians*, p. 249. However, Dunn himself explains the term συστοιχέω (4.25) as introducing to the audience a sequence of parallel antitheses (p. 252).

81. The difference between 'h' and 'ḥ' is often overlooked in Midrash as in the case of *Gen. Rab.* 45.1 (to 16.1). Cf. Nabataic-Aramaic, *ḥgr*, and Arabic, *el-heğr*. Hartmut Gese, *Vom Sinai zum Zion: Alttestamentliche Beiträge zur biblischen Theologie* (BEvT, 64; München: C. Kaiser Verlag, 1984), pp. 59–60. Cf. McNamara, '"To de Hagar"', pp. 34–37. Strabo refers to the city of Agrani/Negrani (Ἀγράνων/Νεγράνων) in the country of Ararene (Ἀραρηνή) in *Geog.* 16.4.24.

totally caught up in allegorizing and was disregarding the ability of the audience to decipher the allegory,[82] or that the audience may have been familiar with such information through the message of circumcisers.[83] Instead of depending on the seemingly least familiar connection for the Galatian audience (i.e. between Hagar and Mt. Sinai as one might hypothesize from the Targumic tradition), one should take note of the obvious connection between Hagar and Mt. Sinai (the Torah) through the common motif of 'slavery'. Torah observance was depicted as enslavement earlier in Paul's discussion (δεδουλωμένοι in Gal. 4.3; cf. δουλεύειν in 4.9; συγκλειόμενοι in 3.23). Then, it is connected with Hagar, because she was a 'slave' (Gal. 4.24). The Galatian audience would probably make the typological connection with Paul based upon the predisposed idea of reversal in the earlier part of Paul's remaking of tradition. In other words, this shifted typology and the rest of the exposition in this pericope function to confirm and cement the newly recreated worldview outlined in the previous two chapters.

The 'present Jerusalem' (νῦν Ἰερουσαλήμ) is introduced here as standing at the end of the unauthentic line of inheritance. The term 'Jerusalem' as in 'present Jerusalem' is generally understood as the centre of Jewish religion and therefore representative of Judaism in general.[84] However, as Martyn points out, Jerusalem is presented as the location of the Jerusalem church in the epistle (Gal. 1.17, 18; 2.1). Therefore, the Galatian audience may have associated 'present Jerusalem' most readily with the Jerusalem church.[85] As seen earlier, Paul treats the problem of the circumcisers in Galatians as a part of the whole problem of the Jewish approach to Gentile incorporation based upon a core ethnic sentiment most readily represented by Torah adherence, which he had experienced in Jerusalem and Antioch. The earlier chapter (Chapter 5) drew attention to Paul's problem with the Jewish mission, which regards Gentile incorporation as creating a 'secondary status'. His severe criticism of the view may be reflected in this outline of the unauthentic and enslaving line of inheritance (the slave woman, the Torah and the present Jerusalem). Therefore, 'present Jerusalem' includes the Jerusalem church, and more urgently for the Galatian community, the circumcisers who may have originated there or at least shared the similar perspective on Gentile incorporation. One may add a qualification to this designation of 'present Jerusalem' that such a negative view of the Torah (Mt. Sinai) and Jerusalem cannot remain neutral to Judaism in general, either. Paul's

82. McNamara, '"To de Hagar"', p. 36; Burton, *Galatians*, p. 259.
83. Cf. Longenecker, *Galatians*, p. 212.
84. Betz, *Galatians*, p. 246.
85. Martyn, *Galatians*, pp. 457–66.

disjunction with Judaism ('Ιουδαϊσμός) seems to accord with this view (Gal. 1.14).[86]

On the other hand, the free woman (ἐλευθέρα) is allegorically understood as the authentic covenant. The Galatian community members are said to inherit this covenant as they are related to the free woman, as the term 'our mother' (Gal. 4.26; μήτηρ ἡμῶν) indicates. And this covenant is compared with the other by way of dualistic contrast between 'Jerusalem above' (ἄνω 'Ιερουσαλήμ) and 'present Jerusalem' (νῦν 'Ιερουσαλήμ). This dualistic 'above/present' contrast makes a sharp distinction between the two covenants,[87] and also gives an explanation for the dissonance between the status of authentic heirship and its present experience of marginalization; i.e. 'why do the authentic heirs suffer?' By introducing this dualism, Paul may be setting the experience of dissonance within the framework of an eschatological scheme. Therefore, within this present and coming evil age (Gal. 1.4), the authentic heirs may experience the injustice of marginalization.[88] It may be that the Jewish apocalyptic tradition was in Paul's thought world, in which the heavenly Jerusalem gives hope for those who despaired of the fate of earthly Jerusalem.[89] However, Paul's dualism is peculiar, in that he negatively describes the Jewish heritage of the Torah (symbol of the core ethnic sentiment) as unauthentic ('slavery' in v. 26) as he makes an antithetical contrast between physical and metaphysical Jerusalems, instead of one reforming the other (Isa. 60–66; Ezek. 40–48; Tob. 13.9–18; *Jub.* 4.26) or simply replacing the other (*1 En.* 90.28–29; *4 Ezra* 7.26; 10.40–44).[90] Currently, the attempt is being made to understand the pericope on the basis of the interpretive framework of recreated worldview, which often plays an important role in the liminal state of social process introduced earlier. One is reminded that the apocalyptic or eschatological ideology or even the sense of imminent crisis often functions to sustain the permanent state or

---

86. Contra Martyn, *Galatians*, pp. 458–59.

87. Cf. Col. 3.1–2; Phil. 3.14 (ἄνω/ἐπὶ τῆς γῆς). A rather odd contrast, for one would naturally expect above/below or present/future. One may understand both contrasts in the comparison. Hans Bietenhard, *Die himmlische Welt im Urchristentum und Spätjudentum* (WUNT, 2; Tübingen: Mohr, 1951), p. 198.

88. Andrew Lincoln, *Paradise Now and Not Yet: Studies in the Role of the Heavenly Dimension in Paul's Thought with Special Reference to his Eschatology* (SNTSMS, 43; Cambridge: Cambridge University Press, 1981), pp. 18–22. While Lincoln finds Paul's motif of the 'heavenly Jerusalem' in the wider Jewish tradition especially based upon Isa. 49.16, he identifies Paul's uniqueness in placing the two in antithetic relation in order to emphasize his view of 'realized eschatology'.

89. Rebuilding of Jerusalem in the eschaton (Isa. 54.10–12.; 60–66; Ezek. 40–48; Tob. 13.9–18; 14.7; Jub. 4.26). Replacement of the old by the new in the eschaton (Rev. 3.12; 21.2–8.).

90. Cf. Betz, *Galatians*, pp. 246–47.

cohesion of such a liminal community.[91] The dualistic contrast between the present Jerusalem and the Jerusalem above may reflect Paul's eschatological persuasion to maintain cohesion of the battered community. This shifted typology creates the recreated worldview, in which authenticity and un-authenticity are exchanged. The marginalized group members 'inherit' the status of the authentic heirship and the marginalizing ones are discredited and disinherited. In this way, the marginalized group members obtain a conceptual framework that strengthens the sense of cohesion among themselves.

In the movement of Mukyokai, the same kind of exchange between authenticity and inauthenticity is carried out over against Western civilization and the denominational churches due to Mukyokai's special emergence situation from the previous social tie. In his biography, Uchimura recalls the early break of his faith from the influence of the West (*How I Became a Christian*).[92] In the early stages of the westernizing policy of the Meiji authority, Western educators played a significant role in the Christian mission. The spread of the gospel and western civilization, therefore, went hand in hand, the natural consequence being that the supremacy of Christianity over against other religions was argued by the supremacy of Western technology and civilization in general.[93] For Uchimura, after rejecting the supremacy of the West, the only way to uphold Christianity was to separate it from the West by disinheriting the West from salvation history. Uchimura says that the West, rather than being a carrier of Christian heritage, is an enemy of Christianity.

> The enemies of Christianity are not Buddhism and Confucianism. The enemies of Christianity are American Hedonism, English Commercialism, French Indifferentism, Russian Nihilism, German Nietzcheism and Tretschkeism, and other hateful and horrible isms of the Western origin. The West in introducing Christianity to the East, has introduced with it its most destructive enemies. The East has nothing to be compared with the unbeliefs of the West. Let not Christian missionaries boast of the easy conquest of heathenism, when enemies far stronger than heathenism are accompanying them from their home and uprooting the very faith they are planting. The Christian West carrying deadly poison in her bosom cannot heal the pagan East. The East needs her own strong Christianity, strong enough to overcome

---

91. Turner, *The Ritual Process*, pp. 153–54. Furthermore, a millennial vision had a significant place in the early process of the Mukyokai movement, particularly in the beginning of its second decade of existence. H. Matsuzawa, 'Kindai Nihon to Uchimura Kanzo' [Modern Japan and Kanzo Uchimura], in H. Matsuzawa (ed.), *Uchimura Kanzo* (Tokyo: Chuo Koron, 1971), pp. 58–70.
92. Uchimura, *Zenshu*, III, p..90.
93. Matsuzawa, 'Kindai Nihon to Uchimura Kanzo', p. 20.

the deadly unbeliefs of the West ('Enemies of Christianity', *Seisho no Kenkyu* 199 [Oct. 1917]).[94]

The previous structural context of Mukyokai was primarily other Christian groups, i.e. denominational churches. In order to justify the *raison d'être* of a newly emergent group, reasons must be given as to why old ones cannot be authentic. Therefore, the sharpest criticism against the churches is also done by dissociating the churches from Christianity and its salvation history. He says:

> The odium of Christianity is in its churches. Men have left and are leaving Christianity because they hate churches ... Christianity minus churches is the Way, the Truth, and the Life. There is no reason for leaving Christ and His Gospel, because churches which are its institutional vestments are soiled and odious. Churchless Christianity will be the Christianity of the future ('Churchless Christianity', *Seisho no Kenkyu* 344 [March 1929]).[95]

Uchimura disinherited the West from salvation history and posited his version of the indigenized Japanese Christian group as authentic in order to create cohesion of the group. This was necessary in order for such a marginalized group to survive in the anti-Christian sentiment of the nation. He also disinherited the conventional denominational churches from the salvation history in order to justify the existence of his group outside the denominational churches. Thus, in these negative descriptions of the West and the church, Uchimura created a cohesion for group members, which helped to offer them a positive identity of their own.

It has been observed in the shifted typology that Paul's intention was to provide a conceptual framework for the marginalized community members to survive and possibly even thrive in spite of devastating disintegrating pressure from significant others. In this new framework or recreated worldview, authentic status is taken away from the powerful and marginalizing groups and given to the marginalized. Just as the West and the church are disinherited from the authentic line of salvation history in the case of Uchimura's rhetoric, a part of the Jewish mission (i.e. the approach of the Jerusalem church to Gentile incorporation), with its emphasis on a core ethnic sentiment, is disinherited from authentic salvation history. It was noted earlier that while Uchimura actively indigenized the religion, Paul regarded pagan practices and cultural motifs as incompatible with his religion. Such a difference is likely due to the difference in their cultural positions, i.e. where the founder is located in relation to the culture of the community. Though the interpretive

---

94. Uchimura, *Zenshu*, XXIII, pp. 167–68.

95. Ibid., XXXII, pp. 51–52. Cf. 'Kyokai to Shinko' [Church and Faith], *Seisho no Kenkyu* (Feb. 1908), in *Zenshu*, XV, p. 386.

approaches differ, both founders of the respective community offered
community members a recreated worldview, in which those significant
other groups are marginalized instead. This effected for the group
members a strong and positive identity, by which they could maintain
their cohesion as authentic entities.

e. *Isaiah 54.1 and Status Elevation (Galatians 4.27)*
For the interpretation of Gal. 4.27, the most common interpretation is on
the basis of 'intertextuality', in which the connection between 'free
woman' and 'Jerusalem above' in v. 26 is substantiated by the wider
context of the quoted passage of LXX Isaiah 54, which is known to the
audience. The consideration of the verse, therefore, starts with the
criticism of this commonly accepted interpretive scheme. It is followed by
an alternative interpretive scheme of recreation of worldview, in which the
concept of 'status reversal/status elevation' and its implication to the
present study will be closely examined.

After the series of typological correlations in vv. 24–26, Paul connects
the 'free woman' (ἐλευθέρα, supposedly Sarah), whom he identifies as
'Jerusalem above' (ἄνω Ἰερουσαλήμ), with the 'barren woman' (στεῖρα) in
v. 27. As her descendants, they (including Paul) can rightly say, 'she is our
mother' (ἥτις ἐστὶν μήτηρ ἡμῶν, v. 26). In order to substantiate the
connection that 'Jerusalem above' is 'our mother' (i.e. Sarah), Paul quotes
LXX Isa. 54.1 in v. 27 (γέγραπται γάρ...), which compares Jerusalem to a
'barren woman' in the context of hope for restoration of the covenant
(Isa. 40–66). Thus, the connection between Jerusalem and Sarah is
confirmed. Moreover, the audience would 'clearly' understand the theme
of restoration behind Isa. 54.1 (cf. Isa. 40–66) or covenant fulfilment that
engulfs nations (Isa. 54.2–3; cf. Gen. 17.16).[96]

There are two concerns about this treatment of the quotation of LXX
Isa. 54.1. One is the assumption of the intertextual echo. As has been
noted earlier, one cannot be certain that the biblical knowledge was so
readily available to the original audience that they would hear the
intertextual echo as much as some commentators would like to affirm.[97]
Therefore, it is difficult to assume that the original audience would hear
the theme of the restoration of Jerusalem in a story of the humiliation and
blessing of a barren woman.[98] The other problem relates to the context of

96. Cf. Longenecker, *Galatians*, p. 215.
97. For the discussion of intertextual echoes, cf. Richard B. Hays, *Echoes of Scripture in
the Letters of Paul* (New Haven and London: Yale University Press, 1989). For the critical
evaluation of Hays's *Echoes*, see Christopher Tuckett, 'Paul, Scripture and Ethics: Some
Reflections', *NTS* 46.3 (2000), pp. 403–24.
98. For example, Lincoln assumes such a prior knowledge of the Jewish tradition among
the Galatian members. Lincoln, *Paradise*, p. 18.

the quoted verse of Isaiah. If the original audience were well-versed with the scripture, they might well note that the features of restoration of Jerusalem in the wider context include the hope of Jewish hegemony over the Gentile nations (Isa. 54.3) and the exclusion of the uncircumcised from Jerusalem (Isa. 52.1). Far from hearing the echo of the covenant promise, the Gentile audience would hear an echo of subjugation under the structure based upon a core ethnic sentiment.[99] A reminder of such an ethno-centred hope of 'restoration' on the basis of the Jewish core ethnic sentiment would contradict Paul's desire to establish the community without the ethnic constraints. Therefore, the interpretation of v. 27 on the basis of intertextual echoes does not seem to be very plausible.

It is suggested here instead that much of the substantiation for the connection between 'Jerusalem above' and 'free woman' in v. 26 is found in the antithetical presentation of the two covenants in the previous verses (vv. 25–26), where Paul places the two pairs (i.e. 'present Jerusalem' and 'Hagar'/'Jerusalem above' and 'free woman') antithetically to each other. The antithetical relationship between 'free woman' and 'slave woman (Hagar)' has already been established in v. 22 and 'present Jerusalem' is connected with 'slave woman'. Therefore, the audience could easily connect 'free woman' with 'Jerusalem above', even without the metaphor behind an unfamiliar scripture. If the connection in v. 26 does not depend on LXX Isa. 54.1, what is the function of the quotation in v. 27? In order to understand the function of the quotation, one should consider the concept of status elevation/status reversal.

This concept of status elevation is an anthropological one found in installation rituals. A leadership figure often inaugurates his or her role in the community through the rite of humiliation, which is followed by the rite of exaltation, in order to establish him or her for the position. For example, a story of resurrection of a mortified deity gives a cultic community a sense of the authenticity of the deity, and thus of the cult as a whole.[100] One may find this concept in the depictions of suffering messiah/suffering Israel which expect future exaltation (cf. Ps. 22) or in the *kenosis* hymn in Phil. 2.6–11.[101] In so-called status elevation, a stigma is explained as a necessary step toward the later glorification, therefore, a mark of authenticity. Thus, in status reversal, a stigma itself comes to possess a positive value (cf. τὰ στίγματα τοῦ Ἰησοῦ ἐν τῷ σώματί μου

99. Therefore, it is one thing to understand the quotation of Isa. 54.1 as a proof of the future growth of the Gentile churches solely on the idea of 'fruitfulness' (πολλὰ τὰ τέκνα), and it is quite another to understand it as such on the basis of the idea of Jewish hegemonic expansion over the nations. Cf. Bruce, *Galatians*, p. 222.

100. Turner, *The Ritual Process*, pp. 170–72.

101. Mödritzer understands this status elevation on the basis of what he calls 'forensic self-stigmatization' (*Ekstase*) in order to transform stigma into charisma. Mödritzer, *Stigma*, pp. 24–25, 267.

βαστάζω, Gal. 6.17).[102] With these approaches to stigma, the marginalized group members maintain their cohesion by resisting and at times glorying in stigma. The biographical sketch of Uchimura reflects how he was caught in the emergence of imperial nationalism and labelled both as a traitor by the general public and as a heretic by denominational churches. The series of unfortunate events leading up to this point, especially following *Fukei Jiken* (Lèse-majesté) brought Uchimura to a strong sense of isolation. In 1893, he used the term *mukyokai* or 'non-church' for the first time in his book *Consolation of a Christian Believer*. The term was originally used not to refer to a particular group, but to describe his extreme sense of loneliness and marginalization, as he said, 'I have become *mukyokai*'.[103] Then, the stigma of Uchimura and thus of Mukyokai was celebrated as the name of his group. That they do not have a church to which they could belong became a mark of authenticity. Elsewhere, Uchimura turns the stigma of 'heresy', of which he was accused, into the mark of an authentic agent of salvation history, saying, 'Blessed is the one who is hated by "orthodoxy" because he is a heretical' ('Seikyo to Itan' [Orthodoxy and Heresy], *Seisho no Kenkyu* 103/104 [Oct.–Nov. 1908]).[104] In both cases, the stigma of the marginalized founder and his community were converted into signs of authenticity.

How does this concept relate to the function of Isa. 54.1 in Gal. 4.27? The connective γάρ in v. 27, instead of substantiating the connection between Jerusalem and Sarah, which the audience would already have made, affirms the covenant as an authentic one by introducing Sarah's experience of status elevation. One may assume here that the original audience had an elementary knowledge of the story of Abraham and his sons through their respective mothers, and therefore made a connection between the barren woman of the quotation in v. 27 and Sarah. Is my dependence on intertextuality arbitrary? One should note that Hays provides the list of criteria for 'intertextual echoes', in which the criterion of 'availability' supports this present assumption on the familiarity of the general knowledge of Abraham's two sons more readily than a particular theme in which a random quotation from Isaiah is located.[105] In the quoted verse, status elevation is clearly depicted: Sarah goes through a form of humiliation by her barrenness, which is followed by a form of

---

102. Cf. Mödritzer, *Stigma*, p. 267. For 'status elevation', cf. Turner, *The Ritual Process*, pp. 170–72. Here, 'status elevation' is explained in the context of the installation ritual. For 'status reversal', cf. Schwimmer, 'Symbolic Competition', pp. 117–55.

103. Uchimura, *Consolation of a Christian Believer*, in *Zenshu*, II, p. 36 (author's translation).

104. Ibid., XVI, p. 82 (author's translation). Cf. 'Itan' [Heresy], *Seisho no Kenkyu* 102 (Sept. 1908) in *Zenshu*, XVI, p. 73.

105. Hays, *Echoes*, pp. 29–32.

exaltation by her fruitful child bearing. The stigma of humiliation (barrenness) was a necessary step for elevation of status as the mother, through whom the descendants enjoy the authentic heirship of Abraham. Thus the quotation of LXX Isa. 54.1 affirms the authenticity of the line of heirship between Abraham and those not under the Torah through Sarah, 'our mother'.

f. *Application to the Present Community (Galatians 4.28–31)*
The Galatian members are once again affirmed as authentic by their connection with Isaac (Gal. 4.28). The introduction of Isaac serves as an additional example of status elevation. It is for this reason that the persecution of 'the one according to the spirit' (τὸν κατὰ πνεῦμα, i.e. Isaac) by 'the one according to the flesh' (ὁ κατὰ σάρκα, i.e. Ishmael) is cited in Gal. 4.29. For the description of the relationship between Isaac and Ishmael, Paul seems to assume simply the Jewish tradition, based upon Gen. 21.9, that Ishmael 'persecuted' (ἐδίωκεν) Isaac.[106] MT reads that Ishmael was simply 'laughing' or 'playing' (מצחק),[107] and LXX seems to translate correctly and specify with παίζοντα μετὰ Ἰσαακ. In it, there is no reference to persecution. Later Jewish tradition inserted the idea of persecution, which was necessary to explain Sarah's harsh response to Ishmael or his conduct, i.e. 'Cast out this slave woman with her son' (גרש האמה הזאת ואת־בנה).[108] Paul draws from Sarah's response a direct application for his community. Isaac's state of authentic heirship is shown by the exclusion of the unauthentic heir who persecutes him (thus, humiliation to exaltation). Paul applies this pattern of authenticity, i.e. status elevation, to the experience of the Galatian community members (οὕτως καὶ νῦν). In other words, Paul interprets for them their recent experience with circumcisers as the same kind of humiliation that leads to exaltation. Instead of circumcision being a mark of authenticity, Paul seeks to persuade that their experience of 'persecution' (marginalization) is the stigma that proves their state of authenticity. Therefore, the application of this interpretation is denouncement and exclusion of the circumcisers as unauthentic descendants (ἔκβαλε, v. 30).

Through the recreated worldview, a marginalized community creates

106. John Skinner, *Critical and Exegetical Commentary on Genesis* (ICC; Edinburgh: T. & T. Clark, 1912), p. 322; H.L. Strack and P. Billerbeck, *Kommentar zum Neuen Testament aus Talmud und Midrash* (6 vols.; München: Beck, 1926), III, pp. 575–76. Cf. *Gen. Rab.* 53; *Pesiq. R.* 48.2; *Pirqe R. El.* 30 for the peculiar interpretation of Gen. 21.9.

107. F. Brown, S.R. Driver and C.A. Briggs, *The New Brown-Driver-Briggs-Gesenius Hebrew and English Lexicon with an Appendix Containing the Biblical Aramaic* (Peabody: Hendrickson, 1979), p. 850.

108. Claus Westermann, *Genesis 12–36: A Commentary* (trans. John J. Scullion; Minneapolis: Ausburg, 1985), p. 339.

and maintains cohesion of the members in the time of adversity. Based upon the recreated worldview, even humiliation becomes a means to achieve exaltation and authenticity of the group. Through this recreated world, the members may gain confidence to face the humiliation and marginalization without yielding to them.

4. *Recreated Worldview as Conceptual Identity*

The pericope of Gal. 4.21–31 has been set within the wider context of a recreated worldview outlined in the third and fourth chapters of the letter. Paul's peculiar exposition of the story of Abraham's heirship through Sarah and Hagar reflects a clear intention of this recreation, i.e. remaking the tradition of Abrahamic inheritance. The question regarding the identity of the authentic heirs of Abraham is important for Paul and for the community members, because it provides a common patriarch, which serves as a clear and positive identity to bind together group members who are uprooted from previous social structures and marginalized by the pressure of the circumcisers and their past compatriots. In the recreated worldview, those with marginalizing power operating under the Torah are discredited from the authentic inheritance of Abraham, thus from the mainline of salvation history. Instead, those marginalized without the Torah inherit the privileges of God through Abraham as his true heirs. This recreated worldview gives the community members a strong sense of authenticity, a *raison d'être* for the fledgling and marginalized group. As the participants in the authentic line of inheritance, the group members should understand their present 'persecution' by the circumcisers as a part of the pattern of humiliation/exaltation that true heirs experience as 'our mother' (Sarah, v.26), who proved herself authentic through her humiliation and subsequent exaltation. This perspective provides a positive identity for the community, in danger of disintegration under pressure from the circumcisers, and it leads to the application of ridding such a devastating negative influence from the community.

This new worldview is intended to help the community members to identify themselves as an authentic religious community. With it, they can resist and even glory in the stigma of marginalization. At the same time, the worldview defines the community clearly against those who are within the previous social structure. For the Jews, participation in this community life means to accept this extraordinary worldview. Therefore, it serves as a clear boundary to resist and regulate negative influences and pressure common among the Galatian community members.

The identity of the Galatian community that is suggested in this chapter is relative to the tradition of the mother religion, Judaism. However, this does not mean that Paul as the community–identity constructor of the instrumental mode was conditioned by a core ethnic sentiment. Instead, he was free to recreate the tradition of the Abrahamic inheritance in such a way as to provide for the benefit and welfare of the members of the newly emerging community. The recreated worldview is offered in order to resist the external categorization as 'secondary status' of uncircumcised sympathizers, which was communicated through pressure to adhere to Mosaic regulations by circumcisers. So far, consideration has been given to a conceptual framework which helps members to identify themselves as an authentic religious community. In the following chapter, I will suggest that such a conceptual dimension of community–identity is concretized in the liminal rite of baptism, which affirms and reaffirms for the members the newly given identity of the community.

Chapter 7

THE DEVELOPMENT AND FUNCTION OF TRIPLE-COUPLETS IN PAUL'S
BAPTISMAL LITURGICAL SAYING (GALATIANS 3.27–28)

A primary interest in this book is to suggest practical ways to help
construct the identity of the Galatian community in the area of materiality
of religion – something that can be seen, heard and/or touched – apart
from concepts and ideologies that have been suggested as identity-
markers. The recreated worldview, which was suggested in the last chapter
as a new identity for the Galatian community, is an example of the
ideological (conceptual) identity-marker. The conclusion of the last
chapter suggested that the rite of baptism may be an actual way to
concretize the conceptual identity of this recreated worldview.[1] Through
the rite of baptism, community members act out the newly constructed
world with the motif of dissolution of social distinction to affirm a new
significance and coherence for themselves, who are categorized as
secondary and marginalized by their significant others.

For the purpose of validating this suggestion concerning baptism, the
analysis starts with the construction of Gal. 3.26–29, where it is suggested
that the passage may be a unique baptismal liturgy that Paul actually
shaped and used during his time of constructing the community in
Galatia. This chapter will continue to use the concept of liminality from
Turner's theory, and particularly the Galatian community will be
understood as existing in a state of so-called 'permanent liminality',
which maintains the state of liminality indefinitely or more precisely for an
extended period of time outside the structural social context (i.e. the
Jewish churches and the larger Jewish context).[2] The rite of baptism with
the peculiar formulaic saying consolidates and justifies life in permanent
liminality as antithetical to life in the previous structure, in order to
maintain the cohesion of the community members and to offer a means of

1. Martyn, *Galatians*, p. 376. Martyn, on the basis of his hermeneutical principle of
revelation vs. religion, undermines the significance of the physical rite of baptism in the letter
to the Galatians.
2. Strecker, *Die liminale Theologie*, p. 111.

resisting pressure from the wider social context.[3] In this sense, the baptismal rite is a positive identity-marking event for the marginalized community members. In this study of the materiality of religion, the case of Mukyokai continues to play an important role as an analogy particularly for the purpose of illustrating the liminal reaction of a fledgling community to the marginalizing pressure of the outside world. In this chapter, 'rite' and 'ritual' are distinguished only by size or degree of complexity. 'Rite' implies the smallest element of sacred actions, while 'ritual' implies an overall event which is made up of rites. Therefore, the term 'rite' is used for baptism, while other feasts and religious acts may be referred to as 'rituals', without making a functional difference solely on the basis of terminology.[4]

1. *Paul's Baptismal Rite in Galatia*

a. *Paul's Baptismal Liturgical Saying*
In Paul's presentation of salvation history (or the discussion of Abraham's authentic heirship), the Torah's secondary nature is pointed out (Gal. 3.19–22). Then the status-shift in v. 25 is followed by a couple of connectives γάρ, but the following verses do not seem to explain directly why 'we will no longer be under a *paidagogos*' (Gal. 3.25). It has been suggested that the connectives γάρ are used here as 'referential' rather than 'explanatory' to refer to an information previously known to the original audience, as in the case of a familiar quotation.[5] In this sense, a thematic correlation is made between 'status-shift' (v. 25) and 'allegiance-shift' of a baptismal liturgy familiar to the Galatians, as the ἐνδύω phraseology suggests (v. 27). Paul explicitly refers to the rite of baptism (ἐβαπτίσθητε) in v. 27. The connection between vv. 27 and 28 is strong, because elsewhere in the Pauline letters, as it is here, the reference to baptism or at least its motif of ἐνδύω phraseology is often connected with the idea of dissolution of distinctions (1 Cor. 12.13; Col. 3.10–11).[6] Therefore, vv. 27 and 28 together seem to form a baptismal liturgical

---

3. Cf. Wedderburn, *Baptism and Resurrection*, pp. 386–87; Moxnes, 'Social Integration', p. 113. Theißen seeks to understand the function of baptism and Eucharist as liminal rites. However, note that Theißen's approach to both rites, as symbolic replacement of cannibalism and symbolic replacement of impurity (in death), may be referring to the temporary liminal rite rather than the permanent liminal rite. Theißen, *Die Religion*, pp. 187–88.

4. Cf. Bernard Lang, 'Ritual/Ritus', in Hubert Cancik, *et al.* (eds.), *Handbuch religionswissenschaftlicher Grundbegriffe* (4 vols.; Stuttgart: Kohlhammer, 1998), IV, pp. 442–44).

5. Cf. Longenecker, *Galatians*, p. 151.

6. In Col. 3.9–11, there is no specific reference to baptism, but the action of ἀπεκδυσάμενοι and ἐνδυσάμενοι remind the reader of the rite. Cf. Wedderburn, *Baptism and Resurrection*, pp. 338–39; Dunn, *Epistles to the Colossians and to Philemon*, pp. 220–21.

saying, which Paul quotes here (the referential use) because it is familiar to the community members. Finally, the quoted baptismal liturgical saying leads to a conclusion in v. 29 on the theme of the larger section concerning the authentic heirship of Abraham. It is therefore plausible that Paul taught the liturgical saying in Galatia when he was founding the community, and now in the letter he is referring to the experience and saying of the rite to strengthen his capacities of persuasion.

The most obvious meaning of baptism prior to Paul relates to the motif of purification or the washing away of impurity in the Hebrew Bible (Lev. 13–17; cf. Ps. 51.2; Isa. 4.4). This custom of purification was widespread in Jewish society and is observed also in the Qumran community (1 QS 3.4–9; 6.14–23). Without implying a direct connection between the Qumran community and John the Baptizer, it is still not too difficult to move from the motif of washing away impurity (ritual impurity) to repentance and remission of transgression (moral impurity) found in the baptismal teaching of John the Baptizer (Mk 1.4, 7, 8). That ritual impurity and moral impurity are sometimes closely connected is observed in how the Gentile problem of moral impurity in the Hebrew Bible was intensified by adding the dimension of ritual impurity to Gentiles in Rabbinic literature (cf. *Sifra perek Zavim* 1.1; *t. Zav.* 2.1).[7] Rabbinic Judaism took it for granted that the water rite had already been necessary for incorporation of Gentiles in the Second Temple period (cf. *m. Pesaḥ* 8.8; *m. Ker.* 2.1).[8] According to Kuhn, the rite of ablution was assumed in the debate on the acceptance of a proselyte to the feast of Passover between Shamaites and Hillelites (*m. Pesaḥ* 8.8).[9] The earliest evidence for Jewish proselyte baptism might be found in a discourse of Epictetus on the distinction between *professing* and *being* (*Diss.* 2.9.19–21) written toward the end of the first century CE. While Oldfather argues that Epictetus probably confused the Christian practice with that of the Jews,[10] it is not likely the

7.   Hayes, *Gentile Impurities*, pp. 122–31.
8.   Schürer, *The History of the Jewish People*, III, pp. 173–74. But this is distinct from the washing for ritual impurity. Cf. Shaye J.D. Cohen, 'Is "Proselyte Baptism" Mentioned in the Mishnah? The Interpretation of *m. Pesaḥ* 8.8 (= *m. Eduyot* 5.2)', in J.C. Reeves and J. Kampen (eds.), *Pursuing the Text* (Festschrift Ben Zion Wacholder; JSOTSup, 184; Sheffield: Sheffield Academic Press, 1994), pp. 278–92 (279–80).
9.   Kuhn, *TDNT*, VI, s.v. 'προσήλυτος'. However, refer to the alternate interpretation of *m. Pesaḥ* 8.8 in Chapter 5 (section 2.b.ii, note 86).
10.   Epictetus, *The Discourses as Reported by Arrian, Books I–II* (trans. W.A. Oldfather; LCL; 2 vols.; Cambridge: Harvard University Press, 1925), I, pp. xxvi, 272–73, note 4. The text reads: '... "He is not a Jew, he is only acting the part". But when he adopts the attitude of mind of the man who has been baptized and has made his choice, then he both is a Jew in fact and is also called one' [ὅταν δ' ἀναλάβῃ τὸ πάθος τὸ τοῦ βεβαμμένου καὶ ᾑρημένου, τότε καὶ ἔστι τῷ ὄντι καὶ καλεῖται Ἰουδαῖος] (*Diss.* 2.9.20).

case, based upon his seemingly clear distinction between the two.[11] However, we should also note that Josephus, Philo, the Hebrew Bible and the New Testament are completely silent about Jewish 'proselyte baptism'.[12] Josephus's account of the Jewish assimilation of King Izates speaks only about circumcision, and this clear case of Jewish incorporation of Gentiles does not refer to baptism (*Ant.* 20.34–48). The same is true for the account of the forceful conversion of two men from Trachonitis (*Life* 113). As long as the dating of Jewish 'proselyte baptism' is not decided, one cannot speak with confidence about its influence on the Christian initiation rite.[13]

In the gospels, no record of Jesus baptizing is found except in the fourth gospel (Jn 3.22; 4.1–2). Here, the rite of baptism is contrasted with that of John the Baptizer, with the motif of repentance and remission of transgression, and the exact function of the baptism by Jesus is ambiguous.[14] Brown equates it with that of John the Baptizer.[15] Jesus' command to baptize in Mt. 28.19 seems to imply a function like that of proselyte baptism because the context in which the rite is referred to is the imperative of preaching to 'all the nations' (πάντα τὰ ἔθνη).[16] However, in the first gospel the only other allusion to the rite is of John the Baptizer (Mt. 3; cf. 21.25), therefore, the reference to baptism as an initiation rite in 28.19 is somewhat surprising. Therefore the function is rather unclear from the gospel.[17] Matthean baptismal formulae with the threefold name may be a later development, as Acts 2.38; 8.16; 10.48; 19.5; Rom. 6.3 and Gal. 3.27 refer only to Jesus' name, which corresponds with the ante-Nicene Eusebian form, 'make disciples *in my name*' (ἐν τῷ ὀνόματί μου, *Hist Eccl.* 3.5.2).[18]

---

11. Stern, *Greek and Latin Authors*, I, p. 543. Epictetus refers to Christians as 'Galilaeans' (οἱ Γαλιλαῖοι) (*Diss.* 4.7.6). Cf. Epictetus, *The Discourses Books III–IV, Fragments, Encheiridion* (trans. W.A. Oldfather; LCL; 2 vols.; Cambridge: Harvard University Press, 1928), II, p. 326, note 1.

12. Cf. Schürer, *The History of the Jewish People*, III, p. 174, note 90. Goodman suggests that what might be taken as a reference to proselyte baptism in *Sib. Or.* 4.165 is most probably speaking of a bath for purification. Goodman, *Mission*, pp. 67–68.

13. G.R. Beasley-Murray, *Baptism in the New Testament* (London: Macmillan, 1962), p. 31.

14. Rudolf Schnackenburg, *Das Johannesevangelium: Einleitung und Kommentar zu Kap. 1–4* (HTKNT, 4.1; Freiburg: Herder, 1965), pp. 449–50. Cf. G.R. Beasley-Murray, *John* (WBC, 36; Dallas: WBP, 1987), p. 52.

15. Raymond E. Brown, *The Gospel according to John* (AB, 29; 2 vols.; New York: Doubleday, 1966), I, pp. 150–51.

16. W.D. Davies and Dale C. Allison, *The Gospel according to St. Matthew* (ICC; 3 vols.; Edinburgh: T. & T. Clark, 1997), III, pp. 684–85.

17. Cf. Donald A. Hagner, *Matthew 14–28* (WBC, 33b; Dallas: WBP, 1995), pp. 887–88.

18. Cf. H. Kosmala, 'The Conclusion of Matthew', *ASTI* 4 (1965), 132–47. Cf. Davies and Allison, *Matthew*, III, p. 685.

While the first gospel's reference to the idea of proselyte baptism may be traced back to Jesus, Paul's clear and specific calling to establish the Gentile mission (Gal. 1.15–16) may have been the occasion for which the initiatory sense of 'new allegiance' was developed in the rite of baptism. The emphasis on new allegiance may be seen in Paul's reference to the symbolic action of 'disrobing/robing' rather than 'washing with water' (cf. Gal. 3.27). The term βαπτίζω is used by Paul ten times and none have to do with the idea of purification, but rather with the idea of allegiance.[19] After the experience of marginalization of Gentile members on account of the core Jewish ethnic sentiment in Antioch, which manifested itself in the issue of Gentile impurity, Paul may have avoided the motif of ablution of impurity for the rite of baptism in order to maintain its suitability for the initiatory rite of a Gentile community (a form of cultural adaptation).[20] It is therefore plausible that Paul is responsible for developing and attaching this distinct significance of new allegiance to the rite of baptism in order for members to gain and maintain cohesion in their newly emerging community.[21]

b. *Origin of the Triple-Couplets Formula and the Rite of Passage*

The motif of 'robing/disrobing' mentioned above together with the rather odd construction of the third of three couplets depicting the eradication of distinction (Gal. 3.28a), has caught the attention of many interpreters.[22] Verse 28a says, 'There is no longer Jew or Greek, there is no longer slave or free, there is no longer male *and* female' (οὐκ ἔνι Ἰουδαῖος οὐδὲ Ἕλλην, οὐκ ἔνι δοῦλος οὐδὲ ἐλεύθερος, οὐκ ἔνι ἄρσεν καὶ θῆλυ).[23] The last couplet

19.   Rom. 6.3; 1 Cor. 1.13, 14, 15, 16, 17; 10.2; 12.13; 15.29; Gal. 3.27. Cf. Acts 22.16 where βαπτίζω is connected to washing away sin.

20.   Contra MacDonald, who is too quick to connect Paul's reference to baptism with water-washing in Rom. 6.3–11; 1 Cor. 15.29; and Gal. 3.26–27, but one does not see baptism and washing connected in these verses. M.Y. MacDonald, *The Pauline Churches*, p. 67.

21.   Martyn notes this peculiar theme in the Pauline baptismal saying and argues that the peculiarity is due to Paul's eschatological interpretation (or signification) of the rite. In his scheme, he undermines the rite's value as a cultic act of initiation. Martyn, *Galatians*, p. 376. One may also consider a possible background influence of the church in Antioch. Jürgen Becker, *Auferstehung der Toten im Urchristentum* (SBS, 82; Stuttgart: KBW Verlag, 1976), pp. 55–56. Becker attempts to locate the theology of Paul, particularly relevant to baptism in Gal. 3.28, among the Hellenistic Jewish Christians in Antioch (Abrogation of the Torah, Eschatological quality, Influence of Hellenistic mystery religions). Cf. Conzelmann, *Geschichte des Urchristentums*, pp. 51–52; Feldtkeller, *Identitätssuche*, p. 138.

22.   Probably the most prominent work on the topic is Wayne A. Meeks, 'The Image of the Androgyne: Some Uses of a Symbol in Earliest Christianity', *HR* 13 (1973–74), pp. 165–208. For the extended bibliography on this topic; cf. Dennis Ronald MacDonald, *There is No Male and Female: The Fate of a Dominical Saying in Paul and Gnosticism* (Philadelphia: Fortress, 1987), pp. 2–3.

23.   Emphasis added.

(ἄρσεν καὶ θῆλυ) is thought to refer to the creation narrative of LXX Gen. 1.27, which says, ἄρσεν καὶ θῆλυ ἐποίησεν αὐτούς. The problem of double-creation accounts (Gen. 1 and 2) invited the speculation of androgyny during the Second Temple and Rabbinic periods (cf. *Quaest. in Gen.* 1.25; *Leg. All.* 1.31–32; *Megilla* 9a; *Gen. Rab.* 8.1; 17.6).[24] Philo, for example, makes an allegorical interpretation of two creation accounts, in which the first account is the creation of 'heavenly man' (ὁ οὐράνοις ἄνθρωπος) who is the image of God, and the second 'earthly man' (ὁ γήϊνος, *Leg. All.* 1.31–32). Therefore, the transformation of the earthly man (into the androgynous state) means a return to the image of God.[25] In the Hellenistic cults, the liminal experience of passage rituals sometimes include the rite of transvestism, where the liminal state of dissolution of gender distinction (an androgynous state) is symbolically acted out by robing and disrobing.[26] The baptismal liturgical saying in Gal. 3.27–28, then, bears resemblance to the Hellenistic passage rituals, and reflects a uniquely Jewish version of reference to an androgynous state. In the New Testament, the idea of 'putting on' in Gal. 3.27 is joined by 'putting off' (Col. 3.9–10), therefore completing the symbolic action of 'disrobing/

24. For example, for the purpose of explaining the meaning of 'rib' in Gen. 2.21–22, Philo employs the image of separation of a bisexual human being, therefore, 'Accordingly the law giver says that woman was made from the side of man, intimating that woman is a half of man's body' (*Quaest. in Gen.* 1.25). However, one is not to connect Paul and Philo too closely and find Platonism of an eclectic kind in Paul after the manner of Philo, as Boyarin suggests. Daniel Boyarin, *Galatians and Gender Trouble: Primal Androgyny and the First-Century Origins of a Feminist Dilemma* (Berkeley: Center for Hermeneutical Studies, 1995), p. 17. Philo may be influenced by a Platonistic understanding of the universe, but he is quite negative about Plato's 'seductive' myth of androgyny in *Vit. Cont.* 63–64. Cf. David M. Hay, 'Things Philo Said and Did Not Say about the *Therapeutae*', in *SBLSP* (Atlanta: Scholars Press, 1992), pp. 673–83 (678).

25. The myth of the androgyne is widely found in the Hellenistic world, for example, in Plato's *Symposium* (*Symp.* 189D-193D) and confirmed in Philo (*Vit. Cont.* 63). The myth goes that there were originally three sexes; male, female and androgyne. The existence in the three modes of the desire for sexual union is explained as the result of their separation into two halves, who seek to regain the primordial state of unity. Concerning the state of androgyny, it says: ἀνδρόγυνον γὰρ ἕν τότε μὲν ἦν καὶ εἶδος καὶ ὄνομα ἐξ ἀμφοτέρων κοινὸν τοῦ τε ἄρρενος καὶ θήλεος [For 'man-woman' was then a unity in form no less than name, composed of both sexes sharing equally in male and female] (*Symp.* 189 E).

26. Meeks, 'The Image of the Androgyne', pp. 195–96. Bultmann, in his analysis based upon a history of school religions, finds a parallel in such cults as Attis, Adonis and Osiris. Bultmann, *Theologie*, I, pp. 138–39. Cf. Lohse, *Umwelt des Neuen Testaments*, p. 242. Cf. Becker, *Auferstehung der Toten*, p. 55. Van Gennep also gives an example of the ritual of transvestism where the male priest dresses like a woman to be incorporated with the deity as his wife. Van Gennep, *Les Rites de Passage*, p. 172. Turner describes the stage of liminal ritual experience as ambiguous and 'betwixt and between' the structural states, and 'they [initiands] may be disguised as monsters, wearing only a strip of clothing, or even go naked, to demonstrate that as liminal [transitional] beings they have no status, property, insignia ...' (Turner, *The Ritual Process*, p. 95) (parentheses added).

robing' in baptism.[27] In Gal. 3.27, it is Christ himself that an initiand puts on, but elsewhere one puts on the 'new self', which is 'according to the image of the creator' (Col. 3.10; cf. Eph. 4.24). In the baptismal rite, one returns to the original image of God (thus 'children of God' in Gal. 3.26); as Meeks concludes in his androgynous speculation, 'the divine image, after which Adam was modeled, was masculofeminine'.[28] MacDonald substantiates Meeks's suggestion by pointing out references to the coexistence of the motif of robing/disrobing and of the dissolution of gender distinction in *Gospel of the Egyptians* found in *Stromateis* 3.13.92 of Clement of Alexandria, *2 Clement* 12.2 and *Gospel of Thomas* 21–22, 37.[29] He argues that this dualistic transvestile saying ('the dominical saying' according to MacDonald) found widely in the Mediterranean coast (Egypt, Syria and Greece) may have been pre-Pauline, known to Paul and in the Pauline churches.[30] This androgynous speculation is attractive in that it offers a plausible explanation of the odd construction of ἄρσεν καὶ θῆλυ in Gal. 3.28a.[31] We cannot assume that the Galatian audience understood the significance of returning to the likeness of God's original creation by hearing the rather odd construction of ἄρσεν καὶ θῆλυ in the formula.[32] Even if the phrase from LXX Gen. 1.27 did not originate with Paul, he may have preserved the phrase in his formulation of the baptismal liturgical saying, because the image of the androgyne as the liminal ritual experience suited on one hand to emphasize the motif of the dissolution of social distinctions and on the other illustrated the idea to those who might have been familiar with such a transvestile (initiatory)

---

27. Meeks, 'The Image of the Androgyne', p. 184. E.g. Apuleius, *Metamorphoses* 11.24.

28. Meeks, 'The Image of the Androgyne', p. 185.

29. He finds a parallel theme and some shared terms among them, of which MacDonald depends primarily on *Gospel of the Egyptian* to identify the (dominical) saying. Clement of Alexandria quotes it as: ὅταν τὸ τῆς αἰσχύνης ἔνδυμα πατήσητε, καὶ ὅταν γένηται τὸ δύο ἕν, καὶ τὸ ἄρρεν μετὰ τῆς θηλείας οὔτε ἄρρεν οὔτε θῆλυ [When you tread upon the *garment* of shame, and when the two become one, and the male with the female *neither male nor female*...] (Clem. Al., *Strom.* 3.13.92; emphasis added).

30. D.R. MacDonald, *Male and Female*, p. 63. The idea of clothing with the redeemer figure has a parallel in gnostic writings other than the three above (cf. *Odes* 7.4; 25.8; *Acts Thom.* 108–12).

31. Also Campbell, who combines MacDonald's thesis with another possible dominical saying of the eschatological angelic state in Lk. 20.36/Mt. 22.30. W.S. Campbell, *Paul's Gospel in an Intercultural Context: Jew and Gentile in the Letter to the Romans* (SIGC, 69; Frankfurt am Main: Lang, 1992), pp. 155–56. Cf. Elisabeth Schüssler Fiorenza, *In Memory of Her: A Feminist Theological Reconstruction of Christian Origins* (London: SCM, 1983), pp. 208–209.

32. However, if it contained such an important theological theme, Paul might have expounded on it while in Galatia.

rite.[33] To be sure, the eradication of the gender distinction may not have been the most urgent issue of Paul for the community.[34] However, at least in his mind, it offered a strong image of the 'liminal experience' of dissolution of social distinction for the passage rite of baptism. Thus, the analyses of the function of rituals and the life situation of the Galatian community through Turner's social/ritual process theory will aid in seeing the significance of this passage rite for community–identity.

2. The Liminal Perspective on Galatian Baptism

a. *Review of Turner's Social/Ritual Process*
The social process theory of Turner was introduced in the theoretical section, and in it I suggested that the Galatian community may be identified as being in the permanently liminal, anti-structural state.[35] The values and indeed worldview of this state are often reversed over against the structural state from which it has emerged. Turner suggests a picture of social process, in which 'structure' and 'anti-structure' pervade one another in a type of teleological process, just as we observe in 'rites of passage' such a process of preliminal (a well-defined life situation) to liminal (very ritual experience, often anti-structural and unconventional) to post-liminal (another well-defined life situation).[36] Therefore, some of the notable characteristic features of both states can be summarized in the columns below:[37]

Structure	**Anti-Structure**
inequality	*equality*
stability	*transience*
complexity	*simplicity*
sagacity	*folly*
purity	*dirt*

33. Wedderburn, *Baptism and Resurrection*, p. 339. Together with the shift from the motif of cleansing to clothing, possibly to avoid association with the Jewish concept of Gentile impurity (Gal. 3.27), the incorporation of the androgynous language for illustration (Gal. 3.28) may be a rare Pauline example of how he sought to render his religion culturally adaptable for Gentile community members.

34. On the priority among the three double-couplets, refer to 2.f in this chapter.

35. Strecker, *Die liminale Theologie*, pp. 96–112. The term 'permanent liminal state' may need a qualification. It is a state that may eventually turn into a post-liminal structure state. In this sense, it may well be called an 'extended liminal state'.

36. Turner, *The Ritual Process*, pp. 96–97, 127–29. Cf. van Gennep, *Les Rites de Passage*.

37. Turner, *The Ritual Process*, pp. 106–107.

Turner clarifies the social process not so much as 'ingroup/outgroup' tension, but as a continual process alternating between structure and liminality. In the former, one may expect one group's total integration of the other once and for all, but in the latter the phases of structure and liminality repeat in the long history of a larger collectivity. Turner sometimes describes this teleological process as 'dialectic' and therefore assumes a tension between the liminal state and the previous structure. Turner's own description of this process is that an exaggerated state of structure may lead to a pathological response 'outside or against "the law"', or 'revolutionary strivings for renewed communitas (liminal state). On the other hand, maximization of the liminal state leads back to the desire for structure'.[38] In the regular social process, this cycle continues. However, this inevitable antithesis in the structure/anti-structure dialectic is amplified in the state of so-called 'permanent liminality', in which is found the peculiar emergent situation of the Galatian community. 'Permanent liminality' usually refers to religious groups that seek to maintain liminality indefinitely (or more precisely extended period of time) outside of a wider structural context as in the case of the early Franciscan movement,[39] and for that matter, the current case of the comparative group of Mukyokai as one observes its emergence patterns.[40]

---

38. Ibid., p. 129.
39. Ibid., p. 145; Bowie, *The Anthropology of Religion*, p. 167.
40. The liminal features of Mukyokai will be referred to in the latter sections through the writings of Uchimura's followers, Yanaihara and Tsukamoto. It was noted earlier that even a permanent liminal community usually finds its way to structure state, thus 'extended period' of liminality to be precise. A curious correlation can be suggested between the teachings of Uchimura and Francis. Turner compares, in the movement's tendency of transition, the opposing features of *simplicity* of liminality and *complexity* of structure, or the 'imaginative/symbolic' nature of liminality and the 'generality/abstraction' of structure. Turner, *The Ritual Process*, pp. 141–55. Lambert notes the highly symbolical teaching of Francis in his Rule. While such strong symbolic sayings as 'the poverty of Christ' and 'the nakedness of Christ' are found, but with no clear definition, others needed to make it into a form of legal regulation in order to maintain the community (a sign of transition from liminality to structure). Lambert, *Franciscan Poverty*, pp. 58–67. Sabatier describes that 'Never was man less capable of making a Rule than Francis. In reality, that [Rule] of 1210 and the one which the pope solemnly approved in November 29, 1223, had little in common except the name'. Paul Sabatier, *Life of St. Francis of Assisi* (trans. Louise Seymour Houghton; London: Hodder & Stoughton, 1894), p. 253. Uchimura's teaching was found at times to lack consistency, so that his disciples recognized their roles as systematizing (or logos-making) the founder's original thoughts in order to provide coherence to the group. Masao Sekine, *Sekine Masao Chosakushu* [Works of Masao Sekine], II, p. 257; Yoshiharu Hakari, *Mukyokai no Ronri* [*Theory of Mukyokai*] (Tokyo: Hokujyu Shuppan, 1988), p. 135.

b. *Galatian Life-Situation and Permanent Liminality*

The previous chapter (Chapter 6) considered the Galatian community as reflecting the characteristic features of permanent liminality, and introduced the idea of 'recreated worldview' as an interpretive framework for Gal. 4.21–31.[41] In this chapter, a close correlation between Turner's theory and the situation of the Galatian community will be made in order to analyse the function of the rite of baptism. Generally speaking, the Galatian community stands in the social process of liminal emergence from the structural state of Jewish collectivity (cf. Gal. 1.13, Ἰουδαϊσμός).[42] In other words, the Jewish founder (Paul) departed from the structural foundation on the basis of a core ethnic sentiment in an attempt to incorporate Gentiles into his religious community, free from pre-set structural confinements. The peculiarity of this process is that it commences a new social process of structure to anti-structure and again to structure, yet not returning to the previous structure of Judaism. Consequently, it eventually repeats its own social process of 'Christian' religious community. This peculiar direction of the social process ('sect emergence' in other words) is often found in religious communities. This process is called 'permanent liminality', in which the state of liminality is extended indefinitely by forever reversing or denying the old structural values of the mother religion (or denomination). The highly confrontational feature observed in the present letter against the previous structure, caused by the peculiar emergent situation of the community in particular and the Gentile mission in general, is within the scope of this concept of 'permanent (or extended period of) liminality'.

This emergent situation of the Galatian community can be outlined briefly in the language of liminal process. Paul situates the local problem of the danger of disintegration (circumcisers' persuasion of circumcision of Gentile members of the community, Gal. 5.2–4, 11–12; 6.12; cf. 2.3) in the larger issue of the tension between the Jewish and Gentile missions, whose approaches to Gentile incorporation are respectively based upon the structural foundation of a core ethnic sentiment and solely upon faith in Christ, free from such a structural foundation (Gal. 2.1–14). As observed in the discussion on the conflicts both in Jerusalem and Antioch in Gal. 2.1–14 in the preceding chapter (Chapter 5), Paul views the Jewish mission, which is based upon a core ethnic sentiment, as threatening his Gentile mission and reducing the Gentile members to subjugation and

---

41. Paul's reinterpretation of the salvation history is due to the community's need to set itself over against the structural context outside, from which the community emerged as a permanent liminal community. The scheme of 'recreated worldview' (more later) is substantiated by A.P. Cohen's concept of symbolic recreation of the influence from the world that the community departed from. Refer to Chapter 1 (section 1.b).

42. Cf. Betz, *Galatians*, pp. 250–51; Martyn, *Galatians*, pp. 440–41.

marginalization (Gal. 2.11–14; cf. 2.3–5; 4.8–11, 17). Therefore, once again the so-called theological (or theoretical) section of the letter (Gal. 3–4) can be interpreted as a remaking of the Abrahamic tradition, i.e. Paul's presentation of a new worldview to the newly emerging community members. This recreated tradition is to replace the core ethnic sentiment, upon which the previous structure has been based.[43] The idea of Abraham's authentic heirship runs throughout the chapters, providing a story of common ancestry for community members who are uprooted from old structural ties.[44] In the peculiar exposition of Abraham's heirship through Sarah and Hagar in the conclusion of the section (Gal. 4.21–31), it was argued that one finds that the statuses of those under the Torah and those not under the Torah are reversed (Chapter 6). This status reversal, or more generally, recreated worldview, is a common reaction of the liminal state against the wider structural social context.

c. *Recreated Worldview and Permanent Liminality*
In order to understand the function of the baptismal rite, it is helpful to revisit Turner's correlation between liminal ritual and liminal community. As a ritual is performed, an individual departs the mundane life pattern and enters the liminal state, then he/she enters back into the mundane life after the ritual is completed (preliminal → liminal → postliminal). One acts out in the ritual itself, either in a symbolic manner or in a more concrete way, a world outside or at the edges of the mundane. In the liminal state, whether it is the temporary liminality of a ritual or the permanent liminality of community life, one experiences anti-structural equality (contra inequality), simplicity (contra complexity), transience (contra stability), foolishness (contra sagacity) and unconvention (contra convention) as noted earlier. The reversal or recreation of values or a worldview (thus 'recreated worldview') are easily observed in the liminal state of anti-structure as response to the structural state. Therefore, a recreated worldview is symbolically acted out in rituals, and in the case of the permanent liminal state the recreated worldview is actually lived out in the community as a new 'norm'.

An example of this recreated worldview of a permanent liminal community is found in the 'gospel' among South African independent churches, which experienced a typical 'ingroup/outgroup' confrontation with the dominant community in the wider social context of colonial social structure.[45] These African-organized churches sought to maintain through recreated worldview the cohesion of those members who were

---

43. Cf. Watson, *Paul*, pp. 61–72.
44. Nash, *The Cauldron of Ethnicity*, pp. 10–11. This sense of possessing a common ancestry is incidentally considered one of the significant features for constructing identity.
45. Turner, *The Ritual Process*, pp. 189–90.

marginalized in the wider structure based upon racial differentiation. The conventional social hierarchy according to skin colour is reversed in the newly created world, whereby the white people are turned away at the gate of heaven because of their earthly status rewards. The white people are the five foolish brides who are denied entry to heaven, while the black people are the five wise brides who enjoy union with Christ.[46]

d. *Rituals' Effects on Community Life*
i. *Ritual in a structural community*

What are the effects of ritual reversal upon community life? One can assume that the effects of a ritual would vary between communities of structural state and of liminal state. First, a ritual's effect upon the structural state is considered. Ritual is a temporary liminal experience, out of the mundane or structural life pattern. The ordinary worldview is temporarily reversed in the ritual. As Turner suggests, 'the feast of love' in the Indian village of Kishan Garhi is a case in point. Marriott reports and comments on this feast. He says:

> The dramatic balancing of Holi – the world destruction and world renewal, the world pollution followed by world purification – occurs not only on the abstract level of structural principles, but also in the person of each participant. Under the tutelage of Krishna, each person plays and for the moment may experience the role of his opposite; the servile wife acts the domineering husband, and vice versa; the ravisher acts the ravished; the menial acts the master; the enemy acts the friend; the strictured youths act the rulers of the republic... Each may thereby learn to play his own routine roles afresh, surely with renewed understanding, possibly with greater grace...[47]

The breach of many pollution rules (a breach of social boundaries) has a cleansing effect on the conventional structure. The deeper understanding of others in the structure actually helps to maintain the conventional structure of the society.[48] Therefore, the effect of the ritual on structural

---

46. Cf. Bengt Sundkler, *Bantu Prophets in South Africa* (Oxford: Oxford University Press, 1961), p. 290. The same type of reversal is also reported among Canadian Indians, particularly the Indians in the Blood Reserve. The Blood Indian Catholics say that their worship of Sun, Moon and the Morning Star corresponds to the worship of Father, Mary and Jesus and thus their worship of God precedes that of white people. Schwimmer, 'Symbolic Competition', pp. 117–55, particularly p. 138.

47. McKim Marriott, 'The Feast of Love', in Milton Singer (ed.), *Krishna, Myths, Rites and Attitudes* (Honolulu: East-West Center, 1966), pp. 210–12.

48. Turner, *The Ritual Process*, p. 188.

community life is ultimately affirmation and revitalization of the structural convention.[49]

ii. *Ritual in a Liminal Community*

What then is the ritual's effect upon the liminal state? Since the community life itself is outside the mundane, a reversal ritual affirms the anti-structural world of the community. In the initiatory rite of the movement of St. Francis, renunciation of property does not turn out to affirm the economic convention of the wider structural context, but affirms instead the permanently held reversed value system or worldview of the community.[50] Therefore, the ritual's effect in the liminal community is affirmation and justification of the recreated worldview of the community, not the conventionality of the previous structure.

The analogical comparative case of Mukyokai is another example of this ritual effect within the liminal community. Mukyokai emerged out of the conventional structural state of the denominational churches. To borrow Turner's description of liminal emergence, Mukyokai's response to the conventional structure may have been a 'pathological' one, outside and against the convention in the sense that the early movement demonstrated a rather harsh response to the church.[51] One of the leading disciples of Uchimura said of Mukyokai: 'It is not just independence from the Christian church of Japan. It is indeed an independence from the universal church. Needless to say that the term "Mukyokai" is a passive term and not a positive and constructive term. However, the term has been a pugnacious term … it cannot be combative unless it denies the enemy'.[52] Another leader, Tsukamoto, articulates the antithetical relation between the church and Mukyokai: 'As long as the church exists as a

49. Ibid., p. 129. The rituals of a recreated worldview are widely observed phenomena. Anthesteria and Hecatombaion are examples of such a ritual from the ancient Hellenistic world (see the subsequent paragraph). Gluckman reports the 'rituals of rebellion', in which Zulu women in South-East Africa enact a ritual protest against authority in order to affirm the social cohesion of the community. Max Gluckman, 'Ritual of Rebellion in South East Africa', in Max Gluckman (ed.), *Order and Rebellion in Tribal Africa: Collected Essays, with an Autobiographical Introduction* (London: Cohen and West, 1963), pp. 110–36 (112). *Kaka-Denka-Matsuri* of the southern island of Kyushu, Japan, is another example, in which male members of the village prepare and serve the feast for the female members of the village once a year in order to affirm the male-oriented social convention for the remainder of the year. *Asahi Newspaper*, http://www.asahi.com/national/update/1211/041.html (12 Dec. 2001). Refer also to the anecdote in the introduction of Shusaku Endo, *Shiroi-hito, Kiroii-hito* [*White People, Yellow People*] (Tokyo: Sincho-sha, 1960).

50. Turner, *The Ritual Process*, p. 145.

51. Ibid., p. 129.

52. Tadao Yanaihara, 'Mukyokai-shugi Ron' [On Mukyokai-ism], in *Yanaihara Tadao Zenshu* [*All Works of Tadao Yanaihara*] (30 vols.; Tokyo: Iwanami Shoten, 1964), XV, p. 10 (author's translation). The article was originally written in 1932.

major part of Christianity, and as long as the church considers itself as being beneficial to salvation of soul, Mukyokai continues its existence'.[53] Mukyokai stood outside the church and refused to form a church. As observed in the previous chapter, the name Mukyokai, which describes a harsh experience of alienation of the founder, was turned around to signify the very *raison d'être* of the community.[54] Gathering outside the church as a non-church (Mukyokai) itself was a sort of ritual experience of permanent liminality, which stood antithetical to the structural state of the church. In the ritual of their religious gathering is affirmed the recreated worldview.

The Galatian community is in a state of permanent liminality. The baptismal rite, with the formulaic saying of dissolution of conventional social differentiations, can be identified as the rite of a recreated worldview. Indeed, the transitional rite of baptism is a reversal rite in a sense that initiands shift their allegiance from one world to another, from the previous structural state to the present liminal state. And in the case of the Galatian baptismal formula, the reversal feature is more apparent because the formula clearly contradicts the value of the wider social convention featuring inequality (over against egalitarianism).

iii. *Summary*

To summarize, one may well stress the distinction between the ritual's function of (1) affirmation of the structural convention in the structural community and (2) affirmation of the newly recreated worldview in the liminal community. The egalitarian motif in the baptismal formula is sometimes compared wrongly with temporary rituals of structural communities of ancient Graeco-Roman cultures. For example, *Hekatombaion* is an annual harvest feast that enacts the Golden Age of Kronos and Phea, in which slaves are allowed to run riot in the streets and are invited to a banquet by their masters. *Anthesteria* is a spring festival, in which the new wine is dedicated to Dionysus. On the first day of the feast, everyone over the age of three participates in wine drinking. Each sits alone silently, thus renouncing the conviviality of the normal banquet or συμπόσιον, and during the feast distinctions of rank and status are abolished.[55] These cases of eradication of boundaries (dissolution of social

---

53. Tsukamoto, 'Mukyokai towa Nanzoya', p. 226 (author's translation).

54. Uchimura, *Consolation of a Christian Believer*, in *Zenshu*, II, p. 36. 'I have become *mukyokai*. No church have I that man made, no hymn do I hear that consoles my soul, nor a minister do I know who prays for me a blessing. I am denied the sanctuary...' (author's translation).

55. The feast of Anthesteria in relation to the feast of Chloe is interpreted as a rite of passage. Cf. Mark W. Padilla (ed.), *Rites of Passage in Ancient Greece: Literature, Religion, Society* (Lewisburg and London: Bucknell University Press/Associated University Presses, 1999).

distinctions) are limited to the ritual itself. Freeman comments on an annual religious ritual of the *Thesmophoria*, in which women are given exclusive access to the ritual, that it may have had the social function of legitimizing the oppression of women for the rest of the year.[56]

The passage rituals with egalitarian motif, therefore, often function to legitimize the structural convention, but it is because these rituals are performed in the structural community.[57] One cannot assume that the function of the rite of baptism in the Galatian community corresponds automatically to such a ritual in a structural community as some have done without examining the nature of the community. Therefore, for example, Paul's baptismal formula, which is a liminal rite in the permanent liminal community, is uncritically correlated with liminal rites in the structural communities (i.e. Hecatombaion, Anthesteria and Thesmophoria).[58] Boyarin maintains that the unrealizability of the eradication of social (gender) differences caused Paul to limit the application of the androgynous speculation within the passage rite.[59] Bultmann, leaving the actual ritual effect ambiguous, postpones to the eschatological future the emancipatory experience expressed in the liturgy.[60] It is suggested instead that the rite of baptism in the case of the Galatian community functions as an affirmation of the recreated worldview in the liminal community, in which the community members have begun to live.

Before focusing on the pericope of the baptismal formula, it will prove beneficial to briefly review the wider structural convention in which the liminal community of the Galatians was located, in order to make a contrast between the convention of the wider social context and the recreated worldview of the Galatian community.

56.   Charles Freeman, *Egypt, Greece, and Rome: Civilizations of the Ancient Mediterranean* (Oxford: Oxford University Press, 1996), pp. 180–81.

57.   Therefore, Fiorenza finds that while the egalitarian ideology is usually confined in the ritual in the case of mystery cults, social consequences accompanied the Christian baptism. Schüssler Fiorenza, *In Memory of Her*, p. 214.

58.   David E. Aune, 'Review of H.D. Betz, *Galatians*', *RelSRev* 7.4 (October 1981), pp. 323–28 (328).

59.   Boyarin, *Galatians and Gender Trouble*, p. 25. On Paul's baptismal formula in Galatians, Boyarin maintains that the unrealizability of the eradication of social (gender) differences caused Paul to limit the application of the androgynous speculation within the passage rite.

60.   Bultmann seems to deny the sociological program and limit the effect within the eschatological congregation, though the actual extent of the ritual effect is ambiguous. Cf. Bultmann, *Theologie*, I, pp. 304–305.

e. *Structural Convention in the Wider Social Context*

In the Hellenistic social background, one finds from time to time a call for abolition of distinction and inequality between ethnic groups, social classes and genders. However, such a call was mostly a poetic nostalgia for the Golden Age or a minority intellectual ideal, which was philosophically explained away or simply ignored.

The ethnic difference was depicted by the phrase, ἕλληνες καὶ βάρβαροι. Βάρβαρος was originally void of a pejorative connotation, and ἕλληνες καὶ βάρβαροι simply meant collectively 'the whole human-kind'.[61] Baldry suggests that the Greek antipathy toward others may have been occasioned by the Persian War, which united the *poleis* against the other people groups.[62] The system of slavery was a norm of the Hellenistic social world, while such a social structure at times caused dissonance with the counterpart ideal of freedom as a moral quality.[63] Probably the earliest voice against slavery was raised by Alcidamas (fourth century BCE) who allegedly said, 'God left all men free; nature has made no man a slave' (quoted in Aristotle, *Rhet.* Book I, 13.2). However, Betz points out that while such an ideal was held by Cynic and Stoic philosophies, the social implementation was not attained, due to their lack of political power. As a result, their ideal was 'internalized' (or redefined) that only men with wisdom were truly free and those who lacked wisdom were indeed slaves.[64] Later Stoics resorted to a type of redefinition of 'equality' in order to affirm the social reality of gender inequality.[65] In principle, they acknowledged that male and female (and slaves over against the free for that matter) possessed equal virtue (Diogenes Laertius, *Vit.* 7.175; Seneca, *Ad Marcian* 16.1). However, the way equal virtue manifested varied according to one's personal character (Cicero, *De Offic.* 1.30.107; 31.110), social and political status (Cicero, *De Offic.* 1.32.115), and individual fortune at any given time (Seneca, *De Beata Vita* 22.11).

---

61. An example is found in Josephus as he tells about the wide influence of Jewish customs in the empire: οὐδ᾽ ἔστιν οὐ πόλις Ἑλλήνων οὐδ᾽ ἥτισουν οὐδε Βάρβαρος [and there is not one city, Greek or barbarian, not a single nation...] (*Apion* 2.282).

62. Harold C. Baldry, *The Unity of Mankind in Greek Thought* (Cambridge: Cambridge University Press, 1965), p. 22. Baldry, however, maintains that such a proposal may not be entirely decisive.

63. Peter Garnsey, *Ideas of Slavery from Aristotle to Augustine* (Cambridge: Cambridge University Press, 1996), p. 238; cf. p. 128.

64. Betz, *Galatians*, pp. 193–94. Betz refers to *Stoicorum Veterum Fragmenta 3*, no. 349–66 and others. Wedderburn finds that, though some parallelism between the Galatian baptismal saying and the Cynics' egalitarian ideology may exist, the image of authentic life in death/dying in Pauline theology is absent from Cynic tradition. Wedderburn, *Baptism and Resurrection*, pp. 388–89.

65. C.E. Manning, 'Seneca and the Stoics on the Equality of the Sexes', *Mnemosyne* 4.26 (1973), pp. 170–77.

Therefore, this redefinition of equality only affirmed the conventional social structure.[66] One may point out as well the egalitarian ideology in the Pythagorean school, but the entrance to the community was highly selective and exclusive.

There are of course exceptions. Meeks points out the cases of upward mobility within the Hellenistic social stratification.[67] Baldry suggests that this social change is due to the process of cosmopolitanism and the influx of non-Greek barbarians (for example, into Athens), to the rise of a 'moneyed middle class' which caused the rejection of traditional respect for the aristocracy, and to the impact of the Peloponnesian war that took more lives of the upper classes.[68] Another exception might be the case of the Epicurean school, which not only admitted women and slaves, but also advanced them to positions of leadership within the school.[69]

However, the general social situation was one that is well depicted by Diogenes Laertius, who attributes the following saying to one of the seven sages, Thales: '... there were three blessings for which he was grateful to Fortune: "first that I was born a human being and not one of the brutes; next, that I was born a man and not a woman; thirdly, a Greek and not a barbarian"' (Diogenes Laertius, *Vit.* 1.33). This social context was shared by the Jews,[70] and perhaps such a saying of Thales above (or possibly Plato) may have been adopted by the Jewish *Tannaim*.[71] Thus *t. Berakot* 7.18 renders, 'R. Judah says: Three blessings one must say daily: Blessed (art thou), who did not make me a gentile; Blessed (art thou), who did not make me a woman; Blessed (art thou), who did not make me a boor (בור)'.[72] One should deal cautiously with the literary evidence of considerably later periods, such as the *Tosefta* and *Babylonian Talmud*. However, together with the general Hellenistic social outlook outlined above, it is possible to locate the Galatian community in a social situation where discrimination and marginalization were assumed on account of ethnic, social class, and gender distinctions.

---

66. Ibid., p. 175. And this is why Seneca is sometimes portrayed as having a double standard for his social dealings (Manning, p. 171) or possessing limited moral sensibilities. Cf. Garnsey, *Ideas of Slavery*, p. 240.

67. Meeks, *The First Urban Christians*, pp. 16–32.

68. Baldry, *The Unity*, pp. 33–34.

69. Meeks, 'The Image of the Androgyne', pp. 172–73. Another example is the case of Deontion, in which is reported a woman president. Adela Yarbrough, 'Christianization in the Fourth Century: The Example of Roman Women', *CH* 45 (1976), pp. 149–65.

70. Eduard Lohse and Günther Mayer (eds.), *Die Tosefta: Seder I: Zeraim* (Stuttgart: Kohlhammer, 1999), p. 99, no. 139.

71. Meeks, 'The Image of the Androgyne', p. 168. ʼ

72. Note that *b. Menaḥ* 43b replaces 'boor' with 'slave'. Lohse and Mayer, *Die Tosefta*, p. 99, no. 140.

f. *Baptism as an Identity-Marking Event*

The Galatian community in particular and the Gentile mission in general have been previously identified as a new entity, emerging from a previous structural context based upon a core ethnic sentiment into a state of permanent liminality. The experience of this state of liminality is outside or at the edges of the wider structural context, thus it is often regarded as anomalous (unclean) and inferior (secondary) from the perspective of the wider social structural context. Therefore, in order to achieve the extended period of cohesion, the stigma of the amorphous state is 'de-stigmatized' or justified by offering a recreated worldview to create a positive identity for the community.[73] Earlier, it was observed that Mukyokai members acted out the ritual of regular gathering outside the church as non-church (Mukyokai) members as an antithetical response to the structural state of the church. That they do not have a church to which they belong was originally a stigma of alienation, but gathering under the name of Mukyokai (non-church) reversed the stigma into a form of celebration.[74] The stigma of the amorphous state was, therefore, 'de-stigmatized' by offering a recreated worldview to create a positive identity for the community. When the ritual of recreated worldview is performed, it has a function of affirming, justifying and celebrating the worldview of the liminal state. It is suggested that the baptism is such a rite of recreated worldview. In the initiatory rite of baptism, the motif of robing/disrobing (ἐνεδύσασθε, 3.27) is introduced to symbolize the act of allegiance transfer, from the world of conventional hierarchy to a world without social distinctions (Gal. 3.28). In the ritual, what was marginalized as anomalous human relatedness is turned into normality or authenticity by dissolving conventional social differentiations. A dissolution motif means equal opportunity (no marginalization) in the religious community – Gentiles are authentic members of the religious community just as they are (without becoming 'Jews' via circumcision). Marginalization as the secondary state based upon a core ethnic sentiment, which is reported as causing the conflicts in Jerusalem and Antioch (Gal. 2.1–14) and is experienced by the Galatian community members, is contested and resisted by acting out the liminal state in the rite of baptism.

One should note, however, that the dissolution motif in the baptismal triple-couplets formula is threefold (Jew/Greek; free/slave; male/female), not merely focusing on the ethnic boundary alone, which is arguably presented as the most urgent concern in the letter due to the experience of

---

73. Refer to Chapter 6 for Gal. 4.21–31 as a recreated worldview. Cf. A.P. Cohen, *The Symbolic Construction*, p. 60.

74. Uchimura, *Consolation of a Christian Believer*, in *Zenshu*, II, p. 36.

marginalization felt both by Paul and the community members.[75] It has earlier been identified in the wider social convention that the overall social differentiation (hierarchical structure) was often summarized in the three categories of ethnicity, class and gender. Therefore, the correlation between the three couplets in v. 28 and this general categorization of hierarchy is strong. At the time of constructing the liturgical saying, Paul's concern may have extended to class and gender differentiations as well as ethnic ones. The motivation for extending the dissolution motif to class and gender differentiations is usually just assumed and not explained.[76] Paul's experience with the Jerusalem apostles and the Jewish mission made a significant impression on him in that the core ethnic sentiment would imply danger of marginalization and subjugation of his mission and community members (Gal. 2.1–14). Therefore, he was led to construct a social framework, in which his community members would be protected and gain security against such a threat of marginalization and subjugation on the point of ethnicity. At this point, Turner's description that 'exaggeration of structure may well lead to pathological manifestations [exaggerated form] of communitas [liminality] outside or against "the law"'[77] may be a helpful insight for the emergence situation of the Gentile mission. Then the inclusion of class and gender differentiations (comprehensive egalitarianism) may reflect the general anti-structural egalitarian response of the community's founder.[78] Then, at least in Paul's thought world, the phrase from LXX Gen. 1.27, infused with the symbolic image of androgynous liminal experience of dissolution of distinction may have

75. It is noted that the order of urgency among the three distinctions may differ according to one's point of view. Some women and slaves, or female slaves, may have felt quite differently. The recent collaboration of African American hermeneutics and feminist hermeneutics breeds awareness of the importance of this point. The history of resistance among the African American theologians to admit to the marginalization of African American women is partially due to male sexism among the very same African American communities. Cf. Brad R. Braxton, *No Longer Slaves: Galatians and African American Experience* (Collegeville: Liturgical Press, 2002), p. 6; Patricia Hill Collins, *Black Feminist Thought: Knowledge, Consciousness and the Politics of Empowerment* (New York: Routledge, 1990). If one takes into consideration the historical situation of Galatia proper in Anatolia, it becomes obvious that the native Phrygians, who were enslaved by the Galati, were either left with the heavy agricultural work or sold off to foreign slave markets. If they made up a part of the constituents in Paul's community, the exigency from their point of view would have been different from Paul's. Cf. Ó Hógáin, *The Celts*, p. 69; Mitchell, *Anatolia*, I, pp. 46–47.

76. Martyn suggests, however, that the ethnic couplet of opposites together with class and gender couplets represent cosmic elements, so that the dissolution of the distinctions means the end of the cosmos and the new age of salvation history. However, one wonders if the primary audience would easily understand such an implication. Moreover, they may be able to connect the dissolution with the actual social hierarchical convention, especially when they belong to the marginalized members of the society. Martyn, *Galatians*, pp. 376, 393.

77. Turner, *The Ritual Process*, p. 129 (parentheses added).

78. Ibid., pp. 106–107.

been a suitable description of the new world, which the members act out in the rite of baptism. Such an egalitarian propensity is also compatible with traditions which reflect the idea of the reversal of fortune (cf. Mt. 5.3–12; Mk 2.17; Lk. 6.20–26).[79] In it also, the marginalized are established in the newly constructed worldview.

There is no way to know how frequently the rite of baptism was being performed in the community prior to the writing of the letter. It seems more plausible to assume that the rite was performed only once for each individual at the initiatory stage rather than performed as a regularly repeated practice for all members, such as the rite of the Eucharist as it is now known. This assumption can be justified by evidence such as that found in 1 Cor. 1.13–17, in which Paul mentions only two names and one household that he has ever baptized in Corinth. If baptism was a part of the regular worship, it may be assumed that he would have baptized more than he mentions here. In this sense, MacDonald is quite right that the former is an 'initiatory rite', while the latter is a 'memorial rite'. The former functions as a one-time transition rite for each initiand at her or his entrance into the community, while the latter functions as a regularly performed rite of remembrance for all members that reinforces religious significance for the community.[80] However, it is plausible that the members were present at each baptismal rite and that the recreated worldview was symbolically acted out each time for all participants (both initiands and observers). The initiands ritually act out departing from the structural convention and entering into the new and reversed world, and at the same time the rite reaffirms and justifies the recreated worldview, thus maintaining cohesion and consolidating the *raison d'être* of the marginalized community for all community members participating in the rite. Therefore, the rite of baptism which symbolically acts out the recreated worldview functions as a significant identity-marking event for the community, which is under threat of marginalization primarily on the point of ethnicity, but also on the points of class and gender for those to whom the categorizations apply.

---

79. For example, Esler suggests that the theme of reversal of fortunes in Luke are both other-worldly and this-worldly. Esler, *Community*, p. 194. Reversal of fortune is a recurrent theme in Lk. (1.53; 6.20; 12.13–31; 16.19–31). Cf. Robert Maddox, *The Purpose of Luke-Acts* (Edinburgh: T. and T. Clark, 1982), p. 103. Or the idea may be described as 'eschatological comfort'. W.D. Davies and Dale C. Allison, *A Critical and Exegetical Commentary on the Gospel according to Saint Matthew* (ICC; 3 vols.; Edinburgh: T. and T. Clark, 1988), I, pp. 466–67.

80. M.Y. MacDonald, *The Pauline Churches*, pp. 65–69.

3. *The Baptismal Rite as an Identity-Marking Event*

The Galatian community was in the state called permanent liminality as it emerged out of the previous structural context, based upon a core ethnic sentiment. Paul interpreted the series of tensions with the previous structure (i.e. the Jerusalem meeting in 2.1–10; the Antioch incident in 2.11–14; the Torah enforcement at the Galatian community) as a threat of marginalization and subjugation of his Gentile mission and the community members. The anti-structural or liminal response to the pressure of the wider structural context is typically the construction of a new worldview different from that of the previous structure. In this recreated worldview, the marginalized community members are offered the sense of significance, the reason and justification for entering and remaining within the community. The dissolution motif of the Galatian triple-couplets formula is such a recreated worldview, acted out symbolically in the rite to affirm a new norm, the new community life in which they find themselves. While a reversal (liminal) ritual of a community in a structural state affirms the status quo of the conventional hierarchical system, the rite of baptism in the permanent liminal state of the community affirms the new norm antithetical to the structural world outside. In this sense, the view that the rite of baptism only symbolically pretended the dissolution overlooks the actual life situation and nature of the community.

However, Paul's reference to the creation order for instruction on the mode of proper prophecy in 1 Cor. 11.2–16 causes some to conclude that he was quite structurally conventional in his approach to the hierarchical structure of the church.[81] MacDonald's approach, which places both Galatians and 1 Corinthians together under the same categorization of 'community-building institutionalization', conditions her to understand the meaning of the Galatian baptismal saying in light of the 'conventional' view in 1 Corinthians.[82] This synthetic approach (or possibly anachronistic one), along with the false understanding of the function of rites, lead some to overlook the impact of the liturgical saying behind baptism (Gal. 3.28), concluding that the gender dissolution motif of the saying was only meant within the temporary ritual experience, in order to affirm the conventional status quo of gender difference.[83] To such a conclusion, the response is threefold. First, it has already been noted that the function of

---

81. Refer again to the conclusions of Bultmann, *Theologie*, I, pp. 304–305; Boyarin, *Primary Androgyny*, p. 25; Aune, 'Review of *Galatians*'. Some feminist interpreters argue that the creation order in 1 Cor. 11.2–3 must be given at least the same weight as Gal. 3.28. Lone Fatum, 'Image of God and Glory of Man: Women in Pauline Congregations', in Kari Elisabeth Børresen (ed.), *Image of God and Gender Models in Judeo-Christian Tradition* (Oslo: Solum Forlag, 1991), pp. 61–80 (64).

82. M.Y. MacDonald, *The Pauline Churches*, pp. 43–44.

83. Bultmann, *Theologie*, I, pp. 304–305; Boyarin, *Primary Androgyny*, p. 25.

passage rites differs according to the nature of the community, i.e. whether it is a structural community or a permanent liminal community.[84] As has been done in this chapter, one should take into account the exact nature of the community in which the passage rite is performed.

Second, one should be aware of the possible tendency of transition in Paul toward the structural state from a liminal state as was earlier pointed out in the discussion of the mode of table fellowship in Chapter 5, and at the same time note the extent and persistence of the social implication of the dissolution motif in the rite despite a tendency of transition toward structure. Paul's attitudinal modification toward the structural state between Galatians and 1 Corinthians can be observed. For instance, he refers to the tradition (παράδοσις) in 1 Cor. 11.2, and if he uses the term as he does elsewhere in 1 Cor. 11.23 and 15.3, this attitude may be understood as a sign of transition from his emphasis on divine revelation over and against human tradition (Gal. 1.15–20 and 2.1–10).[85] In 1 Cor. 15.3–7, Paul aligns himself with the traditions originating from or transmitted through the Jerusalem church. In this sense, Paul came to accept the compatibility between revelation and tradition, and recognized himself fully as a bearer of tradition on the basis of his revelatory experience (cf. Gal. 1.15–16).[86] Indeed, Turner points out that the permanent liminal state of the Franciscan movement finds its way toward structure already beginning a few decades after St. Francis.[87] In the sociological analysis of Mukyokai, I pointed out that the community's peculiar anti-structural (anti-institutional) ideology resulted in a unique form of concretization of its religious experience.[88] Uchimura himself shared his apprehensiveness that the movement might show the tendency to formalization.[89] His followers struggled over their identity between their anti-structural ideology and their need of some degree of organization for the maintenance of the movement.[90] Chiba, a fourth-generation Mukyokai leader, points out that Mukyokai needs 'organization' but not 'institution'. To an outside observer, the difference between organization and institution may be trifling, but those who have struggled to assure maintenance of the community with a strong criticism against the institutionalized church must find a way to express their rightful

84. Refer to this chapter's section 'Rituals' Effects on Community Life' (2.b).

85. Refer to Chapter 3. This shift toward structure is often explained as Paul's later reconciliation with the Jerusalem apostles after the break with them recorded in Gal. 2.11–14. Cf. Bockmuehl, *Jewish Law*, p. 75, note 112.

86. So for Paul, mediator of revelation became also bearer of tradition. Refer to Chapter 8 (section 2.a).

87. Turner, *The Ritual Process*, pp. 146–47.

88. See Chapter 2 (section 2.b).

89. *Zenshu*, XXX, pp. 437–38.

90. Yamagata, 'Byo taru Uchimura Kanzo', p. 207.

identity.[91] Therefore, Paul's argument on the basis of the creation order (1 Cor. 11.3, 7–9) for his instruction on women's prayer and prophetic activities may well be understood as a reflection of this transitional tendency.[92] The apparent development articulated in 1 Corinthians (communal activities as Eucharist, 11.17–34; other modes of commensality, 8.4–13; and worship, 11.2–16; 14.1–40), which is not observed in Galatians, may suggest a transitional tendency toward the structural state in Paul's communities.[93] On the question of more conventional gender relatedness in 1 Cor. 11.2–16, it seems that for Paul the sense of 'orderly' community took precedence, and the radical application of an egalitarian vision in Gal. 3.28 had to be placed under control.[94] Elsewhere, Paul encourages charismatic experiences, but with order (1 Cor. 14.40).[95]

However, this notion of transition in the view of social distinctions needs a qualification. Paul's instruction on head-covering (1 Cor. 11.2–16) needs to be considered against the problem of the gnostic-related confusion, in which some particular individuals confused equality in the community with fusion or amalgamation of sexes to the point of forsaking what Paul considers to be proper 'order'.[96] For Boyarin, this radical kind of application of the egalitarian motive in Gal. 3.28 meant the obliteration of patriarchal marriage, which Paul did not think was appropriate or

---

91. Chiba's comment is based upon my recent conversation with him. Cf. Takahashi, *Mukyokai towa Nani ka*, pp. 12–13.

92. MacDonald hints at the possibility of a formalization in rituals within what she understands generally as the period of 'community-building institutionalization'. M.Y. MacDonald, *The Pauline Churches*, pp. 31–84, especially p. 71. Strecker admits, '...mit Rücksicht auf die innere Einheit sowie die Außenwirkung der missionarisch orientierten Gemeinde mit Strukturwerten angereichert, wodurch freilich der Geist der Communitas (d.h., permanente Liminalität) spürbare Einschränkungen erfährt [...in view of the inner unity, as soon as the activity of the missionary-oriented community necessitated the structure, the freedom of the spirit of *communitas* (i.e. permanent liminality) experienced limitations]' (author's translation and parentheses). Strecker, *Die liminale Theologie*, p. 449.

93. It is not being argued here that there was a direct continuity between the Galatian community and Corinthian community which enables one to determine a developmental pattern; however, one is at least able to see some signs of transition from liminality to structure in the mind of Paul, who founds these communities. Assuming that Paul wrote Galatians during his stay in Corinth (cf. Acts 18.11), there can be at least two years' interval between Galatians and 1 Corinthians.

94. Elisabeth Schüssler Fiorenza, *Rhetoric and Ethic: The Politics of Biblical Studies* (Minneapolis: Fortress, 1999), pp. 169–70. Schüssler Fiorenza suggests that there was a more democratic ecclesiastical relatedness in Corinth that derived from Antioch, which Paul resisted. Cf. Becker, *Auferstehung der Toten*, pp. 55–56.

95. Cf. Schüssler Fiorenza, *In Memory of Her*, p. 236.

96. Anthony C. Thiselton, *The First Epistle to the Corinthians* (NIGTC; Grand Rapids, Eerdmans, 2000), p. 829. Cf. Judith M. Gundry-Volf, 'Gender and Creation in 1 Cor. 11.2–16: A Study in Paul's Theological Method', in J. Adna, *et al.* (eds.), *Evangelium, Schriftauslegung, Kirche* (Festschrift P. Stuhlmacher; Göttingen: Vandenhoeck & Ruprecht, 1997), pp. 151–71 (154).

possible for his community, therefore he confined it only to the baptismal rite.[97] However, on the question as to what Paul may have envisioned in Gal. 3.28 concerning gender distinction, one can only make an assumption by comparison with his vision to dissolve ethnic distinction. As Paul sought to realize equality between Jews and Greeks (and other non-Jews) in their relation to each other and in their access to God and salvation, while Jews did not cease to be Jews and Greeks (and other non-Jews) did not cease to be so, he may have sought equality between male and female in the same sense.

A careful observation should be made of Paul's concern for egalitarian relatedness as well (1 Cor. 11.11–12; cf. 7.2, 4). It is rather significant, according to the contemporary standard, that women are allowed to play an active part in ritual worship by participating in prayer and prophecy (1 Cor. 11.5).[98] Moreover, one does not yet find the same structural convention as is seen, for example, in 1 Tim. 2.11–15. Perhaps Paul refers to the creation order reluctantly for the sake of 'order', for he elaborates on the fact of equal statuses between female and male despite his emphasis on creation order (1 Cor. 11.11–12).[99] Paul's ambiguity in male/female relatedness, observed in 1 Corinthians 7 and 11, may reflect the ongoing dialectic between his original egalitarian motif and the concern for order within the community, leading the community not simply back to the old structural convention (cf. *t. Berakot* 7.18) but to the new structure, reflecting a part of the original egalitarian motif in Gal. 3.28. At this point, one should be reminded of the history of the community development of Mukyokai. Caldarola's analysis of the community led him to conclude that it exhibits a unique sociological phenomenon of perpetuating informality, which should attract the attention of social scientists.[100] However, Mukyokai members who engaged in the translation of Caldarola's work into Japanese are perplexed about his overemphasis of Mukyokai's significance in the field of sociology of religion.[101] They are aware, as noted earlier, of the struggle over their identity in the brief history of the movement and the unique but certain transition from the liminal state to a form of structure, which somehow reflects the original anti-institutional ideology nevertheless. This tendency

97.   Boyarin, *Primal Androgyny*, p. 21. Schüssler Fiorenza finds this perplexing because Paul himself advocates celibacy (1 Cor. 7.7). For her criticism of Boyarin, see Schüssler Fiorenza, *Rhetoric and Ethic*, pp. 166–67.

98.   Mona D. Hooker, 'Authority on her Head: An Examination of 1 Cor xi.10', *NTS* 10 (1964–65), pp. 410–16.

99.   Cf. Schüssler Fiorenza, *In Memory of Her*, p. 230. Kürzinger suggests that χωρίς should be translated as 'different from', thus 'woman is not different from man...' J. Kürzinger, 'Frau und Man nach 1 Kor. 11.11f', *BZ* 22 (1978), pp. 270–75.

100.   Caldarola, *Christianity*, p. 141.

101.   Karudarora, *Uchimura Kanzo*, p. 369.

toward structure seems to correspond to Paul's shift in his relation to the Jerusalem apostles and their values. In 1 Corinthians, Paul stresses the importance of 'tradition' (1 Cor. 11.2, 23; 15.3), and places himself in that tradition. Especially in 1 Cor. 15.3–9, his affirmation of the Jerusalem apostles appears quite a shift from his nuanced stance toward them in Gal. 2.1–14. Though 'structure' does not necessarily mean that Paul is now constrained by old ethno-centred values, he does decide that preserving continuity with the Jerusalem church is beneficial to his Gentile mission.[102] However, this necessitates Paul to be more creative and sensitive in his dealings with inevitably ethno-centred values, as it comes along with continuity with the Jerusalem church, as his writings to the churches in Corinth and Rome seem to convey. Paul's redefinition of such terms as 'circumcision' and 'Jews' (Rom. 2.25–29) and reconsideration of salvation history (Rom. 9–11), which we have considered earlier, are examples of Paul's creativity and sensibility in the process of transition.[103]

There is yet a third response to the false assumption that the baptismal rite only affirms the status quo of gender difference. One should take note of the social implications on the egalitarian motif in the baptismal formula, despite the possible tendency of transition. Therefore, there is among Paul's co-labourers, a female apostle, Junia (Rom. 16.7).[104] Schüssler Fiorenza points out the expectation of actual emancipation of slaves within the Christian communities in the second century CE (Pliny the Younger, *Ep.* 10.96; Ignatius, *Pol.* 4.3).[105] Meeks concludes the social implication of the eradication of the gender distinction in Paul's ministry: 'There are [sic] a number of signs that in the Pauline school women could enjoy a functional equality in leadership roles that would have been unusual in Greco-Roman society as a whole and quite astonishing in comparison with contemporary Judaism'.[106] Taking a close look at the liminal nature of the community, the corresponding function of the passage rite of baptism, and the significant implication for Paul's mission to Gentiles observed above, it can be argued that the rite was a significant identity-marking event for the

---

102. In this sense, Paul's 'instrumental' approach to community–identity construction can be summarized in the more popular language of 'innovation' and 'pragmatism'.

103. Barrett, *Romans*, pp. 57–58; Cranfield, *Romans*, I, pp. 175–76.

104. Junia together with Andronicus is rightly regarded as prominent among the apostles (οἵτινές εἰσιν ἐπίσημοι ἐν τοῖς ἀποστόλοις). Cranfield, *Romans*, II, p. 789; Barrett, *Romans*, p. 259; Fitzmyer, *Romans*, p. 739. See also the contrary view: Theodor von Zahn, *Der Brief des Paulus an die Römer ausgelegt* (Leipzig: A. Deichertsche, 2nd edn, 1910), p. 608, and following Zahn closely, John Murray, *The Epistle to the Romans* (NICNT; 2 vols.; Grand Rapids: Eerdmans, 1965, II, pp. 229–30.

105. Schüssler Fiorenza, *In Memory of Her*, p. 209.

106. Meeks, 'The Image of the Androgyne', p. 198; Schüssler Fiorenza, *In Memory of Her*, pp. 210–11.

marginalized community in Galatia. It is a tangible identity-marker that the community members repeatedly experienced and celebrated whenever an initiand was accepted into the community.

Paul's effort to construct community–identity should be understood as an anti-structural response to the wider structural context. Through efforts of identity construction, he sought to offer cohesion to the newly emerging community. If the baptismal formula was in a sense an egalitarian ideology, it was an internal logic of a small newly emerging community under the threat of disintegration. Therefore, when a postmodern criticism is made against Paul that his baptismal formula contains a hegemonic idea of coercing universal sameness, thus denying the powerless the right to be different,[107] it is evident that the Galatian life situation is being overlooked, in which the teaching was given and the rite was performed.[108] This is not to undermine the important concern against the hegemonic idea of coercing sameness, but one must note who possesses the coercing power.[109] Earlier in chapter 5, it was suggested that

107. Daniel Boyarin, *A Radical Jew: Paul and the Politics of Identity* (Berkeley and London: University of California Press, 1994), p. 233.

108. Cf. Schüssler Fiorenza, *Rhetoric and Ethic*, pp. 158–59. It should be noted that the criticism of Christian identity and its domination has its rightful place. Provision of community–identity as a means to secure safety or stability of an individual or a society is an urgent concern of a fledgling and marginalized group for survival. This has been the assumption of this book. However, because such a provision largely appeals to the human need for security, the notion of community–identity could arguably become an effective rhetoric of social control. We find the most exaggerated form of it expressed in the motto of the *Brave New World*, which happens to be, 'Community, Identity, Stability'. In the fictitious world, 'stability' is controlled solidarity and 'identity' is forced integration. Civilized global community achieved in such a fashion is a perfect state of social stratification and sterilization. Cf. Aldous Huxley, *Brave New World* (Vintage Classics; London: Vintage/ Randomhouse, 2004; originally published by Chatto and Windus, 1932), p. 1. Therefore, my criticism of Boyarin on his approach to the political reading of Paul should be differentiated from the discussion of the value of postmodern criticism of the history of Christian identity and its domination.

109. Boyarin himself makes this very point. Boyarin, *A Radical Jew*, p. 256. A significant issue is raised by Brett in his critique of Boyarin that '*Dominated* communities are not entirely free of *ethical constraints*' (emphases added). Brett, '*Interpreting Ethnicity*', p. 20. However, the focus of the discussion here is 'domination', which often forces individuals or groups to resort to an exaggerated form of resistance as a natural reaction against it. Considering the life situation in which Paul was located in his writing the letter, one may be able to imagine milder expressions that Paul could have used to soften his polemic. Furthermore, the present Christian communities or individuals (even dominated ones) may be encouraged towards ethical discernment in their application of Paul's remarks. However, these meditations and applications of the later Christian communities are different from the ethical evaluation of Paul. Paul's 'ethical constraints' should be evaluated in the context of his own life situation, but not in the context of the devastating consequence of wrong applications of his remarks in the later ecclesial history. By noting this distinction, we may be drawn closer to the reality of Paul's relation to the original followers in the Galatian community.

the unity of the church was sought in two ways.[110] One was by ψευδαδέλφοι who sought the unity by forcing the rite of circumcision on Gentiles, and the other was by Paul who sought the unity by abolishing the ethnic distinction. While one must be sensitive to the social situation in which an ethnic group is in need of protecting its distinctiveness in the still wider social context hostile to their interest, Paul's statement must be understood within the life situation of his fledgling community under the pressure of marginalization.[111] Though Paul's teaching on equality might be easily misused out of context by the powerful, one should take note of the emergent situation of the community to which the formula was given, and realize that the rite of baptism with the formula of dissolution was offering a positive identity and the assurance of authenticity, to those who were denied equal access in the religious community life because they were different.[112]

110.   Refer to Chapter 5 (section 1.b.i–ii). Cf. Segal, *Paul*, p. 198.

111.   Braxton articulates this point from the perspective of African American liberation hermeneutics. He understands Gal. 3.28 as the 'obliteration of dominance'. Braxton, *No Longer Slaves*, pp. 94–95. Cf. Beverly R. Gaventa, 'Is Galatians Just a Guy Thing?: A Theological Reflection', *Interpretation* 54 (2000), pp. 267–78 (267).

112.   We should take heed of the warning of Stegemann concerning the racial implication of the biblical texts that 'anti-semitism and racism are encountered and are not infrequently justified on the basis of biblical texts'. Wolfgang Stegemann, 'Anti-Semitic and Racist Prejudices in Titus 1.10–16', in M.G. Brett (ed.), *Ethnicity and the Bible* (Leiden: E.J. Brill, 1996), pp. 271–94 (293–94). Already in the fourth century, we find a significant example of Christian oppression against paganism recounted by Julian (*Letters* 41B [Bostra]; *Misopogon* 364B). Cf. W.C. Wright's Introduction to the third volume, *Letters 1–73. Letters 74–83 (Apocryphal). Shorter Fragments. Epigrams. Against the Galilaeans. Fragments* (trans. Wilmer C. Wright; LCL; 3 vols.; Cambridge: Harvard University Press, 1923), III, p. xxiv. I argue that the fair and appropriate approach to the biblical texts is first to be sensitive to the life situation in which each statement is made in order to discern the motive of the writer and to evaluate the statement apart from the later history of interpretation and its consequences. Through this differentiation, one may be able to acknowledge and possibly to own responsibility for the historical consequences of the interpretations of the texts.

Chapter 8

COMMUNAL POSSESSION OF A RELIGIOUS WRITING: PAUL'S LETTER
AS A LOCUS OF COMMUNITY–IDENTITY

In this chapter, I will continue to seek a tangible identity-marker for the Galatian community as was done in the previous chapter. Consideration will be given as to how an aspect of Paul's letter to the Galatians may have contributed to constructing the identity of the community. This aspect of the letter does not concern so much the meaning or conceptual content as it does the effect of the communal possession of the physical object of the letter. In this chapter, the latter (the aspect of physical object) is referred to as the 'physico–documentary dimension', as opposed to the 'semantic dimension' of the former. Barton alerts us to the ill-effect of the neglect of this physico–documentary dimension of religious writings, as he says, 'A concentration on the semantic contents of religious works is far from doing justice to the varied purposes and functions of holy books in religious practice'.[1] I suggest in this chapter that Paul's letter to the Galatian community, apart from its semantic content, had a function in helping to construct and maintain the community–identity. This perspective on the function of the letter corresponds with what Graham calls the 'sensorial dimension' of seeing, hearing and touching, which plays a vital role in the religious community life.[2] As noted earlier in the Introduction and Chapter 7, it is necessary to take into consideration this often neglected dimension of religious life of sensorial dimension as a whole (including physico–documentary dimension) in seeking a comprehensive understanding of any religion.[3] Graham says:

> ...seeing, hearing, and touching in particular are essential elements in religious life as we can observe it. Even if they do not admit of easy or exact analysis, they deserve greater attention than our bias in favor of the mental and emotional aspects of religion (in case of scripture,

---

1. Barton, *Holy Writings*, p. 107. Cf. Rosalind Thomas, *Literacy and Orality in Ancient Greece* (Cambridge: Cambridge University Press, 1992), p. 74.
2. Graham, *Beyond the Written Word*, p. 6. Graham himself calls this concept, 'sensual dimension'.
3. Refer to Introduction (3.a).

toward the 'original message' or 'theological meaning' of the text) typically allows.[4]

Needless to say, this present approach does not undermine the importance of the semantic dimension of religious writings. Earlier in the analysis of the remaking of the tradition in Galatians 3–4 and the role of the baptismal rite, the conceptual framework of the recreated worldview was suggested to have been affirmed and concretized through the actual acting out of the reversal in the rite of baptism. In this sense, these two dimensions are, rather than negating one another, at least in many cases contributing together in the life of religious communities. This chapter will attempt to construct a tentative hypothesis, using available evidence, that the letter itself may have functioned as a physical locus that provided the members with cohesion and distinctiveness by communally possessing the letter.[5]

This discussion on this subject matter will start by considering the analogical cases of Mukyokai and Kakure Kirishitan (from this time on, it is shortened as Kakure). A part of the reason why Graham admits the difficulty of exact analysis of the sensorial dimension is that one is left with the text, but with little or no information as to how exactly the text was treated in the original community, and the intention of the author and that of the owners may not necessarily be the same. Barton and others, therefore, take into consideration the genealogical examples of the Jewish veneration of the *Tetragrammaton* and the magical (amuletic) use of the scripture in the early Church as evidences of this non-cognitive dimension of the holy writings.[6] In order to supplement these foregoing studies, examples will be supplied of how the religious writings were treated in the analogical cases in question. In the local groups of Mukyokai, the letters and relics of the charismatic figures function as a locus of the community identity. In the case of Kakure, one finds the possession and ability to recite the commonly held script have a non-cognitive function of creating a locus of community–identity. These observations will serve as a heuristic tool to suggest how Paul's letters, and particularly the letter to the Galatians, may have functioned to provide the community members with

4.   Graham, *Beyond the Written Word*, p. 6.

5.   A question is raised as to why such an important letter addressed to a local community did not survive. The survival and discovery of the ancient manuscripts is a matter of chance, and that is particularly true for the rare possession of a minority community. The lack of tangible evidences does not necessarily forbid a consideration of the topic.

6.   Barton, *Holy Writings*, pp. 106–30; Martin D. Goodman, 'Sacred Scripture and "Defiling the Hand"', *JTS* 41 (1990), pp. 99–107 (103–104); E.A. Judge, 'The Magical Use of Scripture in the Papyri', in E.W. Conrad and E.G. Newing (eds.), *Perspectives in Language and Text* (Winona Lake: Eisenbrauns, 1987), pp. 229–49 (339–40); Johannes Leipoldt and Siegried Morenz, *Heilige Schriften: Beobachtungen zur Religionsgeschichte der antiken Mittelmeerwelt* (Leipzig: VEB Otto Harrassowitz, 1953), pp. 187–88.

a locus of identity. I will particularly note two aspects of the letter that help to provide the community–identity. The first aspect is that the letter replaced the physical presence of the apostle. The physical presence of the apostle was arguably an important locus of the community–identity, therefore, the letter that replaces the presence of the figure in turn had a role of providing the sense of cohesion and distinctiveness of the community. The second aspect is that the letter was a symbol of divine revelation for the community. The awareness of this aspect of the letter would raise the level of importance of the letter as a religious document. The communal possession of such an important religious document may have played the role of providing cohesion and distinctiveness for the community. Then, a further evidence will be sought for this particular physico–documentary function of the letter by considering the function of the autographic signal in Gal. 6.11. In it, I will suggest that the autographic signal in Gal. 6.11 may have served to emphasize for the community members the sense that the letter represents the authority of the apostle, i.e. replaces the physical presence of the apostle.

1. *Analogical Cases of the Physico–Documentary Dimension of Religious Writings and Traditions*

a. *Mukyokai and the Communal Memory of Religious Leaders*
The case of Mukyokai shows a peculiar way of how such a physico–documentary dimension is essential to the life of the religious community, even when the strong attachment of the members to the writings and other objects are regarded as problematic by leaders of the community and Christians outside the community. For example, Caldarola describes how the pupils often collect and preserve the letters and relics given by their *sensei* (teacher-leader). While there is no highly structured hierarchy in the Mukyokai movement, as Mullins suggests, the gatherings of Mukyokai are sustained by the presence of charismatic leaders (*sensei*).[7] The letters and relics of some of these leaders replace their presence especially after their deaths, and continue to function as the vehicle of cohesion for local groups. The communal possession of the collection of relics and letters of those leaders among the religious group members helps to strengthen and sustain the sense of their identity. Because of the peculiar anti-institutional ideology of the movement, the sense of cohesion of each group seems to manifest itself in the members' strong connection with the immediate leader and even letters and relics left by the leader. Caldarola also describes various other ways they express the intensive feeling toward *sensei*:

7. Mullins, *Christianity Made in Japan*, p. 63.

The constant references by Mukyokai members to the *sensei*, his personality, and the living influence of his teachings find further expression in commemorative activities after his death. The first step for the disciples is to edit and publish the *sensei's Zenshu*, or Collected Works. They meet regularly to observe the anniversary of his death and to study various aspects of his life and thought.[8]

This is a case of how a collective memory offers cohesion for a group. Though denominational churches have been critical of this aspect of Mukyokai, a collective memory attached to an 'artefact' (building) often aids the cohesion of the denominational churches as well. In a mission field, a building is often erected to commemorate the work and life of a certain missionary, although it is generally against the sentiment shared among missionaries.[9] Such a phenomenon is of interest to anthropologists, and many devices to preserve and evoke the memory in the material culture (i.e. material aspect of culture, such as artefacts and clothing) are identified. Connerton explains how the Jewish and Christian calendrical festivals with their various rituals (such as Passover, Purim, Hanukka, Sabbath, Easter, Eucharist and Sunday worship) are occasions when those societies remember important 'historical facts' for their religions.[10] In the account of Num. 15.38–39, the Jews used a blue cord on the fringes to remember God's covenant. It functioned as an important object to offer the community their distinctiveness and cohesion as God's people (cf. Josh. 4.3–9 concerning the stones of memorial). The attitude of Mukyokai members to such writings and other objects inevitably became a target of criticism by denominational churches as an excessive devotion and esteem of *sensei,* expressed through the collection of objects and the publication of *sensei's* writings.[11] Therefore, the leaders of Mukyokai have to defend themselves repeatedly against such criticism of their apparent

---

8.   Caldarola, *Christianity*, p. 127.

9.   One example of the commemorative artefact (building) that the author is acquainted with is Meeko Memorial Hall in Yamagata Prefecture, Japan. The general sentiment shared among missionaries is well depicted in 'The New Missionary', an article which introduces the activities of the new generation of missionaries of various church affiliations after the post World War II missionary movement. For example, Richard N. Ostling, *et al.*, 'The New Missionary', *Time Magazine*, 52 (27 Dec. 1982), pp. 38–44.

10.   Paul Connerton, *How Societies Remember* (Themes in the Social Sciences; Cambridge: Cambridge University Press, 1989), pp. 46–47. He uses a nuanced expression that 'to remember is to make the past actual' (p. 46), leaving room for the idea that the memory is susceptible to transformation for the benefit of the preservers of the memory (p. 51). Thus, when one speaks of a device that 'preserves' a memory, a kind of communal control of the memory is usually implied. He goes on to explain a result of 'inscribing' of the oral tradition: that the writing (instead of the memorized tradition) can 'lie around as artefacts and be consulted as required' (p. 76). Cf. Esler, *Conflict and Identity*, pp. 179–80.

11.   Cf. Takahashi, *Mukyokai towa Nanika*, pp. 12–13.

devotion and esteem of *sensei* and their writings.[12] Sekine argues that the strong tie of *sensei*–pupil relationship is evidence of mutual love among the existential community of individuals.[13] Takahashi, the second-generation leader of Mukyokai, admits the intricate bond of *sensei*–pupil to be problematic.[14] Meanwhile, such a physico–documentary dimension of the religious writings continues to be vital for concretizing daily religious experience and thus strengthening a sense of unique identity.

b. *Kakure and the Communal Possession of Oral Tradition*

Let us take another analogy into consideration for this analysis. In the oral transmission of *Orasho no Honyaku* ('Translation of Oracles [*Oratio*]') by a minority Christian group in Japan, a clear case emerges of how the non-semantic dimension of a religious tradition functions to ensure cohesion of the group. The systematic persecution by the first three *Shoguns* of Edo-era in the early part of the seventeenth century against the church, which was founded by Francisco Xavier and other Jesuit missionaries who landed in Japan in 1549, resulted in the martyrdom of about 40,000 believers (13 per cent of the whole Christian population if we count the martyrs of Shimabara revolt), nation-wide seclusion in 1639, and the birth of the minority Christian community called Kakure. Kakure, or literally 'hide-out Christian(s)', is so called because under severe pressure of persecution, peasants and fishermen formed underground Christian communities in small islands and secluded beach villages to preserve both the faith and their lives. They were discovered by Bernard Petitjean of Société de Missions-Etrangères de Paris 266 years later in 1865 just after Commodore Perry forced the Tokugawa Shogunate to forsake its seclusion policy (1854). While some of the members of the community (estimated around 35,000) subsequently attached themselves to the orthodox practice of Roman Catholicism, most remain within distinctive communities of faith, following their own long-cherished and hidden traditions.[15] One of the oral traditions found among the scattered groups of Kakure is the *Orasho no Honyaku*.

Orasho no Honyaku or Translation of Oracles (*Oratio*) was originally a combination of a prayer book and catechism, first published in 1592. During the long period of the underground practice of religion, the Kakure community on the island of Ikitsuki orally preserved one of the

---

12. Cf. Yanaihara, *Mukyokai-Shugi Kirisuto-Kyo Ron*, pp. 191–92; Sekine, *Sekine Masao Zenshu*, II, p. 452.

13. Sekine, *Sekine Masao Zenshu*, II, p. 452.

14. Takahashi, *Mukyokai towa Nani ka*, pp. 12–13.

15. Johannes Laures, *The Catholic Church in Japan* (Connecticut: Greenwood Press, 1954), pp. 178–79. Harrington, *Japan's Hidden Christians*, pp. xiii, 35.

prayers in the *Orasho*, 'Hail Mary'. The Latin prayer of the *Pater Noster* in a corrupted form is also found in their oral tradition. Those who came into contact with Kakure after the period of their hide-out were convinced that the community members did not understand the conceptual content of what they were reciting, not only the *Pater Noster* but also the exact meaning of the Japanese oracles.[16] Whelan reports that the transcription of *Orasho*, with which she came into contact, are written in *kana* (the phonetic letters) and not in the mixture of *kana* and *kanji* (the semantic characters). This enables the transcription without the semantic understanding of the *Orasho*.[17] The communally recited text, though unintelligible, was an important religious marker for the ones who possessed it. The very experience of reciting the text communally helped the members to bind themselves as a unique religious community. Tagita argues that the ability to recite the oracles was a matter of pride and gave the members of Kakure a feeling of superiority.[18] Thus the possession and reciting of the tradition (and later the text) was and is an important factor in constructing and maintaining the community–identity.[19]

It has been observed in the two analogical cases of Mukyokai and Kakure that the possession of a religious document or tradition had a vital role in offering community members a strong sense of cohesion and distinctiveness. In other words, the physico–documentary dimension of the letter is seen to provide a locus of community–identity. There are at least two particular reasons for this physico–documentary function. One, as found in the case of Mukyokai, is that the letters and other documents as well as other artefacts functioned to preserve and evoke the communal memory of the leaders who had a strong tie with members of the local groups. This analogy substantiates the sociological concept of 'social memory'. The other, as found in the case of Kakure, is that the communal possession of a unique oral tradition provided the community members with a sense of pride and distinctiveness of their community in relation to

16. Harrington, *Japan's Hidden Christians*, pp. 70–71. Cf. also Johannes Laures, *Kirishitan Bunko* (Monumenta Nipponica Monographs, 5; Tokyo: Sophia University Press, 3rd edn, 1957).

17. Christal Whelan, *The Beginning of Heaven and Earth* (Honolulu: University of Hawai'i Press, 1996), p. 20.

18. Koya Tagita, 'Kirisuto-Kyo no Nihon-teki Bunka-Henyo' [Modification of Christianity into the Japanese Culture], *Shukyo Kenkyu* [*Study of Religion*] 155 (1958), pp. 65–88.

19. Harrington compares the physico–documentary dimension of this religious tradition with the way some of the Buddhist scriptures are chanted in the original Sanskrit language unintelligible to most chanters, and she argues for the significance of the dimension of the script for the cohesion of the religious group. Harrington, *Japan's Hidden Christians*, p. 72. Cf. also Carmen Blacker, *The Catalpa Bow* (London: Allen & Unwin, 2nd edn, 1986), p. 97. Cf. also Wilfred Cantwell Smith, *What is Scripture?: A Comparative Approach* (London: SCM; Minneapolis: Fortress, 1993), p. 156.

outgroups. These observations will be used heuristically in considering the similar function of the letter to the Galatians in particular and other New Testament writings in general in the following section.

2. *Galatians as a Locus of Community–Identity*

What can be known or surmised about the function of a particular letter of Paul addressed to a specific local community, and particularly in relation to the construction of community–identity? This section seeks to answer this question.

a. *Pauline Letters as Locus of Community–Identity*
As the letter to the Galatians may have functioned as a locus of community–identity on the basis of the observations above, two aspects of the letter will be examined, which may have led the letter to be regarded as a physical locus of community–identity. First, based upon the idea that a religious document functions as a device to preserve and evoke the communal memory, the letter to the Galatians replaced the presence of the apostle, i.e. preserving and evoking his memory in his absence, whose presence was a physical locus that provided the community with a sense of cohesion and distinctiveness. Second, based upon the idea that the communal possession of a unique tradition provides a sense of pride and distinctiveness in the community, Galatians provided for the community a sense of cohesion and distinctiveness because of its religious significance as a record of divine revelation.[20]

i. *The letter as replacing the presence of the apostle*
In order to argue for the letter's function to replace the presence of the apostle, I will consider two factors which seem to have helped to provide for the community a sense of cohesion and distinctiveness. First, I will consider how Paul's very presence may have functioned as a locus of community–identity. Second, I will argue that his letter replaced Paul's presence in his absence and that as a result it functioned as a locus of community–identity.

a. The apostle as the locus of community–identity. That the physical presence of Paul was a significant locus of community–identity can be argued primarily by his awareness of being the apostle to the Gentiles and the practice of founding Gentile communities on the basis of this self-

---

20. While these features may be true of other Pauline letters and the rest of the New Testament writings, and some insights may be drawn from those writings, the primary focus of this discussion is on the function of the letter to the Galatians.

awareness. As the apostle and founder of the community, he felt he could pronounce a curse on those who hindered his mission (Gal. 1.1, 8–9). Paul's description of his relationship to the community members seems to convey that he possessed a considerable authority among them. That he was informed of and perhaps consulted regarding the interference of the circumcisers, which had caused confusion among the community members, seems to indicate that Paul was regarded as being authoritative and responsible for the well-being and destiny of the community in Galatia (Gal. 1.6). The Galatians seem to be familiar with the way Paul received a divine commission to work among them (Gal. 1.13–16). They shared with Paul a vivid charismatic experience that served to remind them of the evidence of his authoritative teaching (Gal. 3.1–5). His original reception by the community is, according to Paul, unusually positive (Gal. 4.14). The Galatians' acceptance of Paul as an 'angel of God' may be a likely event based upon his miraculous works among them (Gal. 3.1–5), especially if Luke's account of the association of Paul (and Barnabas) as Mercury (and Jupiter, Acts 14.12) reflects a kind of expected response to a miracle worker. At the occasion of their acceptance of Paul, he may have explained to them his understanding of 'messenger' based upon the Hebrew verb שׁלֹה (to send): one who is like unto the one who sends (Christ Jesus; cf. *m. Ber.* 5.5), therefore as Christ Jesus (Gal. 4.14, ὡς ἄγγελος θεοῦ ἐδέξασθέ με ὡς Χριστὸν Ἰησοῦν).[21] It is, therefore, plausible to conclude that the founding apostle with such authority played a significant role in providing cohesion and distinctiveness to the community.

Paul's awareness as an apostle of Christ may be expressed in the curious description of his original reception by the Galatians as an 'angel of God/ Christ Jesus' (Gal. 4.14). Indeed, Paul establishes himself as a bearer of the life and death of Christ (Gal. 2.20; cf. 6.17) in his effort to affirm the truthfulness of his gospel and authority. Later, as Paul faced the opposition in Corinth, he again defends his apostleship by pointing out the fact that he shares Christ's affliction, life and death (2 Cor. 4.10; 11.21–29).[22] The authority was passed on to following generations through the 'laying on of hands' (ἐπίθεσις τῶν χειρῶν) ensuring the

---

21. Cf. K.H. Rengstorf, *TDNT*, I, s.v. 'ἀπόστολος' (especially pp. 414–17).

22. Commenting particularly on 2 Cor. 4.10 (4.7–15), Güttgemanns suggests that the mortal body of the apostle is the location of the Kyrios' epiphany, i.e. his suffering demonstrates the presence of the crucified and resurrected one, thus the Lord. See the discussion in the section, 'Die Epiphanie und Präsenz des irdischen Jesus', in Erhardt Güttgemanns, *Der leidende Apostel und sein Herr: Studien zur paulinischen Christologie* (FRLANT, 90; Göttingen: Vandenhoeck & Ruprecht, 1966), pp. 112–19 (particularly pp. 116–17).

continuation of 'tradition' (1 Tim. 4.14; 2 Tim. 1.6; cf. Acts 13.2–3).[23] The authenticity of the tradition is proven by the lifestyle of the bearers of that tradition (1 Tim. 3.1–13; cf. Tit. 1.5–9). Therefore, the idea of passing on tradition should be understood not only in a cognitive sense, i.e. the instructions and information of Jesus (1 Cor. 11.23; 15.1–7), but also as the successive line of bearers of the tradition.[24] The importance of 'tradition-bearer' is clearly spelled out in the writing of the Apostolic Fathers. In the first decade of the second century, Ignatius, the bishop of Antioch, *en route* to his final destination in Rome, explicitly spelled out the importance of the role of bishop (i.e. bearer of the authentic tradition) for the cohesion of communities in threat of disintegration from numerous schismatic movements.[25] He emphasized the continuity of tradition starting from Christ through apostles to bishops (Ignatius, *Trall.* 7; cf. also 2–3).[26] Elsewhere, he says that the mind of God is mediated through Christ to bishops (Ignatius, *Eph.* 3). The church members are instructed to do everything relating to the church in the presence of their bishop (Ignatius, *Smyrn.* 8; cf. *Eph.* 5; *Mag.* 7). Eucharist without the presence of the bishop is not valid (Ignatius, *Smyrn.* 8). Such an enormous

23.   Especially the occasion of the laying of Paul's hands on Timothy is suggested at the occasion of Timothy's enrolment in Paul's Gentile mission. Cf. Luke T. Johnson, *The First and Second Letters to Timothy* (AB, 35a; New York: Doubleday, 2001), p. 345. For various interpretations of the occasion and function of the laying on of hands of Timothy, see I. Howard Marshall, *A Critical and Exegetical Commentary on the Pastoral Epistles* (ICC; Edinburgh: T. & T. Clark, 1999), pp. 697–98.

24.   Cf. James D.G. Dunn, *Unity and Diversity in the New Testament: An Inquiry into the Character of Earliest Christianity* (London: SCM, 1977), pp. 66–69. He classifies the tradition into (1) kerygmatic (1 Cor. 15.1–3), (2) liturgical (1 Cor. 11.23–25), and (3) ethical (1 Cor. 7.10; 1 Thess 4.1) instructions. As was noted in Chapter 7, Paul seems to have found compatibility between his role as a mediator of revelation and bearer of tradition between his writing Galatians and 1 Corinthians. Therefore, when Paul speaks about the tradition of the Eucharist in 1 Cor. 11.23, which may well go back to Jesus' instruction to the immediate disciples, he describes it as 'I received from the Lord' (cf. 1 Cor. 15.3). Cf. Gordon Fee, *The First Epistle to the Corinthians* (NICNT; Grand Rapids: Eerdmans, 1987), p. 548. Fee understands the passage that Paul received the instruction either at Damascus or Antioch from the believers before him, but considered it coming ultimately from Jesus. In 1 Cor., Paul emphasizes the importance of attending to the passing on of tradition (1 Cor. 11.2) both from Jesus (1 Cor. 11.23) and about Jesus (1 Cor. 15.11–17). Especially in 1 Cor. 15.11–17, Paul seeks to make himself a part of that tradition, which may date back to the earliest days of the Christian community in Jerusalem (Fee, *1 Corinthians*, pp. 721–22). Together with these traditions, the tradition bearers seem to have played a significant role in shaping and preserving the communal identity.

25.   Edgar J.A. Goodspeed, *A History of Early Christian Literature* (Chicago: University of Chicago Press, rev. edn, 1966), p. 15.

26.   Ignatius seems to emphasize the importance of hierarchy in the church, i.e. bishop, presbyters and deacons with God, Jesus and the apostles. William R. Schoedel, *Ignatius of Antioch* (Hermeneia; Philadelphia: Fortress, 1985), pp. 141–42.

authority, which was on the basis of continuity of tradition, caused the bishop to function as a physical locus of community–identity. Tradition and its bearers played a role in shaping and preserving the identity of the early church as a whole, and particularly Paul's very presence was a significant locus of the cohesion and distinctiveness of the Galatian community.

b. The letter as replacement for the apostle's presence. Besides sending or assigning a delegate (1 Thess. 3.2; Phil. 2.23, cf. Acts 14.23), Paul's primary means of contact with his communities seems to be his letters.[27] Goodspeed comments on Paul's letters, 'In the hand of Paul this simplest form of composition had developed into a powerful instrument of religious instruction'.[28] In addition to this cognitive dimension, there is yet another non-cognitive, physico–documentary dimension to his letters. Paul's letters signified in one sense absence of the authoritative figure from the addressed communities, but in another they replaced that presence, at least as a substitute for his visit (1 Cor. 5.3; 2 Cor. 10.11; 13.10). It is unclear whether Paul had a definite intention to make his letters a form of religious artefact, besides the intention of the cognitive instruction as Goodspeed suggests. From his letter, it is clear that Paul wished to be with the Galatians and display his emotion to them, but instead he wrote this desire as a substitutionary, next best thing to an actual visit (Gal. 4.20). He elsewhere extended his authoritative 'warning' via letter to those who discredited Paul's authority in his absence in order to prepare them for his visit to exert real authority (2 Cor. 10.11).[29] That Paul probably did not intend his letters to be read once by decision makers within the communities and then set aside as a one-time response to a particular problem is at least supposed by the central role public reading played in early church life (1 Tim. 4.13, cf. 2 Cor. 7.8; 2 Thess. 3.14), in which the reading of the scripture seems to be just as important a ministry of local church leaders as their ministry of preaching and teaching. Johnson comments that it 'was in the context of such public reading, in fact, that Paul's own letters were undoubtedly first read'.[30] Colossians instructs the

27. In Corinth, there are three visits (initial church founding in Acts 18.1–3/painful visit in 2 Cor. 2.1/visit *en route* to Jerusalem in 2 Cor. 12.14; 13.1–2; Acts 20.2–5), two reports (from those from Cloe in 1 Cor. 1.11/another inquiry in 1 Cor. 7.1), delegations (Timothy in 1 Cor. 4.17–19; 16.10–11/Titus in 2 Cor. 7.15), and particularly four letters (lost letter in 1 Cor. 5.9/1 Cor./lost letter in 2 Cor. 2.3–4/2 Cor.).

28. Goodspeed, *A History*, p. 7.

29. P.W. Barnett, *The Second Epistle to the Corinthians* (NICNT; Grand Rapids: Eerdmans, 1997), pp. 277–28.

30. Johnson, *1 & 2 Timothy*, p. 252. Cf. 2 Cor. 7.8; Col. 4.16; 1 Thess. 5.27; 2 Thess. 3.14. Harry Y. Gamble, *Books and Readers in the Early Church: A History of Early Christian Texts* (New Haven and London: Yale University Press, 1995), p. 205. Cf. Justin Martyr, *Apol.* 1.67.

recipients that the letter should be read among them and also among the Laodicean believers (Col. 4.16). Paul requires in 1 Thessalonians that the letter 'be read to all the brothers' (1 Thess. 5.27). It is suggested then that Paul and his immediate followers may have envisioned his letters to be read repeatedly in the communal setting.[31]

If this is as much as can be known about Paul's intention regarding his letters to his communities, what can be gleaned from observation of the analogical cases on the intention or response of the recipients and owners of such letters? In the case of Mukyokai, the community members who had a strong tie with the leader regarded his documents and other relics as a means to preserve and evoke the memory of the leaders. In other words, in the absence of the leaders, their documents substituted for and replaced their presence. Because the leaders played a significant role in shaping the identity of the group, the documents helped members to preserve their identity, in its function of substituting for the leaders' presence. Such a form of religiosity or simply social behaviour was seen in the Hebrew Bible, in which stones and cords on fringes preserved and evoked the memory of God's covenant faithfulness. Such a propensity to sensoriality, i.e. concretization of religious identity through a material object (materiality of religion) may have been operative among the members of Paul's communities. Therefore, the letter to the Galatians may have been a locus of community–identity as a replacement for the presence of the apostle and founder of the community. In order to assist this inference based upon the analogical case, consideration will now be given to another aspect of the Galatian letter.

ii. *The letter as record of God's revelation*
The other aspect of the letter to consider is its religious significance as a record of God's revelation. Galatians comes closer to the Apocalypse than any other NT writings, let alone Pauline letters, because of its revelatory character. A comparison of the Apocalypse and Galatians reveals that both authors take care to describe the occasion of the revelatory experience (Gal. 1.15–16/Rev. 1.12–20), and in both writings there is a clear pronouncement of curse upon the person who alters the revelation (Gal. 1.8–9/Rev. 22.18–19). Together with the pronouncement of curse, Galatians ends with the pronouncement of 'peace/mercy' to those who follow 'this canon' (κανών, Gal. 6.16).[32] In the Apocalypse, the 'integrity formula' (the pronouncement of calamities) suggests, according to Aune, that 'he (the author) regarded his book as the record of a divine revelation

31. Cf. Johnson, *1 & 2 Timothy*, p. 252, also p. 230 on 1 Tim. 3.14; Gamble, *Books and Readers*, p. 213.

32. Cf. Betz, *Galatians*, p. 321. Betz understands Gal. 1.8–9 (conditional curse) and 6.16 (conditional blessing) as book-ending the body of the letter.

that was both complete (therefore unalterable) and sacred'.[33] Similar authority is suggested to be given to the book, with the possible background of the warning in Deuteronomy against false prophets with 'inscriptional sanction and curse'.[34] It is suggested, therefore, that Paul may have written the letter with awareness of such a revelatory authority akin to the Apocalypse, and the recipients may have responded to Paul's description of revelation and authority with seriousness, especially as they were reminded of the occasion when Paul performed miraculous (spiritual) works among them; divine revelation accompanied by divine power (Gal. 3.2–5). Widengren surveys the idea of the giving of the heavenly book via an apostle or prophet in such literature as from Ancient Sumerian, Jewish and Christian gnostic religions and Islam. In it, an apostle (or prophet) ascends to receive the divine revelation or book (e.g. the Torah for Moses) for the religious community on earth. Especially in Mesopotamian religion, the concealment of the book in a sack denotes a sign of inviolability or unalterability of the writing. Paul's self-description as an apostle (or mediator of the divine revelation) in 2 Cor. 12.1–5 and his signification of the divine revelation through a pronouncement of curse upon those who alter it (Gal. 1.8–9) seem to come close to the idea of the apostle and the heavenly book.[35] Therefore, the Galatian community members received the letter with the awareness that it was a record of divine revelation and thus a significant religious writing, directly addressed to them. In it, they would find God's will specifically for them.

The possession of such a special religious writing may have enhanced among community members a sense of special worth. To recall the case of Kakure, the possession of oral tradition and of the ability to recite the unintelligible tradition gave them a sense of pride and significance in relation to the oppressive force of the state outside their underground community. Considering the highly revelatory feature of the letter to the Galatians, the communal possession of such a significant religious writing may well have provided a locus of cohesion and distinctiveness within the community.

I suggest that the letter to the Galatians may have functioned as a locus of community–identity on the basis of two assumptions drawn from consideration of the two analogical cases of Mukyokai and Kakure. It was suggested that the presence of Paul was a significant physical locus of identity to the Galatian community, because of his awareness of being an

---

33.   David E. Aune, *Revelation 17–22* (WBC, 52c; Dallas: WBP, 1998), p. 1231 (author's parentheses).

34.   G.K. Beale, *The Book of Revelation* (NIGNT; Grand Rapids: Eerdmans, 1999), pp. 1150–51. Cf. Deut. 4.1–2; 12.32; 29.19–20.

35.   Geo Widengren, 'The Ascension of the Apostle and the Heavenly Book (King & Saviour III)', *Uppsala Universitets Årsskrift* 7 (1950) in *Uppsala Universitets Årsskrift* (Uppsala: A.-B. Lundequistska Bokhandeln, 1950), pp. 1–117 (12, 84–85).

apostle to Gentiles and his work of founding the Galatian community on the basis of that apostolic awareness. On the basis of the analogical case of Mukyokai, an assumption was made: the letter may have preserved and aroused the communal memory of their apostle and founder, whereby offering to them a sense of cohesion and distinctiveness. I took into consideration as well the revelatory significance of the letter to the Galatians in comparison with the Apocalypse and explained that the letter, with such authority based upon divine revelation, was perceived by community members as a significant religious writing. On the basis of the analogical case of Kakure, it was deduced that the communal possession of such a significant religious writing may have enhanced among the direct recipients of the letter a sense of significance and distinctiveness as an authentic religious group. Considering the effect of the two features discussed here, the letter to the Galatians may have been perceived by community members as an important locus of their identity. The church in general seems to have accepted the Pauline corpus as early as the end of the first century[36] as 'scriptures' (2 Pet. 3.15–16),[37] i.e. inspired and authoritative writing together with the Hebrew Bible.[38] It may be surmised that behind this collective acceptance was the local recognition

---

36. A wide range of possibilities for the date of 2 Pet. (between 60–160 CE) has been suggested. Bauckham's analysis of the literary dependence seems helpful in narrowing the range of possible dates for the letter to 80–100 CE. Refer to Bauckham for 2 Peter's relation in thought and language with *1 Clem.*, *2 Clem.* and *Shepherd of Hermas*. Richard J. Bauckham, *Jude, 2 Peter* (WBC, 50; Waco: WBP, 1983), pp. 149–50, 157–58. Bauckham comments on the historical situation common to these works that '…they were written at a time when either the generation of the apostles or the generation of the first converts in their place of origin had almost or just passed away (*1 Clem.* 23.3; 44.1–3; *2 Clem.* 11.2; *Hermas, Vis.* 3.5.1; *Sim.* 9.15.4)'. See also David G. Horrell, *2nd Peter and Jude* (Epworth Commentaries; Peterborough: Epworth, 1998), pp. 137–38.

37. The letter of Paul in 2 Pet. is identified by some as Galatians because the addressees of 1 Pet. are in Asia Minor (1 Pet. 1.1; cf. 2 Pet. 3.1). Cf. Bauckham, *Jude, 2 Peter*, p. 330. Others argue that the writing of Paul here refers to portions of his letters closely connected to the arguments of 2 Pet. (Rom. 2.4 for 3.14 and 1 Thess. 5.2 for 3.10). Jerome H. Neyrey, *2 Peter, Jude* (AB, 37c; New York: Doubleday, 1993), p. 250. However, the phrase, 'as he does in all his letters' (ὡς ἐν πάσαις ἐπιστολαῖς, 3.16), seems to make better sense if the particular writing refers to one of Paul's letters. Bauckham, *Jude, 2 Peter*, p. 330; cf. Horrell, *2nd Peter and Jude*, pp. 185–86. Schoedel suggests that Polycarp had direct contact with some of the New Testament books including Gal., 1 and 2 Cor., Phil. and Rom., and Lightfoot argues that these NT books are treated at least as authoritative documents. William R. Schoedel, *Polycarp, Martyrdom of Polycarp, Fragments of Papias* V. *The Apostolic Fathers* (ed. Robert M. Grant; 5 vols.; London: Nelson, 1967), pp. 4–5; J.B. Lightfoot and J.R. Harmer (eds.), *The Apostolic Fathers* (Grand Rapids: Baker, 1992), p. 203.

38. Gottlob Schrenk, 'γραφή', in Gerhard Kittel (ed.), *Theological Dictionary of the New Testament* (trans. Geoffrey W. Bromiley; 10 vols.; Grand Rapids: Eerdmans, 1964), I, pp. 742–73. Bauckham, *Jude, 2 Peter*, p. 333.

and treatment of at least some of the individual letters of Paul in the manner suggested in the preceding discussion.

b. *Paul's Autograph as a Sign of his Presence*
i. *Autograph as a sign of Paul's presence*

The concept that a letter represents the author may be understood in light of the function of the autographic section in the Pauline letters, particularly the one in Galatians, which is signalled by a peculiar phrase in Gal. 6.11. In it, Paul temporarily shifts the attention of the audience from the substance or conceptual content of the letter (ongoing theological teachings and moral exhortations) to the subject of his authorship. He says, 'See what large letters I am writing (or I wrote) to you with my hand' ("Ιδετε πηλίκοις ὑμῖν γράμμασιν ἔγραψα τῇ ἐμῇ χειρί). Though no explicit teaching or ideas on the function of the physical form of the letter in Gal. 6.11 are found, it may serve as a window to consider an oft-neglected aspect of letter writing. The study begins with the general consideration of the conventions of amanuensis and autographic endings.

In Gal. 6.11, Paul lets the community members know that either he is writing or wrote (ἔγραψα) by his (own) hand (τῇ ἐμῇ χειρί) in large letters (πηλίκοις... γράμμασιν). In the practice of letter writing, it was common custom to use an amanuensis for the body of the letter and the author of the letter would add a subscription by his or her own hand.[39] Sometimes the practice is explicitly indicated by the author or by the amanuensis (respectively, in 1 Cor. 16.21; Gal. 6.11; Phlm. 19, cf. Rom. 16.22; Col. 4.18; 2 Thess. 3.17). In the case of the original autograph, an implicit indicator such as a change from more practised handwriting (the body of the letter) to rather crude handwriting (the subscription) would sometimes signal that an amanuensis was being used for the writing of a letter.[40]

Various functions of the autograph have been suggested by scholars. Paul explicitly states that he writes the final greeting section by his own hand, primarily so that an audience in the public oral setting would know that Paul's autograph is attached to the letter at the end.[41] Other than this

---

39.   Richard N. Longenecker, 'Ancient Amanuenses and the Pauline Epistles', in R.N. Longenecker and M.C. Tenney (eds.), *New Dimensions in New Testament Study* (Grand Rapids: Zondervan, 1974), p. 283.

40.   Cf. Deissmann, *Licht vom Osten*, pp. 140–41.

41.   Longenecker, *Galatians*, p. 289. Similar to this is the function of authenticating the letter. The autograph of 2 Thess. 3.17 says, 'which is the sign in every letter, in this manner I write' (ὅ ἐστιν σημεῖον ἐν πάσῃ ἐπιστολῇ οὕτως γράφω). Paul supposes that there were letters with heterodox teachings being circulated under his name (2 Thess. 2.2), so he autographs his name and the greeting as the proof (σημεῖον) of the authentic letter of Paul. Abraham J. Malherbe, *The Letters to the Thessalonians* (AB, 32b; New York: Doubleday, 2000), p. 463; I. Howard Marshall, *1 and 2 Thessalonians* (NCBC; London: Marshall,

obvious function, one may find functions relating to both cognitive and non-cognitive dimensions of the letter. Burton suggests a literary device in the autograph of the Galatian letter, relating more to its cognitive dimension. This short verse stands in between two bodies of thought. In the section previous to Gal. 6.11, Paul develops his moral exhortation based upon the antithetical theme of Spirit and flesh, i.e. the contrast between faith in Christ and circumcision (Gal. 5.2–5), the list of fleshly vice and spiritual virtue (Gal. 5.16–26), then the conduct of 'spiritual ones' (οἱ πνευματικοί, Gal. 6.1–10). In the section subsequent to Gal. 6.11, Paul highlights the most urgent practical application of the previous exhortation, which is to warn against the fleshly 'works'of the circumcisers (Gal. 6.12, 13; cf. 5.19–21).[42] Therefore, assuming that the autograph starts here in v. 11, the verse is understood as a literary device highlighting the content in the following section, somewhat akin to the way the bold, underlined or italic typeset is used to highlight meaning.[43] So Paul is saying, according to this suggestion: 'Here I begin to summarize what I have said, so listen carefully!'

Some functions in relation to non-cognitive dimensions are also suggested. For the present discussion, this non-cognitive function of the autograph requires attention. Looking at the autograph of 1 Cor. 16.21, some suggest that it is used as a vehicle to communicate Paul's affection.[44] Besides such affectionate or emotional remarks as Gal. 4.8–16 (or within an autograph, 1 Cor. 16.24), the actual presence of an autograph may add a dimension of personal attachment. Identifying the similarity between 1 Cor. 16.22–24 and the Eucharistic liturgical saying in *Didache* 14, Robinson suggests that the autograph has the function of representing the author's presence at the Eucharistic table, together with the community members.[45] In this sense, the autograph has a function of replacing the presence of the author, i.e. the autograph may have a function of reminding the audience of the author's presence, which the letter replaces. Therefore, a suggestion may be made that the sensorial function of the

---

Morgan and Scott, 1983), p. 232; Wanamaker, *Thessalonians*, p. 293, cf. Dunn, *Epistles to the Colossians and to Philemon*, p. 340. It was not a custom to place a signature at the end of a letter, so one rarely sees the author's name after the formal greeting at the beginning of the letter. Harry Gamble, 'Letters in the New Testament and in the Greco-Roman World', in John Barton (ed.), *The Biblical World* (2 vols.; London and New York: Routledge, 2002), I, p. 192.

42. Burton, *Galatians*, pp. 347, 349.

43. Betz, *Galatians*, p. 314. Others suggest that 'large letters' are caused by Paul's weak eyesight or by his workman's hand for which writing is not an easy thing. Deissmann, *Licht vom Osten*, p. 132, note 6. Cf. also Nigel Turner, *Grammatical Insights into the New Testament* (Edinburgh: T. & T. Clark, 1965), p. 94.

44. Collins, *First Corinthians*, p. 610; Thiselton, *Corinthians*, p. 1347.

45. J.A.T. Robinson, 'Traces of a Liturgical Sequence in 1 Corinthians 16.20–24', *JTS* 4 (1953), pp. 38–41 (38–39).

autograph would enhance the sense of the author's presence which the letter is said to replace.

ii. *Scope and implication of the Galatian autograph*
The attention to the sensorial dimension of the letter causes one to reconsider the scope of the Galatian autograph. Since the original autographed letter is non-extant, one immediately faces the question as to at what point the autograph commences in each letter. It is usually assumed that the autographic section begins with the passage referring to the author's autograph and continues on until the end of the letter (1 Cor. 16.21–24; Gal. 6.11–18; Col. 4.16; 2 Thess. 3.17–18; Phlm. 19–25).[46] Therefore, ἔγραψα in Gal. 6.11 is usually understood as referring to the last eight verses of the final remark and greeting (vv. 11–18). If so, the aorist tense of ἔγραψα must be an epistolary aorist, with which the author writes a letter from the time-frame of the audience. In other words, Paul would be saying, 'I am writing to you (now)', instead of 'I wrote to you' (cf. ἔπεμψα αὐτόν in Phil. 2.28).[47] However, Zahn argues that ἔγραψα for the epistolary aorist is not Paul's customary style.[48] Indeed we find γράφω (the present tense) in Gal. 1.20. The question must be squarely faced as to why Paul uses the present tense in Gal. 1.20 and the aorist in 6.11, if one argues for the epistolary aorist in 6.11. Paul elsewhere uses the present tense form in 1 Cor. 14.37. Some commentators identify Rom. 15.15 and 1 Cor. 5.11; 9.15 as cases demonstrating an epistolary aorist, together with ἔγραψα in Gal. 6.11.[49] However, one cannot simply accept such a conclusion.[50] These cases of the aorist ἔγραψα may well refer to (1) that which Paul 'wrote' previous to what he is writing or (2) that which he 'wrote' elsewhere earlier.[51] Based upon his understanding of the aorist verb, Zahn concludes that, unlike his other letters, Paul autographed

---

46. Except for the peculiar view of Bahr, who argues for a longer subscription based upon the thematic flow and other indicators. So, for example, the subscription of Gal. starts at 5.1, 1 Cor. at 16.15, Col. at 3.8, 2 Thess. at 3.1, Phlm. at 17. Gordon J. Bahr, 'The Subscriptions in the Pauline Letters', *JBL* 87 (1968), pp. 27–41 (34–41). Against this hypothesis, Longenecker criticizes that there is no example of such a long subscription in the conventional non-literary letter writing in the ancient Graeco-Roman literature. Cf. Longenecker, 'Ancient Amanuenses', pp. 291, 296.
47. Bruce, *Galatians*, p. 268; Betz, *Galatians*, p. 314.
48. Von Zahn, *Galater*, p. 277.
49. Longenecker, *Galatians*, p. 289.
50. Thiselton, *1 Corinthians*, p. 413 (for 5.11) and p. 694 (for 9.15).
51. Cf. RSV's decision on these verses for example: 'I wrote …' (1 Cor. 5.11); 'I have written …' (Rom. 15.15), but '… nor am I writing …' (1 Cor. 9.15). See also the same decision in *Die Luther-Revision* (1984) and *Die Einheitsübersetzung* (1979).

Galatians in its entirety.[52] This conclusion, though not widely accepted among recent commentators,[53] follows Chrysostom as he understands the letter being entirely written by Paul unlike his custom (*Com. on Gal.* 6.11).[54] Whether or not Paul wrote the entire letter by his own hand, one cannot be perfectly certain; however, such a possibility cannot be simply dismissed. This suggestion may not be too implausible as one considers the fact that letter writing required by nature the use of comprehensible, therefore, large characters. Cribiore's conclusion of her papyrological analysis is, 'Countless examples of papyrus show that, for the sake of legibility, when people wrote letters, their characters were always more slowly and carefully written and of larger size than those employed for documents'.[55] In light of the evidence above, it seems more plausible to understand Paul's remark Ἴδετε πηλίκοις ὑμῖν γράμμασιν ἔγραψα τῇ ἐμῇ χειρί as referring to the employment of large characters, which was naturally necessitated by writing the (whole) letter himself, than as implying an editorial emphasis on the final comment (such as italic or underline) or as inferring such physical features as Paul's short-sightedness and heavy and stiff handwriting of a manual labourer that prevents him from writing small and intricate characters.[56] What might be the implication if Paul wrote the entire letter by his own hand? If Zahn and others are right that Paul autographed the entire letter, it may be surmised that such a special letter would enhance the sensorial functions of the letter, one of which is, as suggested in this chapter, to provide a physical locus of identity for those who communally possess it.

---

52. Von Zahn, *Galater*, pp. 277–78.

53. Cf. Jerome Murphy-O'Connor, *Paul et l'art épistolaire* (trans. J. Prignaud; Paris: Les éditions du Cerf, 1994), pp. 21–22.

54. Luther also follows the view of Chrysostom. However, he seems to understand πηλίκοις...γράμμασιν as 'how large a document'. Γράμμασιν in the plural can mean 'a document, piece of writing' (cf. *BAGD*, p. 165) while one should note that Paul uses ἐπιστολή for 'a letter'. Martin Luther, *A Commentary on St. Paul's Epistle to the Galatians* (London: James Clarke & Co., 1953), p. 555. There was no uniformity of understanding among the early Fathers on this point. Mark J. Edwards (ed.), *Galatians, Ephesians, Philippians* (Ancient Christian Commentary on Scripture, 8; Downers Grove: IVP, 1999), p. 100.

55. Raffaella Cribiore, *Gymnastics of the Mind: Greek Education in Hellenistic and Roman Egypt* (Princeton and Oxford: Princeton University Press, 2001), p. 89. Cf. also, *idem*, *Writing, Teachers, and Students in Graeco-Roman Egypt* (ASP, 36; Atlanta: Scholars Press, 1996), pp. 5–7.

56. Cf. Frank J. Matera, *Galatians* (SP, 9; Collegeville: The Liturgical Press, 1992), p. 224; Bruce, *Galatians*, p. 268; Deissmann, *Licht vom Osten*, p. 141.

3. *Letter as Locus of Community–Identity*

While the cognitive dimension of a religious writing or of a tradition may define and demarcate a particular local community by its conceptual content as to who they are and who they are not, the community members may identify themselves by the very communal possession of such a religiously significant writing or tradition. Consideration of an often neglected feature of religious writing, the physico–documentary dimension, may help to understand how the communal possession of such a writing may function for constructing the identity of the religious community that possesses it. Therefore, the discussion was conducted in the following manner.

First, analogical cases showed that the religious writings replaced the authority of the leaders and helped to strengthen and maintain the cohesion of the community in his absence. Second, it was suggested that Paul's letters, particularly here Galatians, likewise replaced in his absence the authority of the apostle to the Gentiles and thus the founder of the community. The awareness that the letter contained the divine revelation for those who possessed it may have given them a sense of significance. Third, it was suggested that Paul's autograph in the letter directs the audience's attention to the fact that the letter represents the authority of the author, and that if the entire letter was written by Paul, such a special letter directly addressed to the audience may have increased the sense of his presence. By possessing the letter, they possessed the mark of authenticity as a religious community. Even in the midst of devastating pressure of disintegration, they are assured, by the existence of the special letter among them, that their assembly is the right place to gather as authentic followers of Christ.

A question remains as to how much of this physico–documentary dimension of the letter was due to Paul's wilful intention. Did Paul mean deliberately to provide a 'religious object' to which community members could attach themselves? Some early church documents did later become objects of veneration, in the form of amulets, for example,[57] or possibly also in the form observed as *Nomina Sacra*.[58] How much intention in this direction can be suggested in Paul's writing of the letter? Paul is silent

---

57. Judge, 'The Magical Use', pp. 339–40; Leipoldt and Morenz, *Heilige Schriften*, pp. 187–88.

58. R.F. Hull, 'Called "Christians" at Antioch: Christian Identity and the "Sacred Names" in Early Christian Manuscripts', in G. Weedham (ed.), *Building up the Church* (Johnston City: Milligan College, 1993), pp. 25–50. Cf. Everett Fergason (ed.), *Encyclopedia of Early Christianity* (New York and London: Garland, 2nd edn, 1997), p. 818. See Lightfoot for the comment on *Ep. Barn.* 9.8 for the existence of *Nomina Sacra*. Lightfoot and Harmer (eds.), *The Apostolic Fathers*, p. 299, note 33. However, see Christopher Tuckett, 'P52 and *Nomina Sacra*', *NTS* 47 (2001), pp. 544–48.

about the intention, if he had any of this kind. As Paul's approach to community–identity construction was not constrained by the tradition that expresses a core ethnic sentiment, it is possible to surmise that he may have sought to establish an authority other than the Jewish scripture, even though Paul had to reinterpret and use Jewish scripture to substantiate his persuasion on the basis of his revelatory experience. Does the fact that Paul's letters came to be acknowledged as 'scripture' (2 Pet. 3.15–16) reflect Paul's unrecorded intention? For any further discussion on intentionality, one can only note that religiosity was expressed both in cognitive and non-cognitive fashions in primitive Christianity. On one hand, the New Testament testifies to the importance of the sensory dimension in religious life. An apparent example of this is found in the healing miracle tradition by means of touching the fringe of Jesus' cloth (τοῦ κρασπέδου αὐτοῦ ἅψωνται) in Mk 6.56 (cf. Mt. 14.36; Mt. 9.20/Lk. 8.44). Luke reports similar religious expressions in the ministries of both Peter (Acts 5.15) and Paul (Acts 19.12). On the other hand, Luke reports the case of Bereans who devoted their energies to accurately understand the meaning of the scripture (Acts 17.11–12). As it was noted at the beginning of this chapter, the physico–documentary function of the letter in constructing community–identity remains a tentative hypothesis. However, as long as the sensory dimension is a vital part of religious life in general, this often neglected dimension of the letter begs the attention of further academic discussion on the history of primitive Christianity.

CONCLUSION

The focus for this book was on the context and practices for constructing
an identity of the Galatian community. This approach was based upon the
social-scientific theories of group identity and a socio-historical study of
analogical comparative religious groups. This investigation was particularly interested in the tangible examples of how the identity of a
community may be constructed and maintained (materiality of religion),
in order to add yet another contour to the previous studies of the letter to
the Galatians, which continue to focus at large on the history of ideas.

   For the investigation into the context of community–identity construction, understanding was first sought as to what approach Paul took in
constructing a community–identity. In this study, the early part of Paul's
biographical account in Galatians was noted to determine what kind of
self-understanding he might have had as the result of his revelatory
experience. Paul reckoned his days in 'Judaism' were past. The phenomenon was regarded as 'conversion' with a thematic continuation from the
mother religion of 'Judaism'. He understood himself as an apostle of
Christ, autonomously authorized for the mission to the Gentiles. He
denied the appearance of submission to the Jerusalem apostles. On the
basis of these insights, Paul's approach to community–identity construction was described as the 'instrumental mode', in the language of the
anthropological theory of ethnic identity, by which is meant he is not
constrained by the necessity to preserve a core ethnic sentiment in his
approach to community construction. His firm conviction in his connection with God rather than human institutions and traditions caused him
to approach the ethno-centred traditions and institutions in a critical and
flexible manner, and at the same time he resisted the revelation out of his
experience of christophany from being culturally adapted by the host
environment. His innovation, therefore, was confined within his revelatory experience. In this sense, Paul's innovation is different from that of
Uchimura of Mukyokai, who was freer, as a part of the host culture to the
religion, to indigenize the gospel message. However, Paul's neglect of the
Jewish core sentiment clashed with those whose approaches to community
construction were firmly rooted therein.

   A brief survey of Paul's description of the Jerusalem meeting and the

Antioch incident suggested that the Jerusalem apostles and other constituents of the church were based upon a core ethnic sentiment in their approach to mission and community formation. This suggestion was substantiated with a study of Jewish approaches to proselytism in the Second Temple period. While Gentiles showed various levels of closeness to Jews and Judaism, what later became Noachide regulations generally determined the Gentiles' state of righteousness. Some Jews seem to have insisted on the rite of circumcision for Gentiles to achieve full integration into Judaism, while others did not insist on 'full' integration. The members of the Jerusalem church shared these approaches to Gentile incorporation, in which Jewish ethnic sentiment was an important concern for their efforts of community formation and various degrees of insistence on such an ethnic (physio-cultural) feature as circumcision did exist. The conflicts observed in Galatians 2 may have resulted from conflict between these varying approaches to community–identity construction.

The second chapter of Galatians demonstrates a conflict between so-called ψευδαδέλφοι, who insisted Gentile sympathizers be fully integrated into the Jewish community in order to attain unity of the church; the Jerusalem apostles who would leave Gentile constituents as secondary attachments of sympathizers to the Jewish community; and Paul, who sought to obliterate ethnic concerns to attain a unity of all believers in Christ. Paul, in his retrospective narration of the historical events of the Jerusalem meeting and the incident at Antioch, warned the Galatian community members who were confused by the circumcisers that community construction on the basis of a core ethnic sentiment would be unacceptable, because its effect at best was to render Gentile community members second-class citizens and would exclude those members who were uncircumcised from the people of God as secondary attachments of sympathizers. These various approaches and the resulting conflicts form the context in which Paul sought to construct a positive identity for the Galatian community.

As to how Paul sought to construct this community–identity, special note was taken of the way he recreated the salvation history of Judaism in order to offer community members a positive image of their status as Gentile believers in Christ. The example of Mukyokai demonstrates that this 'recreation of worldview', in which the conventional values and orders are reversed or made inconsequential, gives marginalized believers a *raison d'être* and positive identity. Because Paul was not confined to a core ethnic sentiment in his approach to identity construction, he was free to recreate a tradition favourable to Gentile members of the community. While Paul's recreation of tradition was observed in the entirety of Galatians 3 and 4, special focus was placed on his exposition of the tradition of Abrahamic inheritance in Gal. 4.21–31, in which the recreation affirmed marginalized and stigmatized Gentile members as authentic heirs of God's promise, while those under the Torah were disinherited from the privilege. The stigma of 'persecution' (or rather marginalization) was lifted by Paul as he affirmed that such was the fate or mark of authenticity. While acknowledging that this concept of recreation of tradition or 'recreated worldview' was an ideological framework and not a tangible identity-marker, it is suggested that this recreated worldview was concretely acted out in the physical rite of baptism.

In this analysis of the baptismal rite, Turner's social process theory was closely applied in order to articulate the function of rituals. According to this theory, the Galatian community, in the liminal state, was struggling against structural pressure from outside. In the rite of baptism, the very 'recreated worldview' was acted out to affirm the new order and values suggested by Paul. The tangible rite of baptism was a significant identity-marking event, because those who were otherwise marginalized as secondary attachments were assured of their authentic status within the community. Paul's 'return' to the conventional approach to gender distinction in 1 Corinthians was seen as a sign of the transition from a liminal state to a structural state within Paul's Gentile mission. However, the impact of the egalitarian vision in Paul's baptismal saying persisted in the early church despite the reality of communal transition into a new state of structure. The egalitarian vision has to be understood in a social context, in which the vision was a response against the disintegrating pressure from outside to marginalize and stigmatize the fledgling community and its members, lest one wrongly criticizes Paul through an anachronistic postmodern correlation between his desperate effort to protect the marginalized group with the 'evil' of coercing universalism.

Lastly, a possible function of the non-cognitive (physico–documentary) dimension of Paul's letter was postulated. While the cognitive dimension of the letter provided the content by which the members would know who they were and who they were not, a consideration of the sensorial dimension of the letter suggests that the letter itself represented and replaced the authoritative presence of the apostle of Christ and the founder of the very community, functioning as a catalyst to ensure that community members maintained a strong sense of cohesion and distinctiveness within their new and vulnerable community.

Two particularly notable features of the book, among others, were the use of an analogical comparative case of an emerging and marginalized religious community and the focus on the materiality of religion. These features, as heuristic tools, rendered the study sensitive to the life situation of the Galatian community, perhaps even to the quiet voices of often under-represented community members. So, for example, behind what is usually regarded as the sin of idolatry was suggested a real struggle and sincere effort to make a new faith possible under the pressure of unbelieving compatriots. It was also noted that a marginalized group's struggle to make sense of their existence should be differentiated from a hegemonizing force, whereby the powerless are made to be like the powerful. It was postulated that the letter may have provided not only the conceptual content but also the physical locus of identity for those who communally possess it. Thus, further study of the Pauline communities requires an engaged dialogue with the discipline of comparative religious studies, particularly taking note of the emergence and establishment of communities under marginalizing pressures, reflected both in their teachings and in their actual practices of faith.

BIBLIOGRAPHY

1. General Primary Sources

a. *Biblical and other Jewish Sources*
i. *The Hebrew Bible, Jewish Apocrypha and the New Testament*
New Revised Standard Version with Apocrypha.

Aland, Kurt, *et al.* (eds.), *The Greek New Testament* (Stuttgart: Deutsche Bibelgesellschaft, 27th edn, 1994).

Kittel, R. *et al.* (eds), *Biblia Hebraica Stuttgartensia* (Stuttgart: Deutsche Bibelgesellschaft, 5th edn., 1997).

ii. *Jewish Pseudepigrapha*
Charlesworth, James H. (ed.), *The Old Testament Pseudepigrapha* (2 vols.; New York: Doubleday, 1985).

iii. *Philo*
Philo, *On the Creation, Allegorical Interpretation of Genesis 2 and 3* (trans. F.H. Colson and G.H. Whitaker; LCL; 10 vols.; Cambridge: Harvard University Press, 1929).

—*On the Migration of Abraham* (trans. F.H. Colson and G.H. Whitaker; LCL; 10 vols.; Cambridge: Harvard University Press, 1932).

—*Moses I and II* (trans. F.H. Colson; LCL; 10 vols.; Cambridge: Harvard University Press, 1935).

—*On the Decalogues, On the Special Laws Books I–III* (trans. F.H. Colson; LCL; 10 vols.; Cambridge: Harvard University Press, 1937).

—*Questions and Answers on Genesis* (trans. Ralph Marcus; LCL; Sup. 1; Cambridge: Harvard University Press, 1953).

—*Questions and Answers on Exodus* (trans. Ralph Marcus; LCL; Sup. 2; Cambridge: Harvard University Press, 1953).

iv. *Josephus*
Josephus, *The Life, Against Apion* (trans. H. St. J. Thackeray; LCL; 13 vols.; Cambridge: Harvard University Press, 1926).

—*The Jewish War, Books I–III* (trans. H. St. J. Thackeray; LCL; 13 vols.; Cambridge: Harvard University Press, 1927).

—*The Jewish War, Books IV–VII* (trans. H. St. J. Thackeray; LCL; 13 vols.; Cambridge: Harvard University Press, 1928).

—*The Jewish Antiquities, Books XII–XIV* (trans. Ralph Marcus; LCL; 13 vols.; Cambridge: Harvard University Press, 1933).

—*The Jewish Antiquities, Books XX* (trans. Louis H. Feldman; LCL; 13 vols.; Cambridge: Harvard University Press, 1965).

v. *Dead Sea Scrolls*
Martinez, Florentino Garcia, *The Dead Sea Scrolls Translated: The Qumran Texts in English* (Leiden: E.J. Brill, 2nd edn, 1996).

vi. *Rabbinic Writings*
Danby, Herbert, *The Mishnah: Translated from the Hebrew with Introduction and Brief Explanatory Notes* (Oxford: Oxford University Press, 1933).
Neusner, Jacob (ed.), *The Tosefta: Translation from the Hebrew* (6 vols.; New York: KTAV Publishing House, 1977–86).
—(ed.), *The Talmud of Babylonia: An American Translation, Tractate Sotah* (55 vols.; Chico: Scholars Press, 1984).
—(ed.), *Genesis Rabbah: The Judaic Commentary to the Book of Genesis, A New American Translation* (3 vols.; Atlanta: Scholars Press, 1985).

b. *Graeco-Roman Sources*
Aristotle, *The 'Art' of Rhetoric* (trans. John H. Freese; LCL; 22 vols.; Cambridge: Harvard University Press, 1926).
Augustine, *The City of God, Books 4–7* (trans. W.M. Green; LCL; 7 vols.; Cambridge: Harvard University Press, 1963).
Cicero, *De Officiis* (trans. Walter Miller; LCL; 28 vols.; Cambridge: Harvard University Press, 1913).
Dio Cassius, *Roman History, Books 41–45* (trans. Earnest Cary and Herbert B. Foster; LCL; 9 vols.; Cambridge: Harvard University Press, 1916).
—*Roman History, Books 56–60* (trans. Earnest Cary and Herbert B. Foster; LCL; 9 vols.; Cambridge: Harvard University Press, 1924).
Diognitus Laertius, *Lives of Eminent Philosophers* (trans. R.D. Hicks; LCL; 2 vols.; Cambridge: Harvard University Press, 1925).
Epictetus, *The Discourses as Reported by Arrian, Books I–II* (trans. W.A. Oldfather; LCL; 2 vols.; Cambridge: Harvard University Press, 1925).
—*The Discourses, Books III–IV, Fragments, Encheiridion* (trans. W.A. Oldfather; LCL; 2 vols.; Cambridge: Harvard University Press, 1928).
Julian, *Orations VI-VIII. Letters to Themistius, to the Senate and People of Athens. To a Priest. The Caesars. Misopogon* (trans. Wilmer C. Wright; LCL; 3 vols.; Cambridge: Harvard University Press, 1913).
—*Letters 1–73. Letters 74–83 (Apocryphal). Shorter Fragments. Epigrams. Against the Galilaeans. Fragments* (trans. Wilmer C. Wright; LCL; 3 vols.; Cambridge: Harvard University Press, 1923).
Plato, *Euthyphro. Apology. Crito. Phaedo. Phaedrus* (trans. H.N. Fowler; LCL; 12 vols.; Cambridge: Harvard University Press, 1914).
—*Lysis. Symposium. Gorgias* (trans. W.R.M. Lamb; LCL; 12 vols.; Cambridge: Harvard University Press, 1925).
Pliny, *Natural History, Books 3–7* (trans. H. Rackham; LCL; 10 vols.; Cambridge: Harvard University Press, 1942).

Seneca, *Moral Essays* (trans. John W. Basore; LCL; 10 vols.; Cambridge: Harvard University
    Press, 1932).
Strabo, *Geography: Books 3–5* (trans. Horace L. Jones; LCL; 8 vols.; Cambridge: Harvard
    University Press, 1923).
—*Geography: Books 10–12* (trans. Horace L. Jones; LCL; 8 vols.; Cambridge: Harvard
    University Press, 1928).
Valerius Maximus, *Memorable Doings and Sayings Book 1–5* (trans. D.R. Shackleton Bailey;
    LCL; 2 vols.; Cambridge: Harvard University Press, 2000).

c. *Early Church Fathers*
The Apostolic Fathers (trans. Kirsopp Lake; LCL; 2 vols.; Cambridge: Harvard University
    Press, 1912).
Clement of Alexandria, *Clement of Alexandria* (trans. G.W. Butterworth; LCL; Cambridge:
    Harvard University Press, 1919).

d. *Nag Hammadi Tractates*
Robinson, James (ed.), *The Nag Hammadi Library in English* (San Francisco: Harper & Row,
    rev. edn, 1988).

2. *Japanese Primary Sources*

References to Uchimura are found in the following series of works unless otherwise
indicated. They are abbreviated as *Zenshu* [*All Works*]. The works of Uchimura's followers
    are listed as the secondary works.
Uchimura, Kanzo, *Uchimura Kanzo Zenshu* [*All Works of Kanzo Uchimura*] (41 vols.; Tokyo:
    Iwanami Shoten, 1980–2001).

Included in *Zenshu* are:

1. *Kyu-an Roku [Pursuit of Peace]*, originally published in 1893.
2. Kirisuto-shinto no Nagusame [*Consolation of a Christian Believer*], originally published in
1893.
3. Daihyo-teki Nihon-jin [*Representative Japanese*], originally titled as *Japan and Japanese*
and published in 1894.
4. *Yo wa Ikani-shite Kirisuto-Shinto to Narishi ka [How I Became a Christian: Out of My
Diary]*, originally published in 1895.
5. Articles from the journal, *Seisho no Kenkyu* [*Study of the Bible*].
6. Article from the journal, *The Japan Weekly Mail*.
7. Articles from the journal, *The Japanese Christian Intelligencer*.
8. Articles from the journal, *Tokyo Dokuritsu Zasshi* [*Tokyo Independent Journal*].
9. Article from the journal, *Kokumin Shinbun* [*National Newspaper*].
10. Article from the journal, *Getsuyo Kogi* [*Monday Lecture*].
11. *Letters to Miyabe.*
12. *Letters to Nitobe.*
13. *Letters to Bell.*

14. *Letter to Nobuyoshi Asada.*
15. *Letter to Nijima.*
16. *Letter to A.L. Struthers.*
17. *Diary.*

B. The recorded oral tradition of *Tenchi Hajimari no Koto* of Kakure Kirishitan.

Whelan, Christal, *The Beginning of Heaven and Earth: The Sacred Book of Japan's Hidden Christians* (Honolulu: University of Hawai'i Press, 1996).

3. *Secondary Sources*

Anderson, Benedict, *Imagined Communities: Reflections on the Origin and Spread of Nationalism* (London: Verso Editions, 1983).

Anesaki, Masaharu, *Nichiren: The Buddhist Prophet* (Cambridge: Harvard University Press, 1916).

Asahi Newspaper. (*http://www.asahi.com/national/update/1211/041.html*. Dec. 12, 2001).

Ashton, John, *The Religion of Paul the Apostle* (London: Yale University Press, 2000).

Aune, David E., 'Review of H.D. Betz, *Galatians*', *RelSRev* 7.4 (October 1981), pp. 323–28.

—*Revelation 17–22* (WBC, 52c; Dallas: Word Book Press, 1998).

Bahr, Gordon J., 'The Subscriptions in the Pauline Letters', *JBL* 87 (1968), pp. 27–41.

Baldry, Harold C., *The Unity of Mankind in Greek Thought* (Cambridge: Cambridge University Press, 1965).

Bälz, Erwin, *Das Leben eines deutschen Arztes im erwachenden Japan: Tagebücher, Briefe, Berichte herausgegeben von Toku Bälz* (Stuttgart: J. Engelhorns Nachf, 1913).

Bammel, E., 'πτωχός', in Gerhard Friedrich (ed.), *Theological Dictionary of the New Testament* (trans. Geoffrey W. Bromiley; 10 vols.; Grand Rapids: Eerdmans, 1968), VI, pp. 885–915.

Banks, Marcus, *Ethnicity: Anthropological Constructions* (London and New York: Routledge, 1996).

Banks, Robert, *Paul's Idea of Community: The Early House Churches in their Historical Setting* (Exeter: Paternoster, 1980).

Barclay, John M.G., *Obeying the Truth: A Study of Paul's Ethics in Galatians* (Edinburgh: T. & T. Clark, 1988).

—*Jews in the Mediterranean Diaspora from Alexander to Trajan (323 BCE–117 CE)* (Edinburgh: T. & T. Clark, 1995).

—' "Neither Jew nor Greek": Multiculturalism and the New Perspective on Paul', in M.G. Brett (ed.), *Ethnicity and the Bible* (Leiden: E.J. Brill, 1996), pp. 198–214.

Barnett, P.W., 'Apostle', in Gerald F. Hawthorne, *et al.* (eds.), *Dictionary of Paul and his Letters* (Downers Grove: InterVarsity Press, 1993).

—*The Second Epistle to the Corinthians* (NICNT; Grand Rapids: Eerdmans, 1997).

Baron, S.W., 'Population', in Cecil Roth (ed.), *EncJud*, III (18 vols.; Jerusalem: Keter Publishing House; New York: Macmillan, 1971).

Barrett, C.K., 'Paul and the "Pillar" Apostles', in J.N. Sevenster and W.C. van Unnik (eds.), *Studia Paulina* (Festschrift J. de Zwaan; Haarlem: Bohn, 1953), pp. 1–19.

—'The Allegory of Abraham, Sarah, and Hagar in the Argument of Galatians', in J.

Friedrich, *et al.* (eds.), *Rechtfertigung* (Festschrift Ernst Käsemann; Tübingen: Mohr, 1976), pp. 1–16.

—*A Commentary on the Epistle to the Romans* (BNTC; London: A. & C. Black, 2nd edn, 1991).

Barrett, David, *Schism and Renewal in Africa: An Analysis of Six Thousand Contemporary Religious Movements* (Nairobi: Oxford University Press, 1968).

Barth, Fredrik (ed.), *Ethnic Groups and Boundaries: The Social Organization of Culture Difference* (Oslo: Universitetsforlaget, 1969).

—'Enduring and Emerging Issues in the Analysis of Ethnicity', in H. Vermeulen and C. Govers (eds.), *The Anthropology of Ethnicity: Beyond 'Ethnic Groups and Boundaries'* (Amsterdam: Het Spinhuis, 1994), pp. 11–32.

Bartlett, David L., 'John G. Gager's "Kingdom and Community": A Summary and Response', *Zygon* 13.2 (1978), pp. 109–22.

Barton, John, *Holy Writings, Sacred Text: The Canon in Early Christianity* (Louisville: Westminster/John Knox Press, 1997).

Bastide, Roger, *Les religions africaines au Brésil: vers une sociologie des interpénétrations de civilisations* (Bibliothèque de Sociologie Contempraine; Paris: Presses universitaires de France, 1960).

Bauckham, Richard J., *Jude, 2 Peter* (WBC, 50; Waco: Word Book Press, 1983).

—'James and the Jerusalem Church', in R. Bauckham (ed.), *The Book of Acts in Its Palestinian Setting* (Carlisle: Paternoster, 1995), pp. 415–80.

Bauer, Walter, *A Greek-English Lexicon of the New Testament and Other Early Christian Literature* (trans., rev. and augm. W.F. Armdt, *et al.*; Chicago and London: University of Chicago Press, 2nd edn, 1979).

Baur, Ferdinand Christian, *Das Christentum & die christliche Kirche der drei ersten Jahrhunderte* (Tübingen: L. Fr. Fues, 1860).

—*Paulus, der Apostel Jesu Christi: Sein Leben & Wirken, seine Briefe & seine Lehre* (2 vols.; Leipzig: Fues's Verlag, 2nd edn, 1866).

Beale, G.K., *The Book of Revelation: A Commentary on the Greek Text* (NIGTC; Grand Rapids: Eerdmans, 1999).

Beasley-Murray, G.R., *Baptism in the New Testament* (London: Macmillan, 1962).

—*John* (WBC, 36; Dallas: Word Book Press, 1987).

Becker, H.S., *Outsiders: Studies in the Sociology of Deviance* (New York: Free Press, 1963).

Becker, Jürgen, *Auferstehung der Toten im Urchristentum* (SBS, 82; Stuttgart: KBW Verlag, 1976).

—*Paulus: Der Apostel der Völker* (Tübingen: Mohr, 2nd edn, 1992).

Becker, Ulrich, 'προσήλυτος', in Colin Brown (ed.), *The New International Dictionary of New Testament Theology*, I (4 vols.; Grand Rapids: Zondervan, 1986).

Bediako, Kwame, *Christianity in Africa: The Renewal of a Non-Western Religion* (Edinburgh: Edinburgh University Press, 1995).

Berger, Klaus, *Theologiegeschichte des Urchristentums: Theologie des Neuen Testaments* (Tübingen: Francke, 1994).

Berger, Peter L., *The Sacred Canopy: Elements of a Sociological Theory of Religion* (New York: Anchor Books, 1967).

Berger, Peter L., and Thomas Luckmann, *The Social Construction of Reality: A Treatise in the Sociology of Knowledge* (New York: Penguin, 1966).

Best, Thomas F., 'The Sociological Study of the New Testament: Promise and Peril of a New Discipline', *SJT* 36 (1983), pp. 181–94.

Betz, Hans Dieter, *Galatians: A Commentary on Paul's Letter to the Churches in Galatia* (Hermeneia; Philadelphia: Fortress, 1979).

Bibliotheca Arcana (http://www.cs.utk.edu/~mclennan/BA/index.html#theory).

Bietenhard, Hans, *Die himmlische Welt im Urchristentum & Spätjudentum* (WUNT, 2; Tübingen: Mohr, 1951).

Billerbeck, P., *Die Briefe des Neuen Testaments & die Offenbarung Johannis*, in H.L. Strack and P. Billerbeck (eds.), *Kommentar zum Neuen Testament aus Talmud & Midrash*, III (6 vols.; München: C.H. Beck'sche Verlagsbuchhandlung, 1926).

Blacker, Carmen, *The Catalpa Bow: A Study of Shamanistic Practices in Japan* (London: Allen & Unwin, 2nd edn, 1986).

Bockmuehl, Markus, *Jewish Law in Gentile Churches: Halakhah and the Beginning of Christian Public Ethics* (Edinburgh: T. & T. Clark, 2000).

Borgen, Peder, 'The Early Church and the Hellenistic Synagogue', *ST* 37.1 (1988), pp. 55–78.

Bornkamm, Günther, *Paulus* (Stuttgart: Verlag W. Kohlhammer, 2nd edn, 1969).

Bourdieu, Pierre, 'The Sentiment of Honour in Kabyle Society', in J.G. Peristiany (ed.), *Honour and Shame: The Values of Mediterranean Society* (London: Weidenfeld & Nicolson, 1965), pp. 191–241.

Bowie, Fiona, *The Anthropology of Religion* (Oxford: Blackwell, 2000).

Boyarin, Daniel, *A Radical Jew: Paul and the Politics of Identity* (Berkeley and London: University of California Press, 1994).

—*Galatians and Gender Trouble: Primal Androgyny and the First-Century Origins of a Feminist Dilemma* (Berkeley: Center for Hermeneutical Studies, 1995).

Braxton, Brad R., *No Longer Slaves: Galatians and African American Experience* (Collegeville: Liturgical Press, 2002).

Brett, Mark G. (ed.), 'Interpreting Ethnicity: Methods, Hermeneutics, Ethics' in *idem* (ed), *Ethnicity and the Bible* (Leiden: E.J. Brill, 1996).

—'Interpreting Ethnicity: Method, Hermeneutics, Ethics', in Mark G. Brett (ed.), *Ethnicity and the Bible* (Leiden: E.J. Brill, 1996), pp. 3–22.

Brinsmead, Bernard Hungerford, *Galatians: Dialogical Response to Opponents* (SBLDS, 65; Chico: Scholars, 1982).

Brown, Francis, S.R. Driver and C.A. Briggs, *The New Brown-Driver-Briggs-Gesenius Hebrew and English Lexicon with an Appendix Containing the Biblical Aramaic* (Peabody: Hendrickson, 1979).

Brown, Raymond E., *The Gospel according to John* (AB, 29; 2 vols.; New York: Doubleday, 1966).

—*An Introduction to the New Testament* (New York: Doubleday, 1996).

Bruce, F.F., *Paul: Apostle of the Free Spirit* (Exeter: Paternoster Press, 1977).

—*1 and 2 Thessalonians* (WBC, 45; Waco: Word Book Press, 1982).

—*Commentary on Galatians* (NIGTC; Grand Rapids: Eerdmans, 1982).

Brunner, Emil, *Das Mißverständnis der Kirche* (Zürich: Zwingli-Verlag, 1951).

—'Die christliche Nicht-Kirche-Bewegung in Japan', *Evangelische Theologie* 19 (1959), pp. 147–55.

—*Nihon no Mukyokai Undo* [*Mukyokai Movement of Japan*] (trans. Tadao Yanaihara and Saburo Takahashi; Tokyo: Tokyo Kashin Sha, 1959).

Büchler, Adolf, 'The Levitical Impurity of the Gentile in Palestine Before the Year 70', *JQR* 17 (1926), pp. 1–81.

Bultmann, Rudolf Karl, *Der Stil der paulinischen Predigt & die kynisch-stoische Diatribe* (FRLANT, 13; Göttingen: Vandenhoeck & Ruprecht, 1910).

—*Theologie des Neuen Testaments* (NTG; Tübingen: Mohr, 3rd edn, 1958).

—'πείθω', in Gerhard Friedrich (ed.), *Theological Dictionary of the New Testament* (trans. Geoffrey W. Bromiley; 10 vols.; Grand Rapids: Eerdmans, 1968), VI, pp. 1–11.

—*Die Geschichte der synoptischen Tradition* (Göttingen: Vandenhoeck & Ruprecht, 10th edn, 1995).

Burchard, C., 'Joseph and Aseneth', in James H. Charlesworth (ed.), *The Old Testament Pseudepigrapha* (2 vols.; New York: Doubleday, 1985), II, pp. 177–247.

Burr, David, *The Spiritual Franciscans: From Protest to Persecution in the Century after Saint Francis* (University Park: Penn State University Press, 2001).

Burton, E. DeWitt, *A Critical and Exegetical Commentary on the Epistle to the Galatians* (ICC; Edinburgh: T. & T. Clark, 1921).

Byron, Reginald, 'Identity', in Alan Barnard and Jonathan Spencer (eds.), *Encyclopedia of Social and Cultural Anthropology* (London and New York: Routledge, 1996).

Caldarola, Carlo, *Christianity: The Japanese Way* (Leiden: E.J. Brill, 1979).

Campbell, W.S., *Paul's Gospel in an Intercultural Context: Jew and Gentile in the Letter to the Romans* (SIGC, 69; Frankfurt am Main: Lang, 1992).

Case, Shirley J., *The Social Origins of Christianity* (Chicago: University of Chicago Press, 1923).

—*The Social Triumph of the Ancient Church* (Chicago: University of Chicago Press, 1934).

Chamberlain, Basil Hall, *Things Japanese: Being Notes on Various Subjects Connected with Japan for the Use of Travelers and Others* (London: Kelly and Walsh., 5th edn, 1905).

—*The Invention of a New Religion* (Canton: Pan-Pacific Cultural Association, 1933).

Cicourel, A.V., and J. Kitsuse, *The Educational Decision Makers* (Indianapolis: Bobbs Merrill, 1963).

Cohen, Abner, *Custom and Politics in Urban Africa* (Berkeley: University of California Press, 1969).

Cohen, Anthony P., *The Symbolic Construction of Community* (London and New York: Routledge, 1989).

Cohen, Shaye J.D., 'From the Bible to the Talmud: The Prohibition of Intermarriage', *Hebrew Annual Review* 7 (1983), pp. 23–39.

—*From the Maccabees to the Mishnah* (Philadelphia: Westminster, 1987).

—'Crossing the Boundary and Becoming a Jew', *HTR* 82 (1989), pp. 13–33.

—'Is "Proselyte Baptism" Mentioned in the Mishnah? The Interpretation of *m. Psahim* 8.8 (= *m. Eduyot* 5.2)', in J.C. Reeves and John Kampen (eds.), *Pursuing the Text* (Festschrift Ben Zion Wacholder; JSOTSup, 184; Sheffield: Sheffield Academic Press, 1994), pp. 278–92.

Collins, Patricia Hill, *Black Feminist Thought: Knowledge, Consciousness and the Politics of Empowerment* (New York: Routledge, 1990).

Collins, John J., 'A Symbol of Otherness: Circumcision and Salvation in the First Century', in Jacob Neusner and Ernest S. Frerichs (eds.), *'To See Ourselves as Others See Us': Christians, Jews, 'Others' in Late Antiquity* (Chico, CA: Scholars, 1985), pp. 163–86.

—*Between Athens and Jerusalem: Jewish Identity in the Hellenistic Diaspora* (The Biblical Resource Series; Grand Rapids: Eerdmans, 2nd edn, 2000).

Collins, Raymond F., *First Corinthians* (SP; Collegeville: The Liturgical Press, 1999).

Connerton, Paul, *How Societies Remember* (Themes in the Social Sciences; Cambridge: Cambridge University Press, 1989).

Conzelmann, Hans, *Geschichte des Urchristentums* (GNT, 5; Göttingen: Vandenhoeck & Ruprecht, 1969).

—*1 Corinthians* (Hermeneia; Philadelphia: Fortress, 1975).

—*Acts of the Apostles* (Hermeneia; Philadelphia: Fortress, 1987).

Conzelmann, Hans, and Andreas Lindemann, *Arbeitsbuch zum Neuen Testament* (UniT, 52; Tübingen: Mohr, 1975).

Craigie, Peter C., *The Book of Deuteronomy* (NICOT; Grand Rapids: Eerdmans, 1976), p. 357.

Cranfield, C.E.B., *The Gospel according to Saint Mark* (CGTC; Cambridge: Cambridge University Press, 1959).

—*A Critical and Exegetical Commentary on the Epistle to the Romans* (ICC; 2 vols.; Edinburgh: T. & T. Clark, 1975, 1979).

Cribiore, Raffaella, *Writing, Teachers, and Students in Graeco-Roman Egypt* (American Studies in Papyrology, 36; Atlanta: Scholars Press, 1996).

—*Gymnastics of the Mind: Greek Education in Hellenistic and Roman Egypt* (Princeton and Oxford: Princeton University Press, 2001).

Cullmann, Oskar, 'Πέτρος', in Gerhard Friedrich (ed.), *Theological Dictionary of the New Testament* (trans. Geoffrey W. Bromiley; 10 vols.; Grand Rapids: Eerdmans, 1968), VI, pp. 100–12.

Daniélou, Jean, *L'Eglise des Apôtres* (Paris: Edition du Seuil, 1970).

Davies, W.D., and Dale C. Allison, *A Critical and Exegetical Commentary on The Gospel according to Saint Matthew* (ICC; 3 vols.; Edinburgh: T. & T. Clark, 1988–97).

Deissmann, Adolf, *Licht vom Osten: Das Neue Testament & die neuentdeckten Texte der hellenistisch-römischen Welt* (Tübingen: Mohr, 4th edn, 1923).

Dibelius, Martin, *Urchristentum & Kultur: Rektoratsrede gehalten bei der Stiftungsfeier der Universität am 22. November 1927* (Heidelberg: C. Winters Universitätsbuchhandlung, 1928).

Douglas, Mary, *Purity and Danger: An Analysis of Concepts of Pollution and Taboo* (London and New York: Routledge, 1966).

Dunn, James D.G., *Jesus and the Spirit: A Study of the Religious and Charismatic Experience of Jesus and the First Christians as Reflected in the New Testament* (London: SCM, 1975).

—*Unity and Diversity in the New Testament: An Inquiry into the Character of Earliest Christianity* (London: SCM, 1977).

—'The Relationship between Paul and Jerusalem according to Galatians 1 and 2', *NTS* 28 (1982), pp. 461–78.

—*Romans 9–16* (WBC, 38b; Dallas: Word Book Press, 1988).

—*Jesus, Paul and the Law: Studies in Mark and Galatians* (Louiseville: W/JKP, 1990).

—'What was the Issue between Paul and "Those of the Circumcision"?', in Martin Hengel and Ulrich Heckel (eds.), *Paulus & das antike Judentum* (WUNT, 58; Tübingen: Mohr, 1991), pp. 295–317.

—*The Epistle to the Galatians* (BNTC; Peabody: Hendrickson, 1993).

—*The Theology of Paul's Letter to the Galatians* (NTT; Cambridge: Cambridge University Press, 1993).

—*The Epistles to the Colossians and to Philemon: A Commentary on the Greek Text* (NIGTC; Grand Rapids: Eerdmans, 1996).

Durkheim, Émil, *De la division du travail social* (Paris: Librairie Félix Alcan, 6th edn, 1932).

—*Suicide: Étude de Sociologie* (Paris: Librairie Félix Alcan, rev. edn, 1930).

Eastman, Susan, 'The Evil Eye and the Curse of the Law: Galatians 3.1 Revisited', *JSNT* 83 (2001), pp. 69–87.

Edwards, Mark J. (ed.), *Galatians, Ephesians, Philippians* (Ancient Christian Commentary on Scripture: New Testament, 8; Downers Grove: InterVarsity Press, 1999).

Eidheim, Harald, 'When Ethnic Identity is a Social Stigma', in F. Barth (ed.), *Ethnic Groups and Boundaries: The Social Organization of Culture Difference* (Oslo: Universitetsforlaget, 1969), pp. 39–57.

Eller, Jack David, and Reed M. Coughlan, 'The Poverty of Primordialism: The Demystification of Ethnic Attachments', *Ethnic and Racial Studies* 16.2 (1993), pp. 183–202.

Elliott, John H., 'Paul, Galatians, and the Evil Eye', *Currents in Theology and Mission* 17 (August 1990), pp. 262–73.

—*Social-Scientific Criticism of the New Testament: An Introduction* (London: SPCK, 1993).

—'The Evil Eye and the Sermon on the Mount: Contours of a Pervasive Belief in Social Scientific Perspective', *BibInt* 2 (March 1994), pp. 51–84.

Endo, Shusaku, *Shiroi-hito, Kiiroi-hito* [*White People, Yellow People*] (Tokyo: Shincho-sha, 1960).

Epstein, A.L., *Ethos and Identity: Three Studies in Ethnicity* (London: Tavistock, 1978).

Epstein, Louis, *Marriage Laws in the Bible and Talmud* (Cambridge: Harvard University Press, 1942).

Eriksen, Thomas Hylland, *Ethnicity and Nationalism: Anthropological Perspectives* (London: Pluto, 1993).

Esler, Philip F., *Community and Gospel in Luke-Acts: The Social and Political Motivations of Lukan Theology* (SNTSMS, 57; Cambridge: Cambridge University Press, 1987).

—*The First Christians in their Social Worlds: Social-Scientific Approaches to New Testament Interpretation* (London and New York: Routledge, 1994).

—'Making and Breaking an Agreement Mediterranean Style: A New Reading of Galatians 2.1–14', *BibInt* 3.3 (1995), pp. 285–314.

—*Galatians* (NTR; London and New York: Routledge, 1998).

—*Conflict and Identity in Romans: The Social Setting of Paul's Letter* (Minneapolis: Fortress Press, 2003).

Fatum, Lone, 'Image of God and Glory of Man: Women in Pauline Congregations', in Kari Elisabeth Børresen (ed.), *Image of God and Gender Models in Judeo-Christian Tradition* (Oslo: Solum Forlag, 1991), pp. 61–80.

Fee, Gordon, *The First Epistle to the Corinthians* (NICNT; Grand Rapids: Eerdmans, 1987).

—*Paul's Letter to the Philippians* (NICNT; Grand Rapids: Eerdmans, 1995).

Feldman, Louis H., 'Jewish Proselytism', in H.W. Attridge and Gohei Hata (eds.), *Eusebius, Christianity, and Judaism* (Detroit: Wayne University Press, 1992), pp. 372–407.

—'The Omnipresence of the God-Fearers', *BARev* 12.5 (September–October 1986), pp. 58–63.

—*Jew and Gentile in the Ancient World* (Princeton: Princeton University Press, 1993).

Feldtkeller, Andreas, *Identitätssuche des syrischen Urchristentum: Mission, Inkulturation &*

Pluralität im älten Heidenchristentum (NTOA, 25; Freiburg: Universitätsverlag/ Göttingen: Vandenhoeck & Ruprecht, 1993).

Fergason, Everett (ed.), *Encyclopedia of Early Christianity* (New York and London: Garland, 2nd edn, 1997).

Fitzmyer, Joseph A., *The Gospel according to Luke X-XXIV: A New Translation with Introduction and Commentary* (AB, 28a; New York: Doubleday, 1985).

—*Romans: A New Translation with Introduction and Commentary* (AB, 33; New York: Doubleday, 1993).

—*The Acts of the Apostles: A New Translation with Introduction and Commentary* (AB, 31; New York: Doubleday, 1998).

Fredriksen, Paula, 'Paul and Augustine: Conversion Narratives, Orthodox Traditions, and the Retrospective Self', *JTS* 37 (1986), pp. 3–34.

Freeman, Charles, *Egypt, Greece, and Rome: Civilizations of the Ancient Mediterranean* (Oxford: Oxford University Press, 1996).

Furukawa, Tetsufumi, 'Bushido', in *Nihon Rekishi Dai-Jiten* [*Grand Dictionary of Japanese History*], VIII (22 vols.; Tokyo: Kawade Shobo, 1970).

Furuya, Yasuo, and Hideo Oki, *Nihon no Shingaku* [*Japan's Theology*] (Tokyo: Yorudan-sha, 1989).

Gager, John G., *Kingdom and Community: The Social World of Early Christianity* (New Jersey: Prentice-Hall, 1975).

Gamble, Harry Y., *Books and Readers in the Early Church: A History of Early Christian Texts* (New Haven and London: Yale University Press, 1995).

—'Letters in the New Testament and in the Greco-Roman World', in John Barton (ed.), *The Biblical World* (2 vols.; London and New York: Routledge, 2002), I, pp. 188–204.

Gardiner, Edward Norman, *Athletics of the Ancient World* (Oxford: Oxford University Press, 1930).

Garnsey, Peter, *Ideas of Slavery from Aristotle to Augustine* (Cambridge: Cambridge University Press, 1996).

Gaston, Lloyd, 'Paul and Jerusalem', in P. Richardson and J.C. Hurd (eds.), *From Jesus to Paul* (Waterloo: Wilfrid Laurier University Press, 1984), pp. 61–71.

Gaventa, Beverly R., *From Darkness to Light: Aspects of Conversion in the New Testament* (Philadelphia: Fortress, 1986).

—'Galatians 1 and 2: Autobiography as Paradigm', *NTS* 28 (1986), pp. 309–26.

—'Is Galatians Just a Guy Thing?: A Theological Reflection', *Interpretation* 54 (2000), pp. 267–78.

Geertz, Clifford, 'The Integrative Revolution: Primordial Sentiments and Civil Politics in the New States', in C. Geertz (ed.), *Old Societies and New States: The Quest for Modernity in Asia and Africa* (New York: The Free Press, 1963), pp. 108–13.

—*The Interpretation of Cultures: Selected Essays by Clifford Geertz* (New York: Basic Books, 1973).

Gese, Hartmut, *Vom Sinai zum Zion: Alttestamentliche Beiträge zur biblischen Theologie* (BEvT, 64; München: C. Kaiser Verlag, 1984).

Gilbert, Gary, 'The Making of a Jew: "God-Fearer" or Convert in the Story of Izates', *Union Seminary Quarterly Review* 44.3–4 (1991), pp. 299–313.

Gluckman, Max, 'Ritual of Rebellion in South East Africa', in Max Gluckman (ed.), *Order and Rebellion in Tribal Africa: Collected Essays, with an Autobiographical Introduction* (London: Cohen and West, 1963), pp. 110–36.

240   *Community–Identity Construction in Galatians*

Goodman, Martin D., 'Sacred Scripture and "Defiling the Hand"', *JTS* 41 (1990), pp. 99–107.

—'Identity and Authority', *Judaism* 39 (1990), pp. 192–201.

—*Mission and Conversion: Proselytizing in the Religious History of the Roman Empire* (Oxford: Clarendon, 1994).

Goulder, Michael, *A Tale of Two Missions* (London: SCM Press, 1994).

Graham, W.A., *Beyond the Written Word: Oral Aspects of Scripture in the History of Religion* (Cambridge: Cambridge University Press, 1987).

Green, Miranda J., *The Gods of the Celts* (Gloucester: Sutton, 1986).

—*Dictionary of Celtic Myth and Legend* (London: Thomas & Hudson, 1992).

Green, M., *The Second Epistle of Peter and the General Epistle of Jude* (TNTC; Leicester: InterVarsity Press, 1968).

Grundmann, Walter, 'δεξιός', in Gerhard F. Kittel (ed.), *Theological Dictionary of the New Testament* (trans. Geoffrey W. Bromiley; 10 vols.; Grand Rapids: Eerdmans, 1964), II, pp. 37–40.

Gundry, Robert H., *Mark: A Commentary on His Apology for the Cross* (Grand Rapids: Eerdmans, 1993).

Gundry-Volf, J.M., 'Gender and Creation in 1 Cor 11.2–16: A Study in Paul's Theological Method', in J. Adna, *et al.* (eds.), *Evangelium, Schriftauslegung, Kirche* (Festschrift Peter Stuhlmacher; Göttingen: Vandenhoeck & Ruprecht, 1997), pp. 151–71.

Gutrod, Walter, 'Ἰουδαΐζειν', in Gerhard Friedrich (ed.), *Theological Dictionary of the New Testament* (trans. Geoffrey W. Bromiley; 10 vols.; Grand Rapids: Eerdmans, 1965), III, pp. 369–91.

Güttgemanns, Erhardt, *Der leidende Apostel & sein Herr: Studien zur paulinischen Christologie* (FRLANT, 90; Göttingen: Vandenhoeck & Ruprecht, 1966).

Haenchen, Ernst, *Die Apostelgeschichte* (Göttingen: Vandenhoeck & Ruprecht, 13th edn, 1961).

—'Petrus-Probleme', *NTS* 7 (1960–61), pp. 187–97.

Hagner, D.A., *Matthew 14–28* (WBC, 33b; Dallas: Word Book Press, 1995).

Hakari, Yoshiharu, *Mukyokai no Ronri* [*Theory of Mukyokai*] (Tokyo: Hokujyu Shuppan, 1988).

Hansen, G. Walter, *Abraham in Galatians: Epistolary and Rhetorical Contexts* (JSNTSup, 29; Sheffield: JSOT Press, 1989).

Hanson, R.P.C., *Allegory and Event: A Study of the Sources and Significance of Origen's Interpretation of Scripture* (London: SCM, 1959).

Harrington, Ann H., *Japan's Hidden Christians* (Chicago: Loyola University Press, 1993).

Hata, Gohei, 'The Origin of the Greek Bible: Another Explanation' (Paper presented at Jewish Studies Seminar at Wolfson College, Oxford, March 4, 2003).

Hawthorne, Gerald F., *Philippians* (WBC, 43; Dallas: Word Book Press, 1983).

Hay, David M., 'Things Philo Said and Did Not Say about the *Therapeutae*', in *SBLSP* (Atlanta: Scholars Press, 1992), pp. 673–83.

Hayes, Christine E., *Gentile Impurities and Jewish Identities: Intermarriage and Conversion from the Bible to the Talmud* (Oxford: Oxford University Press, 2002).

Hays, Richard B., *Echoes of Scripture in the Letters of Paul* (New Haven and London: Yale University Press, 1989).

Hengel, Martin, *Die Zeloten: Untersuchungen zur Jüdischen Freiheits-Bewegung in der Zeit von Herodes 1. bis 70 n. Chr.* (Leiden and Köln: E.J. Brill, 1961).

—*Judentum & Hellenismus: Studien zu ihrer Begegnung unter besonderer Berücksichtigung Palästinas bis zur Mitte des 2. Jh. v. Chr.* (WUNT, 10.1; Tübingen: Mohr, 1969).

—'Der vorchristliche Paulus', in M. Hengel and Ulrich Heckel (eds.), *Paulus & das antike Judentum* (WUNT, 58; Tübingen: Mohr, 1991), pp. 177–293.

—'Ἰουδαία in der geographischen Liste Apg 2, 9–11 und Syrien als "Grossjudäa"', *RHPR* 80 (2000), pp. 51–68.

Hengel, Martin and Anna M. Schwemer, *Paulus zwischen Damascus & Antiochien: Die unbekannten Jahre des Apostels* (WUNT, 108; Tübingen: Mohr, 1998).

Hill, Craig C., *Hellenists and Hebrews: Reappraising Division within the Earliest Church* (Minneapolis: Fortress, 1992).

Himmelfarb, Martha, 'Levi, Phinehas, and the Problem of Intermarriage at the Time of the Maccabean Revolt', *Jewish Studies Quarterly* 6 (1999), pp. 1–24.

Hogg, Michael A., and Dominic Abrams, *Social Identifications: A Social Psychology of Intergroup Relations and Group Processes* (London and New York: Routledge, 1988).

Holmberg, Bengt, *Paul and Power: The Structure of Authority in the Primitive Church as Reflected in the Pauline Epistles* (Philadelphia: Fortress, 1980).

—*Sociology and the New Testament: An Appraisal* (Minneapolis: Fortress, 1990).

Hooker, Mona D., 'Authority on her Head: An Examination of 1 Cor. xi.10', *NTS* 10 (1964–65), pp. 410–16.

Horrell, David G., *2nd Peter and Jude* (Epworth Commentaries; Peterborough: Epworth, 1998).

Horsley, Greg, 'Anatolia, from the Celts to the Christians', *Buried History: Quarterly Journal of the Australian Institute of Archaeology* 36.1–2 (March–June 2000), pp. 49–55.

Horsley, Richard A., *Hearing the Whole Story: The Politics of Plot in Mark's Gospel* (Louisville: Westminster/John Knox Press, 2001).

Hort, F.J.A., *Judaistic Christianity* (London: Macmillan, 1904).

Hull, R.F., 'Called "Christians" at Antioch: Christian Identity and the "Sacred Names" in Early Christian Manuscripts', in G. Weedham (ed.), *Building up the Church* (Festschrift Henry E. Webb; Johnston City: Milligan College, 1993), pp. 25–50.

Hurtado, Larry W., 'Convert, Apostate or Apostle to the Nations: The "Conversion" of Paul in Recent Scholarship', *SR* 22.3 (1993), pp. 273–84.

Hutchinson, John, and Anthony D. Smith, 'Ethnicity, Religion, and Language', in J. Hutchinson and A.D. Smith (eds.), *Ethnicity* (Oxford and New York: Oxford University Press, 1996), pp. 32–34.

Huxley, Aldous, *Brave New World* (Vintage Classics; London: Vintage, 2004, originally published by Chatto and Windus, 1932).

Ishida, Takeshi, 'The Meaning of "Independence" in the Thought of Uchimura Kanzo', in Ray A. Moore (ed.), *Culture and Religion in Japanese-American Relation: Essays on Uchimura Kanzo, 1891–1930* (Ann Arbor: University of Michigan Press, 1981), pp. 7–19.

Jenkins, Richard, *Social Identity* (London and New York: Routledge, 1996).

Jeremias, Joachim, *Jesus' Promise to the Nations* (trans. S.H. Hooke; SBT; London: SCM, 1958).

Jewett, Robert, 'The Agitators and the Galatian Congregation', *NTS* 17 (1970–71), pp. 198–212.

Johnson, Luke T., 'Review: The Pauline Churches', *JAAR* 58 (Winter 1990), pp. 716–19.

—*Letters to Paul's Delegates, 1 Timothy, 2 Timothy, Titus* (The New Testament in Context; Valley Forge: Trinity, 1996).

—*The First and Second Letters to Timothy: A New Translation with Introduction and Commentary* (AB, 35a; New York: Doubleday, 2001).

Judge, Edwin A., *The Social Pattern of the Christian Groups in the First Century: Some Prolegomena to the Study of New Testament Ideas of Social Obligation* (London: Tyndale, 1960).

—'The Magical Use of Scripture in the Papyri', in E.W. Conrad and E.G. Newing (eds.), *Perspectives in Language and Text* (Winona Lake: Eisenbrauns, 1987), pp. 339–49.

Just, Roger, 'Some Problems for Mediterranean Anthropology', *Journal of the Anthropological Society of Oxford* 9.2 (Trinity, 1978), pp. 81–97.

Kang, Sang-jung, *Nashonarizumu* [*Nationalism*] (Tokyo: Iwanami, 2001).

Kamei, Shunsuke, *Uchimura Kanzo: Meiji Seishin no Dohyo* [*Kanzo Uchimura: A Milestone of Meiji Spirit*] (Tokyo: Chuo-Koronsha, 1977).

Karudarora, Karuro, *Uchimura Kanzo to Mukyokai* (trans. Mitsuzo Tamura, *et al.*; Tokyo: Shinkyo Shuppan, 1978).

Käsemann, Ernst, *Exegetische Versuche & Besinnungen* (2 vols.; Göttingen: Vandenhoeck and Ruprecht, 1960).

—*Commentary on Romans* (Grand Rapids: Eerdmans, 1980).

Kasher, Aryeh, *Jews, Idumaeans, and Ancient Arabs: Relations of the Jews in* Eretz Israel *with the Nations of the Frontier and the Desert during the Hellenistic and Roman Era (332 BCE–70 CE)* (Tübingen: Mohr, 1988).

Kautsky, Karl, *Der Ursprung des Christentums: Eine historische Untersuchung* (Stuttgart: JNM Dietz Nachfolger, 12th edn, 1922).

Keene, Donald, *Landscapes and Portraits: Appreciations of Japanese Culture* (London: Secker and Warburg, 1972).

—*Dawn to the West: Japanese Literature of the Modern Era* (New York: Holt, Rinehart and Winston, 1984).

Kirk, J. Andrew, 'Apostleship since Rengstorf: Toward a Synthesis', *NTS* 21 (1975), pp. 249–64.

Kishimoto, Hideo (ed.), *Japanese Religion in the Meiji Era* (trans. John F. Howes; Centenary Culture Council Series; Tokyo: Obunsha, 1956).

Kittel, Gerhardt F., 'δοκέω', in G.F. Kittel (ed.), *Theological Dictionary of the New Testament* (trans. Geoffrey W. Bromiley; 10 vols.; Grand Rapids: Eerdmans, 1964), II, pp. 242–55.

Klawans, Jonathan, 'Notions of Gentile Impurity in Ancient Judaism', *Association for Jewish Studies Review* 20.2 (1995), pp. 285–312.

—*Impurity and Sin in Ancient Israel* (Oxford: Oxford University Press, 2000).

Klein, Günter, 'Galater 2.6–9 & die Geschichte der Jerusalemer Urgemeinde', *Zeitschrift für Theologie & Kirche* 57 (1960), pp. 275–95.

—*Die zwölf Apostel: Ursprung & Gehalt einer Idee* (Zürich: Zwingli-Verlag, 1951).

Klinghardt, Matthias, *Gesetz & Volk Gottes: Das lukanische Verständnis des Gesetzes nach Herkunft, Funktion & seinem Ort in der Geschichte des Urchristentums* (WUNT, 2.32; Tübingen: Mohr, 1988).

Knox, John, *Chapters in a Life of Paul* (London: SCM, rev. edn, 1989).

Kolb, Frank, 'Antiochia in der frühen Kaiserzeit', in H. Cancik, *et al.* (eds.), *Geschichte*

Tradition – Reflexion (Festschrift Martin Hengel; 3 vols.; Tübingen: Mohr, 1996), II, pp. 97–118.

Kosmala, H.,'The Conclusion of Matthew', *ASTI* 4 (1965), pp. 132–47.

Kraabel, A.T., 'Review: Paul, Judaism and the Gentiles, etc.', *JBL* 108 (Spring 1989), pp. 160–63.

Kraemer, Ross Shepard, *When Aseneth Met Joseph: A Late Antique Tale of the Biblical Patriarch and His Egyptian Wife, Reconsidered* (Oxford and New York: Oxford University Press, 1998).

Kruse, C.G., 'Apostle', in J.B. Green and S. McKnight (eds.), *Dictionary of Jesus and the Gospels* (Downers Grove: InterVarsity Press, 1992).

Kuhn, Karl G., ''Ιουδαϊσμος', in Gerhard Friedrich (ed.), *Theological Dictionary of the New Testament* (trans. Geoffrey W. Bromiley; 10 vols.; Grand Rapids: Eerdmans, 1965), III, pp. 359–69.

—'προσήλυτος', in Gerhard Friedrich (ed.), *Theological Dictionary of the New Testament* (trans. Geoffrey W. Bromiley; 10 vols.; Grand Rapids: Eerdmans, 1968), VI, pp. 727–44.

Kümmel, Werner Georg, *Einleitung in das Neue Testament* (Heidelberg: Quelle and Meyer, 21st edn, 1983).

Kürzinger, J., 'Frau & Man nach 1 Kor 11.11f', *BZ* 22 (1978), pp. 270–75.

Lambert, Malcolm, *Franciscan Poverty: The Doctrine of the Absolute Poverty of Christ and the Apostles in the Franciscan Order 1210–1323* (London: SPCK, 1961).

Lang, Bernard, 'Ritual/Ritus', in Hubert Cancik, *et al.* (eds.), *Handbuch religionswissenschaftlicher Grundbegriffe* (5 vols; Stuttgart: Kohlhammer, 1998), IV, pp. 442–58.

Latto, Timo, *Paulus & das Judentum: Anthropologische Erwägnungen* (Åbo: Åbo Akademis Förlag, 1991).

Laures, Johannes, *The Catholic Church in Japan: A Short History* (Connecticut: Greenwood, 1954).

—*Kirishitan Bunko: A Manual Books and Documents on Early Christian Mission in Japan* (Monumenta Nipponica Monographs, 5; Tokyo: Sophia University Press, 3rd edn, 1957).

Le Grys, Alan, *Preaching to the Nations: The Origins of Mission in the Early Church* (London: SPCK, 1998).

Leipoldt, Johannes, and Siegried Morenz, *Heilige Schriften: Beobachtungen zur Religionsgeschichte der antiken Mittelmeerwelt* (Leipzig: VEB Otto Harrassowitz, 1953).

Lemert, E.M., *Human Deviant: Social Problem and Social Controls* (Englewood Cliffs: Prentice-Hall, 2nd edn, 1972).

Lightfoot, J.B., *Saint Paul's Epistle to the Philippians* (London: Macmillan, 8th edn, 1888).

—*Saint Paul's Epistle to the Galatians* (London and New York: Macmillan, 9th edn, 1888).

—*The Apostolic Fathers: Revised Texts with Introductions, Notes, Dissertations, and Translations* (Peabody: Hendrickson, 1989).

Lightfoot, J.B., and J.R. Harmer (eds.), *The Apostolic Fathers: Greek Texts and English Translations and their Writings* (Grand Rapids: Baker, 2nd edn, 1992).

Lincoln, Andrew T., *Paradise Now and Not Yet: Studies in the Role of the Heavenly Dimension in Paul's Thought with Special Reference to his Eschatology* (SNTSMS, 43; Cambridge: Cambridge University Press, 1981).

Lindstrom, Lamont, 'syncretism', in Alan Barnard and Jonathan Spencer (eds.),

244   *Community–Identity Construction in Galatians*

Encyclopedia of Social and Cultural Anthropology (London and New York: Routledge, 1996).

Linton, R., 'One Hundred Per-Cent American', *The American Mercury* 40 (1937), pp. 427–29.

Lipp, Wolfgang, 'Selbststigmatisierung', in M. Brusten and J. Hohmeier (eds.), *Stigmatisierung 1: Zur Produktion gesellschaftlicher Randgruppen* (Neuwied und Darmstadt: Hermann Luchterhand Verlag, 1975), pp. 25–53.

—'Charisma – Social Deviation, Leadership and Cultural Change: A Sociology of Deviance Approach', *The Annual Review of the Social Sciences of Religion* 1 (1997), pp. 59–77.

Lohse, Eduard, *Umwelt des Neuen Testaments* (GNT, 1; Göttingen: Vandenhoeck & Ruprecht, 1971).

Lohse, Eduard, and Günther Mayer (eds.), *Die Tosefta: Seder I: Zeraim* (Stuttgart: Kohlhammer, 1999).

Longenecker, Richard N., 'Ancient Amanuenses and the Pauline Epistles', in R.N. Longenecker and M.C. Tenney (eds.), *New Dimensions in New Testament Study* (Grand Rapids: Zondervan, 1974), pp. 281–97.

—*Galatians* (WBC, 41; Dallas: Word Book Press, 1990).

Lüdemann, Gerd, *Paulus, der Heidenapostel: Studien zur Chronologie*, I (FRLANT, 123.1; 2 vols.; Göttingen: Vandenhoeck & Ruprecht, 1980).

Lührmann, Dieter, 'Tage, Monate, Jahreszeiten, Jahre (Gal. 4.10)', in Rainer Albertz, *et al.* (eds.), *Werde & Wirken des Alten Testaments* (Festschrift C. Westermann; Göttingen: Vandenhoeck & Ruprecht, 1980), pp. 428–45.

Lütgert, Wilhelm, *Gesetz & Geist: Eine Untersuchung zur Vorgeschichte des Galaterbriefes* (Gütersloh: C. Bertelsmann, 1919).

Luther, Martin, *A Commentary on St. Paul's Epistle to the Galatians* (London: James Clarke, 1953; orig. trans. and ed. 1575).

Lyons, George, *Pauline Autobiography: Toward a New Understanding* (SBLDS, 73; Atlanta: Scholars, 1985).

MacDonald, Dennis Ronald, *There is No Male and Female: The Fate of a Dominical Saying in Paul and Gnosticism* (Philadelphia: Fortress, 1987).

MacDonald, Margaret Y., *The Pauline Churches: A Socio-Historical Study of Institutionalization in the Pauline and Deutero-Pauline Writings* (SNTSMS, 60; Cambridge: Cambridge University Press, 1988).

MacLennan, Robert S., and A. Thomas Kraabel, 'The God-Fearers – a Literary and Theological Invention', *BARev* 12.5 (September/October 1986), pp. 46–53.

Maddox, Robert, *The Purpose of Luke-Acts* (Edinburgh: T. & T. Clark, 1982).

Malherbe, Abraham J., *Social Aspects of Early Christianity* (Philadelphia: Fortress, 1983).

—*The Letters to the Thessalonians* (AB, 32b; New York: Doubleday, 2000).

Malina, Bruce J., 'The Social Sciences and Biblical Interpretation', *Interpretation* 36 (1982), pp. 229–42.

—*The New Testament World: Insights from Cultural Anthropology* (Louisville, KY: W/JKP, rev. edn, 1993).

Malina, B.J., and Jerome H. Neyrey, *Portraits of Paul: An Anthropology of Ancient Personality* (Louisville, KY: W/JKP, 1996).

Manning, C.E., 'Seneca and the Stoics on the Equality of the Sexes', *Mnemosyne* 4.26 (1973), pp. 170–77.

Manson, Thomas W., *Studies in the Gospels and Epistles* (Manchester: Manchester University Press, 1962).

Marriott, McKim, 'The Feast of Love', in Milton Singer (ed.), *Krishna: Myths, Rites and Attitudes* (Honolulu: East-West Center, 1966), pp. 200–12.

Marrou, Henri Irénée, *Histoire de l'Education dans l'Antiquit* (Paris: Editions du Seuil, 6th edn, 1965).

Marshall, Gordon (ed.), *Dictionary of Sociology* (Oxford and New York: Oxford University Press, 2nd edn, 1998).

Marshall, I. Howard, *Commentary on Luke* (NIGTC; Grand Rapids: Eerdmans, 1978).

—*1 and 2 Thessalonians* (NCBC; London: Marshall, Morgan and Scott, 1983).

—*A Critical and Exegetical Commentary on the Pastoral Epistles* (ICC; Edinburgh: T. & T. Clark, 1999).

Martin, Ralph P., *2 Corinthians* (WBC, 40; Dallas: Word Book Press, 1986).

Martin, Troy, 'Pagan and Judeo-Christian Time-Keeping Schemes in Gal. 4.10 and Col. 2.16', *NTS* 42 (1996), pp. 105–19.

Martyn, J. Louis, 'A Law-Observant Mission to Gentiles: The Background of Galatians', *SJT* 38 (1985), pp. 307–24.

—*Galatians: A New Translation with Introduction and Commentary* (AB, 33a; New York: Doubleday, 1997).

Maruyama, Masao, *Thought and Behaviour in Modern Japanese Politics* (Oxford: Oxford University Press, 1963).

Masaike, Hitoshi, *Uchimura Kanzo Den* [*Life of Kanzo Uchimura*] (Tokyo: Kyobun-Kan, 1977).

Mason, Steve, *Josephus and the New Testament* (Peabody: Hendrickson, 2nd edn, 2003).

Matera, Frank J., *Galatians* (SP, 9; Collegeville: The Liturgical Press, 1992).

Mathews, Shailer, *The Social Teaching of Jesus: An Essay in Christian Sociology* (New York: Hodder and Stoughton, 1897).

Matsuzawa, Hiroaki, 'Kindai Nihon to Uchimura Kanzo' [Modern Japan and Kanzo Uchimura], in Hiroaki Matsuzawa (ed.), *Uchimura Kanzo* (Tokyo: Chuo Koron, 1971), pp. 7–78.

Mayor, J.B., *The Epistle of St. Jude and the Second Epistle of St. Peter* (London: Macmillan, 1907).

McEleney, Neil J., 'Conversion, Circumcision and the Law', *NTS* 20 (1974), pp. 319–41.

McKnight, Scot, *A Light among the Gentiles: Jewish Missionary Activity in the Second Temple Period* (Minneapolis: Fortress, 1990).

McNamara, M., ' "To de (Hagar) Sina oros estin en te Arabia" (Gal. 4.25a): Paul and Petra', *Milltown Studies* 2 (1978), pp. 24–41.

Meeks, Wayne A., 'The Man from Heaven in Johannine Sectarianism', *JBL* 91 (1972), pp. 44–73.

—'The Image of the Androgyne: Some Uses of a Symbol in Earliest Christianity', *HR* 13 (1973–74), pp. 165–208.

—*The First Urban Christians: The Social World of the Apostle Paul* (New Haven and London: Yale University Press, 1983).

Meggitt, Justin J., *Paul, Poverty and Survival* (SNTW; Edinburgh: T. & T. Clark, 1998).

Mehan, H., A. Hertweck and J.L. Meihls, *Handicapping the Handicapped: Decision Making in Students' Educational Careers* (Stanford: Stanford University Press, 1986).

Menoud, Philippe-H., 'Le sense du verbe πορθεῖν', in Franz H. Kettler (ed.), *Apophoreta* (Festschrift Ernst Haenchen; BZNWKAK, 30; Berlin: Töpelmann, 1964), pp. 178–86.

Mercer, J.R., *Labeling the Mentally Retarded: Clinical and Social System Perspectives on Mental Retardation* (Berkeley: University of California Press, 1973).

Metzger, Bruce M., *A Textual Commentary on the Greek New Testament* (Stuttgart: United Bible Society, 1975).

Milgrom, Jacob, *Leviticus 17–22* (AB, 3a; New York: Doubleday, 2000).

Mitchell, Stephen, 'Galatia', in David Noel Freedman (ed.), *Anchor Bible Dictionary*, II (6 vols.; New York: Doubleday, 1992), pp. 270–72.

—*The Celts in Anatolia and the Impact of Roman Rule*. I. *Anatolia: Land, Men, and Gods in Asia Minor* (2 vols.; (Oxford: Clarendon Press, 1993).

—*The Rise of the Church*. II. *Anatolia: Land, Men, and Gods in Asia Minor* (2 vols.; Oxford: Clarendon Press, 1993).

Miura, Hiroshi, *The Life and Thought of Kanzo Uchimura, 1861–1930* (Grand Rapids: Eerdmans, 1996).

Mödritzer, Helmut, *Stigma & Charisma im Neuen Testament & seiner Umwelt: Zur Soziologie des Urchristentums* (NTOA, 28; Freiburg: Universitätsverlag/Göttingen: Vandenhoeck & Ruprecht, 1994).

Montefiore, Claude J.G., *Judaism and St. Paul: Two Essays* (London: Max Goschen, 1973).

Moo, Douglas, 'Paul and the Law in the Last Ten Years', *SJT* 40 (1987), pp. 287–307.

—*The Epistle to the Romans* (NICNT; Grand Rapids: Eerdmans, 1996).

Moore, Carey A., *Judith: A New Translation with Introduction and Commentary* (AB, 40; New York: Doubleday, 1985).

Morton, Russell, 'Review: *Paulus & das Judentum*', *CBQ* 55 (April 1993), pp. 375–77.

Moxnes, H., 'Social Integration and the Problem of Gender in St. Paul's Letters', *ST* 43 (1989), pp. 99–113.

Muddiman, John, 'An Anatomy of Galatians', in Stanley E. Porter, *et al.* (eds.), *Crossing the Boundaries: Essays in Biblical Interpretation in Honour of Michael D. Goulder* (Leiden: E.J. Brill, 1994), pp. 257–70.

Mukyokai-Shi Kenkyu Henshu-Sha (ed.), *Mukyokai-Shi* [*History of Mukyokai*] (4 vols.; Tokyo: Shinkyo-sha, 1991).

Mullins, Mark R., *Christianity Made in Japan: A Study of Indigenous Movements* (Honolulu: University of Hawai'i Press, 1998).

Munck, Johannes, 'Paul, the Apostles, and the Twelve', *ST* 3 (1949), pp. 96–110.

—*Paul and the Salvation of Mankind* (London: SCM Press, 1959).

Murphy-O'Connor, Jerome, 'Tradition and Redaction in 1 Cor. 15.3–7', *CBQ* 43 (1981), pp. 582–89.

—'Pauline Missions before the Jerusalem Conference', *RB* 89 (1982), pp. 71–91.

—*Paul et l'art épistolaire: contexte et structure littéraires* (trans. Jean Prignaud; Paris: Les editions du Cerf, 1994).

—*Paul: A Critical Life* (Oxford and New York: Oxford University Press, 1996).

Murray, John, *The Epistle to the Romans* (NICNT; Grand Rapids: Eerdmans, 1965).

Mußner, Franz, *Der Galaterbrief* (HTKNT, 9; Freiburg: Herder, 1974).

Nanos, Mark D., *The Irony of Galatians: Paul's Letter in First-Century Context* (Minneapolis: Fortress Press, 2002).

Nash, Manning, *The Cauldron of Ethnicity in the Modern World* (Chicago and London: University of Chicago Press, 1989).

Nelson, Geoffrey, *Spiritualism and Society* (London: Routledge & Kegan Paul, 1969).

Neyrey, Jerome H., *2 Peter, Jude: A New Translation with Introduction and Commentary* (AB, 37c; New York: Doubleday, 1993).

Nitobe, Inazo, *Bushido, the Soul of Japan: An Exposition of Japanese Thought* (Tokyo: Shokwado, 1901).

Nogakko, Sapporo, *Second Annual Report of Sapporo Agricultural College, 1878* (Tokei: Kaitakusha, 1878).

Nolland, John, 'Uncircumcised Proselytes?', *JSJ* 12 (1981), pp. 173–94.

Ó Hógáin, Dáithí, *The Celts: A History* (Woodbridge: Boydell Press, 2002).

Oepke, Albrecht, *Der Brief des Paulus an die Galater* (Berlin: Evangelische Verlagsanstalt, 1964).

—'κενός', in Gerhard Friedrich (ed.), *Theological Dictionary of the New Testament* (trans. Geoffrey W. Bromiley; 10 vols.; Grand Rapids: Eerdmans, 1965), III, pp. 659–62.

Ostling, Richard N., *et al.*, 'The New Missionary', *Time Magazine* 52 (27 Dec. 1982), pp. 38–44.

Oswald, Hilton C. (ed.), *Luther's Works*, XXVI (trans. Jaroslav Pelikan; 56 vols.; St Louis: Concordia, 1963).

Ota, Yuzo, *Uchimura Kanzo: Sono Sekai-Shugi to Nihon-Shugi wo Megutte [Kanzo Uchimura: On His Globalism and Nationalism]* (Tokyo: Kenkyusha Shuppan, 1977).

—'Mediation between Cultures', in John F. Howes (ed.), *Nitobe Inazo: Japan's Bridge across the Pacific* (Oxford: Westview Press, 1995), pp. 237–52.

Overman, J. Andrew, 'The God-Fearers: Some Neglected Features', *JSNT* 32 (1988), pp. 17–26.

Padilla, Mark W. (ed.), *Rites of Passage in Ancient Greece: Literature, Religion, Society* (Lewisburg and London: Bucknell University Press/Associated University Presses, 1999).

Park, Robert, 'The City: Suggestions for the Investigation of Human Behavior in the Human Environment', in R. Park, *et al.* (eds.), *The City* (Chicago: University of Chicago Press, 1925), pp. 1–46.

Peristiany, J.G. (ed.), *Honour and Shame: The Values of Mediterranean Society* (London: Weidenfeld and Nicolson, 1965).

Peristiany, J.G., and J. Pitt-Rivers (eds.), *Honour and Grace in Anthropology* (Cambridge: Cambridge University Press, 1992).

Porton, Gary G., 'Halakah', in David Noel Freedman (ed.), *Anchor Bible Dictionary*, III (6 vols.; New York: Doubleday, 1992).

—*The Stranger within your Gates: Converts and Conversion in Rabbinic Literature* (Chicago: University of Chicago Press, 1994).

Powles, Cyril H., 'Foreign Missionaries and Japanese Culture in the Late 19th Century: Four Patterns of Approach', *The Northeast Journal of Theology* (Sept. 1969), pp. 14–28.

—'Bushido: Its Admirers and Critics', in John F. Howes (ed.), *Nitobe Inazo: Japan's Bridge across the Pacific* (Oxford: Westview Press, 1995), pp. 107–18.

Quell, G., and S. Schulz, 'σπέρμα', in Gerhard Friedrich (ed.), *Theological Dictionary of the New Testament* (trans. Geoffrey W. Bromiley; 10 vols.; Grand Rapids: Eerdmans, 1971), VII, pp. 536–38.

Räisänen, Heikki, *Paul and the Law* (WUNT, 29; Tübingen: Mohr, 1987).

Rengstorf, K.H., 'ἀπόστολος', in Gerhard F. Kittel (ed.), *Theological Dictionary of the New*

Testament (trans. Geoffrey W. Bromiley; 10 vols.; Grand Rapids: Eerdmans, 1964), I, pp. 398–447.

Richter, Philip J., 'Recent Sociological Approaches to the Study of the New Testament', *Religion* 14 (1984), pp. 77–90.

Riesenfeld, Harald, 'τηρέω', in Gerhard Friedrich (ed.), *Theological Dictionary of the New Testament* (trans. Geoffrey W. Bromiley; 10 vols.; Grand Rapids: Eerdmans, 1972), VIII, pp. 140–51.

Robinson, D.W.B., 'The Circumcision of Titus, and Paul's "Liberty"', *Australian Biblical Review* 12 (1964), pp. 24–42.

Robinson, J.A.T., 'Traces of a Liturgical Sequence in 1 Corinthians 16.20–24', *JTS* 4 (1953), pp. 38–41.

Rowland, Christopher, *Christian Origins: An Account of the Setting and Character of the Most Important Messianic Sect of Judaism* (London: SPCK, 1985).

—*Radical Christianity: A Reading of Recovery* (Cambridge: Polity Press, 1988).

Sabatier, Paul, *Life of St. Francis of Assisi* (trans. Louise Seymour Houghton; London: Hodder and Stoughton, 1894).

Sanders, E.P., *Paul and Palestinian Judaism* (Minneapolis: Fortress, 1977).

—*Paul, the Law and the Jewish People* (Minneapolis: Fortress, 1983).

—'Jewish Association with Gentiles and Galatians 2.11–14', in R.T. Fortna and B.R. Gaventa (eds.), *The Conversation Continues: Studies in Paul and John in Honor of J. Louis Martyn* (Nashville: Abingdon, 1990), pp. 170–88.

—*Judaism: Practice and Belief 63 BCE–66 CE* (London: SCM, 1992).

Sanders, Jack T., *Schismatics, Sectarians, Dissidents, Deviants: The First One Hundred Years of Jewish-Christian Relations* (London: SCM, 1993).

Satake, Akira, 'Apostolat & Gnade bei Paulus', *NTS* 15 (1968–69), pp. 96–107.

Schlier, Heinrich, *Der Brief an die Galater: Übersetzt & erklärt* (Göttingen: Vandenhoeck & Ruprecht, 10th edn, 1949).

Schmidt, K.L., 'ἐκκλησία', in Gerhard Friedrich (ed.), *Theological Dictionary of the New Testament* (trans. Geoffrey W. Bromiley; 10 vols.; Grand Rapids: Eerdmans, 1965), III, pp. 501–36.

Schmithals, Walter, *Das kirchliche Apostelamt: Eine historische Untersuchung* (FRLANT, 79; Göttingen: Vandenhoeck & Ruprecht, 1961).

—*Paulus & Jakobus* (FRLANT, 85; Göttingen: Vandenhoeck & Ruprecht, 1963).

Schnackenburg, Rudolf, *Das Johannesevangelium: Einleitung & Kommentar zu Kap. 1–4* (HTKNT, 4.1; Freiburg: Herder, 1965).

Schneider, Gerhard, *Apostelgeschichte: Kommentar* (HTKNT, 5; Freiburg im Beisgau: Herder, 1982).

Schoedel, William R., *Polycarp, Martyrdom of Polycarp, Fragments of Papias*. V. *The Apostolic Fathers: A New Translation and Commentary* (ed. Robert M. Grant; 5 vols.; London: Thomas Nelson & Sons, 1967).

—*Ignatius of Antioch: A Commentary on the Letters of Ignatius of Antioch* (Hermeneia; Philadelphia: Fortress: 1985).

Schoeps, Hans Joachim, *Paulus: Die Theologie des Apostels im Lichte der jüdischen Religionsgeschichte* (Tübingen: Mohr, 1959).

Schottroff, Luise, '"Not Many Powerful": Approaches to a Sociology of Early Christianity', in David G. Horrell (ed.), *Social-Scientific Approaches to New Testament Interpretation* (Edinburgh: T. & T. Clark, 1999), pp. 275–87.

Schreiner, Thomas, *The Law and Its Fulfillment: A Pauline Theology of Law* (Grand Rapids: Baker, 1993).

Schrenk, Gottlob, 'γραφή', in Gerhard F. Kittel (ed.), *Theological Dictionary of the New Testament* (trans. Geoffrey W. Bromiley; 10 vols.; Grand Rapids: Eerdmans, 1964), I, pp. 742–73.

Schröter, Jens, 'Review: *Die liminale Theologie des Paulus*', *JBL* 120.4 (Winter 2001), pp. 777–80.

Schürer, Emil, *Geschichte des jüdischen Volkes im Zeitalter Jesu Christi*, II (4 vols.; Leipzig: J.C. Hinrichs'sche, 4th edn, 1907).

—*The History of the Jewish People in the Age of Jesus Christ (175 BC–AD 135)* (rev. and ed. Geza Vermes, Fergus Millar and Matthew Black; 3 vols. in 4; Edinburgh: T. & T. Clark, 1973–87).

Schüssler Fiorenza, Elisabeth, *In Memory of Her: A Feminist Theological Reconstruction of Christian Origins* (London: SCM, 1983).

—*Rhetoric and Ethic: The Politics of Biblical Studies* (Minneapolis: Fortress, 1999).

Schwarzfuchs, Simon R., 'Noachide Laws', in Cecil Roth (ed.), *EncJud*, XII (18 vols.; Jerusalem: Keter Publishing House/New York: Macmillan, 1971).

Schweitzer, Albert, *Die Mystik des Apostels Paulus* (Tübingen: Mohr, 1930).

Schwimmer, E.G., 'Symbolic Competition', *Anthropologica* XIV.2 (1972), pp. 117–55.

Scott, James C., *Domination and the Arts of Resistance: Hidden Transcript* (New Haven and London: Yale University Press, 1990).

Scott, James M., *Paul and the Nations: The Old Testament and Jewish Background of Paul's Mission to the Nations with Special Reference to the Destination of Galatians* (WUNT, 84; Tübingen: Mohr, 1995).

Scroggs, Robin, 'The Earliest Christian Communities as Sectarian Movement', in Jacob Neusner (ed.), *Christianity, Judaism and Other Greco-Roman Cults* (Festschrift Morton Smith; 4 vols.; Leiden: E.J. Brill, 1975), II pp. 164–79.

Segal, Alan F., 'The Costs of Proselytism and Conversion', in David J. Lull (ed.), *SBLSP* (Atlanta: Scholars, 1988), pp. 336–69.

—*Paul the Convert: The Apostolate and Apostasy of Saul the Pharisee* (New Haven and London: Yale University Press, 1990).

Seifrid, Mark A., *Justification by Faith: The Origin and Development of a Central Pauline Theme* (Leiden: E.J. Brill, 1992).

Sekine, Maso, *Sekine Masao Chosakushu [All Works of Masao Sekine]* II, (20 vols.; Shin-chi Shobo, 1981).

Shimazaki, Toson, *Sakura no Mi no Jukusuru Toki [When Cherry Fruits Ripen]* (Tokyo: Shincho-Sha, 1955, originally published by Shunyo-Do in 1912).

Shively, Donald H., 'The Japanization of the Middle Meiji', in Donald H. Shively (ed.), *Tradition and Modernization in Japanese Culture* (Studies in the Modernization of Japan; Princeton, NJ: Princeton University Press, 1971), pp. 77–119.

—'Motoda Eifu: Confucian Lecturer to the Meiji Emperor', in D.S. Nivison and A.F. Wright (eds.), *Confucianism in Action* (Stanford: Stanford University Press, 1959), pp. 302–33.

Siker, Jeffrey S., *Disinheriting the Jews: Abraham in Early Christian Controversy* (Louisville: W/JKP, 1991).

Silva, Moisés, *Interpreting Galatians: Explorations in Exegetical Method* (Grand Rapids: Baker, 2nd edn, 2001).

Simon, Marcel, *Verus Israel: Etude sur les Relations entre Chrétiens et Juifs dans l'Empire Romain (135–425)* (Paris: E. de Boccard, 1948).

Skinner, John, *Critical and Exegetical Commentary on Genesis* (ICC; Edinburgh: T. & T. Clark, 1912).

Slee, Michelle, *The Church in Antioch in the First Century CE: Communion and Conflict* (JSNTSup, 244; London and New York: T. & T. Clark/Continuum, 2003).

Smith, Anthony D., 'Chosen People: Why Ethnic Groups Survive', *Ethnic and Racial Studies* 15.3 (1992), pp. 440–49.

Smith, Jonathan Z., 'Too Much Kingdom, Too Little Community', *Zygon* 13.2 (June 1978), pp. 123–30.

—*Drudgery Divine: On the Comparison of Early Christianities and the Religions of Late Antiquity* (London and Chicago: University of London, 1990).

Smith, Wilfred Cantwell, *What is Scripture?: A Comparative Approach* (London: SCM; Minneapolis: Fortress, 1993).

Snow, David, and Richard Machalek, 'The Convert as a Social Type', in R. Collins (ed.), *Sociological Theory* (San Francisco: Jossey-Bass, 1983), pp. 259–89.

Soeda, Yoshiya, *Kyoiku-Chokugo no Shakai-shi [Social-History of the Rescript of Education]* (Tokyo: Yushindo-Kobunsha, 1997).

Sokolovskii, Sergey, 'Ethnicity', in Alan Barnard and Jonathan Spencer (eds.), *Encyclopedia of Social and Cultural Anthropology* (London and New York: Routledge, 1996, pp. 190–93).

Stark, Rodney, and William Sims Bainbridge, 'Of Churches, Sects, and Cults: Preliminary Concepts for a Theory of Religious Movements', *JSSR* 18.2 (1979), pp. 117–33.

Stegemann, Wolfgang, 'Anti-Semitic and Racist Prejudices in Titus 1.10–16', in M.G. Brett (ed.), *Ethnicity and the Bible* (Leiden: E.J. Brill, 1996), pp. 271–94.

Stendahl, Krister, *Paul among Jews and Gentiles* (Philadelphia: Fortress, 1976).

Stern, Menahem, *Greek and Latin Authors on Jews and Judaism* (3 vols.; Jerusalem: The Israel Academy of Sciences and Humanities, 1974–84).

Strack, H.L., and P. Billerbeck (eds.), *Kommentar zum Neuen Testament aus Talmud und Midrash. III. Exkurse zu einzenen Stellen des Neuen Testaments: Abhandlungen zur neutestamentlichen Theologie & Archäologie* (6 vols. München: 1926).

Strecker, Christian, *Die liminale Theologie des Paulus: Zugänge zu paulinischen Theologie aus kulturanthropologischen Perspektive* (FRLANT, 185; Göttingen: Vandenhoeck & Ruprecht, 1999).

Stuart, Ninian, *Dimension of the Sacred: An Anatomy of the World's Beliefs* (London: HarperCollins, 1996).

Stuehrenberg, Paul F., 'Proselyte', in David Noel Freedman (ed.), *Anchor Bible Dictionary*, V (6 vols.; New York: Doubleday, 1992, pp. 503–504).

Sundkler, Bengt, *Bantu Prophets in South Africa* (Oxford: Oxford University Press, 1961).

Suzuki, Toshiro (ed.), *Kaiso no Uchimura Kanzo [Memories of Kanzo Uchimura]* (Tokyo: Iwanami Shoten, 1956).

Tagita, Koya, 'Kirisuto-Kyo no Nihon-teki Bunka-Henyo' [Modification of Christianity into the Japanese Culture], *Shukyo Kenkyu [Religious Studies]* 155 (1958), pp. 65–88.

Tajfel, Henri (ed.), *Differentiation between Social Groups: Studies in the Social Psychology of Intergroup Relations* (London and New York: Academic, 1978).

Tajfel, Henri, and J.C. Turner, 'An Integrative Theory of Intergroup Conflict', in W.G.

Austin and S. Worchel (eds.), *The Social Psychology of Intergroup Relations* (Monterey: Brooks-Cole, 1979, pp. 33–47).

Takahashi, Saburo, *Mukyokai towa Nani ka [What is Mukyokai]* (Tokyo: Kyobun-Kan, 1994).

Takahashi, Yoshio, 'Jinshu kaizo-ron' *[On Transformation of the Race]*, in Ikujiro Wantabe (ed.), *Kyoiku Chokugo no Hongi to Kampatsu no Yurai* (Tokyo: Fukumura Shoten, 1931).

Tannenbaum, Robert E., 'Jews and God-Fearers in the Holy City of Aphrodite', *BARev* 12.5 (September–October 1986), pp. 54–57.

Taylor, John J., 'Why Were the Disciples First Called "Christians" at Antioch?', *RB* 101 (1994), pp. 75–94.

Taylor, Vincent, *The Gospel according to St. Mark* (London: Macmillan, 2nd edn, 1966).

Theißen, Gerd, 'Die soziologische Auswertung religiöser Überlieferungen: Ihre methodologischen Probleme am Beispiel des Urchristentums', *Kairos* 17 (1975), pp. 284–99.

—'Die Starken & Schwachen in Korinth: Soziologische Analyse eines theologischen Streites', *EvT* 35 (1975), pp. 155–72.

—*The Social Setting of Pauline Christianity* (trans. and ed. John H. Schütz; Minneapolis: Fortress, 1982).

—*Studien zur Soziologie des Urchristentums* (WUNT, 19.2; Tübingen: Mohr, rev. edn, 1983).

—*Psychologische Aspekte paulinischer Theologie* (FRLANT, 131; Göttingen: Vandenhoeck & Ruprecht, 1983).

—'Judentum und Christentum bei Paulus: Sozialgeschichtliche Überlegungen zu einem beginnenden Schisma', in Martin Hendgel and Ulrich Heckel (eds.), *Paulus und das antike Judentum* (WUNT, 58; Tübingen: Mohr, 1991), pp. 331–56.

—*Die Religion der ersten Christen: Eine Theorie des Urchristentums* (Gütersloh: Chr. Kaiser/ Gütersloher Verlagshaus, 2000).

Thiselton, Anthony C., *The First Epistle to the Corinthians: A Commentary on the Greek Text* (NIGTC; Grand Rapids: Eerdmans, 2000).

Thomas, Rosalind, *Literacy and Orality in Ancient Greece* (Cambridge: Cambridge University Press, 1992).

Thomson, Peter J., *Paul and the Jewish Law: Halakha in the Letter of the Apostle to the Gentiles* (Minneapolis: Fortress, 1990).

Thrall, Margaret E., *A Critical and Exegetical Commentary on the Second Epistle to the Corinthians* (ICC; 2 vols.; Edinburgh: T. & T. Clark, 2000).

Trebilco, Paul R., *Jewish Communities in Asia Minor* (SNTSMS, 69; Cambridge: Cambridge University Press, 1991).

Troeltsch, Ernst, *The Social Teaching of the Christian Churches* (trans. Olive Wyon; 2 vols.; London and New York: Macmillan, 1931).

Tsukamoto, Toraji, 'Mukyokai towa Nanzoya' [What is Mukyokai?], in *Tsukamoto Toraji Chosaku Zenshu Zoku [All Works of Tsukamoto Toraji II]*, I (8 vols.; Seisho Chishikisha, 1927).

Tsunoda, Ryusaku, *et al.* (eds.), *Sources of Japanese Tradition* (Records of Civilization: Sources and Studies, 54; New York and London: Columbia University Press, 1958).

Tuckett, Christopher, 'Paul, Scripture and Ethics: Some Reflections', *NTS* 463 (2000), pp. 403–24.

—'P₅₂ and *Nomina Sacra*', *NTS* 47 (2001), pp. 544–48.

Turner, Nigel, 'Second Thoughts: Papyrus Finds', *ExpTim* LXXVI (1964), pp. 44–48.

—*Grammatical Insights into the New Testament* (Edinburgh: T. & T. Clark, 1965).

Turner, Victor, *The Ritual Process: Structure and Anti-Structure* (New York: Cornell University Press, 1969).

Tyson, Joseph B., 'Paul's Opponents in Galatia', *NovT* 10 (1968), pp. 241–54.

van Gennep, Arnold, *Les rites de passage: études systématique des rites* (Paris: Librairie Critique, 1909).

van der Horst, P.W., 'Juden & Christen in Aphrodisias im Licht ihrer Beziehungen in anderen Städten Kleinasiens', in J. van Amersfoort and J. van Oort (eds.), *Juden & Christen in der Antike* (Kampe: Kok, 1990), pp. 125–43.

Vogt, Thea, *Angst & Identität im Markusevangelium: Ein text-psychologischer & sozial-geschichtlicher Beitrag* (NTOA, 26; Freiburg: Universitätsverlag/Göttingen: Vandenhoeck & Ruprecht, 1993).

von Harnack, Adolf, *Die Mission & Ausbreitung des Christentums in der ersten drei Jahrhunderten* (2 vols.; Leipzig: J.C. Hinrich, 4th edn, 1924).

von Zahn, Theodor, *Der Brief des Paulus an die Galater ausgelegt* (Leipzig: Deichertsche, 1905).

—*Der Brief des Paulus an die Römer ausgelegt* (Leipiz: Deichertsche, 2nd edn, 1910).

Wanamaker, Charles A., *The Epistles to the Thessalonians: A Commentary on the Greek Text* (NIGTC; Grand Rapids: Eerdmans, 1990).

Waswo, Ann, *Modern Japanese Society* (Oxford: Oxford University Press, 1996).

Watson, Francis, *Paul, Judaism and the Gentiles: A Sociological Approach* (SNTSMS, 56; Cambridge: Cambridge University Press, 1986).

—*Text, Church and World: Biblical Interpretation in Theological Perspective* (Edinburgh: T. & T. Clark, 1994).

Weber, Max, *The Methodology of the Social Sciences* (trans. and ed. Edward A. Shils and Henry A. Finch; Glencoe: Free Press, 1949).

—*Economy and Society: An Outline of Interpretive Sociology* (trans. Günther Roth and Claus Wittich; 3 vols.; New York: Bedminster, 1968).

Wedderburn, Alexander J.M., *Baptism and Resurrection: Studies in Pauline Theology against its Graeco-Roman Background* (WUNT, 44; Tübingen: Mohr, 1987).

Westermann, Claus, *Genesis 12–36: A Commentary* (trans. John J. Scullion; Minneapolis: Ausburg, 1985).

Whelan, Christal, *The Beginning of Heaven and Earth* (Honolulu: University of Hawai'i Press, 1996), p. 20.

Widengren, Geo, 'The Ascension of the Apostle and the Heavenly Book (King & Saviour III)', *Uppsala Universitets Årsskrift* 7 (1950), pp. 1–117, in *Uppsala Universitets Årsskrift: Acta Universtatis Uppsalienssis 1950* (Uppsala: A.-B. Lundequistska Bokhandeln, 1950).

Wilson, Bryan R., 'An Analysis of Sect Development', in B.R. Wilson (ed.), *Patterns of Sectarianism: Organization and Ideology in Social and Religious Movements* (London: Heinemann, 1967), pp. 22–45.

—*Magic and the Millennium: A Sociological Study of Religious Movements of Protest among Tribal and Third-World Peoples* (London: Heinemann, 1973).

—*Religion in Sociological Perspective* (Oxford: Oxford University Press, 1982).

Worsley, Peter, *The Trumpet Shall Sound: A Study of 'Cargo' Cults in Melanesia* (New York: Schlocken Books, 1968).

Wrede, W., *Paul* (trans. Edward Lummis; London: Philip Green, 1907).

Wright, N.T., *The Climax of the Covenant: Christ and the Law in Pauline Theology* (Minneapolis: Fortress, 1992).

Yamagata, Iso'o, 'Byo taru Uchimura Kanzo' [Squint-Eyed Kanzo Uchimura], in Toshiro Suzuki (ed.), *Kaiso no Uchimura Kanzo* [*Memories of Kanzo Uchimura*] (Tokyo: Iwanami Shoten, 1956, pp. 203–208).

Yamamoto, Taijiro, *Uchimura Kanzo no Konpon Mondai* [*Fundamental Problems of Kanzo Uchimura*] (Tokyo: Kyobun-Kan, 1968).

Yanaihara, Tadao, *Yanaihara Tadao Zenshu* [*All Works of Tadao Yanaihara*] (30 vols.; Tokyo: Iwanami Shoten, 1964).

—*Mukyokai-Shugi Kirisuto-Kyo Ron* [*On Mukyokai Christianity*] (Tokyo: Iwanami Shoten, 1982).

Yarbrough, Adela, 'Christianization in the Fourth Century: The Example of Roman Women', *CH* 45 (1976), pp. 149–65.

INDICES

INDEX OF REFERENCES

DEAD SEA SCROLLS
1QS
3.4–9, 6.14–23 182

4QMMT
B75–82   138

JOSEPHUS
Jewish Wars
2.118–19   39, 118n.14
2.454   103
3.453   95n.59
4.141   95n.59
4.159   95n.59
7.3.3   101, 129n.57

Antiquities of the Jews
2.39   137, 139
4.6.10–12   157n.31
4.7.3   133n.73
10.135   83n.6
11.346   159n.37
12.119   129
13.9.1   133
13.15.5   133
13.257   79
14.110   105
14.403   79, 112n.53, 155
18.1.1   39
19.229–334 143
20.34–48   24, 111, 113n.54, 119, 183
20.38–39   111
20.43   111, 119
20.113–17   143
20.118–20   143

Life of Flavius Josephus
112–13   103
113   111, 183

Against Apion
1.67   95n.59
2.10.123   102n.9
2.79–81   118n.14
2.179–81   39
2.279–95   102
2.282   107, 121, 195n.61

2.283   106

PHILO
De Decalogo
81   102
1.320–33   104

Legum Allegoriae
1.31–32   185

Legatio ad Gaium
44.349   139

De Migratione Abrahami
89–90   157n.31
89–93   110
92   110

Quaestiones in Exodum
2.2   105, 107, 110

Quaestiones in Genesin
1.25   185, 185n.24

De Specialibus Legibus
1.51   105, 111

De Vita Contemplativa
63–64   185n.24, n.25

De Vita Mosis
1.5.23–24   137, 139
2.17   101
2.36   102
2.41   102
2.44   102

NEW TESTAMENT
Matthew
3   183
5.3–12   199
9.20   225
14.36   225
21.25   183
22.30   186n.31
23.15   101n.6, 103, 103n.18
28.19   183